ECONOMIC INTEGRATION WORLDWIDE

Also by Ali M. El-Agraa

BRITAIN WITHIN THE EUROPEAN COMMUNITY (*editor*)
INTERNATIONAL ECONOMIC INTEGRATION (*editor*)
INTERNATIONAL TRADE
JAPAN'S TRADE FRICTIONS
PROTECTION, COOPERATION, INTEGRATION AND DEVELOPMENT (*editor*)
PUBLIC AND INTERNATIONAL ECONOMICS (*editor*)
THEORY OF CUSTOMS UNIONS (*with A. J. Jones*)
THE ECONOMICS OF THE EUROPEAN COMMUNITY
THE THEORY AND MEASUREMENT OF INTERNATIONAL ECONOMIC INTEGRATION
THE THEORY OF INTERNATIONAL TRADE
TRADE THEORY AND POLICY

Economic Integration Worldwide

Ali M. El-Agraa
Professor of International Economics
and European and American Economies
Faculty of Commerce
Fukuoka University
Japan

Other contributors:
Victor Bulmer-Thomas, Victoria Curzon Price,
Enzo Grilli, David G. Mayes, Shelton M. A. Nicholls,
Richard Pomfret, Peter Robson, Sidney Weintraub

St. Martin's Press
New York

ECONOMIC INTEGRATION WORLDWIDE

For information, address:

St. Martin's Press, Scholarly and Reference Division,
175 Fifth Avenue, New York, N.Y. 10010

This book is printed on paper suitable for recycling and made from fully managed and sustained forest sources.

First published in the United States of America in 1997

Printed in Great Britain

ISBN 0–312–16354–1 (cloth)
ISBN 0–312–16355–X (paperback)

Library of Congress Cataloging-in-Publication Data
Economic integration worldwide / Ali M. El-Agraa.
p. cm.
Includes bibliographical references and index.
ISBN 0–312–16354–1 (cloth). — ISBN 0–312–16355–X (pbk.)
1. International economic integration—Case studies. I. El-Agraa, A. M. .
HF1418.5.E27 1996
337.1—dc20 96–18823
CIP

To Diana, Mark and Frances

Contents

List of Tables and Figures

TABLES

FIGURES

Preface and Acknowledgements

In the Preface and Acknowledgements to the first edition of my *International Economic Integration*, published by Macmillan and St Martin's Press in 1982, I wrote:

> Those interested in the field of international economic integration probably share my concern regarding the scope of most books under that title: the majority refer to the European Community and some make additional occasional references to other schemes such as the European Free Trade Association (EFTA), the Council for Mutual Economic Assistance (CMEA, or COMECON as it is generally known in the West) or the Latin-American Free Trade Association (LAFTA). Since international economic integration is defined as the act of two nations or more agreeing to pursue common aims and policies (see Chapter 1) and since the world contains numerous schemes of this nature, it would seem appropriate that such books should give adequate discussion and coverage of *all* significant schemes. My aim with this book is to do precisely that in a brief and concise manner.

I repeated the same paragraph in the second edition of the book, issued by the same publishers in 1988, simply because nothing had happened by then to necessitate any change. Since then, there has not only been a proliferation in international economic integration schemes, but also a tremendous drive towards the deepening and widening of the European Community, including a change in its title to the European Union (EU) to reflect them. The latter resulted in the publication of many books, especially on the EU's *Single Market* drive, and of the new schemes, the North American Free Trade Agreement (NAFTA) and its predecessor, the Canada–US Free Trade Area (CUFTA), have also led to the publication of many volumes. Nevertheless, it remains the case that there are still very few books which provide a global and comprehensive coverage; hence this book.

The reader may wonder why this is not a third edition of *International Economic Integration*, especially when both editions of that book were well received by the profession and widely used by many universities all over the world for the teaching of courses on this subject. There are several reasons. First, although some of the chapters may have the familiar titles, not only have their contents changed dramatically, but some of them have been written by completely different invited contributors. Second, the book contains new chapters covering schemes which were either not in existence before or have become significant since then. Third, the book also contains a new chapter dealing with pertinent issues concerning worry by the international community regarding developments suggesting that the world may become split into three dominant trading blocs. Fourth, my team has changed so much: of the original contributors, I could extend invitations to only three. Fifth, some chapters have completely disappeared due to the demise of the relevant schemes. Finally, I have assumed more responsibility than before in terms of writing many of the chapters myself.

The book could not have taken its present form or structure without the cooperation of my distinguished and truly international group of contributors to all of whom I am extremely grateful. Professor Victor Bulmer-Thomas of Queen Mary and Westfield College, University of London, who is also Director of the University's Institute of Latin American Studies and an Editor of the *Journal of Latin American Studies*, contributed two chapters on Latin American economic integration before and after the 'debt crisis'. Professor Victoria Curzon Price of the University of Geneva, who is also Director of the European Institute of the same University, has contributed the chapter on that scheme. Dr Enzo Grilli of the IMF, where he is Executive Director for Italy (and constituency), having been an Executive Director with the World Bank before that, also lectures at the Johns Hopkins and Bocconi universities and has written several books and numerous articles on the EU's trade and aid policies towards the LDCs and the Central and Eastern European countries, has contributed the chapter on these issues. Dr David Mayes, Chief Manager of the Economics Department at the Reserve Bank of New Zealand, a former Coordinator of the UK's Economic and Social Research Council *Single European Market Research Programme*, and an Editor of the *Economic Journal*, who has written extensively on the quantitative estimation of economic integration effects, has contributed the chapter covering this important field. Dr Shelton Nicholls, a Lecturer in the Department of Economics, University of the West Indies, has done some research on the Caribbean Community and Common

Market and has collaborated with me in writing the chapter on CARICOM. Professor Richard Pomfret of the University of Adelaide and the Johns Hopkins School of Advanced International Studies before that, who is a leading expert on economic integration and has many publications on ASEAN and Australasian integration, has contributed the chapter on ASEAN. Peter Robson, who has published extensively, especially on the African dimension of international economic integration, was the Professor (now Honorary) of Economics with St Andrews University and Editor of the *Journal of Common Market Studies*, has contributed the chapter on economic integration in Africa. Professor Sidney Weintraub, who holds the William E. Simon Chair in Political Economy at the Centre for Strategic and International Studies in Washington DC and is also the Dean Rusk Professor of International Affairs at the Lyndon B. Johnson School of Public Affairs at the University of Texas, Austin, has written extensively on NAFTA and contributed the chapter on it.

The analysis of schemes of international economic integration requires knowledge of the theory of international economic integration as well as the problems regarding the empirical estimation of integration effects. So as to highlight the issues involved, to avoid repetition and make the chapters on actual schemes and related matters more accessible to a wider readership (by reducing technical discussion in those chapters to a minimum), separate chapters have been provided for these aspects.

ALI M. EL-AGRAA

Fukuoka

Notes on the Contributors

Victor Bulmer-Thomas is Director of the Institute of Latin American Studies, University of London, and Professor of Economics at Queen Mary and Westfield College. He is also an Editor of the *Journal of Latin American Studies*. His most recent books include (ed.) *The New Economic Model in Latin America and Its Impact on Income Distribution and Poverty*, *The Economic History of Latin America since Independence*, (with N. Craske and M. Serrano) *Mexico and the North American Free Trade Agreement: Who Will Benefit?*

Victoria Curzon Price is Professor of Economics at the University of Geneva and Director of the European Institute at the same University. From 1969 to 1977 she was Editor of the *Journal of World Trade Law*. She is currently working on an 'Austrian' interpretation of international trade. Her publications include *The Essentials of Economic Integration: Lessons of EFTA Experience* (1974), (with Gerard Curzon) *The Management of Trade Relations in the GATT* (1976), *Unemployment and Other Non-work Issues* (1980) and *Industrial Policies in the European Community* (1981). Her latest article is entitled 'The European Economic Area: Implications for Non-members in General and Mediterranean Countries in Particular' in Ahiram and Tovias (eds), *Whither EU–Israeli Relations* (1995).

Enzo Grilli is Executive Director for Italy (and constituency) at the International Monetary Fund, having been Executive Director at the World Bank before then. He is also a Professorial Lecturer in Economics at the School of Advanced International Studies of the Johns Hopkins University in Washington DC, and teaches at the Bocconi University in Milan, Italy. He is the author of numerous books and articles on trade and development issues. His latest books include *The European Community and the Developing Countries* (1993) and *Interdependenze Macro Economiche Nord-Sud* (1995).

David G. Mayes, formerly Coordinator of the Economic and Social Research Council (ESRC; UK) 'Single European Market Research Programme' and Chairman of the 'COST A7' action on 'The Evolution of Rules for a Single European Market', is Chief Manager of the Economics Department at the Reserve Bank of New Zealand. He is consultant at the National Institute for Economic and Social Research (NIESR) in London, a Research Associate of the New Zealand Institute of Economic Research and has been an Editor of the *Economic Journal* since 1976. He has published numerous articles and books.

Shelton M. A. Nicholls is Lecturer in the Department of Economics, University of the West Indies, St Augustine Campus, Trinidad and Tobago. He obtained his first degree from the same university, and his Ph.D from Queen Mary and Westfield College, University of London. He has published in the areas of large-scale macroeconometrics and time series modelling and is currently involved in research and teaching in trading blocs, economic integration, the World Trade Organisation (WTO) and financial economics.

Richard Pomfret has been Professor of Economics at the University of Adelaide, Australia, since 1992. Before that he was Professor of Economics at the Johns Hopkins University's School of Advanced International Studies in Washington DC, Bologna and Nanjing, and previously worked at Concordia University in Montréal and the Institut für Weltwirtschft at the University of Kiel, Germany. In 1993 he was seconded to the United Nation's Economic Commission for Asia and the Pacific for a year, acting as adviser on macroeconomic policy to the Asian republics of the former Soviet Union. He has also been consultant to the World Bank, the Arab Monetary Fund and the European Union/ASEAN. He has written thirteen books and numerous journal articles. His books include *The Economic Development of Canada* (1981, 1993), *Mediterranean Policy in the European Community* (1986), *Unequal Trade* (1988), *Investing in China 1979–89* (1991), *The Economics of Central Asia* (1995), *Asian Economies in Transition* (1996) and textbooks on international trade and economic development.

Peter Robson is currently Honorary Professor of Economics at St Andrews University, having previously held the Chair of Economics there from 1968 to 1987. He was earlier Professor of Economics at the University of Nairobi, Kenya. He has undertaken empirical studies of several regional groupings in Africa, Latin America and South East Asia. He was the Editor of the *Journal of Common Market Studies* from 1985 to 1991. His publications include: (ed.) *Economic Integration in Africa* (1968), *International Economic Integration* (1971), *Intégration, Dévelopment et Equité* (1987), *The Economics of International*

Integration (1987) and *Transnational Corporations and Regional Integration* (1993).

Sidney Weintraub holds the William E. Simon Chair in Political Economy at the Center for Strategic and International Studies in Washington DC and is Dean Rusk Professor of International Affairs at the Lyndon B. Johnson School of Public Affairs at the University of Texas at Austin. He is entered in the first edition of *Who's Who in Economics*. He has published numerous articles and books. Some of his latest books include *A Marriage of Convenience* (1990), *The US–Mexico Free Trade Agreement* (1992) and *NAFTA: What Comes Next?* (1994).

1 General Introduction

Ali M. El-Agraa

INTERNATIONAL ECONOMIC INTEGRATION

'International economic integration' (hereafter, simply economic integration) is one aspect of 'international economics' which has been growing in importance for well over four decades. The term itself has a rather short history; indeed, Machlup (1977) was unable to find a single instance of its use prior to 1942. Since then the term has been used at various times to refer to practically any area of international economic relations. By 1950, however, the term had been given a specific definition by economists specialising in international trade: 'it denotes a state of affairs or a process which involves the amalgamation of separate economies into larger free trading regions'. It is in this more limited sense that the term is used today. However, one should hasten to add that economists not familiar with this branch of international economics have for quite a while been using the term to mean simply increasing economic interdependence between nations.

More specifically, economic integration is concerned with the discriminatory removal of all trade impediments between at least two participating nations and with the establishment of certain elements of cooperation and coordination between them. The latter depends entirely on the actual form that integration takes. Different forms of economic integration can be envisaged and many have actually been implemented (see Table 1.1 for a schematic presentation):

1. *Free trade areas*, where the member nations remove all trade impediments amongst themselves but retain their freedom with regard to the determination of their own policies *vis-à-vis* the outside world (the non-participants – for example, the European Free Trade Association (EFTA) and the demised Latin American Free Trade Area (LAFTA).
2. *Customs unions*, which are very similar to free trade areas except that member nations must conduct and pursue common external commercial relations – for instance, they must adopt common external tariffs (CETs) on imports from the non-participants as

Table 1.1 Schematic presentation of economic integration schemes

Scheme	*Free intra-scheme trade*	*Common commercial policy*	*Free factor mobility*	*Common monetary & fiscal policy*	*One government*
Free trade area	yes	no	no	no	no
Customs union	yes	yes	no	no	no
Common market	yes	yes	yes	no	no
Economic union	yes	yes	yes	yes	no
Political union	yes	yes	yes	yes	yes

is the case in, *inter alia*, the European Union (EU, which is in this particular sense a customs union, but, as we shall presently see, it is more than that), the Central American Common Market (CACM) and the Caribbean Community and Common Market (CARICOM).

3. *Common markets*, which are customs unions that allow also for free factor mobility across national member frontiers, i.e. capital, labour, technology and enterprises should move unhindered between the participating countries – for example, the EU (but again it is more complex).
4. *Complete economic unions*, which are common markets that ask for complete unification of monetary and fiscal policies, i.e. the participants must introduce a central authority to exercise control over these matters so that member nations effectively become regions of the same nation – the EU is heading in this direction.
5. *Complete political unions*, where the participating countries become literally one nation, i.e. the central authority needed in complete economic unions should be paralled by a common parliament and other necessary institutions needed to guarantee the sovereignty of one state – an example of this is the unification of the two Germanies in 1990.

However, one should hasten to add that political integration need not be, and in the majority of cases will never be, part of this list. Nevertheless, it can of course be introduced as a form of unity and for no economic reason whatsoever, as was the case with the two Germanies and as is the case with the pursuit of the unification of the Korean Peninsula, although one should naturally be interested in its economic consequences (see below). More generally, one should indeed stress that each of these forms of economic integration can be introduced in its own right; hence they should not be confused with *stages* in a *process* which eventually leads to either complete economic or political union.

It should also be noted that there may be *sectoral* integration, as distinct from general across-the-board integration, in particular areas of the economy as was the case with the European Coal and Steel Community (ECSC), created in 1950, but sectoral integration is a form of cooperation not only because it is inconsistent with the accepted definition of economic integration but also because it may contravene the rules of the General Agreement on Tariffs and Trade (GATT), now called the World Trade Organisation (WTO) – see below. Sectoral integration may also occur within any of the mentioned schemes, as is the case with the EU's Common Agricultural Policy (CAP), but then it is nothing more than a 'policy'.

One should further point out that it has been claimed that economic integration can be *negative* or *positive*. The term negative integration was coined by Tinbergen (1954) to refer to the removal of impediments on trade between the participating nations or to the elimination of any restrictions on the process of trade liberalisation. The term positive integration relates to the modification of existing instruments and institutions and, more importantly, to the creation of new ones so as to enable the market of the integrated area to function properly and effectively and also to promote other broader policy aims of the scheme. Hence, at the risk of oversimplification, according to this classification, it can be stated that sectoral integration and free trade areas are forms of economic integration which require only negative integration, while the remaining types require positive integration, since, as a minimum, they need the positive act of adopting common relations. However, in reality this distinction is oversimplistic not only because practically all existing types of economic integration have found it essential to introduce some elements of positive integration, but also because theoretical considerations clearly indicate that no scheme of economic integration is viable without certain elements of positive integration, for example, even the ECSC deemed it necessary to establish new institutions to tackle its specified tasks – see Chapter 5.

ECONOMIC INTEGRATION AND WTO RULES

The rules of WTO, GATT's successor, allow the formation of economic integration schemes on the understanding that, although free trade areas, customs unions, etc. are discriminatory associations, they may not pursue policies which increase the level of their discrimination beyond that which existed prior to their formation, and that tariffs and other trade restrictions (with some exceptions) are removed on *substantially* all the trade amongst the participants. Hence, once allowance was made for the proviso regarding the external trade relations of the economic integration scheme (the CET level, or the common level of discrimination against extra-area trade, in a customs union, and the average tariff or trade discrimination level in a free trade area), it seemed to the drafters of Article XXIV (see Appendix to this chapter) that economic integration did not contradict the basic principles of WTO – trade *liberalisation* on a most-favoured-nation (MFN) basis, *non-discrimination*, *transparency* of instruments used to restrict trade and the promotion of *growth and stability* of the world economy – or more generally the principles of *non-discrimination*, *transparency* and *reciprocity*.

There are more serious arguments suggesting that Article XXIV is in direct contradiction to the spirit of WTO – see Chapter 3 and, *inter alia*, Dam (1970). However, Wolf (1983, p. 156) argues that if nations decide to treat one another as if they are part of a single economy, nothing can be done to prevent them, and that economic integration schemes, particularly like the EU at the time of its formation in 1957, have a strong impulse towards liberalisation; in the case of the EU at the mentioned time, the setting of the CETs happened to coincide with GATT's Kennedy Round of tariff reductions. However, recent experience, especially in the case of the EU, has proved otherwise since there has been a proliferation of non-tariff barriers (see Chapters 5 and 15), but the point about WTO not being able to deter countries from pursuing economic integration has general validity: WTO has no means for enforcing its rules; it has no coersion powers.

Of course, these considerations are more complicated than is suggested here, particularly since there are those who would argue that nothing could be more discriminatory than for a group of nations to remove all tariffs and trade impediments on their mutual trade while *at the same time* maintaining the initial levels against outsiders. Indeed, it it would be difficult to find 'clubs' which extend equal privileges to non-subscribers. Moreover, as we shall see in Chapter 3, economic integration schemes may lead to resource reallocation effects which are economically undesirable. However, to have denied nations the right to form such associations, particularly when the main driving force may be political rather than economic, would have been a major set back for the world community. Hence, all that needs to be stated here is that as much as Article XXIV raises serious problems regarding how it fits in with the general spirit of WTO, it also reflects its drafters' deep understanding of the future development of the world economy.

MOTIVES FOR ECONOMIC INTEGRATION

We shall see in Chapters 2 and 5 that the driving force behind the formation of the EU, the earliest and most influential of all existing integration schemes, was the political unity of Europe with the aim of realising eternal peace in the Continent. Some analysts would also argue that the recent attempts by the EU for more intensive economic integration can be cast in the same vein, especially since they are accompanied by common foreign and defence policies. At the same time, during the late 1950s and early 1960s economic integration amongst developing nations was perceived as the only viable way for them to make some real economic progress; indeed that was the rationale behind the United Nation's encouragement and support of such efforts. However, no matter what the motives for economic integration may be, it is still necessary to analyse the economic implications of such geographically discriminatory associations, that is one of the reasons why I have included political unification as one of the possible schemes.

At the customs union and free trade area levels, the possible sources of economic gain from economic integration can be attributed to:

(a) enhanced efficiency in production made possible by increased specialisation in accordance with the law of comparative advantage, due to the liberalised market of the participating nations;
(b) increased production levels due to better exploitation of economies of scale made possible by the increased size of the market;
(c) an improved international bargaining position, made possible by the larger size, leading to better terms of trade (cheaper imports from the outside world and higher prices for exports to them);
(d) enforced changes in efficiency brought about by intensified competition between firms; and
(e) changes affecting both the amount and quality of the factors of production due to technological advances, themselves encouraged by (d).

If the level of economic integration is to go beyond the free trade area and customs union levels, then further sources of economic gain also become possible:

(f) factor mobility across the borders of the member nations will materialise only if there is a net economic incentive for them, thus leading to higher national incomes;
(g) the coordination of monetary and fiscal policies may result in cost reductions since the pooling of efforts may enable the achievement of economies of scale; and
(h) the unification of efforts to achieve better employment levels, lower inflation rates, balanced trade, higher rates of economic growth and better income distribution may make it cheaper to attain these targets.

It should be apparent that some of these possible gains relate to static resource reallocation effects while the rest relate to long-term or dynamic effects. It should also be emphasised that these are *possible* economic gains, i.e. there is no guarantee that they can ever be achieved; everything would depend on the nature of the particular scheme and the type of competitive behaviour prevailing prior to integration. Indeed, it is quite feasible that in the absence of 'appropriate' competitive behaviour, economic integration may worsen the situation. Thus the possible attainment of these benefits must be considered with great caution:

> Membership of an economic grouping cannot of itself guarantee to a member state or the group a satisfactory economic performance, or even a better performance than in the past. The static gains from integration, although significant, can be – and often are – swamped by the influence of factors of domestic or international origin that have nothing to do with integration. The more fundamental factors influencing a country's economic performance (the dynamic factors) are unlikely to be affected by integration except in the long run. It is clearly not a necessary condition for economic success that a country should be a member of an economic community as the experience of several small countries confirms, although such countries might have done better as members of a suitable group. Equally, a large integrated market is in itself no guarantee of performance, as the experience of India suggests. However, although integration is clearly no panacea for all economic ills,

nor indispensable to success, there are many convincing reasons for supposing that significant economic benefits may be derived from properly conceived arrangements for economic integration. (Robson, 1984)

PLAN OF THE BOOK

This book is concerned with economic integration, defined in the limited sense of a state of affairs or a process which involves the amalgamation of separate economies into larger regions. Hence schemes of sectoral integration or international cooperation do not constitute a part of the book. This does not mean that OPEC, OAPEC, RCD, OECD, the Nordic Community, OAU, etc. (see Chapter 2) are not important, but simply that they are different in both nature and scope, and space limitations do not permit an adequate consideration of every conceivable scheme and institution. Had the book been about international institutions dealing with both economic and other relations, there would of course have been a justification for a comprehensive coverage of all such organisations. Moreover, of the schemes which qualify according to this limited definition, the book contains individual chapters on only those which have a fair degree of firm experience behind them, such as the EU and EFTA. Although there is ample justification for separate chapters on the CACM, ALADI and the Andean Pact, economic integration in Central and Latin America has taken such a completely different turn since the middle 1980s that it is both logical and meaningful to consider the schemes in the region together. Thus there are two chapters, respectively tackling integration there prior to and after 1985, but with clear sections on the appropriate schemes. Despite its young age, NAFTA has a separate chapter simply because it is an expanded and slightly changed CUFTA, thus it does have experience behind it. All Arab and African schemes are dealt with in single respective chapters: Arab integration because it is fluid and largely dormant; African integration because members belong to numerous and overlapping schemes and have had no record of success behind them. On the other hand, apart from being the most significant and influential scheme, the EU also has extensive relationships with some African, Caribbean and Pacific countries, as well as with many developing nations and the Eastern European nations that used to belong to the CMEA; hence two chapters are warranted. APEC is obviously too much of an infant at this stage to merit a separate chapter. And so on and so forth.

Hence the general plan of the book is such that Chapter 2 introduces all schemes briefly yet comprehensively, but devotes more space to such schemes as APEC and the CMEA; the former because of its embryonic nature and the latter not only because although it lasted for a long time, it has met its demise and left no solid achievements behind it. The reader will also find two chapters on the theory of economic integration and the problems of the quantitative estimation of integration effects. The theoretical considerations (Chapter 3), methodological aspects and the difficulties of statistical estimation (Chapter 4) are common to all schemes: it would therefore seem wise to tackle these problems separately in order that the chapters on actual integration schemes should be relieved of this task. There then follow chapters on the EU (5), EU Trade Policies towards the LDCs and CEECs (Central and East European Countries; 6), EFTA (7), NAFTA (8), Latin America before the Debt Crisis (9), Latin America since 1985 (10), CARICOM (11), ASEAN (12), the Arab League (13), and Africa (14). There then follows the first of the two final chapters (15), which is devoted to recent debates concerning allegations of increasing protectionism in the EU and NAFTA, and the need for a third trading bloc in East Asia (15). The final chapter (16) deals with the policy considerations emanating from the theoretical aspects of integration, asks the LDCs pertinent questions regarding economic integration, states overall conclusions and prognosticates on the future for economic integration.

APPENDIX

Article XXIV

Territorial Application – Frontier Traffic – Customs Unions and Free-Trade Areas

1. The provisions of this agreement shall apply to the metropolitan customs territories of the contracting parties and to any other customs territories in respect of which this Agreement has been accepted under Article XXVI or is being applied under Article XXXIII or pursuant to the Protocol of Provisional Application. Each such customs territory shall, exclusively for the purposes of the territorial application of this Agreement, be treated as though it were a contracting party; *Provided* that the provisions of this

paragraph shall not be construed to create any rights or obligations as between two or more customs territories in respect of which this Agreement has been accepted under Article XXVI or is being applied under Article XXXIII or pursuant to the Protocol of Provisional Application by a single contracting party.

2. For the purposes of this Agreement a customs territory shall be understood to mean any territory with respect to which separate tariffs or other regulations of commerce are maintained for a substantial part of the trade of such territory with other territories.

3. The provisions of this Agreement shall not be construed to prevent:
   (a) Advantages accorded by any contracting party to adjacent countries in order to facilitate frontier traffic;
   (b) Advantages accorded to the trade with the Free Territory of Trieste by countries contiguous to that territory, provided that such advantages are not in conflict with the Treaties of Peace arising out of the Second World War.

4. The contracting parties recognize the desirability of increasing freedom of trade by the development, through voluntary agreements, of closer integration between the economies of the countries parties to such agreements. They also recognize that the purpose of a customs union or of a free-trade area should be to facilitate trade between the constituent territories and not to raise barriers to the trade of other contracting parties with such territories.

5. Accordingly, the provisions of this Agreement shall not prevent, as between the territories of contracting parties, the formation of a customs union or of a free-trade area or the adoption of an interim agreement necessary for the formation of a customs union or of a free-trade area; *Provided* that:
   (a) with respect to a customs union, or an interim agreement leading to the formation of a customs union, the duties and other regulations of commerce imposed at the institution of any such union or interim agreement in respect of trade with contracting parties not parties to such union or agreement shall not on the whole be higher or more restrictive than the general incidence of the duties and regulations of commerce applicable in the constituent territories prior to the formation of such union or the adoption of such interim agreement, as the case may be;
   (b) with respect to a free-trade area, or an interim agreement leading to the formation of a free-trade area, the duties and other regulations of commerce maintained in each of the constituent territories and applicable at the formation of such free-trade area or the adoption of such interim agreement to the trade of contracting parties not included in

such area or not parties to such agreement shall not be higher or more restrictive than the corresponding duties and other regulations of commerce existing in the same constituent territories prior to the formation of the free-trade area, or interim agreement, as the case may be; and

(c) any interim agreement referred to in sub-paragraphs (a) and (b) shall include a plan and schedule for the formation of such a customs union or of such a free-trade area within a reasonable length of time.

6. If, in fulfilling the requirements of sub-paragraph 5(a), a contracting party proposes to increase any rate of duty inconsistently with the provisions of Article II, the procedure set forth in Article XXVIII shall apply. In providing for compensatory adjustment, due account shall be taken of the compensation already afforded by the reductions brought about in the corresponding duty of the other constituents of the union.

7. (a) Any contracting party deciding to enter into a customs union or free-trade area, or an interim agreement leading to the formation of such a union or area, shall promptly notify the CONTRACTING PARTIES and shall make available to them such information regarding the proposed union or area as will enable them to make such reports and recommendations to contracting parties as they may deem appropriate.

(b) If, after having studied the plan and schedule included in an interim agreement referred to in paragraph 5 in consultation with the parties to that agreement and taking due account of the information made available in accordance with the provisions of sub-paragraph (a), the CONTRACTING PARTIES find that such agreement is not likely to result in the formation of a customs union or of a free-trade area within the period contemplated by the parties to the agreement or that such period is not a reasonable one, the CONTRACTING PARTIES shall make recommendations to the parties to the agreement. The parties shall not maintain or put into force, as the case may be, such agreement if they are not prepared to modify it in accordance with these recommendations.

(c) Any substantial change in the plan or schedule referred to in paragraph 5(c) shall be communicated to the CONTRACTING PARTIES, which may request the contracting parties concerned to consult with them if the change seems likely to jeopardize or delay unduly the formation of the customs union or of the free-trade area.

8. For the purposes of this Agreement:

(a) A customs union shall be understood to mean the substitution of a single customs territory for two or more customs territories, so that

(i) duties and other restrictive regulations of commerce (except, where necessary, those permitted under Articles XI, XII, XIII, XIV, XV and XX) are eliminated with respect to substantially all the trade between the constituent territories of the union or at least with respect to substantially all the trade in products originating in such territories, and,

(ii) subject to the provisions of paragraph 9, substantially the same duties and other regulations of commerce are applied by each of the members of the union to the trade territories not included in the union;

(b) A free-trade area shall be understood to mean a group of two or more customs territories in which the duties and other restrictive regulations of commerce (except, where necessary, those permitted under Articles XI, XII, XIII, XIV, XV and XX) are eliminated on substantially all the trade between the constituent territories in products originating in such territories.

9. The preferences referred to in paragraph 2 of Article I shall not be affected by the formation of a customs union or of a free-trade area but may be eliminated or adjusted by means of negotiations with contracting parties affected. This procedure of negotiations with affected contracting parties shall, in particular, apply to the elimination of preferences required to conform with the provisions of paragraph 8(a)(i) and paragraph 8(b).

10. The CONTRACTING PARTIES may by a two-thirds majority approve proposals which do not fully comply with the requirements of paragraphs 5 to 9 inclusive, provided that such proposals lead to the formation of a customs union or a free-trade area in the sense of this Article.

11. Taking into account the exceptional circumstances arising out of the establishment of India and Pakistan as independent States and recognizing the fact that they have long constituted an economic unit, the contracting parties agree that the provisions of this Agreement shall not prevent the two countries from entering into special arrangements with respect to the trade between them, pending the establishment of their mutual trade relations on a definitive basis.

12. Each contracting party shall take such reasonable measures as may be available to it to ensure observance of the provisions of this Agreement by the regional and local governments and authorities within its territory.

2 Regional Trade Arrangements Worldwide

Ali M. El-Agraa

INTRODUCTION

Since the end of the Second World War various forms of international economic integration have been proposed and numerous schemes have actually been implemented. Even though some of those introduced were later discontinued or completely reformulated, the number adopted during the decade commencing in 1957 was so great as to prompt Haberler in 1964 to describe that period as the 'age of integration'. After 1964, however, there has been such a proliferation of integration schemes that Haberler's description may be more apt for the post-1964 era.

This book contains chapters on practically every significant scheme of international economic integration that is in existence today. Such a detailed and comprehensive treatment risks the danger of distracting the reader from the global perspective. Therefore this chapter is devoted to a comprehensive yet basic coverage of all the economic integration schemes and their trade arrangements.

ECONOMIC INTEGRATION IN EUROPE

The European Union (EU)

The EU is the most significant and influential of these arrangements since it comprises some of the most advanced nations of Western Europe: Austria, Belgium, Denmark, Finland, France, Germany, Greece, Ireland, Italy, Luxemburg, the Netherlands, Portugal, Spain, Sweden and the United Kingdom (UK) – see Table 2.1 for a visual display and Table 2.2 for data on GDP, population and per capita GNP; note that all the tables include arrangements not specified in the text but which are self-explanatory.

The EU was founded by six (not quite since Germany was then not yet united) of these nations (Belgium, France, West Germany, Italy,

Luxemburg and the Netherlands, usually referred to as the *Original Six*, simply the Six hereafter) by two treaties, signed in Rome on the same day in 1957, creating the *European Economic Community* (EEC) and the *European Atomic Energy Community* (Euratom). However, the Six had then been members of the *European Coal and Steel Community* (ECSC) which was established by the Treaty of Paris in 1951. Thus, in 1957 the Six belonged to three communities, but in 1965 it was deemed sensible to merge the three entities into one and called it the *European Communities* (EC). Three of the remaining nine (Denmark, Ireland and the UK) joined later in 1973. Greece became a full member in January 1981, Portugal and Spain in 1986, and Austria, Finland and Sweden in 1995.

Presently, the EU is in receipt of applications for membership from Cyprus, Hungary, Malta, Poland, Turkey and Switzerland. Also, most of the remaining Eastern European nations have not only signed *Agreements of Association* with the EU, but also intend to join as soon as possible, especially the Czech Republic and Slovakia. Moreover, the EU, Iceland, Liechtenstein and Norway belong to the *European Economic Area* (EEA), a scheme which provides Iceland and Norway with virtual membership of the EU, but without having a say in EU decisions; indeed the EEA is seen as stepping stone in the direction of full EU membership. Thus, if all goes according to plan, the EU is set to comprise the whole of Europe.

Although the EEC Treaty relates simply to the formation of a customs union and provides the basis for a common market in terms of free factor mobility, many of the orginators of the EEC saw it as a phase in a process culminating in complete economic and political union. Thus the *Treaty on European Union* (the Maastricht Treaty), which transformed the EC into the EU in 1994 and which intends, *inter alia*, to provide the EU with a single central bank, a single currency, and common foreign and defence policies by the end of this century, should be seen as positive steps towards the attainment of the founding fathers' desired goal.

The European Free Trade Association (EFTA)

EFTA is the other major scheme of international economic integration in Europe. To understand its membership one has to learn something about its history. In the mid-1950s when an EEC of the Six plus the UK was being contemplated, the UK was unprepared to commit itself to some of the economic and political aims envisaged for that

Table 2.1 Economic integration in Europe

	Existing schemes and arrangements									*Prospective arrangements*		
Aim	*EU 1957 CM*[a]	*EFTA*[b] 1960 FTA[a]	*EEA CU*[a]	*EFTA/ East Europe*[c] *FTA*[a]	*EU/ Czech R. FTA*[a]	*EU Slovakia FTA*[a]	*EU/ Hungary FTA*[a]	*EU/ Poland FTA*[a]	*EU/ Israel*[d]	EU/ Bulgaria FTA[a]	EFTA/ Israel[e] FTA[a]	EU/ GCC[f] FTA[a]
Austria	*		*		*	*	*	*	*	*		*
Belgium	*		*		*	*	*	*	*	*		*
Denmark	*		*		*	*	*	*	*	*		*
Finland	*		*		*	*	*	*	*	*		*
France	*		*		*	*	*	*	*	*		*
Germany	*		*		*	*	*	*	*	*		*
Greece	*		*		*	*	*	*	*	*		*
Ireland	*		*		*	*	*	*	*	*		*
Italy	*		*		*	*	*	*	*	*		*
Luxemburg	*		*		*	*	*	*	*	*		*
Netherlands	*		*		*	*	*	*	*	*		*
Portugal	*		*		*	*	*	*	*	*		*
Spain	*		*		*	*	*	*	*	*		*
Sweden	*		*		*	*	*	*	*	*		*
UK	*		*		*	*	*	*	*	*		*

Iceland	*	*	*							*	
Norway	*	*	*							*	
Switzerland	*		*							*	
Bulgaria			*						*		
Czech Rep.			*	*							
Hungary			*			*					
Poland			*				*				
Romania			*								
Slovakia			*		*						
GCC											*
Israel								*		*	

Notes

[a] FTA = free trade area; CU = customs union; CM = common market.
[b] Finland was an associate member until its accession in 1986, and Liechtenstein became a full member in 1991.
[c] The countries involved have agreed to examine conditions for the gradual establishment of a FTA.
[d] The EU and Israel reached an agreement similar to the EEA in 1995.
[e] Currently being negotiated.
[f] See Table 2.7 for members of the Gulf Cooperation Council (GCC).

Table 2.2 Economic indicators for European countries

	GDP		*Population*		*GNP per capita*	
Country	*US$m*	*Annual growth rate (%) 1980–93*	*million*	*Annual growth rate (%) 1980–93*	*US$*	*Annual growth rate (%) 1980–93*
Austria	182,067	2.3	8	0.3	23,510	2.0
Belgium	210,576	2.1	10	0.2	21,650	1.9
Denmark	117,587	2.0	5	0.1	26,730	2.0
Finland	74,124	2.0	5	0.4	19,300	1.5
France	1,251,689	2.1	57	0.5	22,490	1.6
Germany[a]	1,910,760	2.6	81	0.2	23,560	2.1
Greece	63,240	1.3	10	0.6	7,390	0.9
Ireland	42,962	3.8	4	0.3	13,000	3.6
Italy	991,386	2.2	57	0.1	19,840	2.1
Luxemburg	na	na	0.4	na	37,320	2.8
Netherlands	309,227	2.3	15	0.6	20,950	1.7
Portugal	85,665	3.0	10	0.1	9,130	3.3
Spain	478,582	3.1	39	0.4	13,590	2.7
Sweden	166,745	1.7	9	0.3	24,740	1.3
UK	819,038	2.5	58	0.2	18,069	2.3
Iceland	na	na	0.3	na	24,950	1.2
Norway	103,419	2.6	4	0.4	25,970	2.2
Switzerland	232,161	1.9	7	0.8	35,760	1.1
Bulgaria	10,369	0.9	9	0.0	1,140	0.5
Czech Rep.	31,613	na	10	0.0	2,710	na
Hungary	38,099	−0.1	10	−0.4	3,350	1.2
Poland	85,853	0.7	38	0.6	2,260	0.4
Romania	25,969	−2.5	23	0.2	1,140	−2.4
Russian Fed.	329,432	−0.5	149	0.5	2,340	−1.0
Slovak Rep.	11,076	na	5	0.5	1,950	na
Israel	69,739	4.1	5	2.3	13,920	2.0

Note

[a] Except for population, data refer to the Federal Republic of Germany before unification.

Source: unless otherwise indicated, the sources for all the tables are various issues of the World Bank's *World Development Report*, especially for 1993 and 1995.

community. For example, the adoption of a common agricultural policy and the eventual political unity of Western Europe were seen as aims which were in direct conflict with the UK's powerful position in the world and its interests in the Commonwealth, particularly with regard to 'Commonwealth preference' which granted special access to the markets of the Commonwealth. Hence the UK favoured the idea of a Western Europe which adopted free trade in industrial products only, thus securing for itself the advantages offered by the Commonwealth as well as opening up Western Europe as a free market for her industrial goods. In short, the UK sought to achieve the best of both worlds for itself, which is of course quite understandable. However, it is equally understandable that such an arrangement was not acceptable to those seriously contemplating the formation of the EEC, especially France which stood to lose in an arrangement excluding a common policy for agriculture. As a result the UK approached those Western European nations who had similar interests with the purpose of forming an alternative scheme of economic integration to counteract any possible damage due to the formation of the EEC. The outcome was EFTA which was established in 1960 by the Stockholm Convention with the object of creating a free market for industrial products only; there were some agreements on non-manufactures but these were relatively unimportant.

The membership of EFTA consisted of: Austria, Denmark, Norway, Portugal, Sweden, Switzerland (and Liechtenstein) and the UK. Finland became an associate member in 1961, and Iceland joined in 1970 as a full member. But, as already stated, Denmark and the UK (together with Ireland), joined the EC in 1973; Portugal (together with Spain) joined in 1986; and Austria, Finland and Sweden joined the EU in 1995. This left EFTA with a membership consisting mainly of a few and relatively smaller nations of Western Europe – see Tables 2.1 and 2.2.

The Council for Mutual Economic Assistance (CMEA)

Until recently, economic integration schemes in Europe were not confined to the EU and EFTA. Indeed, before the dramatic events of 1989–90, the socialist planned economies of Eastern Europe had their own arrangement which operated under the CMEA, or COMECON as it was generally known in the West. The CMEA was formed in 1949 by Bulgaria, Czechoslovakia, the German Democratic Republic, Hungary, Poland, Romania and the USSR; they were later joined by three non-European countries: Mongolia (1962), Cuba (1972) and Vietnam (1978). In its earlier days, before the death of Stalin, the activities of the CMEA were confined to the collation of the plans of the member states, the development of a uniform system of reporting statistical data and the recording of foreign trade statistics. However, during the 1970s a series of measures was adopted by the CMEA to implement their 'Comprehensive Programme of Socialist Integration', hence indicating that the organisation was moving towards a form of integration based principally on methods of plan coordination and joint planning activity, rather than on market levers (Smith, 1977). Finally, attention should be drawn to the fact that the CMEA comprised a group of relatively small countries and one 'super power' and that the long-term aim of the association was to achieve a highly organised and integrated bloc, without any agreement ever having been made on how or when that was to be accomplished.

The dramatic changes that have recently taken place in Eastern Europe and the former USSR have inevitably led to the demise of the CMEA. This, together with the fact that the CMEA did not really achieve much in the nature of economic integration, indeed some analysts have argued that the entire organisation was simply an instrument for the USSR to dictate its wishes on the rest, are the reasons why this book does not contain a chapter on the CMEA; the interested reader will find a chapter in El-Agraa (1988a). However, one should hasten to add that soon after the demise of the USSR, Russia and seventeen former USSR republics formed the Commonwealth of Independent States (CIS) which makes them effectively one nation.

Before leaving Europe it should be mentioned that another scheme exists in the form of a regional bloc between the five Nordic countries (the Nordic Community): Denmark, Finland, Iceland, Norway and Sweden. However, in spite of claims to the contrary (Sundelius and Wiklund, 1979), the Nordic scheme is of one of cooperation rather than economic integration since its members belong either to the EU or EFTA, and, as we have seen, the EU and EFTA are closely linked through the EEA.

ECONOMIC INTEGRATION IN AFRICA

In Africa, there are numerous schemes of economic integration – see Tables 2.3 and 2.4.

The *Union Douanière et Economique de l'Afrique Centrale* (UDEAC), a free trade area, comprises the People's Republic of the Congo, Gabon, Cameroon and the Central African Republic. Member nations of UDEAC plus Chad, a former member, constitute a monetary union. The *Communauté Economique de l'Afrique de l'Ouest* (CEAO), which was formed under the Treaty of Abidjan in 1973, is a free trade area consisting of the Ivory Coast (Côte d'Ivoire), Mali,

Mauritania, Niger, Senegal and Upper Volta (now Burkina Faso); Benin joined in 1984. Member countries of the CEAO, except for Mauritania, plus Benin and Togo, have replaced the CEAO by an Act constituting an economic and monetary union. In 1973 the *Mano Riven Union* (MRU) was established between Liberia and Sierra Leone; they were joined by Guinea in 1980. The MRU is a customs union which involves a certain degree of cooperation particularly in the industrial sector. The *Economic Community of West African States* (ECOWAS) was formed in 1975 with fifteen signatories: its membership consists of all those countries participating in UDEAC, CEAO, MRU plus some other West African States. Despite its name, ECOWAS is a free trade area. Its total membership today is seventeen.

In 1969 the *Southern African Customs Union* (SACU) was established between Botswana, Lesotho, Swaziland and the Republic of South Africa; they were later joined by Namibia. The *Economic Community of the Countries of the Great Lakes* (CEPGL), a free trade area, was created in 1976 by Rwanda, Burundi and Zaire. Until its collapse in 1978, there was the *East African Community* (EAC) between Kenya, Tanzania and Uganda. In 1981 the *Preferential Trade Area* (PTA), a free trade area, was created by fifteen nations from Eastern and Southern Africa: Angola, Botswana, the Comoros, Djibouti, Ethiopia, Kenya, Losetho, Malawai, Mauritius, Mozambique, Swaziland, Tanzania, Uganda, Zambia and Zimbabwe; they were later joined by another five nations. The PTA has been replaced by the much more ambitious *Common Market for Eastern and Southern Africa* (COMESA). In 1983 the *Economic Community of Central African States* (EEAC, the acronym is from French) was created by eleven nations in Equatorial and Central Africa. In 1985 the *Benin Union* (BU) was formed by Benin, Ghana, Nigeria and Togo. In 1980, the *Lagos Plan of Action* was inaugurated with a membership which included practically the whole of Africa. There are also many smaller sub-regional groupings such as the Kagera River Basin organisation (KBO), the Lake Tanganyika and Kivu Basin organisation (LTKBC) and the Southern African Development Coordination Council (SADCC).

Moreover, there are schemes involving the Nothern African nations (see Tables 2.7 and 2.8). In August 1984 a treaty was signed by Libya and Morocco to establish the *Arab–African Union*, whose main aim is to tackle their political conflicts in the Sahara Desert. In 1989 the *Arab Maghreb Union* (AMU), a common market, was created by Algeria, Libya, Morocco and Tunisia. Egypt participates in the *Arab Cooperation Council* (ACC) which was formed in 1990 (see p. 32).

Table 2.3 Regional trade arrangements in Africa

	CEAO[a]	*CEPGL*	*EAC*[b]	*ECOWAS*	*MRU*[a]	*COMESA*[c]	*SACU*	*UDEAC*[d]	*Sene/ Gambia*	*Lagos Plan of Action*
Founded	*1972*	*1976*	*1967*	*1975*	*1973*	*1981*	*1969*	*1964*	*1981*	*1980*
Aim	*FTA*	*FTA*	*EU*	*FTA*	*CU*	*FTA*	*CU*	*FTA*	*CON*[e]	*EU*
Angola						*				*
Benin	*			*						*
Botswana						*	*			*
Burkina Faso	*			*						*
Burundi		*				*				*
Cameroon								*		*
Cape Verde				*						
CAR								*		*
Chad								*		*
Comros						*				*
Congo								*		*
Côte d'Ivoire	*			*						*
Djibouti						*				*
Eq. Guinea								*		*
Ethiopia						*				*
Gabon				*				*		*
Gambia				*					*	*
Ghana				*						*
Guinea				*	*[f]					*
Guinea-Bissau				*						*
Kenya			*			*				*
Lesotho						*	*			*
Liberia				*	*					*
Madagascar						*				*
Malawi						*				*

Mali	*			*						*
Mauritania	*			*						*
Mauritius						*				*
Mozambique						*				*
Namibia							*			*
Niger	*			*						*
Nigeria				*						*
Rwanda		*				*				*
Senegal	*			*					*	*
Seychelles										*
Sierra Leone				*	*					*
Somalia						*				*
South Africa							*			*
Sudan						*				*
Swaziland						*	*			*
Tanzania			*			*				*
Togo				*						*
Uganda			*			*				*
Zaire		*								*
Zambia						*				*
Zimbabwe						*				*

Notes

[a] In effect since 1974.

[b] Dismantled in 1978.

[c] The Common Market for eastern and southern Africa is an ambitious recent replacement of the PTA which was in effect since 1984.

[d] In effect since 1966.

[e] CON = confederation.

[f] Joined in 1980.

Table 2.4 Economic indicators for the African countries

Country	GDP US$m	GDP Annual Growth Rate (%) 1980–93	Population million	Population Annual Growth Rate (%) 1980–93	GNP per capita US$	GNP per capita Annual Growth Rate (%) 1980–93
Angola	na	na	10	na	b	na
Benin	2,125	2.7	5	3.0	430	−0.4
Botswana	3,813	9.6	1	3.4	2,790	6.2
Burkina Faso	2,698	3.7	10	2.6	300	0.8
Burundi	855	3.6	6	2.9	180	0.9
Cameroon	11,082	0.0	13	2.8	820	−2.2
Cape Verde	na	na	0.4	na	920	3.0
CAR[a]	1,172	1.0	3	2.4	400	−1.6
Chad	1,133	4.8	6	2.3	210	3.2
Comros	na	na	0.5	na	560	−0.4
Congo	2,385	2.7	2	2.9	950	−0.3
Côte d'Ivoire	8,087	0.1	13	3.7	630	−4.6
Djibouti	na	na	0.6	na	780	na
Eq. Guinea	na	na	0.4	na	420	1.2
Ethiopia	5,750	1.8	52	2.7	100	na
Gabon	5,420	1.2	1	1.7	4,960	−1.6
Gambia, The	303	2.4	1	3.7	350	−0.2
Ghana	6,084	3.5	16	3.3	430	0.1
Guinea	3,172	3.7	1	2.0	500	na
Guinea-Bissau	241	4.8	1	2.0	240	2.8
Kenya	4,691	3.8	25	3.3	270	0.3
Lesotho	609	5.5	2	2.9	650	−0.5
Liberia	na	na	3	na	c	na
Madagascar	3,126	0.9	14	3.3	220	−2.6
Malawi	1,810	3.0	11	na	200	−1.2
Mali	2,662	1.9	10	3.0	270	−1.0
Mauritania	859	2.0	2	2.6	500	−0.8
Mauritius	2,780	6.0	1	0.9	3,030	5.5
Mozambique	1,367	1.0	15	1.7	90	−1.5
Namibia	2,109	1.3	1	2.7	1,820	0.7
Niger	2,220	−0.6	9	3.3	270	−4.1
Nigeria	31,344	2.7	105	2.9	300	−0.1
Rwanda	1,359	1.1	8	2.9	210	−1.2
Senegal	5,770	2.8	8	2.7	750	0.0
Seychelles	na	na	0.1	na	6,280	3.4
Sierra Leone	660	1.1	4	2.5	150	−1.5
Somalia	na	na	9	na	c	na
South Africa	105,636	0.9	40	2.4	2,980	−0.2
Sudan	na	na	27	na	c	na
Swaziland	na	na	0.9	na	1,190	2.3
Tanzania	2,086	3.6	28	3.2	90	0.1
Togo	1,249	0.7	4	3.0	340	−2.1
Uganda	3,037	3.8	18	2.4	180	na
Zaire	na	na	41	na	c	na
Zambia	3,685	0.9	9	3.4	380	−3.1
Zimbabwe	4,986	2.7	11	3.2	520	−0.3

Notes
[a] Central African Republic.
b = Estimated to be between $696 and $2,785.
c = Estimated to be $695 or less.

Hence, a unique characteristic of economic integration in Africa is the multiplicity and overlapping of its schemes. For example, in the West alone, there was a total of thirty-three schemes and intergovernmental cooperation organisations, which is why the United Nations Economic Commission for Africa (UNECA) recommended in 1984 that there should be some rationalisation in the economic cooperation attempts in West Africa. However, as Table 2.3 partially shows, the diversity and overlapping is not confined to West Africa alone. Needless to add, the Lagos Plan of Action is no solution since, apart from encompassing the whole of Africa and being a weaker association, it exists on top of the other schemes. When this uniqueness is combined with proliferation in schemes, one cannot disagree with Robson (see Chapter 14) when he declares:

> *Reculer pour mieux sauter* is not a dictum that seems to carry much weight among African governments involved in regional integration. On the contrary, if a certain level of integration cannot be made to work, the reaction of policy makers has typically been to embark on something more elaborate, more advanced and more demanding in terms of administrative requirements and political commitment.

That is why this book contains only a single and brief chapter on African integration; indeed, one can even argue that such a chapter has no place in this book.

ECONOMIC INTEGRATION IN WESTERN HEMISPHERE

Latin America and the Caribbean

Economic integration in Latin America has been too volatile to describe in simple terms since the post-1985 experience has been very different from that in the 1960s and 1970s. At the risk of misleadling, one can state that there are four schemes of economic integration in this region – see Tables 2.5 and 2.6. Under the 1960 Treaty of Montevideo, the *Latin American Free Trade Association* (LAFTA) was formed between Mexico and all the countries of South America except for Guyana and Surinam. LAFTA came to an end in the late 1970s but was promptly succeeded by the *Association for Latin American Integration* (ALADI or LAIA) in 1980. The Managua Treaty of

Table 2.5 Regional trade arrangements in the western hemisphere[a]

	Existing arrangements								
	NA-FTA	*CACM*[b]	*LAFTA-LAIA*	*CARI-COM*[c]	*Andean Pact*[d]	*US-Canada*	*MER-COSUR*[e]	*OECS*[f]	*US-Israel*
Founded	*1993*	*1961*	*1960/80*	*1973*	*1969*	*1988*	*1991*	*1991*	*1989*
aim	*FTA*	*FTA*	*FTA*	*CU*	*FTA*	*FTA*	*FTA*	*CI*	*FTA*
Canada	*					*			
Mexico	*		*			*			
USA	*					*			*
Belize				*					
Costa Rica		*							
El Salvador		*							
Guatemala		*							
Honduras		*							
Nicaragua		*							
Panama[g]		*							
Antiqua/Bermuda				*				*	
Bahamas				*					
Barbados				*					
Dominica				*				*	
Grenada				*				*	
Jamaica				*					
Monserrat				*				*	
St Kitts/Nevis				*				*	
St Lucia				*				*	
St Vincent				*				*	
Trinidad/Tobago				*					
Argentina			*				*		
Bolivia			*		*				
Brazil			*				*		
Chile			*		*				
Colombia			*		*				
Ecuador			*		*				
Guyana				*					
Paraguay			*				*		
Peru			*		*				
Uruguay			*				*		
Venezuela			*		*				
Israel									*

Notes

[a] Does not include unilateral trade preferences and exclusive countries with no arrangements.

[b] Revived in 1990; aimed to establish a common market by 1992.

[c] Aimed to achieve a common external tariff by 1994.

[d] Efforts were being made to revive the AP and to create a common market by 1994.

[e] Aims to achieve a common market by 1995.

[f] Organization of East Caribbean States.

[g] Effective in October 1991.

Argentina-Brazil 1990 FTA	*Chile-Mexico 1991 FTA*	*El Salvador-Guatemala*[g] *1991 FTA*	*EAI (US)*[h] *1991 FTA*	*Prospective arrangements* *Mexico-Central America*[i]	*Chile-Colombia-Venezuela*	*Colombia-Mexico-Venezuela*[j]	*Venezuela-Central America*[k]	*RIO Group*
	*			*		*		*
		*						
			*	*			*	
		*	*	*			*	
		*		*			*	
			*	*			*	
			*	*			*	
			*	*			*	
			*					
			*					
			*					
			*					
			*					
			*					
			*					
			*					
			*					
			*					
			*					
*			*					*
			*					
*			*					
	*		*					*
			*		*	*		*
			*					
			*					
	*		*					
			*					*
			*					*
			*		*	*	*	*

[h] The Enterprise of the Americas Initiative aims to achieve a hemisphere free trade zone. By October 1991, the US had signed framework agreements with 29 countries, including: the 13 CARICOM nations; the 4 MERCOSUR states, Chile, Colombia, Costa Rica, Ecuador, El Salvador, Honduras, Panama, Peru, Nicaragua and Venezuela.

[i] These countries aim to form a Central America-Mexican free trade zone by 1996.

[j] Signature of the trade and investment agreement occurred in 1991 and trilateral limited free trade was supposed to happen by the end of 1993.

[k] The agreement aims to phase out tariffs on trade in the area.

[l] Panama participates in summits but is not ready to participate fully in regional integration.

Table 2.6 Economic indicators for the western hemisphere, 1993

	GDP		*Population*		*GNP per capita*	
Country	*US$m*	*Annual growth rate (%) 1980–93*	*million*	*Annual growth rate (%) 1980–93*	*US$*	*Annual growth rate (%) 1980–93*
Canada	477,468	2.6	29	1.2	19,970	1.4
Mexico	343,472	1.6	90	2.3	3,610	−0.5
USA	6,259,899	2.7	258	1.0	24,740	1.7
Belize	na	na	0.204	na	2,450	2.9
Costa Rica	7,577	3.6	3	na	2,150	1.1
El Salvador	7,625	1.6	6	1.5	1,320	0.2
Guatemala	11,309	1.7	10	2.9	1,100	−1.2
Honduras	2,867	2.9	5	3.1	600	−0.3
Nicaragua	1,800	−1.8	4	3.0	340	−5.7
Panama	6,565	1.3	2.5	2.6	2,600	−0.7
Antiqua/Bermuda	na	na	0.065	na	6,540	5.2
Bahamas, The	na	na	0.268	na	11,420	1.4
Barbados	na	na	0.260	na	6,230	0.5
Dominica	na	na	0.071	na	2,720	4.6
Grenada	na	na	0.092	na	2,380	3.8
Jamaica	3,825	2.3	2	0.9	1,440	−0.3
Monserrat	na	na	0.012	na	na	na
St Kitts/Nevis	na	na	0.042	na	4,410	5.4
St Lucia	na	na	0.142	na	3,380	4.4
St Vincent	na	na	0.110	na	2,120	5.0
Trinidad/Tobago	4,487	−3.6	1	1.3	3,830	−2.8
Argentina	255,595	0.8	34	1.4	7,220	−0.5
Bolivia	5,382	1.1	7	2.1	760	−0.7
Brazil	444,205	2.1	156	2.0	2,930	0.3
Chile	43,684	5.1	14	1.7	3,170	3.6
Colombia	54,076	3.7	36	2.3	1,400	1.5
Ecuador	14,421	2.4	11	2.5	1,200	0.0
Guyana	na	na	0.816	na	350	−3.6
Paraguay	6,825	2.8	5	3.1	1,510	0.7
Peru	41,061	−0.5	23	2.1	1,490	−2.7
Uruguay	13,144	1.3	3	0.6	3,830	−2.8
Venezuela	59,995	2.1	21	2.5	2,840	−0.7
Israel	69,739	4.1	5	2.3	13,920	2.0

1960 established the *Central American Common Market* (CACM) between Costa Rica, El Salvador, Guatemala, Honduras and Nicaragua. In 1969 the *Andean Pact* (AP) was established under the Cartegena Agreement between Bolivia, Chile, Colombia, Ecuador,

Peru and Venezuela; the AP forms a closer link between some of the least developed nations of LAFTA, now LAIA.

Since the debt crisis in the 1980s, economic integration in Latin America has taken a new turn with Mexico joining Canada and the US (see below) and Argentina, Brazil, Paraguay and Uruguay, the more developed nations of LAIA, creating *MERCOSUR* in 1991. MERCOSUR became a customs union by 1 January 1995 but aims to become more than a common market by 2013. Bolivia and Chile became associate members in mid-1995, a move which Brazil sees as merley a first step towards the creation of a *South American Free Trade Area* (SAFTA), a counterweight to the efforts in the north (see p. 260).

There is one scheme of economic integration in the Caribbean. In 1973 the *Caribbean Common Market and Community* (CARICOM) was formed between Antigua, Barbados, Belize, Dominica, Grenada, Guyana, Jamaica, Monstserrat, St Kitts-Nevis-Anguilla, St Lucia, St Vincent, and Trinidad and Tobago. CARICOM replaced the *Caribbean Free Trade Association* (CARIFTA) which was established in 1968.

North and Central America

In 1988 Canada and the United States established the *Canada–US Free Trade Agreement* (CUFTA), and, together with Mexico, they formed the *North American Free Trade Agreement* (NAFTA) in 1993 which started to operate from 1 January 1994. Despite its name, NAFTA also covers investment. The enlargement of NAFTA to include the rest of the western hemisphere was suggested by George Bush while US President who hoped to construct what is now referred to as the *Free Trade Area of the Americas* (FTAA), which is under negotiation, aiming for a conclusion by 2005. Chile has been negotiating membership of NAFTA.

ECONOMIC INTEGRATION IN ASIA-PACIFIC

Asia does not figure prominently in the league of economic integration schemes (see Tables 2.7 and 2.8) but this is not surprising given the existence of such large (if only in terms of population) countries as China and India. The *Regional Cooperation for Development* (RCD) was a very limited arrangement for sectoral integration between Iran, Pakistan and Turkey. The *Association for South-East Asian Nations* (ASEAN) comprises seven nations: Brunei, Indonesia, Malaysia, the

Table 2.7 Regional trade arrangements in Asia-Pacific and the Middle East

	Existing arrangements							*Prospective arrangement*
	CER	*ASEAN*	*ACM*	*ECO*[a]	*GCC*	*AFTA*[b]	*APEC*[c]	EAEC[d]
Founded	*1983*	*1967*	*1964*	*1985*	*1981*			
Aim	*FTA*	*FTA*	*CU*		*CU*			
Australia	*						*	
Brunei		*				*	*	*
Chile							*	
China							*	*
Hong Kong							*	*
Indonesia		*				*	*	*
Japan							*	*
Malaysia		*				*	*	*
New Zealand	*						*	
Papua New Guinea							*	
Philippines		*				*	*	*
Singapore		*				*	*	*
South Korea							*	*
Taiwan							*	*
Thailand		*				*	*	*
Bahrain					*			
Egypt			*					
Iran				*				
Iraq			*					
Jordan			*					
Kuwait					*			
Libya			*					
Oman					*			
Qatar					*			
Saudi Arabia					*			
Syria			*					
UAE					*			
Yemen			*					
Canada							*	
Mauritania					*			
Pakistan						*		
Turkey						*		
USA							*	

Notes

[a] The purpose of this group is bilateral trade promotion and coperation in industrial planning.

[b] Thailand proposal endorsed by ASEAN Ministers in 1991.

[c] Originally a regional grouping to represent members' views in multilateral negotiating fora, now committed to freeing trade and investment among its richer members by 2010 and by 2020 for the rest.

[d] This grouping was initially proposed by Malaysia in 1990.

Table 2.8 Economic indicators for Asia-Pacific countries, 1993

Country	GDP US$m	GDP Annual growth rate (%) 1980–93	Population million	Population Annual growth rate (%) 1980–93	GNP per capita US$	GNP per capita Annual growth rate (%) 1980–93
Australia	289,390	3.1	18	1.5	17,500	1.6
Brunei	na	na	0.3	na	a	na
Chile	43,684	5.1	14	1.7	3,170	3.6
China	425,611	9.6	1,178	1.4	490	8.2
Hong Kong	89,997	6.5	6	1.1	18,060	5.4
Indonesia	144,707	5.8	187	1.7	740	4.2
Japan	4,214,204	4.0	124	0.5	31,490	2.0
Malaysia	64,450	6.2	19	2.5	3,140	3.5
New Zealand	43,699	1.5	3	0.9	12,600	0.7
Papua New Guinea	5,091	3.1	4	2.2	1,130	0.6
Philippines	54,068	1.4	65	2.3	850	−0.6
Singapore	55,153	6.9	3	1.1	19,850	2.1
South Korea	330,831	9.1	44	1.1	7,660	8.2
Taiwan[d]	226,243	na	21	na	10,852	na
Thailand	124,862	8.2	58	1.7	2,110	6.4
Bahrain	na	na	0.5	na	8,030	−2.9
Egypt	35,784	4.3	56	2.0	660	2.8
Iran	107,335	2.6	64	na	na	na
Iraq	na	na	20	na	b	na
Jordan	4,441	1.2	4	4.9	1,190	na
Kuwait	22,402	na	2	1.9	19,360	−4.3
Libya	na	na	5	na	c	na
Oman	11,686	7.6	2	4.5	4,850	3.4
Qatar	na	na	0.5	na	15,030	−7.2
Saudi Arabia	121,530	0.4	17	4.4	na	-3.6
Syria	na	na	14	na	b	na
UAE	34,935	0.3	2	4.4	21,430	−4.4
Yemen	11,958	na	13	3.6	na	na
Canada	477,468	2.6	29	1.2	19,970	1.4
Mauritania	859	2.0	2	2.6	500	−0.8
Pakistan	46,360	6.0	123	2.8	430	3.1
Turkey	156,413	4.6	60	2.3	2,970	2.4
USA	6,259,899	2.7	258	1.0	24,740	1.3

Notes
a = Estimated to be more than $8,626.
b = Estimated to be $695 or less.
c = Estimated to be between $696 and $2,785.
[d] The data are from national accounts with the first column referring to GNP.

Philippines, Singapore, Thailand and Vietnam. ASEAN was founded in 1967 by these countries minus Brunei and Vietnam in the shadow of the Vietnam War. Brunei joined in 1984 and Vietnam in July 1995. After almost a decade of inactivity 'it was galvanized into renewed vigour in 1976 by the security problems which the reunification of Vietnam seemed to present to its membership' (Arndt and Garnaut,

1979). The drive for the establishment of ASEAN and for its vigorous reactivation in 1976 was both political and strategic. However, right from the start, economic cooperation was one of the most important aims of ASEAN, indeed most of the vigorous activities of the group since 1976 have been predominantly in the economic field, and the admission of Vietnam in 1995 is a clear manifestation of this. Moreover, ASEAN has recently been discussing proposals to accelerate its own plan for a free trade area to the year 2000 from 2003, itself an advance on the original target of 2008.

In 1965 Australia and New Zealand entered into a free trade arrangement called the *New Zealand Australia Free Trade Area.* This was replaced in 1983 by the more important *Australia New Zealand Closer Economic Relations and Trade Agreement* (CER, for short): not only have major trade barriers been removed, but significant effects on the New Zealand economy have been experienced as a result.

A scheme for the Pacific Basin integration-cum-cooperation was being hotly discussed during the 1980s. In the late 1980s I (El-Agraa, 1988a, 1988b) argued that 'given the diversity of countries within the Pacific region, it would seem highly unlikely that a very involved scheme of integration would evolve over the next decade or so'. This was in spite of the fact that there already existed:

1. The *Pacific Economic Cooperation Conference* (PECC) which is a tripartite structured organisation with representatives from governments, business and academic circles and with the secretariat work being handled between general meetings by the country next hosting a meeting.
2. The *Pacific Trade and Development Centre* (PAFTAD) which is an academically oriented organisation.
3. The *Pacific Basin Economic Council* (PBEC) which is a private-sector business organisation for regional cooperation.
4. The *Pacific Telecommunications Conference* (PTC) which is a specialised organisation for regional cooperation in this particular field.

The reason for the pessimism was that the

> region under consideration covers the whole of North America and Southeast Asia, with Pacific South America, the People's Republic of China and the USSR all claiming interest since they are all on

> the Pacific. Even if one were to exclude this latter group, there still remains the cultural diversity of such countries as Australia, Canada, Japan, New Zealand and the USA, plus the diversity that already exists within ASEAN. It would seem that unless the group of participants is severely limited, Pacific Basin *cooperation* will be the logical outcome. (El-Agraa, 1988a, p. 8)

However, in an attempt to provide a rational basis for resolving Japan's trade frictions, I may appear to have contradicted myself:

> it may be concluded that . . . Pacific Basin cooperation-cum-integration is the only genuine solution to the problems of Japan and the USA (as well as the other nations in this area). Given what is stated above about the nature of the nations of the Pacific Basin, that would be a broad generalisation: what is needed is a very strong relationship between Japan and the USA within a much looser association with the rest of SE Asia. Hence, what is being advocated is a form of involved economic integration between Japan and the USA (and Canada, if the present negotiations for a free trade area of Canada and the USA lead to that outcome), within the broad context of 'Pacifc Basin Cooperation', or, more likely, within a free trade area with the most advanced nations of SE Asia: Australia, New Zealand, South Korea, the nations of ASEAN, etc. (El-Agraa, 1988b, pp. 203–4)

I added that the proposed scheme should not be a protectionist one. Members of such a scheme should promote cooperation with the rest of the world through their membership of GATT (now WTO) and should coordinate their policies with regard to overseas development assistance, both financially and in terms of the transfer of technology, for the benefit not only of the poorer nations of SE Asia, but also for the whole developing world.

Thus the *Asia Pacific Economic Cooperation* (APEC) forum can be considered as the appropriate response to my suggestion. It was established in 1989 by ASEAN plus Australia, Canada, Japan, New Zealand, South Korea the US. These were joined by China, Hong Kong and Taiwan in 1991. In 1993 President Clinton galvanised it into its present form and size of eighteen nations. In Bogor, Indonesia, in 1994 APEC declared its intention (vision) to create a free trade and investment area by the year 2010 by its advanced members, with the rest to follow suit ten years later. APEC tried to chart the route for realising this vision in Osaka, Japan, in November 1995, and came up with the interesting resolution that each member nation should unilaterally declare its own measures for freeing trade and investment, with agriculture completely left out of the reckoning.

ECONOMIC INTEGRATION IN THE MIDDLE EAST

There are several schemes in the Middle East, but some of them extend beyond the geographical area traditionally designated as such. This is natural since there are nations with Middle Eastern characteristics in parts of Africa. The *Arab League* (AL) clearly demonstrates this reality since it comprises twenty-two nations, extending from the Gulf in the East to Mauritania and Morocco in the West. Hence the geographical area covered by the scheme includes the whole of North Africa, a large part of the Middle East, plus Djibouti and Somalia. The purpose of the AL is to strengthen the close ties linking Arab states, to coordinate their policies and activities, direct them to their common good, and mediate in disputes between them. These may seem like vague terms of reference, but the *Arab Economic Council*, whose membership consists of all Arab Ministers of Economic Affairs, was entrusted with suggesting ways for economic development, cooperation, organisation and coordination. The *Council for Arab Economic Unity* (CAEU), which was formed in 1957, had the aim of establishing an integrated economy of all AL states. Moreover, in 1964 the *Arab Common Market* was formed (but practically never got off the ground) between Egypt, Iraq, Jordan and Syria, and in 1981 the *Gulf Cooperation Council* (GCC) was established between Bahrain, Kuwait, Oman, Qatar, Saudi Arabia and United Arab Emirates to bring together the Gulf states and prepare the ground for them to join forces in the economic, political and military spheres.

The latest schemes of economic integration in the Middle East have already been mentioned, but only in passing in the context of Africa. The ACC was founded on 16 February 1989 by Egypt, Iraq, Jordan and the Arab Yemen Republic with the aim of boosting Arab solidarity and acting as 'yet another link in the chain of Arab efforts towards integration'. Moreover, on 18 February 1989 the AMU was formed by Algeria, Libya, Mauritania, Morocco and Tunisia. The AMU aims to create an organisation similar to the EU.

SECTORAL COOPERATION SCHEMES

There are two schemes of sectoral economic integration which are not based on geographical proximity. The first is the *Organisation for Petroleum Exporting Countries* (OPEC), founded in 1960 with a truly international membership. Its aim was to protect the main interest of its member nations: petroleum. After verging close to liquidation, OPEC seems to have been revived, but it has lost some of its political clout. The second is the *Organisation for Arab Petroleum Exporting Countries* (OAPEC), established in January 1968 by Kuwait, Libya and Saudi Arabia. These were joined in May 1970 by Algeria, and the four Arab Gulf Emirates: Abu Dhabi, Bahrain, Dubai and Qatar. In March 1972 Egypt, Iraq and Syria became members. OAPEC was temporarily liquidated in June 1971 and Dubai is no longer a member. The agreement establishing OAPEC states that the

> principal objective of the Organization is the cooperation of the members in various forms of economic activity... the realization of the closest ties among them... the determination of ways and means of safeguarding the legitimate interests of its members... the unification of efforts to ensure the flow of petroleum to its consumption markets on equitable and reasonable terms and the creation of a suitable climate for the capital and expertise invested in the petroleum industry in the member countries. (*Middle East Economic Survey*, 1968)

However, in the late 1960s OAPEC flexed its muscle within OPEC to force the latter to use petroleum as a weapon against Israeli occupation of certain Arab areas. Many analysts would argue that the tactic was to no avail; indeed many believe that it accomplished no more than to undermine OAPEC's reputation, especially since there is nothing in the aims quoted above to vindicate such action. Since then, OAPEC has undertaken a number of projects both within and outside the organisation – see, for example, Mingst (1977–8).

Finally, there are also the *Organisation for African Unity* (OAU), *Organisation for Economic Cooperation and Development* (OECD) and the *World Trade Organisation* (WTO). However, these and the above are schemes for intergovernmental cooperation rather than for economic integration. Therefore, except where appropriate, nothing more shall be said about them.

3 The Theory of Economic Integration

Ali M. El-Agraa

INTRODUCTION

In reality, almost all existing cases of economic integration were either proposed or formed for political reasons even though the arguments popularly put forward in their favour were expressed in terms of possible economic gains. However, no matter what the motives for economic integration are, it is still necessary to analyse the economic implications of such geographically discriminatory groupings.

As mentioned in chapter 1, at the customs union (and free trade area) level, the possible sources of economic gain can be attributed to:

(a) enhanced efficiency in production made possible by increased specialisation in accordance with the law of comparative advantage;
(b) increased production levels due to better exploitation of economies of scale made possible by the increased size of the market;
(c) an improved international bargaining position, made possible by the larger size, leading to better terms of trade;
(d) enforced changes in economic efficiency brought about by enhanced competition; and
(e) changes affecting both the amount and quality of the factors of production due to technological advances.

If the level of economic integration is to proceed beyond the customs union (CU) level, to the economic union level, then further sources of gain become possible due to:

(f) factor mobility across the borders of member nations;
(g) the coordination of monetary and fiscal policies; and

(h) the goals of near full employment, higher rates of economic growth and better income distribution becoming unified targets.

I shall now discuss these considerations in some detail.

THE CUSTOMS UNION ASPECTS

The Basic Concepts

Before the theory of second-best was introduced (Meade, 1955; Lipsey and Lancaster, 1956–7), it used to be the accepted tradition that CU formation should be encouraged. The rationale for this was that since free trade maximised world welfare and since CU formation was a move towards free trade, CUs increased welfare even though they did not maximise it. This rationale certainly lies behind the guidelines of GATT's (now the World Trade Organisation, (WTO)) Article XXIV (see Appendix to Chapter 1) which permits the formation of CUs and free trade areas as the special exceptions to the rules against international discrimination.

Viner (1950) and Byé (1950) challenged this proposition by stressing the point that CU formation is by no means equivalent to a move to free trade since it amounts to free trade *between* the members and *protection vis-à-vis* the outside world. This combination of free trade and protectionism could result in 'trade creation' and/or 'trade diversion'. Trade creation is the replacement of expensive domestic production by cheaper imports from a partner and trade diversion is the replacement of cheaper *initial* imports from the outside world by more expensive imports from a partner. Viner and Byé stressed the point that trade creation is beneficial since it does not affect the rest of the world while trade diversion is harmful and it is therefore the relative strength of these two effects which determines whether or not CU formation should be advocated. It is therefore important to understand the implications of these concepts.

Assuming perfect competition in both the commodity and factor markets, automatic full employment of all resources, costless adjustment procedures, perfect factor mobility nationally but perfect immobility across national boundaries, prices determined by cost, three countries *H* (the home country), *P* (the potential customs union partner) and *W* (the outside world), plus all the traditional assumptions employed in tariff theory, we can use a simple diagram to illustrate these two concepts.

In Figure 3.1 (I am using partial-equilibrium diagrams because it has been demonstrated that partial- and general-equilibrium analyses are, under certain circumstances, equivalent – see El-Agraa and Jones 1981), S_W is *W*'s perfectly elastic tariff free supply curve for this commodity; S_H is *H*'s supply curve while S_{H+P} is the joint *H* and *P* tariff free supply curve. With a non-discriminatory tariff imposition by *H* of *AD* (t_H), the effective supply curve facing *H* is *BREFQT*, i.e. its own supply curve up to *E* and *W*'s, subject to the tariff $[S_W\ (1 + t_H)]$ after that. The domestic price is therefore *0D* which gives domestic production of $0q_2$, domestic consumption of $0q_3$ and imports of q_2q_3. *H* pays q_2LMq_3 for these imports while the domestic consumer pays q_2EFq_3, with the difference (*LEFM*) being the tariff revenue which accrues to the *H* government. This

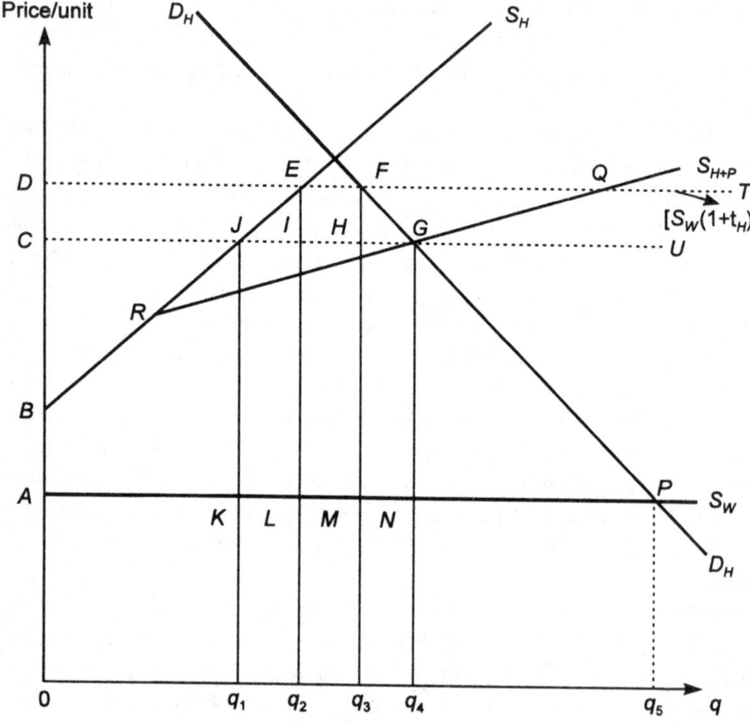

Figure 3.1 Trade creation and trade diversion

government revenue can be viewed as a transfer from the consumers to the government with the implication that when the government spends it, the marginal valuation of that expenditure should be exactly equal to its valuation by the private consumers so that no distortions should occur.

If *H* and *W* form a CU, the free trade position will be restored so that $0q_5$ will be consumed in *H* and this amount will be imported from *W*. Hence free trade is obviously the ideal situation. But if *H* and *P* form a CU, the tariff imposition will still apply to *W* while it is removed from *P*. The effective supply curve in this case is *BRGQT*. The union price falls to *0C* resulting in a fall in domestic production to $0q_1$, an increase in consumption to $0q_4$ and an increase in imports to q_1q_4. These imports now come from *P*.

The welfare implications of these changes can be examined by employing the concepts of consumers' and producers' surpluses. As a result of increased consumption, consumers' surplus rises by *CDFG*. Part of this (*CDEJ*) is a fall in producers' surplus due to the decline in domestic production and another part (*IEFH*) is a portion of the tariff revenue now transferred back to the consumer subject to the same condition of equal marginal valuation. This leaves the triangles *JEI* and *HFG* as gains from CU formation. However, before we conclude whether or not these triangles represent *net* gains we need to consider the overall effects more carefully.

The fall in domestic production from $0q_2$ to $0q_1$ leads to increased imports of q_1q_2. These cost q_1JIq_2 to import from *P* while they originally cost q_1JEq_2 to produce domestically. (Note that these resources are assumed to be employed elsewhere in the economy without any adjustment costs or redundancies!) There is therefore a saving of *JEI*. The increase in consumption from $0q_3$ to $0q_4$ leads to new imports of q_3q_4 which cost q_3HGq_4 to import from *P*. These give a welfare satisfaction to the consumers equal to q_3FGq_4. There is therefore an increase in satisfaction of *HFG*. However, the *initial* imports of q_2q_3 cost the country q_2LMq_3 but these imports now come from *P* costing q_2IHq_3. Therefore these imports lead to a loss equal to the loss in government revenue of *LIHM* (*IEFH* being a retransfer). It follows that the triangle gains (*JEI* + *HFG*) have to be compared with the loss of tariff revenue (*LIHM*) before a definite conclusion can be made regarding whether or not the net effect of CU formation has been one of gain or loss.

It should be apparent that q_2q_3 represents, in terms of our definition, trade diversion, and $q_1q_2 + q_3q_4$ represent trade creation, or alternatively that areas *JEI* plus *HFG* are trade creation (benefits) while area *LIHM* is trade diversion (loss). (The reader should note that I am using Johnson's 1974 definition so as to avoid the unnecessary literature relating to a trade-diverting welfare-improving CU promoted by Gehrels, 1956–7, Lipsey, 1960 and Bhagwati, 1971.) It is then obvious that trade creation is economically desirable while trade diversion is undesirable. Hence Viner and Byé's conclusion that it is the relative strength of these two effects which should determine whether or not CU formation is beneficial or harmful.

The reader should note that if the initial price is that given by the intersection of D_H and S_H (due to a higher tariff rate), the CU would result in pure trade creation since the tariff rate is prohibitive. If the price is initially $0C$ (due to a lower tariff rate), then CU formation would result in pure trade diversion. It should also be apparent that the size of the gains and losses depends on the price elasticities of S_H, and S_{H+P} and D_H and on the divergence between S_W and S_{H+P}, i.e. cost differences.

The Cooper–Massell Criticism

Viner and Byé's conclusion was challenged by Cooper and Massell (1965a). They suggested that the reduction in price from $0D$ to $0C$ should be considered in two stages: firstly, reduce the tariff level indiscriminately (i.e. for both *W* and *P*) to *AC* which gives the same union price and production, consumption and import changes; secondly, introduce the CU starting from the new price $0C$. The effect of these two steps is that the gains from trade creation (*JEI* + *HFG*) still accrue while the losses from trade diversion (*LIHM*) no longer apply since the new effective supply curve facing *H* is *BJGU* which ensures that imports continue to come from *W* at the cost of q_2LMq_3. In addition, the new imports due to trade creation ($q_1q_2 + q_3q_4$) now cost less leading to a further gain of *KJIL* plus *MHGN*. Cooper and Massell then conclude that *a policy of unilateral tariff reduction is superior to customs union formation.*

Further Contributions

Following the Cooper–Massell criticism have come two independent but somewhat similar contributions to the theory of CUs. The first development is by Cooper and Massell (1965b) themselves, the essence of which is that two countries acting together can do better than each acting in isolation. The second is by Johnson (1965a) which is a private plus social costs and benefits analysis expressed in political economy terms. Both contributions utilise a 'public good' argument with Cooper and Massell's expressed in practical terms and Johnson's in theoretical terms. However, since the Johnson approach is expressed in familiar terms this section is devoted to it – space limitations do not permit a consideration of both.

Johnson's method is based on four major assumptions:

(a) governments use tariffs to achieve certain non-economic (political, etc.) objectives;
(b) actions taken by governments are aimed at offsetting differences between private and social costs. They are, therefore, rational efforts;
(c) government policy is a rational response to the demands of the electorate;
(d) countries have a preference for industrial production.

In addition to these assumptions, Johnson makes a distinction between private and public consumption goods, real income (utility enjoyed from both private and public consumption, where consumption is the sum of planned consumption expenditure and planned investment expenditure) and real product (defined as total production of privately appropriate goods and services).

These assumptions have important implications. First, competition among political parties will make the government adopt policies that will tend to maximise consumer satisfaction from both 'private' and 'collective' consumption goods. Satisfaction is obviously maximised when the *rate of satisfaction per unit of resources is the same in both types of consumption goods*. Secondly, 'collective preference' for industrial production implies that consumers are willing to expand industrial production (and industrial employment) beyond what it would be under free international trade.

Tariffs are the main source of financing this policy simply because GATT (now WTO) regulations rule out the use of export subsidies and domestic political considerations make tariffs, rather than the more efficient production subsidies, the usual instruments of protection.

Protection will be carried to the point where *the value of the marginal utility derived from collective consumption of domestic and industrial activity is just equal to the marginal excess private cost of protected industrial production.*

The marginal excess cost of protected industrial production consists of two parts: the marginal production cost and the marginal private consumption cost. The marginal production cost is equal to the proportion by which domestic cost exceeds world market cost. In a very simple model this is equal to the tariff rate. The marginal private consumption cost is equal to the loss of consumer surplus due to the fall in consumption brought about by the tariff rate which is necessary to induce the marginal unit of domestic production. This depends on the tariff rate and the price elasticities of supply and demand.

In equilibrium, the proportional marginal excess private cost of protected production measures the marginal 'degree of preference' for industrial production. This is illustrated in Figure 3.2 where: S_W is the world supply curve at world market prices; D_H is the constant-utility demand curve (at free trade private utility level); S_H is the domestic supply curve; S_{H+u} is the marginal private cost curve of protected industrial production, including the excess private consumption cost (*FE* is the first component of marginal excess cost – determined by the excess marginal cost of domestic production in relation to the free trade situation due to the tariff imposition (*AB*) – and the area *GED* (= *IHJ*) is the second component which is the dead loss in consumer surplus due to the tariff imposition); the height of *vv* above S_W represents the marginal value of industrial production in collective consumption and *vv* represents the preference for industrial production which is assumed to yield a diminishing marginal rate of satisfaction.

The maximisation of *real* income is achieved at the intersection of *vv* with S_{H+u} requiring the use of tariff rate *AB*/*0A* to increase industrial production from $0q_1$ to $0q_2$ and involving the marginal degree of preference for industrial production *v*. Note that the higher the value of *v*, the higher the tariff rate, and that the degree of protection will tend to vary inversely with the ability to compete with foreign industrial producers. It is also important to note that, in equilibrium, the government is maximising real income, not real product: maximisation of real income makes it necessary to sacrifice real product in order to gratify the preference for collective consumption of industrial production. It is also important to note that this analysis is not confined to net importing countries. It is equally applicable to net exporters, but lack of space prevents such elaboration – see El-Agraa (1984a) for a detailed explanation.

The above model helps to explain the significance of Johnson's assumptions. It does not, however, throw any light on the CU issue.

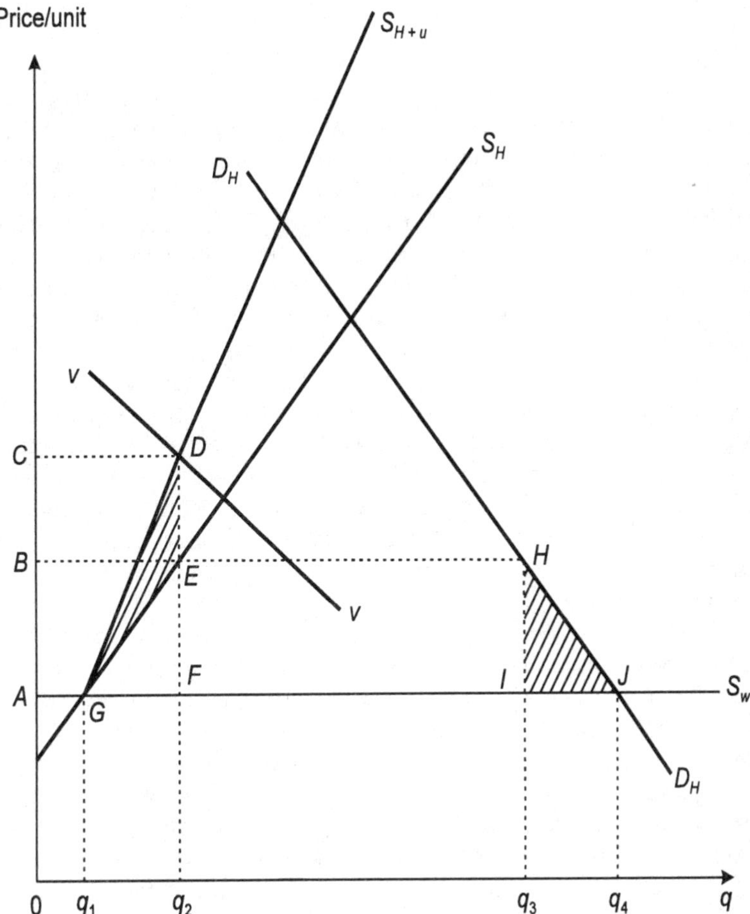

Figure 3.2 Preference for industrial production

To make the model useful for this purpose it is necessary to alter some of the assumptions. Let us assume that industrial production is not one aggregate but a variety of products in which countries have varying degrees of comparative advantage; that countries differ in their overall comparative advantage in industry as compared with non-industrial production; that no country has monopoly/monopsony power (conditions for optimum tariffs do not exist); and that no export subsidies are allowed (GATT/WTO).

The variety of industrial production allows countries to be both importers and exporters of industrial products. This, in combination with the 'preference for industrial production', will motivate each country to practise some degree of protection.

Given the third assumption, a country can gratify its preference for industrial production only by protecting the domestic producers of the commodities it imports (import-competing industries). Hence the condition for equilibrium remains the same: $vv = S_{H+u}$. The condition must now be reckoned differently, however: S_{H+u} is slightly different because, first, the protection of import-competing industries will reduce exports of both industrial and non-industrial products (for balance of payments purposes). Hence, in order to increase total industrial production by one unit it will be necessary to increase protected industrial production by more than one unit so as to compensate for the induced loss of industrial exports. Secondly, the protection of import-competing industries reduces industrial exports by raising their production costs (due to perfect factor mobility). The stronger this effect, *ceteris paribus*, the higher the marginal excess cost of industrial production.

These will be greater, the larger the industrial sector compared with the non-industrial sector and the larger the protected industrial sector relative to the exporting industrial sector.

If the world consists of two countries, one must be a net exporter and the other necessarily a net importer of industrial products and the balance of payments is settled in terms of the non-industrial sector. Hence both countries can expand industrial production at the expense of the non-industrial sector. Therefore for each country the prospective gain from reciprocal tariff reduction must lie in the expansion of exports of industrial products. The reduction of a country's own tariff rate is therefore a source of loss which can only be compensated for by a reduction of the other country's tariff rate (for an alternative, orthodox, explanation see El-Agraa, 1979b).

What if there are more than two countries? If reciprocal tariff reductions are arrived at on a 'most-favoured nation' basis, then the reduction of a country's tariff rate will increase imports from *all* the other countries. If the tariff rate reduction is, however, discriminatory (starting from a position of non-discrimination), then there are two advantages: first, a country can offer its partner an increase in exports of industrial products without any loss of its own industrial production by diverting imports from third countries (trade diversion); secondly, when trade diversion is exhausted any increase in partner industrial exports to this country is exactly equal to the reduction in industrial production in the same country (trade creation), hence eliminating the gain to third countries.

Therefore, discriminatory reciprocal tariff reduction costs each partner country less, in terms of the reduction in domestic industrial production (if any) incurred per unit increase in partner industrial production, than does non-discriminatory reciprocal tariff reduction. On the other hand, preferential tariff reduction imposes an additional cost on the tariff reducing country: the excess of the costs of imports from the partner country over their cost in the world market.

The implications of this analysis are:

(a) both trade creation and trade diversion yield a gain to the CU partners;
(b) trade diversion is preferable to trade creation for the preference granting country since a sacrifice of domestic industrial production is not required;
(c) both trade creation and trade diversion may lead to increased efficiency due to economies of scale.

Johnson's contribution has not achieved the popularity it deserves because of the alleged nature of his assumptions. However, a careful consideration of these assumptions indicates that they are neither extreme nor unique: they are the kind of assumptions that are adopted in any analysis dealing with differences between social and private costs and benefits. It can, of course, be claimed that an

> economic rationale for customs unions on public goods grounds can only be established if for political or some such reasons governments are denied the use of direct production subsidies – and while this may be the case in certain countries at certain periods in their economic evolution, there would appear to be no acceptable reason why this should generally be true. Johnson's analysis demonstrates that customs union and other acts of commercial policy may make economic sense under certain restricted conditions, but in no way does it establish or seek to establish a general argument for these acts. (Krauss, 1972)

While this is a legitimate criticism it is of no relevance to the world we live in: subsidies are superior to tariffs, yet all countries prefer the use of tariffs to subsidies! It is a criticism related to a first-best view of the world. Therefore, it seems unfair to criticise an analysis on grounds which do not portray what actually exists; it is what prevails in practice that matters. That is what Johnson's approach is all about and that is what the theory of second-best tries to tackle. In short, the lack of belief in this approach is tantamount to a lack of belief in the validity of the distinction between social and private costs and benefits.

General Equilibrium Analysis

The conclusions of the partial equilibrium analysis can easily be illustrated in general equilibrium terms. To simplify the analysis we shall assume that *H* is a 'small' country while *P* and *W* are 'large' countries, i.e. *H* faces constant *t/t* (t_P and t_W) throughout the analysis. Also, in order to avoid repetition, the analysis proceeds immediately to the Cooper–Massell proposition.

In Figure 3.3, *HH* is the production possibility frontier for *H*. Initially, *H* is imposing a prohibitive non-discriminatory tariff which results in P_1 as both the production and consumption point, given that t_W is the most favourable t/t, i.e. *W* is the most efficient country in the production of clothing (*C*). The formation of the CU leads to free trade with the partner, *P*, hence production moves to P_2 where t_P is at a tangent to *HH*, and consumption to C_3 where CIC_5 is at a tangent to t_P. A unilateral tariff reduction (UTR) which results in P_2 as the production point results in consumption at C_4 on CIC_6 (if the tariff revenue is returned to the consumers as a lump sum) or at C_3 (if the tariff revenue is retained by the government). Note that at C_4 trade is with *W* only.

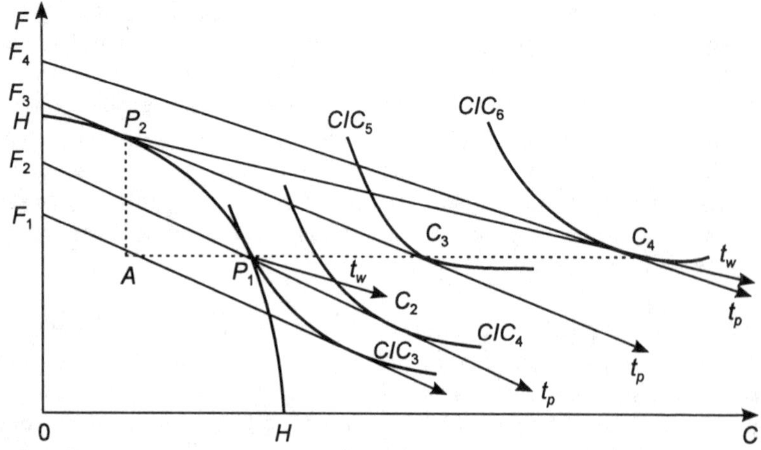

Figure 3.3 General equilibrium of the Cooper–Massell argument

Given standard analysis, it should be apparent that the situation of UTR and trade with *W* results in exports of AP_2 which are exchanged for imports of AC_4 of which C_3C_4 is the tariff revenue. In terms of Johnson's distinction between consumption and production gains and his method of calculating them (see El-Agraa, 1983b, chapters 4 and 10), these effects can be expressed in relation to food (*F*) only. Given a Hicksian income compensation variation, it should be clear that: (i) F_1F_2 is the positive consumption effect; (ii) F_2F_3 is the production effect (positive due to curtailing production of the protected commodity); and (iii) F_3F_4 is the tariff revenue effect. Hence the difference between CU formation and a UTR (with the tariff revenue returned to the consumer) is the loss of tariff revenue F_3F_4 (C_4 compared with C_3). In other words, the consumption gain F_1F_2 is positive and applies in both cases but in the Cooper-Massell analysis the production effect comprises two parts: (i) a *pure* TC effect equal to F_2F_4; and (ii) a *pure* TD effect equal to F_3F_4. Hence F_2F_3 is the difference between these two effects and is, therefore, rightly termed the *net* TC effect.

Of course, the above analysis falls short of a general equilibrium one since the model does not endogenously determine the t/t – see ibid., chapter 5). However, as suggested above, such analysis would require the use of offer curves for all three countries both with and without tariffs. Unfortunately such an analysis is still awaited – the attempt by Vanek (1965) to derive an 'excess offer curve' for the potential union partners leads to no more than a specification of various possibilities; and the contention of Wonnacott and Wonnacott (1981) to have provided an analysis incorporating a tariff by *W* is unsatisfactory since they assume that *W*'s offer curve is perfectly elastic – see p. 53.

Dynamic Effects

The so-called dynamic effects (Balassa, 1962) relate to the numerous means by which economic integration may influence the rate of growth of GNP of the participating nations. These ways include the following:

(a) scale economies made possible by the increased size of the market for both firms and industries operating below optimum capacity before integration occurs;
(b) economies external to the firm and industry which may have a downward influence on both specific and general cost structures;

(c) the polarisation effect, by which is meant the cumulative decline either in relative or absolute terms of the economic situation of a particular participating nation or of a specific region within it due either to the benefits of trade creation becoming concentrated in one region or to the fact that an area may develop a tendency to attract factors of production;
(d) the influence on the location and volume of real investment; and
(e) the effect on economic efficiency and the smoothness with which trade transactions are carried out due to enhanced competition and changes in uncertainty.

Hence these dynamic effects include various and completely different phenomena. Apart from economies of scale, the possible gains are extremely long term in nature and cannot be tackled in orthodox economic terms: for example, intensified competition leading to the adoption of best business practices and to an American-type of attitude, etc. (Scitovsky, 1958) seems like a naive socio-psychological abstraction that has no solid foundation with regard to both the aspirations of those countries contemplating economic integration and to its actually materialising!

Economies of scale can, however, be analysed in orthodox economic terms. In a highly simplistic model, like that depicted in Figure 3.4 where scale economies are internal to the industry, their effects can easily be demonstrated – a mathematical discussion can be found in, *inter alia*, Choi and Yu (1985), but the reader must be warned that the assumptions made about the nature of the economies concerned are extremely limited, e.g. H and P are 'similar'. $D_{H,P}$ is the identical demand curve for this commodity in both H and P and D_{H+P} is their joint demand curve; S_W is the world supply curve; AC_P and AC_H are the average cost curves for this commodity in P and H respectively. Note that the diagram is drawn in such a manner that W has constant average costs and that it is the most efficient supplier of this commodity. Hence free trade is the best policy resulting in price $0A$ with consumption which is satisfied entirely by imports of $0q_4$ in each of H and P giving a total of $0q_6$.

If H and P impose tariffs, the only justification for this is that uncorrected distortions exist between the privately and socially valued costs in these countries – see Jones (1979) and El-Agraa and Jones (1981). The best tariff rates to impose are Corden's (1972a) made-to-measure tariffs which can be defined as those which encourage domestic production to a level that just satisfies domestic consumption

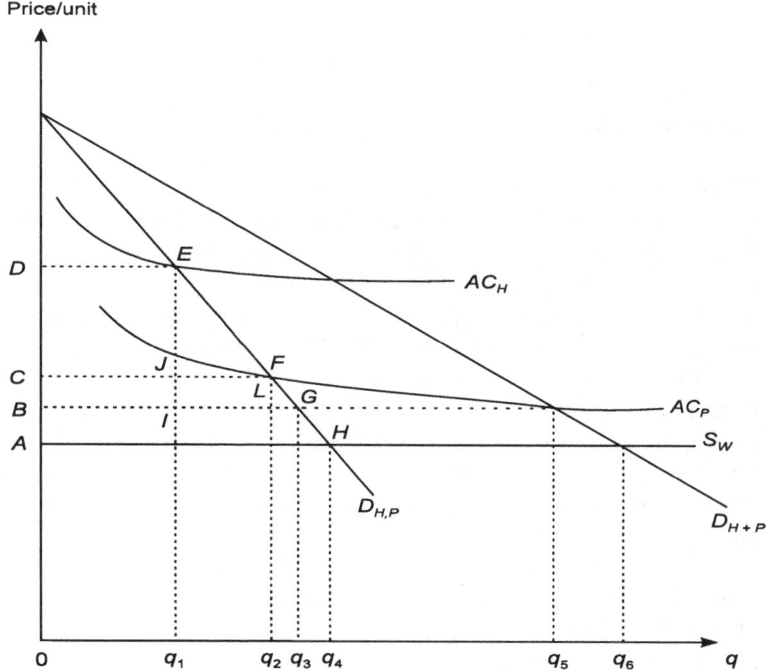

Figure 3.4 Economies of scale and customs unions

without giving rise to monopoly profits. These tariffs are equal to *AD* and *AC* for *H* and *P* respectively, resulting in $0q_1$ and $0q_2$ production in *H* and *P* respectively.

When *H* and *P* enter into a CU, *P*, being the cheaper producer, will produce the entire union output – $0q_5$ at a price *0B*. This gives rise to consumption in each of *H* and *P* of $0q_3$ with gains of *BDEG* and *BCFG* for *H* and *P* respectively. Parts of these gains, *BDEI* for *H* and *BCFL* for *P*, are 'cost-reduction' effects. There also results a production gain for *P* and a production loss in *H* due to abandoning production altogether.

Whether or not CU formation can be justified in terms of the existence of economies of scale will depend on whether or not the net effect is a gain or a loss, since in this example *P* gains and *H* loses, as the loss from abandoning production in *H* must outweigh the consumption gain in order for the tariff to have been imposed in the first place. If the overall result is net gain, then the distribution of these gains becomes an important consideration. Alternatively, if economies of scale accrue to an integrated industry, then the locational distribution of the production units becomes an essential issue.

Domestic Distortions

A substantial literature tried to tackle the important question of whether or not the formation of a CU may be economically desirable when there are domestic distortions. Such distortions could be attributed to the presence of trade unions which negotiate wage rates in excess of the equilibrium rates or to governments introducing minimum wage legislation – both of which are widespread activities in most countries. It is usually assumed that the domestic distortion results in a *social* average cost curve which lies below the private one. Hence, in Figure 3.5, which is adapted from Figure 3.4, I have incorporated AC_H^s and AC_P^s as the *social* curves in the context of economies of scale and a separate representation of countries *H* and *P*.

Note that AC_H^s is drawn to be consistently above AP_W, while AC_P^s is below it for higher levels of output. Before the formation of a CU, *H* may have been adopting a made-to-measure tariff to protect its industry, but the first-best policy would have been one of free trade, as argued in the previous section. Hence, the formation of the CU will lead to the same effects as in the previous section, with the exception that the cost-reduction effect (*b*) will be less by DD' times $0q_1$. For *P*, the effects will be: (i) as before, a consumption gain of area *c*; (ii) a cost-reduction effect of area *e* due to calculations relating to social rather than private costs; (iii) gains from sales to *H* of areas d_1 and d_2, with d_1 being an income transfer from *H* to *P*, and d_2 the difference between domestic social costs in *P* and P_W – the world price; and (iv) the social benefits accruing from extra production made possible by the CU – area *f* – which is measured by the extra consumption multiplied by the difference between P_W and the domestic social costs.

However, this analysis does not lead to an economic rationale for the formation of CUs, since *P* could have used first-best policy instruments to eliminate the divergence between private and social cost. This would have made AC_P^s the operative cost curve, and assuming that D_{H+P+W} is the world demand curve, this would have led to a world price of *OF* and exports of q_3q_5 and q_5q_6 to *H* and *W* respectively, with obviously greater benefits than those offered by the CU. Hence the economic rationale for the CU will have to depend on factors that can explain why first-best instruments could not have

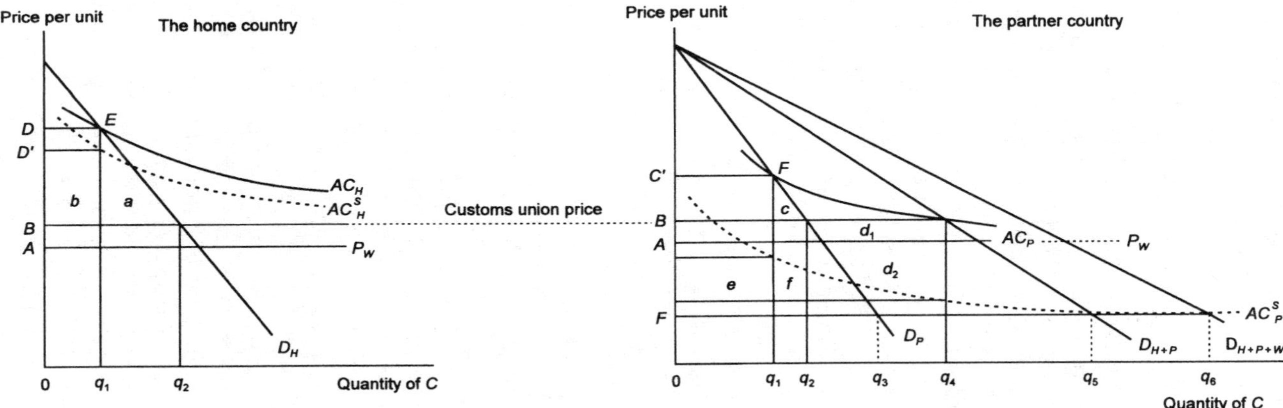

Figure 3.5 A customs union with economies of scale and domestic distortions

been employed in the first instance (Jones, 1980). In short, this is not an absolute argument for CU formation.

Terms of Trade Effects

So far the analysis has been conducted on the assumption that CU formation has no effect on the terms of trade (*t/t*). This implies that the countries concerned are too insignificant to have any appreciable influence on the international economy. Particularly in the context of the EU and groupings of a similar size, this is a very unrealistic assumption.

The analysis of the effects of CU formation on the *t/t* is not only extremely complicated but is also unsatisfactory since a convincing model incorporating tariffs by all three areas of the world is still awaited – see Mundell (1964), Arndt (1968) and Wonnacott and Wonnacott (1981). To demonstrate this, let us consider Arndt's analysis, which is directly concerned with this issue and the Wonnacotts' analysis, whose main concern is the Cooper–Massell criticism but which has some bearing on this matter.

In Figure 3.6, 0_H, 0_P and 0_W are the respective offer curves of *H*, *P* and *W*. In section (a) of the figure, *H* is assumed to be the most efficient producer of commodity *Y*, while in section (b), *H* and *P* are assumed to be equally efficient. Assuming that the free trade *t/t* are given by $0T_0$, *H* will export q_6h_1 of *Y* to *W* in exchange for $0q_6$ imports of commodity *X*, while *P* will export q_1p_1 of *Y* in exchange for $0q_1$, of commodity *X*, with the sum of *H* and *P*'s exports being exactly equal to $0X_3$.

When *H* imposes an *ad valorem* tariff, its tariff revenue-distributed curve is assumed to be displaced to $0'H'$ altering the *t/t* to $0T_1$. This leads to a contraction of *H*'s trade with *W* and, at the same time, increases *P*'s trade with *W*. In section (a) of the figure, it is assumed that the net effect of *H* and *P*'s trade changes (contraction in *H*'s exports and expansion in *P*'s) will result in a contraction in world trade. It should be apparent that, from *H*'s point of view, the competition of *P* in her exports market has reduced the appropriateness of the Cooper–Massell alternative of a (non-discriminatory) UTR.

Note, however, that *H*'s welfare may still be increased in these unfavourable circumstances, provided that the move from h_1 to h_2 is accompanied by two conditions. It should be apparent that the larger the size of *P* relative to *H* and the more elastic the two countries' offer curves over the relevant ranges, the more likely it is that *H* will lose as a result of the tariff imposition. Moreover, given the various offer

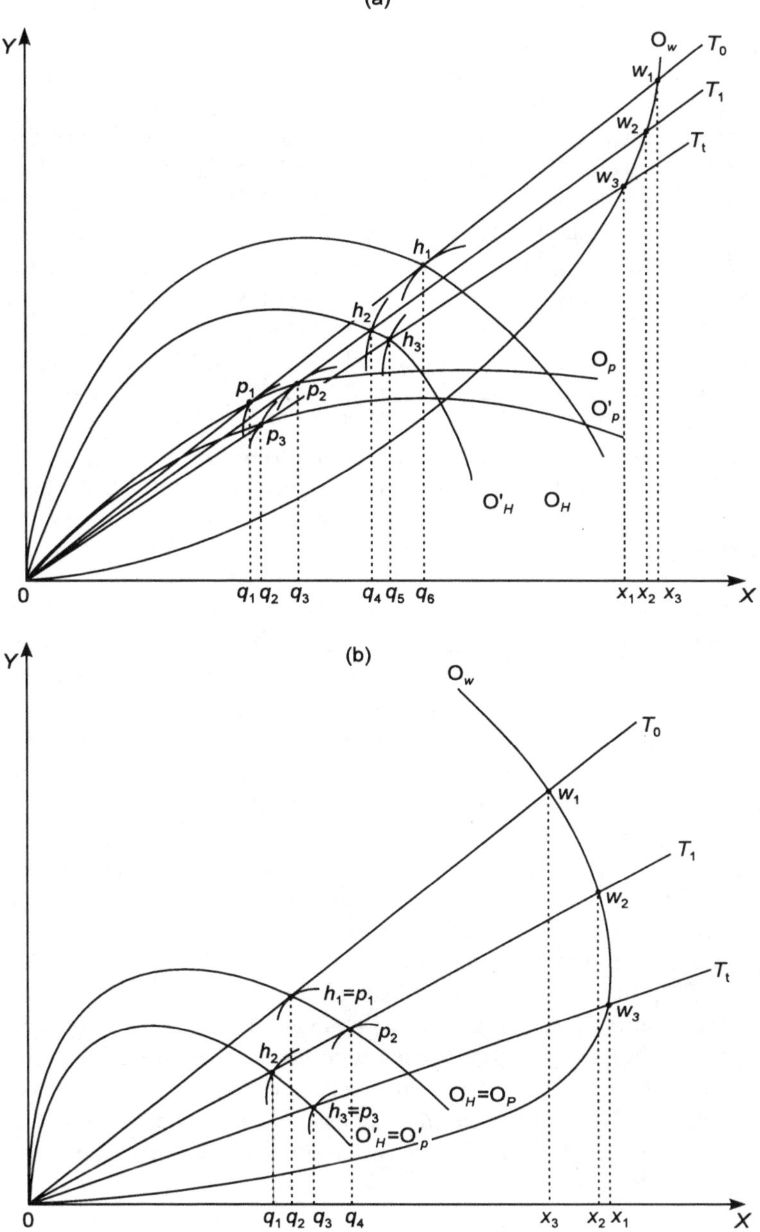

Figure 3.6 Customs unions and the terms of trade

curves and *H*'s tariff, *H* is more likely to sustain a loss in welfare, the lower her own marginal propensity to spend on her export commodity, *X*. If, in terms of consumption, commodity *Y* is a 'Giffen' good in country *H*, h_2 will be inferior to h_1.

In this illustration, country *H* experiences a loss of welfare in case (a) but an increase in case (b), while country *P* experiences a welfare improvement in both cases. Hence, it is to *H*'s advantage to persuade *P* to adopt restrictive trade practices. For example, let *P* impose an *ad valorem* tariff and, in order to simplify the analysis, assume that in section (b) *H* and *P* are identical in all respects such that their revenue-redistributed offer curves completely coincide. In both sections of the figure, the *t/t* will shift to $0T_t$, with h_3, P_3 and w_2 being the equilibrium trading points. In both cases, *P*'s tariff improves *H*'s welfare but *P* gains only in case (b), and is better off with unrestricted trade in case (a) in the presence of tariff imposition by *H*.

The situation depicted in Figure 3.6 illustrates the fundamental problem that the interests, hence the policies, of *H* and *P* may be incompatible:

> Country [*H*] stands to gain from restrictive trade practices in [*P*], but the latter is better off without restrictions – provided that [*H*] maintains its tariff. The dilemma in which [*H*] finds itself in trying to improve its terms of trade is brought about by its inadequate control of the market for its export commodity. Its optimum trade policies and their effects are functions not only of the demand elasticity in [*W*] but also of supply conditions in [*P*] and of the latter's reaction to a given policy in [*H*].
>
> Country [*H*] will attempt to influence policy making in [*P*]. In view of the fact that the latter may have considerable inducement to pursue independent policies, country [*H*] may encounter formidable difficulties in this respect. It could attempt to handle this problem in a relatively loose arrangement along the lines of international commodity agreements, or in a tightly controlled and more restrictive set-up involving an international cartel. The difficulty is that neither alternative may provide effective control over the maverick who stands to gain from independent policies. In that case a [CU] with common tariff and sufficient incentives may work where other arrangements do not. (Arndt, 1968, p. 978)

Of course, the above analysis relates to potential partners who have similar economies and who trade with *W*, with no trading relationships between them. Hence, it could be argued that such countries are ruled out, by definition, from forming a CU. Such an argument would be misleading since this analysis is not concerned with the static concepts of TC and TD; the concern is entirely with *t/t* effects, and a joint trade policy aimed at achieving an advantage in this regard is perfectly within the realm of international economic integration.

One could ask about the nature of this conclusion in a model which depicts the potential CU partners in a different light. Here, Wonnacott and Wonnacott's (1981) analysis may be useful, even though the aim of their paper was to question the general validity of the Cooper–Massell criticism, when the *t/t* remain unaltered as a result of CU formation. However, this is precisely why it is useful to explain the Wonnacotts' analysis at this juncture: it has some bearing on the *t/t* effects and it questions the Cooper–Massell criticism.

The main point of the Wonnacotts' paper was to contest the proposition that UTR is superior to the formation of a CU, hence the *t/t* argument was a side issue. They argued that this proposition does not hold generally if the following assumptions are rejected:

(a) that the tariff imposed by a partner (P) can be ignored;
(b) that W has no tariffs; and
(c) that there are no transport costs between members of the CU (P and H) and W.

Their approach was not based on *t/t* effects or economies of scale and, except for their rejection of these three assumptions, their argument is also set entirely in the context of the standard two-commodity, three-country framework of CU theory.

The basic framework of their analysis is set out in Figure 3.7. 0_H and 0_P are the free trade offer curves of the potential partners whilst 0^t_H and 0^t_P are their initial tariff-inclusive offer curves. 0^1_W and 0^2_W are W's offer curves depending on whether the prospective partners wish to import commodity X (0^l_W) or export it (0^2_W). The inclusion of both 0^t_H and 0^t_P meets the Wonnacotts' desire to reject assumption (i) whilst the gap between 0^1_W and 0^2_W may be interpreted as the rejection of (ii) and/or of (iii) – see ibid., pp. 708–9.

In addition to these offer curves, I have inserted in Figure 3.7 various trade indifference curves for countries H and P ($T_H \ldots$ and $T_P \ldots$ respectively) and the pre-CU domestic *t/t* in H (0_t). 0^2_W is drawn parallel to 0^2_W from the point c where 0_P intersects 0_t.

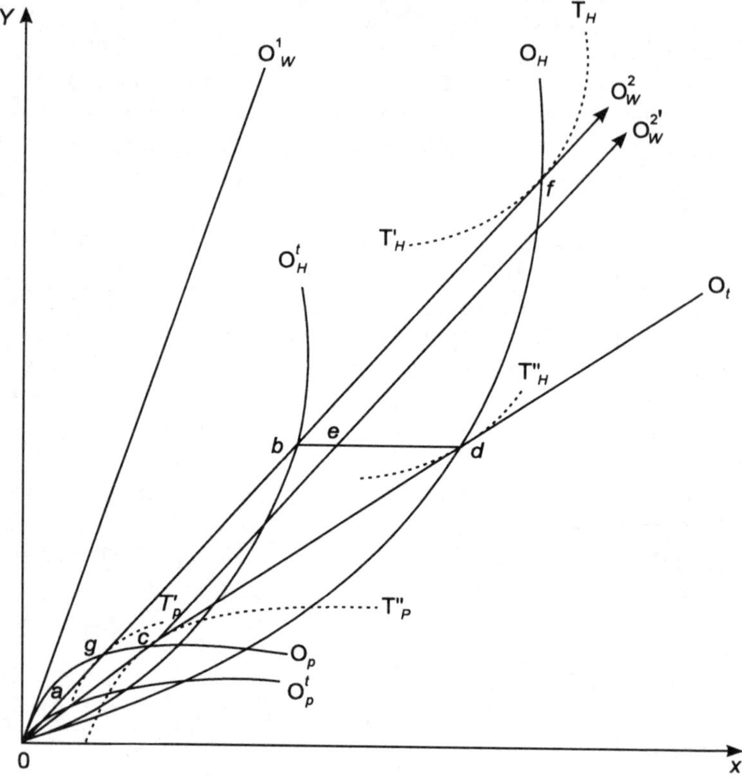

Figure 3.7 UTR versus customs unions

The diagram is drawn to illustrate the case where a CU is formed between *H* and *P* with the CET set at the same rate as *H*'s initial tariff on imports of *X* and where the domestic *t/t* in *H* remain unaltered so that trade with *W* continues after the formation of the CU. With its initial non-discriminatory tariff, *H* will trade along 0^2_W with both *P* (0_a) and with *W* (*ab*). The formation of the CU means that *H* and *P*'s trade is determined by where 0_P intersects 0_t (i.e. at *c*) and that *H* will trade with *W* along $c0^2_W$ (drawn parallel to 00^2_W). The final outcome for *H* will depend on the choice of assumptions about what happens to the tariff revenue generated by the remaining external trade. If there is no redistribution of tariff revenue in *H*, then traders in that country will remain at point *d*. The tariff revenue generated by the external trade of the CU with *W* is then shown to be equal to *ed* (measured in units of commodity *X*) which represents a reduction of *be* compared with the pre-CU tariff revenue in *H*. Further, if procedures similar to those of the European Union were adopted, the revenue *ed* would be used as an 'own resource' (see chapter 5, p. 18 and El-Agraa 1994c, chapter 15) to be spent/distributed for the benefit of both members of the CU whereas the pre-union tariff revenue (*bd*) would be kept by country *H*.

It can be seen that country *P* will benefit from the formation of the CU even if it receives none of this revenue, but that *H* will undoubtedly lose even if it keeps all the post-union tariff revenue. This is the case of pure TD and, in the absence of additional income transfers from *P*, *H* clearly cannot be expected to join the CU even if it considers that this is the only alternative to its initial tariff policy. There is no rationale, however, for so restricting the choice of policy alternatives. UTR is unambiguously superior to the initial tariff policy for both *H* and *P* and, compared with the non-discriminatory free trade policies available to both countries (which take country *H* to T'_H at *f* and country *P* to T'_P at *g*), there is no possible system of income transfers from *P* to *H* which can make the formation of a CU Pareto-superior to free trade for both countries. It remains true, of course, that country *P* would gain more from membership of a CU with *H* than it could achieve by UTR but, provided that *H* pursues its optimal strategy, which is UTR, country *P* itself can do no better than follow suit so that the optimal outcome for both countries is multilateral free trade (MFT).

Of course, there is no *a priori* reason why the CU, if created, should set its CET at the level of country *H*'s initial tariff. Indeed, it is instructive to consider the consequences of forming a CU with a lower CET. The implications of this can be seen by considering the effect of rotating 0_t anti-clockwise towards 0^t_W. In this context, the moving 0_t line will show the post-union *t/t* in countries *H* and *P*. Clearly, the lowering of the CET will improve the domestic *t/t* for *H* compared with the original form of the CU and it will have a trade creating effect as the external trade of the CU will increase more rapidly than the decline in intra-union trade. Compared with the original CU, *H* would gain and *P* would lose. Indeed, the lower the level of the CET, the more likely is *H* to gain from the formation of the CU *compared with the initial non-discriminatory tariff*. As long as the CET remains positive, however, *H* would be unambiguously worse off from membership of the CU than from UTR and, although *P* would gain from such a CU compared with any initial tariff policy it may adopt, it remains true that there is no conceivable set of income transfers associated with the formation of the CU which would make both *H* and *P* simultaneously better off than they would be if, after *H*'s UTR, *P* also pursued the optimal unilateral action available – the move to free trade.

It is of course true that, if the CET is set at zero, so that the rotated 0_t coincides with 0^2_W, then the outcome is identical with that for the unilateral adoption of free trade for both countries. This, however, merely illustrates how misleading it would be to describe such a policy as 'the formation of a CU'; a CU with a zero CET is indistinguishable from a free trade policy by both countries and should surely be described solely in the latter terms.

One can extend and generalise this approach beyond what has been done here – see El-Agraa (1984a) and Berglas (1983). The important point, however, is what the analysis clearly demonstrates: the assumption that the *t/t* should remain constant for members of a CU, even if both countries are 'small', leaves a lot to be desired. But it should also be stressed that the Wonnacotts' analysis does not take into consideration the tariffs of *H* and *P* on trade with *W* nor does it deal with a genuine three-country model since *W* is assumed to be very large: *W* has constant *t/t*.

CUSTOMS UNIONS VERSUS FREE TRADE AREAS

The analysis so far has been conducted on the premise that differences between CUs and free trade areas can be ignored. However, the ability of the member nations of free trade areas to decide their own commercial policies *vis-à-vis* the outside world raises certain issues. Balassa (1962) pointed out that free trade areas may result in deflection of trade, production and investment. Deflection of trade occurs when imports from *W* (the cheapest source of supply) come via the member country with the lower tariff rate, assuming that transport and administrative costs do not outweigh the tariff differential. Deflection of production and investment occur in commodities whose production requires a substantial quantity of raw materials imported from *W* – the tariff differential regarding these materials might distort the true comparative advantage in domestic materials therefore resulting in resource allocations according to overall comparative disadvantage.

If deflection of trade does occur, then the free trade area effectively becomes a CU with a CET equal to the lowest tariff rate which is obviously beneficial for the world – see Price (1974). However, most free trade areas seem to adopt 'rules of origin' so that only those commodities which originate in a member state are exempt from tariff imposition. If deflection of production and investment does take place, we have the case of the so-called 'tariff factories' but the necessary conditions for this to occur are extremely limited – see El-Agraa in El-Agraa and Jones (1981, ch. 3) and El-Agraa (1984b).

COMMON MARKETS AND ECONOMIC UNIONS

The analysis of CUs needs drastic extension when applied to common markets (CMs) and economic unions (EUs). First, the introduction of free factor mobility may enhance efficiency through a more rational reallocation of resources but it may also result in depressed areas therefore creating or aggravating regional problems and imbalances – see Mayes (1983) and Robson (1984). Secondly, fiscal harmonisation may also improve efficiency by eliminating non-tariff trade barriers (NTBs) and distortions and by equalising their effective protective rates. Thirdly, the coordination of monetary and fiscal policies which is implied by monetary integration may ease unnecessarily severe imbalances, hence resulting in the promotion of the right atmosphere for stability in the economies of the member nations.

These CM and EU elements must be tackled *simultaneously* with trade creation and diversion as well as economies of scale and market distortions. However, such interactions are too complicated to consider here – the interested reader should consult El-Agraa (1983a, b; 1984a; 1985a). Hence, this section will be devoted to a brief discussion of factor mobility, fiscal harmonisation and monetary integration.

With regard to *factor mobility*, it should be apparent that the removal (or harmonisation) of all barriers to labour (L) and capital (K) will encourage both L and K to move. L will move to those areas where it can fetch the highest possible reward, i.e. 'net advantage'. This encouragement need not necessarily lead to an increase in actual mobility since there are socio-political factors which normally result in people remaining near their birthplace – social proximity is a dominant consideration, which is why the average person does not move. If the reward to K is not equalised, i.e. differences in marginal productivities (mps) exist before the formation of an EU, K will move until the mps are equalised. This will result in benefits which can be clearly described in terms of Figure 3.8 which depicts the production characteristics in H and P. M_H and M_P are the schedules which relate the K stocks to their mps in H and P respectively, given the quantity of L in each country; assuming only two factors of production.

Prior to EU formation, the K stock (which is assumed to remain constant throughout the analysis) is $0q_2$ in H and $0q_1^*$ in P. Assuming that K is immobile internationally, all K stocks must be nationally owned and, ignoring taxation, profit per unit of K will be equal to its mp, given conditions of perfect competition. Hence the total profit in H is equal to $b + e$ and $i + k$ in P. Total output is, of course, the whole area below the M_P curve but within $0q_2$ in H and $0q_1^*$ in P, i.e. areas $a + b + c + d + e$ in H and $j + i + k$ in P. Therefore, L's share is $a + c + d$ in H and j in P.

Since the mp in P exceeds that in H, the removal of barriers to K mobility or the harmonisation of such barriers will induce K to move away from H and into P. This is because nothing has happened to affect K in W. Such movement will continue until the mp of K is the same in both H and P. This results in q_1q_2 ($= q_1^*q_2^*$) of K moving from H to P. Hence the output of H falls to $a + b + c$ while its *national* product including the return of the profit earned on K in P ($= g + f$) increases by $(g - c)$. In P, *domestic* product rises by $(f + g + h)$ while *national* product (excluding the remittance of profits to H) increases by area h only. Both H and P experience a change in the relative share of L and K in national product, with K-owners being unfavourably disposed in H and favourably disposed in P.

Of course, this analysis is too simplistic since, apart from the fact that K and L are never perfectly immobile at the international level and multinational corporations have their own ways of transferring K (see McManus, 1972; Buckley and Casson; 1976; Dunning, 1977), the analysis does not take into account the fact that K may actually move to areas with low wages after the formation of an EU. Moreover, if K moves predominantly in only one direction, one country may become a depressed area; hence the 'social' costs and benefits of such an occurrence need to be taken into consideration, particularly if the EU deems it important that the economies of both H and P should be balanced. Therefore, the above gains have to be discounted or supplemented by such costs and benefits.

Fiscal harmonisation is an integral part of fiscal policy. Very widely interpreted, fiscal policy comprises a whole corpus of 'public finance' issues: the relative size of the public sector, taxation and expenditure, and the allocation of public sector responsibilities between different

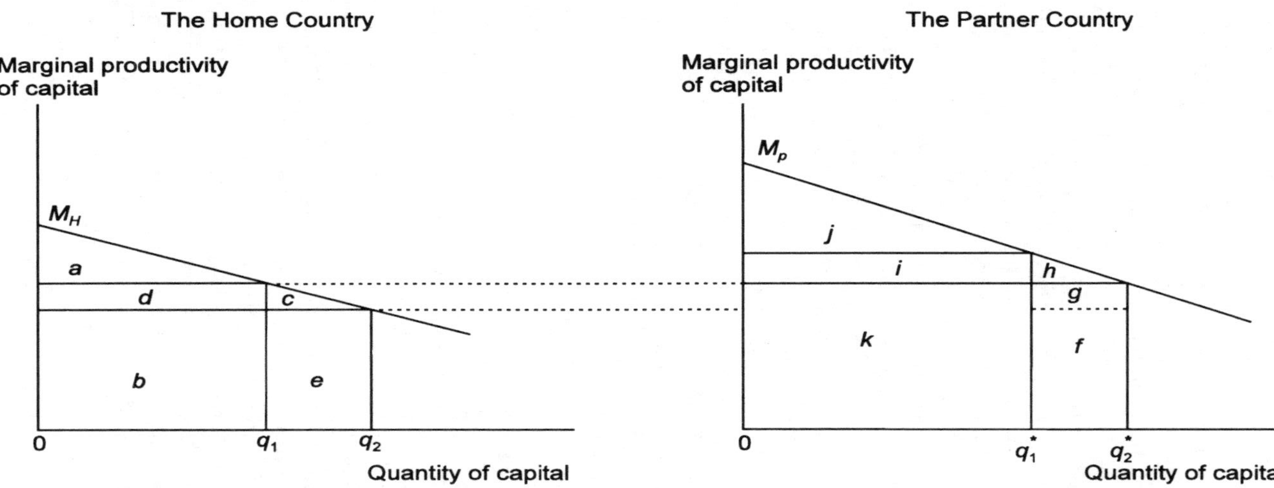

Figure 3.8 The economic implications of free factor mobility in the home and partner countries

tiers of government (Prest, 1979). Hence fiscal policy is concerned with a far wider area than that commonly associated with it, namely, the aggregate management of the economy in terms of controlling inflation and employment levels.

Experts in the field of public finance (Musgrave and Musgrave, 1976) rightly stress that public finance is a misleading term, since the subject also deals with *real* issues, have identified a number of problems associated with these fiscal policy concerns. For instance, the *relative size of the public sector* raises questions regarding the definition and measurement of government revenue and expenditure (Prest, 1972), and the attempts at understanding and explaining revenue and expenditure have produced more than one theoretical model (Peacock and Wiseman, 1967; Musgrave and Musgrave, 1976). The *division of public sector responsibilities* raises the delicate question of which fiscal aspects should be dealt with at the central government level and which aspects should be tackled at the local level. Finally, the area of *taxation and expenditure criteria* has resulted in general agreement about the basic criteria of *allocation* (the process by which the utilisation of resources is split between private and social goods and by which the 'basket' of social goods is chosen), *equity* (the use of the budget as an instrument for achieving a fair distribution), *stabilisation* (the use of the budget as an instrument for achieving and maintaining a 'reasonable' level of employment, prices and economic growth and for achieving equilibrium and stability in the balance of payments), and *administration* (the practical possibilities of implementing a particular tax system and the cost to the society of operating such a system). However, a number of very trickly problems are involved in a consideration of these criteria. In discussing the efficiency of resource allocation, the choice between work and leisure, for example, or between private and public goods, is an important and controversial one. With regard to the equity of distribution, there is the problem of what is meant by equity: is it personal, class or regional equity? In a discussion of the stabilisation of the economy, there exists the perennial problem of controlling unemployment and inflation and the trade-off between them. A consideration of administration must take into account the problem of efficiency versus practicality. Finally, there is the obvious conflict between the four criteria in that the achievement of one aim is usually at the expense of another; for example, what is most efficient in terms of collection may prove less (or more) equitable than what is considered to be socially desirable.

The above relates to a discussion of the problems of fiscal policy in very broad national terms. When considering fiscal policy in the context of economic integration, there are certain elements of the international dimension that need spelling out and there are also some interregional (intra-integrated area) elements that have to be introduced.

Consider the case of taxes (and of course subsidies since they are negative taxes). Very briefly, internationally, it has always been recognised that taxes (and equivalent instruments) have similar effects to tariffs on the international flow of goods and services – non-tariff distortions of international trade (Baldwin, 1970). Other elements have also been recognised as operating similar distortions on the international flow of factors of production (Johnson, 1965b; Bhagwati, 1969; Johnson and Krauss, 1974).

In the particular context of CMs and EUs, it should be remembered that their formation, at least from the economic viewpoint, is meant to facilitate the free and unimpeded flow of goods, services and factors between the member nations. Since tariffs are not the only distorting factor in this respect, the proper establishment of intra-CM/EU free trade necessitates the removal of all non-tariff distortions that have an equivalent effect. Hence, the removal of tariffs may give the impression of establishing free trade inside such schemes of economic integration, but this is by no means automatically guaranteed, since the existence of sales taxes, excise duties, corporation taxes, income taxes, etc. may impede this freedom. The moral is that not only tariffs, but also all equivalent distortions, must be eliminated or harmonised.

In short, there are at least two basic elements to fiscal policy: the instruments available to the government for fiscal policy purposes (i.e. the total tax structure) and the overall impact of the joint manoeuvring of the instruments (i.e. the role played by the budget). As the following discussion will no doubt demonstrate, these two aspects are so intertwined that it is very difficult to handle them separately; this is due to the fact that a tax raises government revenue which, depending on how it is spent, results in macroeconomic effects.

With this background in mind, one should ask: what is tax harmonisation and why is it needed in CMs and EUs? To answer these questions, it may be instructive to examine the experience of the European Union (EU) in this respect. In earlier years, tax harmonisation was defined as tax coordination. Ideally, in a *fully* integrated EU, it could be defined as the identical unification of both base and rates, given the same tax system and assuming that everything else is also unified. Prest (1979, p. 78) rightly argues that *coordination* is tantamount to a low-level meaning of tax harmonisation, since it could be interpreted to be some process of consultation between member countries or, possibly, loose agreements between them to levy tax on a similar sort of base or at similar sorts of rates. Hence it is not surprising that tax harmonisation has, in practice, come to mean a compromise between a low level of coordination (the EU is more than a low level of integration) and the ideal level of standardisation (the EU is nowhere near its ultimate objective of complete political unity).

In case it is not obvious why taxes should give rise to trade distortions, it may be useful to examine the nature of taxes before the inception of the EU, as well as to consider the treatment given at the time to indirect taxation on internationally traded commodities.

Before considering these aspects, however, one should recall that there are two basic types of taxation: direct and indirect. Direct taxes, like income and corporation taxes, come into operation at the end of the process of personal and industrial activities. They are levied on wages and salaries when activities have been performed and payment has been met (income taxes), or on the profits of industrial or professional business at the end of annual activity (corporation taxes). Hence, direct taxes are not intended to play any significant role in the pricing of commodities or professional services. Indirect taxes are levied specifically on consumption and are, therefore, in a simplistic model, very significant in determining the pricing of commodities given their real costs of production.

Historically speaking, in the EU there existed four types of sales, or turnover, taxes: the *cumulative multi-stage cascade system* (operated in West Germany until the end of 1967, in Luxemburg until the end of 1969 and in the Netherlands until the end of 1968) in which the tax was levied on the gross value of the commodity in question at each and every stage of production without any rebate on taxes paid at earlier stages; *value added tax* which has operated in France since 1954 where it is known as TVA – *Taxe sur la Valeur Ajoutée* – which is basically a non-cumulative multistage system; the *mixed systems* (operated in Belgium and Italy) which were cumulative multi-stage systems that were applied down to the wholesale stage, but incorporated taxes which were applied at a single point for certain products; and finally, *purchase tax* (operated in the UK) which was a single-stage tax normally charged at the wholesale stage by registered manufacturers or wholesalers – this meant that manufacturers could trade with each other without paying tax. Although all these tax systems had the common characteristic that no tax was paid on exports, so that each country levied its tax at the point of entry, one should still consider the need for harmonising them.

A variety of taxes also existed in the form of excise duties. The number of commodities subjected to this duty ranged from the usual (or 'classical') five of manufactured tobacco products, hydrocarbon oils, beer, wine and spirits, to an extensive number including coffee, sugar, salt, matches, etc. (in Italy). Also, the means by which the government collected its revenues from excise duties ranged from government-controlled manufacturing, e.g. tobacco goods in France and Italy, to fiscal imports based on value, weight, strength, quality, etc.

As far as corporation tax is concerned, three basic schemes existed and still exist, but not in any single country at *all* times. The first is the *separate system* which was used in the UK – the system calls for the complete separation of corporation tax from personal income tax and was usually referred to as the 'classical system'. The second is the *two-rate system* or *split-rate system* which was the German practice and was recommended as an alternative system for the UK in the Green Paper of 1971 (HMSO, Cmnd 4630). The third is the *credit* or *imputation system* – this was the French system and was proposed for the UK in the White Paper of 1972 (HMSO, Cmnd 4955).

Generally speaking, the corporation tax varied from being totally indistinguishable from other systems (Italy) to being quite separate from personal income tax with a single or split-rate which varied between 'distributed' and 'undistributed' profits, to being partially integrated with the personal income tax systems, so that part of the corporation tax paid on distributed profits could be credited against a shareholder's income tax liability.

The personal income tax system itself was differentiated in very many aspects among the six founder countries of the EC, not just as regards rates and allowances, but also administration procedures, compliance and enforcement.

Finally, the variety in the para-tax system relating to social security arrangements was even more striking. The balance between sickness, industrial injury, unemployment and pensions was very different indeed, and the methods of financing these benefits were even more so – see El-Agraa (1985b, tables 14.4 and 14.5).

In order to explain the distorting nature of taxes, it may be instructive to have a closer look at the problems relating to the EU's taxes, especially its turnover tax: VAT. The first problem relates to the point at which the tax should be levied. Here, two basic principles have been recognised and a choice between them has to be made: the 'destination' and 'origin' principles. Taxation under the destination principle specifies that commodities going to the same destination must bear the same tax load irrespective of their origin. For example, if Italy levies a general sales tax at 8 per cent and France a similar tax at 16 per cent, a commodity exported from Italy to France would be exempt from Italy's 8 per cent tax but would be subjected to France's 16 per cent tax. Hence, the Italian export commodity would compete on equal terms with French commodities sold in the French market. Taxation under the origin principle specifies that commodities with the same origin must pay exactly the same tax, irrespective of their destination. Hence a commodity exported by Italy to France would pay the Italian tax (8 per cent) and would be exempt from the French tax (16 per cent). Hence, the commodity that originated from Italy would compete unfairly against a similar French commodity.

The second problem relates to the range of coverage of the tax. If some countries are allowed to include certain stages, e.g. the retail stage, and others make allowances for certain fixed capital expenditures and raw materials, the tax base will not be the same. This point is very important, because one has to be clear about whether the tax base (vital for an economically integrated area which adopts a general budget; note also that this is the clearest example of a tax which directly influences budget revenue) should be consumption or net national income. To illustrate, in a 'closed' economy

$$Y \equiv W + P \equiv C + I$$

where Y = GNP, W = wages and salaries, P = gross profits, C = consumption and I = gross capital expenditure. If value-added is defined as $W + P - I$ (i.e. GNP minus gross capital expenditure), then consumption will form the tax base. If instead of gross capital expenditure one deducts only capital consumption (depreciation), then Net National Product will become the tax base. Obviously, the argument holds true in an open economy. It is therefore important that members of a CM or an EU should have a common base for the financing of a common general budget as is the case in the EU.

The third problem relates to exemptions that may defeat the aim of VAT being a tax on consumption. For example, in a three-stage production process, exempting the first stage does not create any problem, since the tax levies on the second and third stages together will be equivalent to a tax levied on all three stages. Exempting the third stage will obviously reduce the tax collection, provided of course that the rates levied at all stages were the same. If the second stage is exempt, the tax base will be in excess of that where no exemptions are allowed for, since the tax on the first stage cannot be transferred as an input tax on the second stage, and the third stage will be unable to claim any input tax from items bought from the second stage. The outcome will be a tax based on the total sum of the turnover of stages one and three only, rather than a tax levied on the total sum of the value added at all three stages.

With regard to the corporation tax, the important question is the treatment of investment in the different member nations, since, if *K* mobility within the EU is to be encouraged, investors must receive equal treatment irrespective of their native country (region). Here, Dosser (1973, p. 95) highly recommends the *separate system* since it is 'neutral' in its tax treatment between domestic investment at home and abroad, and between domestic and foreign investment at home, provided both member countries practise the same system. Prest (1979, pp. 85–6) argues that even though a *separate system* does not discriminate against partner (foreign) investment, it does discriminate between 'distributed' and 'undistributed' profits, and that the *imputation system* even though it is 'neutral' between 'distributed' and 'undistributed' profits, actually discriminates against partner (foreign) investment. Prest therefore claims that neither system can be given 'full marks'.

Excise duties are intended basically for revenue-raising purposes. For example, in the UK, excise duties on tobacco products, petroleum and alcoholic drinks account for about a quarter of central government revenue. Hence, the issues raised by the harmonisation of these taxes are specifically those relating to the revenue-raising function of these taxes and to the equity, as opposed to the efficiency, of these methods.

Finally, the income tax structure has a lot to do with the freedom of *L* mobility. Ideally, one would expect equality of treatment in every single tax that is covered within this structure, but it is apparent that since there is more than one rate, the harmonisation of a 'package' of rates might achieve the specified overall objective.

In conclusion, one hopes that the digression to the particular case of the EU has clarified the need for tax harmonisation, and has also answered the question regarding why fiscal harmonisation is needed only in CMs and more involved schemes of economic integration, although even CUs may find it necessary to have a very close examination of the effect of taxation on member nations' product competitiveness.

Monetary integration has two essential components: an exchange rate union and *K* market integration. An exchange rate union is established when member countries have what is in effect one currency. The actual existence of one currency is not necessary, however, because if member countries have *permanently* fixed exchange rates amongst themselves, the result is effectively the same.

Convertibility refers to the *permanent* absence of all exchange controls for both current and *K* transactions, including interest and dividend payments (and the harmonisation of relevant taxes and measures affecting the *K* market) within the union. It is, of course, absolutely necessary to have complete convertibility for trade transactions, as otherwise an important requirement of CU formation is threatened, namely the promotion of free trade between members of the CU, which is an integral part of an EU. Convertibility for *K* transactions is related to free factor mobility and is therefore an important aspect of *K* market integration which is necessary in common markets, not in CUs or free trade areas.

In practice, this definition of monetary integration should specifically include: (i) an explicit harmonisation of monetary policies; (ii) a common pool of foreign exchange reserves; and (iii) a single central bank. There are important reasons for including these elements. Suppose union members decide either that one of their currencies will be a reference currency, or that a new unit of account will be established. Also assume that each member country has its own foreign exchange reserves and conducts its own monetary and fiscal policies. If a member finds itself running out of reserves, it will have to engage in a monetary and fiscal contraction sufficient to restore the reserve position. This will necessitate the fairly frequent meeting of the finance ministers or central bank governors, to consider whether or not to change the parity of the reference currency. If they do decide to change it, then all the member currencies will have to move with it. Such a situation could create the kinds of difficulty which plagued the Bretton Woods System (see El-Agraa, 1985a, ch. 5).

In order to avoid such difficulties, it is necessary to include the above three elements in the definition of monetary integration. The central bank would operate in the market so as permanently to maintain the exchange parities among the union currencies and, at the same time, it would allow the rate of the reference currency to fluctuate, or to alter intermittently, relative to the outside reserve currency. For instance, if the foreign exchange reserves in the common pool were running down, the bank would allow the reference currency, and with it all the partner currencies, to depreciate. This would have the advantage of economising in the use of foreign exchange reserves, since all partners would not tend to be in deficit or surplus at the same time. Also surplus countries would automatically be helping deficit countries.

However, without explicit policy coordination, a monetary union would not be effective. If each country conducted its own monetary policy, and hence could engage in as much domestic credit creation as it wished, surplus countries would be financing deficit nations without any incentives for the deficit countries to restore equilibrium. If one country ran a large deficit, the union exchange rate would depreciate, but this might put some partner countries into surplus. If wage rates were rising in the member countries at different rates, while productivity growth did not differ in such a way as to offset the effects on relative prices, those partners with the smaller inflation rates would be permanently financing the other partners.

Therefore, monetary integration which explicitly includes the three requirements specified removes all these problems. Incidentally, this also suggests the advantages of having a single currency.

The benefits of monetary integration should by now be clear (see Robson, 1984; El-Agraa, 1985a). However, there is no consensus of opinion with regard to its costs, if any, simply because those who stress the costs entirely ignore the basic reality that although a member nation loses its individual ability to alter its exchange rate, the EU's exchange rate can be altered. Moreover, the economic rationale for exchange rate flexibility depends heavily on Tinbergen's (1952) criterion of at least an equal number of policy instruments and policy objectives. Orthodoxy has it that there are two macroeconomic policy targets (internal and external equilibrium) and two policy instruments (financial instruments, which have their greatest impact on the level of aggregate demand, hence on the internal equilibrium, and the exchange rate which operates mainly on the external equilibrium). Of course, financial instruments can be activated via both monetary and fiscal policies and may have a varied impact on both the internal and external equilibria. Given this understanding, the case for maintaining flexibility in exchange rates depends entirely on the presumption that the loss of one of the two policy instruments will conflict with the achievement of both internal and external equilibria.

Assuming that there is a Phillips (1958) curve relationship (a negative response of rates of change in money wages – $\dot{W}$ – and the level of unemployment – *U*), Fleming (1971) and Corden (1972b) can explain these aspects by using a simple diagram which was first devised by De Grauwe (1975). Hence, in Figure 3.9 the top half depicts the position of *H* while the lower half depicts that of *P*. The top right and the lower left corners represent the two countries' Phillips curves while the remaining quadrants show their inflation rates – $\dot{P}$. *WI* and WI_P are, of course, determined by the share of *L* in total GNP, the rate of change in the productivity of *L* and the degree of competition in both the factor and commodity markets, with perfect competition resulting in the *WI*s being straight lines. Note that the intersection of the *WI*s with the vertical axes will be determined by the rates of change of *L*'s share in GNP and its rate of productivity change. The diagram has been drawn on the presumption that the *L* productivity changes are positive.

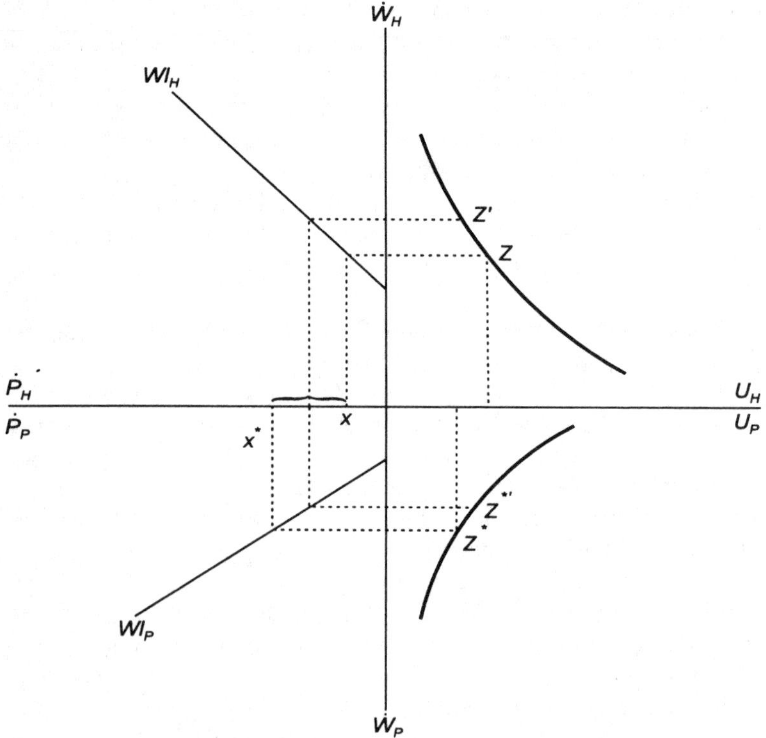

Figure 3.9 The Fleming/Corden analysis of monetary integration

The diagram is drawn in such a way that countries *H* and *P* differ in all respects: the positions of their Phillips curves; their preferred trade-offs between $\dot{W}$ and $\dot{P}$; and their rates of productivity growth. *H* has a lower rate of inflation, *x*, than *P*, x^* (equilibria being at *z* and z^*), hence, without monetary integration, *P*'s currency should depreciate relative to *H*'s; note that it is almost impossible that the two countries' inflation rates would coincide. Altering the exchange rates would then enable each country to maintain its preferred internal equilibrium: *z* and z^* for respectively countries *H* and *P*.

When *H* and *P* enter into an exchange rate union, i.e. have irrevocably fixed exchange rates *vis-à-vis* each other, their inflation rates cannot differ from each other, given a model without traded goods. Hence, each country will have to settle for a combination of *U* and $\dot{P}$ different from that which it would have liked. Therefore, the Fleming–Corden conclusion is vindicated.

It does not require much imagination to see that if this crude version of the Phillips curve is replaced by an expectations adjusted one along the lines suggested by Phelps (1968) and Friedman (1975), i.e. the Phillips curves become vertical in the long run, the Fleming–Corden conclusion need no longer hold. Moreover, once non-traded goods are incorporated into the model and/or *K* and *L* mobility are allowed for, it follows that the losses due to deviating from internal equilibrium vanish into oblivion. Finally, this model does not allow for the fact that monetary integration involves at least three countries, hence *W* has to be explicitly included in the model.

In addition, one should point out a fundamental contradiction in the analysis of those who exaggerate the costs. If a nation decides to become a member of a monetary union, this implies that it accedes to the notion that the benefits of such a union must outweigh any possible losses and/or that it feels that a monetary union is essential for maintaining a rational EU. It will want to do so because its economy is more interdependent with its partners than with *W*. Why then would such a country prize the availability of the exchange rate as a policy instrument for its own domestic purposes? The answer is that there is no conceivable rational reason for its doing so: it will want to have an inflation rate, monetary growth target and unemployment rate which are consistent with those of its partners. Also, the use of the union's exchange rate *vis-à-vis W* plus the rational operations of the common central bank and its general activities should ensure that any worries on the part of *H* are alleviated. Hence, for such a country to feel that there is something intrinsically good about having such a policy instrument at its own disposal is tantamount to its not having any faith in or true commitment to the EU to which it has voluntarily decided to belong!

MACROECONOMICS OF INTEGRATION

We have seen that trade creation and trade diversion are the two concepts most widely used in international economic integration. We have also seen that their economic implications for resource reallocation are usually tackled in terms of particular commodities under conditions of global full employment. However, the economic consequences for the outside world and their repercussions on the integrated area are usually left to intuition. Moreover, their implications for employment are usually ruled out by assumption.

In an effort to rectify these serious shortcomings, I have used a macroeconomic model (see chapters 6–8 of El-Agraa and Jones, 1981) with the purpose of investigating these aspects. The model is still in its infancy and a sophisticated model is now being constructed (see Jones, 1983). However, even the crude model so far published indicates that the advantages of using a macro model are that it clearly demonstrates the once-and-for-all nature of trade creation and trade diversion. It also shows the insignificance of their overall impact given realistic values of the relevant coefficients: marginal propensities to import; marginal propensities to consume; tariff rates, etc. The model also demonstrates that trade creation is beneficial for the partner gaining the new output and exports but is detrimental to the other partner and the outside world. Also that trade diversion is beneficial for the partner now exporting the commodity but is detrimental for the other partner and the outside world. The author feels that a more sophisticated model will corroborate these conclusions.

ECONOMIC INTEGRATION IN DEVELOPING COUNTRIES

It has been claimed that the body of economic integration theory as so far developed has no relevance for the Third World. This is due to the fact that the theory suggested that there would be more scope for trade creation if the countries concerned were initially very competitive in production but potentially very complementary and that a CU would be more likely to be trade creating if the partners conducted most of their foreign trade amongst themselves – see Meade (1955) and Lipsey (1960). These conditions are unlikely to be satisfied in the majority of the developing nations. Moreover, most of the effects of integration are initially bound to be trade diverting, particularly since most of the Third World seeks to industrialise.

On the other hand, it was also realised that an important obstacle to the development of industry in these countries is the inadequate size of their individual markets – see Brown (1961), Hazlewood (1967, 1975) and Robson (1980, 1983, 1984). It is therefore necessary to increase the market size so as to encourage optimum plant installations – hence the need for economic integration. This would, however, result in industries clustering together in the relatively more advanced of these nations – those that have already commenced the process of industrialisation.

I have demonstrated elsewhere (El-Agraa, 1979a, 1994b) that there is essentially *no theoretical difference* between economic integration in the Advanced World and the Third World but that there is a major difference in terms of the *type* of economic integration that suits the particular *circumstances* of developing countries and that is politically feasible: the need for an equitable distribution of the gains from industrialisation and the location of industries is an important issue (see p. 00). This suggests that any type of economic integration that is being contemplated must incorporate as an essential element a common fiscal authority and some coordination of economic policies. But then one could equally well argue that *some degree* of these elements is necessary in *any* type of integration – see the Raisman Committee recommendations for the EAC (1961).

ECONOMIC INTEGRATION AMONG SOCIALIST COUNTRIES

The only example up to now of economic integration among communist countries was the CMEA. However, here the economic system perpetuated a fundamental lack of interest of domestic producers in becoming integrated with both consumers and producers in other member countries. As Marer and Montias (1988) emphasise, the integration policies of member nations had to focus on the mechanism of state-to-state relations rather than on domestic economic policies which would have made CMEA integration more attractive to producers and consumers alike. That is, integration had to be planned by the state at the highest possible level and imposed on ministries, trusts and enterprises. It should also be stated that the CMEA operated different pricing mechanisms for intra- and extra-area trade. Moreover, the attitude of the USSR was extremely important since the policies of the East European members of the CMEA were somewhat constrained by the policies adopted by the organisation's most powerful member, for economic as well as political reasons. CMEA integration, therefore, had to be approached within an entirely different framework. However, now that the CMEA has met its demise, there is no justification in pursuing this issue further.

CONCLUSIONS

The conclusions reached here are consistent with my 1979 conclusions and with those of Jones in El-Agraa and Jones (1981). They are:

First, that the rationale for regional economic integration rests upon the existence of constraints on the use of first-best policy instruments. Economic analysis has had little to say about the nature of these constraints, and presumably the evaluation of any regional scheme of economic integration should incorporate a consideration of the validity of the view that such constraints do exist to justify the pursuit of second- rather than first-best solutions.

Secondly, that even when the existence of constraints on superior policy instruments is acknowledged, it is misleading to identify the results of regional economic integration by comparing an arbitrarily chosen common policy with an arbitrarily chosen national policy. Of course, ignorance and inertia provide sufficient reasons why existing policies may be non-optimal but it is clearly wrong to attribute gains which would have been achieved by appropriate unilateral action to a policy of regional integration. Equally, although it is appropriate to use the optimal common policy as a point of reference, it must be recognised that this may overstate the gains to be achieved if, as seems highly likely, constraints and inefficiencies in the political processes by which policies are agreed prove to be greater among a group of countries than within any individual country.

Although the first two conclusions raise doubts about the case for regional economic integration, in principle at least, a strong general case for economic integration does exist. In unions where economies of scale may be in part external to national industries, the rationale for unions rests essentially upon the recognition of the externalities and market imperfections which extend beyond the boundaries of national states. In such circumstances, unilateral national action will not be optimal whilst integrated action offers the scope for potential gain.

As with the solution to most problems of externalities and market imperfections, however, customs union theory frequently illustrates the proposition that a major stumbling block to obtaining the gains from joint optimal action lies in agreeing an acceptable distribution of such gains. Thus the fourth conclusion is that the achievement of the potential gains from economic integration will be limited to countries able and willing to cooperate to distribute the gains from integration so that all partners may benefit compared to the results achieved by independent action. It is easy to argue from this that regional economic integration may be more readily achieved than global solutions but, as the debate about monetary integration in the EU illustrates (see Chapter 5), the chances of obtaining potential mutual gain may well founder in the presence of disparate views about the distribution of such gains and weak arrangements for redistribution.

4 The Problems of the Quantitative Estimation of Integration Effects

David G. Mayes

Over the last few years there has been a quantum leap forward in the estimation of the impact of economic integration generated by the need for the European Commission to assess the costs and benefits, first of completing the 'Internal Market' and secondly of moving to Economic and Monetary Union (EMU). The first, set out in Emerson *et al.* (1988), was a very substantial work involving a large number of consultants and generating some seventeen volumes of reports under the title *The Costs of Non-Europe.* These studies are distinguished by the fact that they explore not only a much wider range of the characteristics of integration than does most previous work but they adopt specific macro- and micro-economic approaches to the problem. The study of the effects of EMU, 'One Market One Money' (in *European Economy*, no. 44, October 1990) is a less precise assessment but still one which advances understanding of the problems involved. The renewed enthusiasm for integration in the late 1980s and early 1990s has led to substantial progress on empirical analysis on several fronts. The North American Free Trade Area negotiations stimulated a further raft of work, much of it following more of a general equilibrium approach.

In this chapter, therefore, I begin by setting out the conceptual framework for measuring the effects of integration before going on to explain how the analysis progressed up to 1987 and then setting out, in the light of subsequent progress, how the impact might be assessed.

A FRAMEWORK FOR ESTIMATING THE EFFECTS OF ECONOMIC INTEGRATION

Economic integration tends to proceed in steps beginning with reducing the barriers to trade, moving on to lowering the barriers to the movement of factors, labour and capital and then to removing barriers posed by the existence of a whole host of regulatory measures, which were intended primarily for the treatment of domestic issues but in practice restrict trade or factor movements. Beyond this, one can move towards macro and microeconomic policy coordination and the implementation of common policies. Integration of macroeconomic policy as proposed by the European Union in the Maastricht Treaty of 1993 tends to be one of the last stages before political union, as it involves the giving up of control over key policy instruments and hence a significant loss of sovereignty. It is difficult to specify the end of the process as national states themselves exhibit varying degrees of integration. The former Soviet Union probably provides the most striking example where many aspects of industry were highly integrated with one or two plants supplying the whole union, indeed in some cases supplying the whole of the COMECON bloc. Yet the experiences of the last few years have shown the extent of the underlying divisions. Therefore, rather than speculate on how far the process will or could go in the European or other contexts, this analysis stops with EMU.

Although the steps in this analysis follow the sequence of European integration, there is no required ordering of these events. Australia and New Zealand had free movement of labour long before they achieved free movement of goods and services.

Estimation of the effects of integration have followed a similar path as the process of closer integration has proceeded, starting with trade and moving on to full EMU. There is, however, one important distinction which affects the way in which quantification can be approached. The initial stages of integration tend to involve the removal of barriers: tariffs, quotas, immigration and capital controls. Following the work of Pinder (1968) and Tinbergen (1954), these steps can be classified as 'negative' integration – it is just necessary to stop doing something. Whereas the later stages of integration involve more 'positive' measures, creating common regulations, developing common policies. However, there are also aspects of integration which are less formalised such as development of social and business customs, tastes and informal codes of behaviour. All of these pose problems for quantitative estimation.

CUSTOMS UNIONS, FREE TRADE AREAS AND THE EFFECTS ON TRADE

Customs unions and free trade areas provide the most straightforward aspect of integration for estimating the impact. Although many agreements are complex (the NAFTA agreement is an inch thick), most estimation usually conceives the problem as involving merely the progressive removal of tariffs between partner countries, and, in the former case, the forming of a common external tariff with respect to the rest of the world. The removal of quotas and other barriers to trade is usually subsumed within the tariff changes for the purpose of estimation by computing a tariff equivalent. This is, of course, not really correct as the tariff revenue accrues largely to the importing country, while, unless quotas are auctioned, the revenue from the ensuing higher price accrues largely to the foreign exporter. These tariff changes are expected to result in a series of relative price changes. The price of imports from partner countries falls, for commodities where the tariff is cut, relative to the price of the same commodity produced in the domestic country. For third countries, which are excluded from the union, relative prices may change for more than one reason. They will change differently if the tariff with respect to third countries is shifted from its pre-integration level or it may change if producers in third countries have different pricing reactions to the change in price competition. Some third country producers may decide to absorb more of the potential change by reducing profits rather than by increasing prices relative to those of domestic producers. The relative price of different commodities is also likely to change and hence there is a complex set of interrelated income and substitution effects to be explained. More recently it has been possible to explore how firms react to these changes in barriers (Smith and Venables, 1988). As soon as we relax the implicit assumption of perfect competition which underlies much of the published analysis and admit that the number of important firms in each industry may be limited and hence able to influence selling prices, the analysis becomes more complex as an assumption has to be made about the nature of the process of price determination.

The immediate difficulty is thus the translation of tariff changes and other agreed measures in the customs union treaty into changes in prices and other variables which are known to have an impact on economic behaviour. Such evidence as there is suggests that there are wide discrepancies among the reactions of importers benefiting from tariff cuts and also among competitors adversely affected by them (EFTA, 1968), and that reactions of trade to changes in tariffs are different from those to changes in prices (Kreinin, 1961). Two routes would appear to be open, one is to estimate the effect of tariff changes on prices and then estimate the effects of these derived price changes on trade patterns, and the other is to operate directly with observed relative price movements. This latter course exemplifies a problem which runs right through the estimation of the effects of economic integration and makes the obtaining of generally satisfactory results almost impossible. It is that to measure the effect of integration one must decide what would have happened if integration had not occurred. Thus, if in the present instance any observed change in relative prices were assumed to be the result of the adjustment to tariff changes, all other sources of variation in prices would be ignored, which is clearly an exaggeration and could be subject to important biases if other factors were affecting trade at the same time.

The Appropriate Procedure

If economic integration were treated like any other change in exogenous or policy variables in a model, the correct econometric procedure would be to estimate a model which was large enough to reflect all the influences in the economy which we thought were important. Having estimated the model using data from some period in the past, one would first fit it to the data from the period of integration and then rerun the model inserting the values of the appropriate explanatory variables as they would have been without integration to calculate the second set of values. The difference between the two estimates is then the identifiable effects of integration according to our model of behaviour.

Unfortunately, this is no mean task and can only be approached by use of large models of the international economy such as those of the National Institute, NIGEM (NIESR, 1995), Oxford Economic Forecasting (Burridge *et al.*, 1991) or the European Commission's HERMES and OECD's INTERLINK (Emerson *et al.*, 1988). The main problems are: (i) the size of model required; and (ii) the constancy of parameters over time. I shall deal with these in turn. The normal response in practice (see Mayes, 1978) has been to estimate a highly simplified model and make a further simple assumption about changes in parameters. Furthermore, one of the stages in the argument is usually left out and, instead of comparing what the model predicts with integration to what it predicts without integration, authors tend to compare actual behaviour with what would have happened without integration attributing all the difference to the effects of integration. Given the simplicity of the models and the assumptions about changes in parameters this can result in substantial biases in estimates (Mayes, 1984).

The Size of the Model

There are two basic issues over the size of model: the first is one of aggregation and the second of how many relations are necessary to capture the effects of integration throughout the economy and not just the initial impact on trade flows. The aggregation issue is well known (see Barker, 1970 for a very clear example relating to the United Kingdom) and occurs, first because the direct price and substitution elasticities of demand for imports vary very considerably over different commodities, running from direct price elasticities near zero for essential commodities which cannot be produced locally to quite substantial values for finished manufactures, such as consumer durables for which there are many close substitutes. Secondly, both the level of tariffs and the changes in them which have been agreed vary, sometimes quite considerably, so taking a uniform value across all trade could be very misleading. It is thirdly emphasised by the changing commodity composition of trade which tends to result in a downward bias in the estimates (see Orcutt, 1950 for the original exposition and Morgan, 1970 for a more recent example). A more trivial reason for disaggregation can be advanced as in the case of EFTA Secretariat (1969), which looked at the effects of integration on a thirty-six-commodity breakdown of trade for its member states. Here it is necessary to know the results in some detail otherwise it is difficult to assess which are important, especially in so far as the interest is in examining whether *inter*-industry specialisation has taken place rather than the *intra*-industry specialisation which took place in the EU (see *inter alia*, Grubel and Lloyd, 1975; Kreinin, 1979). In many cases the level of disaggregation is driven not so much by relevance to the problem at hand as by the availability of data. Thus our use of ninety-one sectors in Burridge and Mayes (1990) when exploring the impact of the Single Market was dictated by the maximum amount of information available in the UK input–output tables.

The second issue regarding which influences to incorporate is a much harsher problem. Using a simple logarithmic import function in prices and incomes, like Houthakker and Magee (1969) for example,

$$ln\, M = a + b\, ln\, RP + c\, ln\, Y + e \qquad (4.1)$$

where M is imports, $RP = PM/PD$, the relative price of imports to the domestic product and Y is a measure of income, a, b and c are parameters and *e* an unobservable residual, one could estimate the direct price effect of integration by multiplying our estimate of the price elasticity, *b*, by the calculated change in relative prices due to integration (Mayes, 1971; Kreinin, 1973). (A more complex *RP* term can allow for substitution between imports from partners and non-members as well as substitution between imports and domestic products to be incorporated (Verdoorn and Schwartz, 1972).) However, the relative fall in the price of imports will have other consequences in the economy. If output prices are a mark-up on costs then they will tend to be lower as some of the imports are inputs to domestic output. Imports going both to final and intermediate demand will tend to lower the rate of price inflation and this in turn will have consequences for the wage rate through the usual inflationary spiral and for the price of exports and hence export demand.

Exports will in any case be affected by the change in tariffs in partner countries. In so far as the increased export demand is met by increased output, demand will also increase both at the intermediate and final levels creating the usual progressive process of the feedback step by step through the economy. The model must also be able to take account of the effects of increased imports on domestic output which will in turn have a deflationary influence on domestic demand. At the very least it is also necessary to have some balance of payments/exchange rate relation.

Therefore, without disaggregating over commodities or countries we are considering a model of at least ten equations for each identified country that we need to examine, to say nothing of the constraints across countries which are necessary to make sure that the estimates for transactions between them are consistent. It is thus immediately clear why this route was avoided in practice on many occasions as it requires an immense amount of data collection and work on estimation.

Whatever model is adopted we do need to be able to explain imports and exports disaggregated at the very least by trading area and usually by country as well if we are to obtain estimates of trade creation, trade diversion, and the effects on the balance of payments and welfare.

In more recent years there has been substantial use of Computable General Equilibrium (CGE) models (see, for example, Stoeckel *et al.* 1990) in the case of European integration and for NAFTA. While they may not indicate the time path of change and may have imposed rather than estimated coefficients which have been directly empirically estimated, they nevertheless have the clear advantage of completeness.

Constancy of Parameters

If some of the expected effects of integration take place, such as the exploitation of economies of scale and the changes in economic efficiency, it will not be just the variables in the model which change with integration, but also the parameters. Thus it would not be possible to use a model estimated in a period with integration to suggest what would have happened without integration by changing the values of variables alone or vice versa. Furthermore, if we take periods such as the formulation of EFTA and the EC during the 1950s and 1960s, or the enlargement of the EC in 1973 there is a good argument that general economic conditions were not similar in the periods before and after integration. Certainly the years after the oil crisis of 1973–4 and the period of floating exchange rates are not readily comparable with preceding periods. Balassa (1967, 1974) actually uses changes in the income elasticity of demand for imports as a means of estimating the effects of the formation of the EC.

The Disadvantages of Simple Models

The advantages of simple models are clear as is shown in Kreinin (1979). Even with a more sophisticated model we can only get an idea of an order of magnitude not an accurate single number, hence if it is possible to use only a relatively limited amount of readily available information to estimate the magnitude, we can make much more efficient use of our resources by adopting the simple model. In Mayes (1978) I showed in a survey of the estimates of trade creation and trade diversion in the EC that the approximate bounds for the likely size of trade creation were, in the view of the authors surveyed, 8–15 billion US dollars, or to put it differently, between approximately 9 and 17 per cent of total EC trade in that year. If that degree of accuracy is acceptable then it might be possible to stop there and merely advise that, providing appropriate bounds are set by varying the assumptions behind the simple model, this is sufficient.

However, I would argue that this is not the case and that these orders of magnitude could easily be substantially incorrect. On the whole these simplified models work by projecting either shares of trade or shares in total consumption from the pre-integration period into the post-integration period, perhaps 'normalised' by the behaviour of third countries during the post-integration period or by the share of member countries in the market of third countries in the post-integration period. Normalisation in this context means, for example, that if imports in the rest of the world increased their share in total consumption by a certain percentage, then, without integration, import shares in the integrating countries would also have increased by that amount.

Normalisation of some form is certainly necessary otherwise all differences in the general level of world trade and activity, which lead to differences in activity and trade among the integrating countries, will be attributed to integration. Thus, in the period up to 1969–70 trade creation in the EC is approximately halved by appropriate normalisation (Kreinin, 1972), whereas in the post-enlargement period since 1973 trade creation is increased by normalisation, world trade and activity having grown more slowly than formerly. However, there is no means of deciding what portion of the increase in activity in the integrating countries is due to integration, nor of separating changes due to technology, movement of factors rather than goods, changes in consumption patterns, etc. (Mayes, 1984).

Thus the final figure is an amalgam of effects. It shows us how trade patterns have changed in the integrating countries compared to normalisation. This is certainly interesting and useful information, but whether it is a measure of trade creation or trade diversion as described in the last chapter is another matter. Because it has no explicit explanation of how changes in trade from integration take place, all changes from whatever source (after normalisation) are included in measured trade creation and diversion; they might be positive or negative, but we have no information about their sign or size.

It is worth noting before leaving this section that the main emphasis on quantitative work on these static effects on trade is largely in the context of the exploitation of comparative advantage, yet the work of Petith (1977) suggests that the effects from the change in the terms of trade on the EC and EFTA may have been between two and six times as important at 0.34 to 0.93 per cent of GDP as that from trade creation.

Furthermore, the calculated changes in trade flows are frequently classed in empirical work as 'trade creation' if they increase total trade or 'trade diversion' if they are switches from trade with non-member to trade with a member country, while the correct definitions of the two concepts are in fact the *welfare* consequences of the changes in trade flows (Pelkmans, 1984).

THE DYNAMIC EFFECTS

While the discussion of the exploitation of comparative advantage, the gains from a favourable movement in the terms of trade and often those from economies of scale is expressed in terms of comparative statics, as we explained in the previous section, it is difficult to disentangle them from feedback onto incomes and activity. Indeed it is difficult to see why one would want to restrict consideration to such 'first round' effects. The essence of the gains from increased efficiency and technological change is that the economy should reap dynamic gains. Even small dynamic changes will rapidly swamp the static effects as the former grow year by year while the latter are fixed. In other words, integration should enhance the rate of growth of GDP rather than just giving a single step increase in the level of welfare. Again, it is necessary to explain how this might come about explicitly.

There are two generalised ways in which this can take place, first, through increased productivity growth at a given investment ratio, or secondly, through increased investment itself. This is true whether the increased sales are generated internally or through the pressures of demand for exports from abroad through integration. Growth gains can, of course, occur temporarily in so far as there are slack resources in the economy. Again, it is possible to observe whether the rate of growth has changed but it is much more difficult to decide whether that is attributable to integration.

Krause (1968) attempted to apply a version of Denison's (1967) method of identifying the causes of economic growth but suggested that *all* changes in the rate of business investment were due to the formation of the EC (or EFTA in the case of those countries). In Mayes (1978) I showed that if the same contrast between business investment before and after the formation of the EC (EFTA) were applied to Japan the estimated effect was larger than in any of the integrating countries! Clearly changes in the rate of business investment can occur for reasons other than integration.

In order to identify what the contribution of integration is to the rate of economic growth, a model of behaviour must be used which can explain how such influences can take place. A partial approach which identifies one of the five main routes of effect on the economy identified by Lipsey (1957), namely the exploitation of economies of scale, is tackled by Owen (1983) in a dynamic framework. In this case, if one can identify the degree to which demand is increased by integration it is then possible to identify the extent to which unit costs are reduced as a result of increased output, largely through the greater specialisation which is expected from the exploitation of comparative advantage whether on an inter- or intra-industry basis. While the description I have given is in a static form, Owen also explains the process in a dynamic framework. However, this is still the estimation of only a part of the dynamic effects, it will only be complete if a full model, explaining how the gains from economies of scale are fed back into economic activity, is used.

The most complete example comes from Baldwin (1989), who suggested that the effects of completion of the European single market could be substantially underestimated by Emerson *et al.* (1988) as they did not take account of the full dynamic feedbacks. Over the medium-term (5–7 years) horizon that Emerson *et al.* consider the dynamic effects could add 13–135 per cent to the estimates, with a suggested mean addition of 65 per cent. (Ironically, almost identical to the 67 per cent increase suggested using a much more elementary model in Mayes (1971).)

THE MOVEMENT OF FACTORS

Although the proposals for a single market (Commission of the European Communities, 1985) emphasised the importance of establishing the four freedoms of movements in goods, services, labour and capital, such freedoms had been envisaged even from the early stages of European integration. Estimation of the impact of movements in labour and capital complicate the estimation of the effects of integration of the markets for goods and services. Factor movements can be both substitutes and complements for movements in goods and services. A new foreign investment may require an inflow of skilled labour, imports for some of its inputs and may export part of its output. On the other hand, a company may decide to invest in a new plant using local labour to supply the local market, both substituting for goods or services it previously supplied from its home market. Most of the models we have discussed thus far ignore the possibility of factor movements and hence any impact they may have on trade flows – a further aspect of their incompleteness.

Unlike the study of trade flows, the theory of factor movements is relatively underdeveloped. This makes the quantification of the effects difficult right from the outset. It is possible to measure the flows of labour and of direct and portfolio investment, although data on the latter are sometimes rather inaccurate and definitions vary widely from one country to another. However, it is much more difficult to decide what proportion of any change which takes place after integration is due to the integration. This is the same problem as in the case of trade flows and, with a lack of suitable well-determined models of factor movements, reliance is likely to have to be placed on an analysis of trends.

The assumption at the outset of the present discussion is that economic integration reduces or possibly eliminates the barriers to factor movements. This assumption is not a necessary condition for factor movements to take place and is not applicable in the case of some free trade areas which refer only to products. It is used to simplify the analysis. Changes in factor movements may still take place even if barriers remain unchanged (provided, naturally, that they are not prohibitive), because of the changes in trade and activity stemming from the free trade area.

Freedom of movement of capital and labour have been restricted for more than one reason. There have been natural fears of being taken over by an influx of foreign nationals or capital but the flow of capital in particular has been restricted because of problems of macroeconomic management. Without a fully operating market system, short-run capital flows can destablise foreign exchange markets. In what follows we do not deal with these stabilisation issues but they would, of course, have needed to be borne in mind at the time.

Increased trade may require increased distribution networks or complementary production – greater familiarity with some countries may increase both capital and labour migration. As in all such cases, there are incentives for capital and labour to leave one country and incentives for them to enter specific other countries (often described as push and pull factors).

There are clear relations between the movement of labour and the movement of capital: relatively low wages in one country compared with another encourage labour to move from the lower wage to the higher wage country to obtain higher incomes and capital to move in the opposite direction to exploit lower costs, although, of course, many other considerations, for example marginal tax rates, will tend to modify these decisions. Nevertheless, we shall treat the labour and capital movements separately for ease of exposition. In the limit, movements of capital will increase the number of jobs available in the destination country and, in relative terms, decrease it in the source country, to such an extent that, coupled with the movement of labour in the opposite direction, factor prices will tend towards equalisation in the absence of other distortions. This, however, is sufficiently far from reality that we only need consider it as a means of determining the theoretical signs of the changes rather than the likely magnitude. The degree to which factor prices move towards equalisation will, of course, in itself be a measure of the movement towards integration.

The labour movement decision is perhaps the easier to consider as it reflects household behaviour in the light of the push and pull factors. While the nature of the relative wage incentive and the relative employment opportunities may be clear and measurable, the effects of other determinants, such as language, division of the family if only the worker concerned is permitted to move, the availability of housing – which certainly acts as a barrier to internal labour movements in the UK – and similar social considerations are immensely difficult to quantify. What is clear in the European case is that, with the exception of the Irish in the UK, there has been relatively little labour movement among the northern European countries (Emerson, 1979). The major movements have been from southern European countries, whether or not in the Community, and from Turkey.

Although the need for an integrated theory of trade and investment has been stated on many occasions, actual steps to implement it have been limited. Such attempts as there have been, Casson (1980) and Grey (1980), for example, have not been applied to actual data, let alone to the quantification of the effects of integration. Although portfolio capital can be invested abroad by the personal sector and the government largely in response to relative expected yields (assessed through relative interest rates, expected inflation and exchange rates) and risks, as explained in Cuthbertson *et al.* (1980), the interesting decision lies in the choice by firms whether to export to a particular country, buy participation in the activity of other companies already operating there through portfolio investment or invest directly in that country themselves.

The interaction of possible effects under the formation of a customs union which also eases restrictions on the movement of factors is complex. In so far as direct investment in a particular market has taken place to enable operation inside a market which has tariffs restricting trade, one might expect that trade might be used as a substitute for direct investment if that country is included in a customs union. If one thought of equivalent concepts to trade creation and trade diversion as investment creation and investment diversion, on this argument they might both have opposite signs to their trade counterparts. The freeing of trade would tend to make trade relatively attractive compared with investment hence leading to an overall reduction in direct investment in partner countries. Secondly, direct investment in non-member countries would become relatively attractive thus diverting investment away from the member countries.

Against these influences there are three sets of offsetting factors. In the first place, the removal of controls on factor movements within the customs union will encourage direct investment as well as trade. Secondly, any increase in growth occurring within the member countries will attract investment relative to that in third countries, and thirdly, trade and investment have a large measure of complementarity as well as substitutability. According to Panić (1980) a UK Department of Trade enquiry in 1976 revealed that 'about 29 per cent of the exports covered ... went to related enterprises'. It may be easier to transport goods at some stages of production rather than others thus requiring both direct investment and trade. In addition, other distortions, such as internal tax systems, which are not specifically related to trade may encourage multinational operation.

The overall picture is thus confused and it is not surprising that there has been a tendency to develop an eclectic explanation of the phenomenon, such as Dunning (1980) who suggests that perceived advantages to the firm of direct investment abroad can be classified under the three headings of ownership, internalisation and location. The empirical evidence, such as is available, is also difficult to interpret. Direct investment in both directions with Western Europe increased rapidly before the UK joined the EC as well as subsequently. To some extent this is also explicable by Dunning's theory of the development of direct investment: countries with very low per capita incomes have a low capacity to absorb direct investment, but as the country grows the inflow of capital builds up until it reaches a maximum somewhere in the range of incomes between Singapore and New Zealand. Beyond this point domestic industrial and financial activity is such that the country can support an increasing outflow of direct investment. At some point the net movement of capital changes from an inflow to an outflow and for the EC countries (other than the UK) this tended to be reached during the period 1967 to 1975. Clearly the nature of countries' financial institutions themselves affects the exact timing.

Flows of direct investment, particularly those involved with takeovers and mergers, tend to go in cycles. While there was a major boom in such flows in Europe during the implementation of the legislation for the completion of the European internal market the boom also extended to North America. Assessing the impact of capital flows thus faces all the same difficulties of establishing a counter-factual. The size of the boom was such that it is implausible to suggest that it was unrelated to European integration. However, it is difficult to get beyond the realms of speculation to suggest what part of the worldwide increase might have been a spin-off from the movements in Europe as firms tried to rebalance their position, or, of course, the extent to which the European boom was just part of a worldwide move not driven primarily by European integration.

Such a loose form of quantification is clearly unsatisfactory if one wants to explain not just the approximate level of capital flows but the effects of change in their determinants, as is necessary in the case of integration. However, at least some important steps have been made in this direction, rather more than can be said for the quantification of the effects of positive integration which is considered in the next section.

POSITIVE INTEGRATION AND THE QUANTIFICATION OF THE EFFECTS OF COMMON POLICIES

The emphasis on the effects of positive integration, within the EU at any rate, has been on agriculture. As the Common Agriculture Policy (CAP) takes over half of the total EU budget this is to be expected. However, the issues which it raises can be applied to the other areas of common policies which occur as integration develops, whether they apply to fisheries, regional or monetary and technology policies. The essential feature is that positive integration will normally entail the transfer of resources between member states. These transfers may occur either through direct payments from one country to another (or to a central authority) or through the need to maintain relative price levels which are different from those which would obtain under free trade and payments.

Thus, for example, the CAP imposes two costs on the UK, the first because it contributes more than it receives under the European Agricultural Guidance and Guarantee Fund, EAGGF (or FEOGA), and secondly, because it has to pay higher prices for its food than would otherwise be the case. Clearly, producers gain from this second form of resource adjustment, and these effects tend to amplify those from the net receipts from the EAGGF.

If these resource flows result in a deficit on the balance of payments, a country has three solutions to the problem. The first is to depreciate its rate of exchange in the hope that the balance of payments will be improved through the relative price effect, the second is to deflate and attempt to improve the balance through the relative income effect and the third is to obtain a continuing capital inflow. Without integration this last course is not usually open (countries such as Australia and New Zealand are, of course, exceptions) but with integration this is no different from the continuing regional deficits and surpluses which exist within countries virtually indefinitely. The existence of a common currency precludes depreciation and deflation is likely to be the exact opposite of the intentions of regional policy because the deficit region tends to be relatively depressed already (as in the case of Scotland, Northern Ireland, Wales and part of Northern England in the case of the UK).

The assessment of costs of common policies depends on the route which is chosen for adjustment to the required resource flows. Under a common currency system or a managed adjustable set of aligned parities, as in the European Monetary System (EMS), the pressure has tended to be on the deficit rather than the surplus countries to adjust. In this way, *on balance*, the adjustment to the costs of the common policies is deflationary and welfare is foregone in the community as a whole. Similarly, if depreciation is chosen as the method under fully employed resources, it is necessary to reduce domestic demands in order to realise resources for increased exporting. Furthermore, Kaldor (1971) points out that if a country tries to resist the pressure to depreciate it may enter a vicious circle of low competitiveness, deflation, reduced investment and hence even lower competitiveness and so on.

A second cost must also be considered, namely that of inflation. The greater the weight placed on adjustment by surplus countries the greater the likely overall rate of inflation within the EU. It is clear, therefore, that positive integration through the implementation of common policies has led to the search for common solutions to the effects on member countries. Thus although the original attempt to move towards monetary union following the Werner Plan may have petered out, it has been replaced by a more comprehensive attempt to move to EMU through the Maastricht Treaty.

The most comprehensive attempt to look at common policies (Franzmeyer *et al.*, 1991) is concerned with their regional impact rather than their impact at the level of the individual member state.

However, their concern is with the redistributive effect of the policies, not with their impact on economic activity. Structural policy, for example, as administered through the regional and social funds, is intended to increase the growth potential of the regions in which it is spent. As pointed out in Begg *et al.* (1991), the European Commission does not monitor the real impact, just whether the funds have been spent in the intended manner on the approved programmes. There has been some narrowing of the differentials over recent years (Begg and Mayes, 1993) but it is not possible to show how much of this is due to the structural policies. Nam and Reuter (1991) show that increasing infrastructure and improving human capital through training are not on their own enough to ensure that investment is attracted to disadvantaged regions. However, such findings are qualitative. Some firms require other features such as ready access to large markets, networks of suppliers and business services which may only be available in the main centres.

We are thus largely dependent on assessments such as that of Franzmeyer *et al.* (1991) which shows that although structural policy does indeed redistribute funds to the less advantaged regions, technology policy does not. The Coal and Steel Community funds go primarily to the old industrial areas, which in general do not show the lowest GDP per head in Europe, while the CAP redistributes away from the poorer areas of southern Europe as it is primarily focused on 'northern' products (reflecting the characteristics of the original six members).

An analysis of the budgetary flows thus gives a limited view of the impact and needs complementing by microeconomic studies that explore the economic impact of programmes. Even so aggregating these is difficult as the counter-factual must calculate the impact of the alternative use of these funds as it is only their net impact on efficiency and growth that is relevant.

A SINGLE MARKET

Although the original phraseology of the European Community talked in terms of a 'common market', what that entailed in practice was simply the removal of various external barriers with relatively limited positive integration outside agriculture where there was substantial harmonisation. The moves to create the single European market following the 1985 White Paper (Commission of the European

Communities, 1985) were much more pervasive. Although they deliberately did not follow the example of agriculture in trying to harmonise product specification and process standards in detail, the approach was primarily regulatory, seeking to remove the host of national regulations which effectively made the movement of goods, services, labour and capital across the borders of the member states more difficult.

The majority of nearly 300 areas of barrier identified related to differences in technical requirements, whether product standards, required qualifications for workers, location for financial services or domestic ownership for public procurement. The remainder were labelled as fiscal barriers, through the differential operation of tax systems, or physical barriers, such as border controls.

The sheer complexity of these changes represents a challenge for quantification. While trying to convert quotas into their tariff equivalent might have appeared a heroic exercise, this pales into insignificance. The challenge, therefore, was not merely to try to list the relevant barriers but to quantify their importance. This would appear to be in the first instance a fairly microeconomic task, requiring an assessment of the degree to which each measure could be translated into a value equivalent.

However, the European Commission, as probably the only body with the resources to do so, took up the challenge and its assessment, 'The Economics of 1992' (Emerson *et al.*, 1988), pursued a novel approach to exploring the impact of integration by measuring the departures from it. This inverts the procedure of trying to explain what the counter-factual might be if integration were not to take place. Instead the comparison becomes one with a specified view of what the integrated economy might look like. In such an economy there would be little price dispersion and enterprises would operate on a Europe-wide level. Thus in setting out the potential impact the study looked at the extent of departures from the lowest prices and the extent to which economies of scale have not been exploited. This approach does not estimate the likely impact of integration but provides an estimate of the scope for gains. Unfortunately, the estimates have widely been interpreted as forecasts and substantial effort has not been devoted to trying to find empirical means of deciding the extent to which these potential gains will be realised.

The results of this assessment on an industry by industry and barrier by barrier basis, set out in Table 4.1, suggest potential gain of around 80 billion EU in 1985 prices. The drawback of such an

Table 4.1 Estimated costs of barriers, EC12 1985 (billion ECU)

1. Specific types of barriers	
Customs formalities	8–9
Public procurement	21
2. Barriers in specific industries	
Food	0.5–1
Pharmaceuticals	0.3–0.6
Automobiles	2.6
Textiles and clothing	0.7–1.3
Building materials	2.8
Telecommunications equipment	3–4.8
3. Barriers in specific services	
Financial services	22
Business services	3.3
Road transport	5
Air transport	3
Telecommunication services	6

Source: Emerson *et al.* (1988).

approach is that it does not consider the response of producers nor the extent of the continuing ability to segment markets either because of market power or differences in tastes and customs. In part this was covered by the study by Smith and Venables (1988) which formed part of the Commission's programme. They considered how firms in imperfect competition might respond, allowing the number of firms to change so that economies of scale could be exploited.

Taking the sector by sector studies and a view on possible feedback gave an estimate of the scope for gain of around 6 per cent of EU GDP (Table 4.2) This then provided the input to the use of macroeconomic models (their own HERMES and OECD's INTERLINK) to trace through the economy-wide feedback of the realisation of these possible microeconomic effects (Table 4.3). This procedure follows the practice advocated above of using a full macroeconomic model to evaluate not just the first round impact of changes but the feedbacks thereafter. However, even so it is necessary for the model to be able to accommodate the impact on growth rates and it is not clear that the longer run performance of these models is sufficiently affected (Baldwin, 1989), as they tend to converge to an equilibrium.

Furthermore, as Stoeckel *et al.* (1990) point out in their general equilibrium analysis of the international impact of the single market,

Table 4.2 Partial equilibrium calculations of the costs of non-Europe (percentage of real GDP, EC7 1985)

	Variant	
	A	*B*
Costs of barriers affecting trade only	0.2	0.3
Costs of barriers affecting all production	2.0	2.4
Economies of scale from restructuring and increased production	2.0	2.1
Competition effects on X-inefficiency and monopoly rents	1.6	1.6
Total	5.8	6.4

Note
Variants A and B relate to the use of different primary source material.
Source: As Table 4.1.

it is not clear that the full feedback through exchange rates, changes in foreign demand and re-equilibration of the balance of payments across the world has been fully accounted for. It is likely, as in previous steps of European integration, that trade creation will outweigh trade diversion and hence there will be a favourable stimulus to the rest of the world.

These estimates are all *ex-ante*. We have argued (Burridge and Mayes, 1993) that in practice not only will the ability of the single market legislation to 'complete' the internal market be less than 100 per cent (and the scope for some changes such as exploitation of economies of scale exaggerated (Geroski, 1989)) but the impact will be spread over a longer period. Some changes will be anticipated as firms try to achieve a market position before the competition, while others will be attenuated as the final measures only start to take their

Table 4.3 Macroeconomic consequences of completing the internal market (percentage change from base, EC12)

	1 Year	*2 Years*	*Medium term*	
			Simulation	*Range*
Real GDP	1.1	2.3	4.5	3.2 to 5.7
Consumer prices	−1.5	−2.4	−6.1	−4.5 to −7.7
Employment, 000	−525	−35	1,804	1,350 to 2,300

Source: As Table 4.1.

effect near the end of the decade, not in 1992. The jury must therefore be out for some time, although the European Commission is currently organising a major estimation of progress to be reported in 1996.

One study – Buigues and Sheehy (1993) – does attempt to estimate the effects up to 1992 but it commits the fallacy mentioned above of extrapolating previous trends to establish the counter-factual and attributing all the residual to integration. At the time the European economy was at a cyclical peak. Had the analysis been repeated in 1993–4 instead of estimating an impact of the order of 3.5 per cent of the GDP, the outcome might well have been negative.

ECONOMIC AND MONETARY UNION

The final steps in the sequence outlined above in moving to EMU present the most straightforward of the quantitative problems in the sense that they fall into the traditional mould of a policy shock. There will be some microeconomic effects. Transaction costs will be reduced and high inflation countries will incur less of the 'menu' costs involved each time prices are changed when they become part of the low inflation union. Similarly, there are some costs to be borne in the changeover to the single currency – not just the bringing forward of the printing of notes and the minting of coins but the need to change accounting systems, coin operated machines, all posted prices and to inform the population fully. It is clearly possible to approach these changes in an identical manner to the changes involved in the completion of the internal market.

The main changes will be the adjustments in fiscal and monetary policy necessary, first, to meet the convergence criteria laid down in the Maastricht Treaty, and secondly, in the operation of stage 3 of EMU. Monetary policy will follow a single low inflation target, while the extent to which fiscal policy can be used to counter shocks will be limited. The constraints on debt and deficit ratios will continue in stage 3. It is thus necessary in simulating the convergence to EMU to impose constraints on fiscal policy, see Barrell *et al.* (1996), for example. Similarly, in stage 3 it will be necessary to build new policy reaction functions for both fiscal and monetary policy into macroeconomic models of the European economy.

The wrinkle in this analysis is the presumption that the member states will function in stage 3 after 1999 in the way they have done in recent years. The extent of structural change in New Zealand, for example, which included moving from high inflation to price stability has meant that econometric models estimated on past data (such as the Reserve Bank's Model XII) have broken down. The new models which are being developed have very different characteristics. The pass through from the price level to wages is considerably weakened and the sustainable rate of growth has increased markedly. Existing models will therefore tend to underestimate the benefits of EMU.

The Commission's own estimates of the impact of EMU, One Market, One Money (Commission of the European Communities, 1990) is rather cautious. The transactions cost gain is estimated to be 0.1 to 0.2 per cent of GDP, although it might be as high as 1 per cent for the high inflation countries. Similarly, the increased credibility of the new rules is thought likely to reduce the risk premium by around 0.5 per cent. This fall in long-run interest rates is likely to stimulate the rate of growth. This might raise income in the Community significantly, possibly up to 5–10 per cent in the long run (ibid, p. 63). These calculations are only outlined and do not involve the sorts of structural change that we have discussed. What is clear is that only small changes in the rate of growth readily offset any costs of reducing inflation in the first instance. However, it is several years before the arithmetic turns favourable. This is a disappointing conclusion for those member states who have so much difficulty in meeting the Maastricht convergence criteria that they fail to join the initial participants in stage 3. They experience the costs but do not reach the point of reaping the full benefits of credibility, lower interest rates and increased growth.

This conclusion emphasises the importance of the time path of the responses to steps towards integration. Simple comparison of end points through comparative static models or some CGE models will be inadequate if the transition costs are so great that the favourable post integration environment is never achieved.

CONCLUSION

It is clear from the preceding discussion that quantification of the effects of integration has been relatively rudimentary partly due to the lack of consideration of the many problems involved, but more importantly due to the inherent complexity of the effects. While changes in tariffs may exert straightforward static effects on trading partners, these effects are observed in a dynamic context of evolving trade payments and activity. That evolution must be explained when attempting to measure the effects of integration. The use of the difference between actual behaviour and some hypothetical 'anti-monde', which might have occurred without integration, based on the extrapolation of previous trends and concurrent behaviour in other countries and markets, is bound to result in biases because all residual changes in behaviour are attributed to integration, not just those which can be directly explained by it. Furthermore, such analyses often exclude the feedback of reactions to tariff and relative price changes onto incomes and efficiency. Given the very small size of the static effects on trade and payments compared with a change in the rate of economic growth by half of 1 per cent, it would be very easy to draw totally erroneous conclusions over the size or even the sign of the aggregate effect.

As soon as the analysis is extended to include changes in economic growth, efficiency and the movement of factors rather than just trade in goods and services, the problems of quantification become immense. There is no well-developed theory of the interrelated movements of trade, payments, incomes and factors, let alone one which can be clearly applied and estimated to calculate the effects of integration.

Many of the barriers to integration such as language and customs are inherently difficult to quantify, so the overwhelming tendency is to try to use generalised methods which can at least determine the order of magnitude of the effects. However, it is not just the pressures which are placed upon countries which matter. The responses of an economic community to the resource costs of common policies as well as that from tariff reduction affects their overall consequence. In particular the less coordinated the response the more likely it is to be deflationary. It is difficult enough to measure the effects of integration where the result depends upon the aggregated reaction of firms and households, but where it also depends on the hypothetical reactions of government policy to different economic pressures, it is only possible to attempt to quantify the results of different policy choices and no single conclusion can be reached.

Research on the quantification of the effects of integration languished in the second half of the 1970s and well on into the 1980s. However, the surge in progress towards integration with the single market and EMU in Europe and NAFTA has breathed new life into the subject. This has been aided by progress in economic modelling over the intervening years. Econometric models have been built which cover all fifteen EU member states and the main influences (see NIGEM (NIESR, 1995), for example). At the same time, there has been substantial progress with CGE models and of models which integrate international trade theory and industrial economics (Krugman, 1986).

Much still remains to be done and there is no shortage of plans and examples of integration to investigate, not just as the internal market, NAFTA and EMU take effect but as Central and Eastern Europe are drawn into the EU and other American countries into NAFTA.

5 The European Union

Ali M. El-Agraa

INTRODUCTION

The European Union (EU, hereafter) is the most significant and influential of international economic integration schemes. Three reasons account for the significance. First, the EU comprises some of the most advanced nations of Western Europe, each with its own unique and complicated economic and political system: Austria, Belgium, Denmark, Finland, France, Germany, Greece, Ireland, Italy, Luxembourg, the Netherlands, Portugal, Spain, Sweden and the UK. Second, from a voluntary viewpoint, it is the oldest such scheme. Third, and most importantly, it is the only scheme seeking the most involved and demanding type of international integration. The influence is simply due to the relative global weight of the EU: the data in Table 5.1 clearly show not only that both EU population (98 per cent) and GDP (83 per cent, but this does not include the GDP for the former Federal German Republic) are similar to those of NAFTA, the only comparable trading bloc, but also its *per capita* GNP is in excess of that of NAFTA.

The EU was founded by Belgium, France, West Germany, Italy, Luxembourg and the Netherlands (the Six, hereafter). Three of the remaining nine (Denmark, Ireland and the UK) joined later in 1973. Greece acceeded as a full member in January 1981, having been an *Associate Member* for a long time before then. Portugal and Spain were admitted in 1986 after a lengthy period of negotiations. Austria, Finland and Sweden joined in January 1995. Other nations, including Cyprus, Hungary, Malta, Poland, Turkey and Switzerland, have applied for membership, and most of the Eastern European countries, including Hungary and Poland, have not only signed *Association Treaties* with the EU, but have also openly expressed their desire for full membership, especially the Czech and Slovak republics (see Chapter 6). Norway successfully negotiated EU membership and was set to join at the time of the first enlargement in 1973, but its citizens decided

Table 5.1 Economic and demographic data, 1993

Country	*Population (millions)*	*GDP ($ billion)*	*GNP per capita ($)*	*Exports ($ billion)*	*Imports ($ billion)*
Austria	7.9	182.1	23,510	40.2	48.6
Belgium	10.0	210.6	21,650	112.5	125.1
Denmark	5.2	117.6	26,730	35.9	29.5
Finland	5.1	74.1	19,300	23.5	18.0
France	57.5	1,251.7	22,490	206.3	202.3
Germany	80.7	1,910.8	23,560	380.2	348.6
Greece	10.4	63.2	7,390	8.0	20.5
Ireland	3.5	43.0	13,000	28.6	21.4
Italy	57.1	991.4	19,840	168.5	146.8
Luxembourg	0.4	14.8	37,320	na	na
Netherlands	15.3	309.2	20,950	139.1	126.6
Portugal	9.8	85.7	9,130	15.4	24.6
Spain	39.5	478.6	13,590	62.9	78.6
Sweden	8.7	166.8	24,740	49.9	42.7
UK	57.9	819.0	18,060	180.6	206.3
EU	369.0	5,899.6	17,596	1,451.6	1,439.6
NAFTA	377.0	7,080.9	16,107	640.2	785.2
Cyprus	0.7	7.5	10,380	na	na
Hungary	10.2	38.1	3,350	8.9	12.6
Iceland	0.3	6.6	24,950	na	na
Malta	0.4	2.9	7,970	na	na
Norway	4.3	103.4	25,970	31.9	24.0
Poland	38.3	85.9	2,260	14.0	18.8
Switzerland	7.1	232.2	35,760	61.4	56.7
Turkey	59.6	156.4	2,970	15.3	29.2

Notes
1. Germany's data is that for only the former West Germany.
2. na Means not available.

Source: World Bank, *World Development Report, 1995*.

(by 53 per cent) against ratification of the agreement, and it repeated the same act when it was set to join at the time of the last enlargement in 1995, but its citizens again opted against ratification (by 52.2 per cent). However, Norway, together with Iceland and Liechtenstein, i.e. the European Free Trade Association (EFTA) minus Switzerland (which is odd, given its application for full membership) are locked in together with the EU in the *European Economic Area* (EEA, see Chapter 7), which provides the EU and EFTA countries with full access to each others markets for most manufactured products, but without the EFTA nations being able to influence EU policy decisions. Thus, if all goes according to plan, the EU is set to comprise the whole of Europe, and as Table 5.1 shows, just the inclusion of the immediate potential EU members will make the EU a formidable association.

In a world presently dominated by purely economic considerations, the driving force behind European integration is often forgotten. Therefore, this chapter begins with a brief history of European unity and adopts a historical perspective throughout so that the reader can make sense of the ongoing debate on this issue. It then goes on to consider its aims, institutions and the progress it has achieved to date. Since EU activities are wide ranging, the following chapter by Grilli deals with EU policies towards Eastern Europe and the developing countries. Moreover, as is obvious from the above, the EU and EFTA are closely linked, hence Chapter 7 by Price has direct relevance to the EU. Furthermore, since Chapter 4 by Mayes is inevitably coloured by EU studies, it also has a direct bearing on the EU. Thus a thorough understanding requires going through all four chapters. Of course, the impatient reader may find this approach inconvenient, but as the author of the book not only do I have to eliminate unnecessary repetition but also to accommodate my invited contributors.

A SHORT HISTORY OF EUROPEAN UNITY

Philosophical Underpinnings

Most, if not all, actual steps taken to achieve economic and political unity in Europe originated after 1945 (see Collins, 1980, 1994; Lipgens, 1982; Swann, 1988). However, the idea of such unity is not confined to the past five decades or so. Indeed, the opposite is the case. History shows that there have been a number of proposals and arrangements designed to create European unity: in the fourteenth century, the idea of a united Christendom inspired Pierre Dubois to propose a *European Confederation* to be ruled by a *European Council* of wise, expert and faithful men; in the seventeenth century, Sully proposed to keep peace in Europe by means of a *European Army*; in 1693, William Penn, the English Quaker, proposed the creation of a *European Diet*, *Parliament* or *State* in his *Essay Towards the Present and Future Peace of Europe*; in the nineteenth century, Proudhon was strongly in favour of the formation of a *European Federation* and predicted that the twentieth century would witness an era of federations, forecasting disaster in the absence of such a development; and immediately after the First World War, politicians began to give serious consideration to the concept of European unity, for example in 1923, Count Coudenhove Kalergi, the Austrian founder-leader of the *Pan-European Movement*, called for the formation of a *United States of Europe*, his reason being the successful assertion of Swiss unity in 1848, the forging of the German Empire in 1871 and, most significantly, the independence of the United States in 1776 (see Borchardt, 1995), and on 5 September 1929, in a renowned speech, delivered to the *League of Nations Assembly* in Geneva, the French Foreign Minister, Aristide Briand, with the backing of his German counterpart, Gustav Stresmann, proposed the creation of a *European Union* within the framework of the League of Nations and reiterated this later, when Prime Minister, by declaring that part of his political manifesto was the building of a *United States of Europe*.

The main reason for the pursuit of European unity was the achievement of lasting peace in Europe; it was realised that there was no other means of putting an end to the Continent's woeful history of conflict, bloodshed, suffering and destruction. However, economic reasons were also a contributing factor. These were influenced by the tradition of free trade and Adam Smith's (1776) argument that 'the division of labour is limited by the extent of the market' which the German philosopher Friedrich Naumann utilised to propose in 1915 that European nation states were no longer large enough to compete on their own in world markets, therefore, they had to unite in order to survive.

Despite the fact that there was no shortage of plans for creating a united Europe, nevertheless it was not until 1945 that a combination of new forces and an intensification of old ones prompted action. First, Europe had been at the centre of yet another devastating war, caused by the ambitions of nation states. Those who sought and still seek a united Europe have always had at the forefront of their minds the desire to prevent any further outbreak of war in Europe. It was felt that if the nations of Europe could be brought closer together, such war would become unthinkable. Second, the Second World War left Europe economically exhausted, and this led to the view that if Europe were to recover, it would require a concerted effort on the part of the European states. Third, the Second World War also soon revealed that for a long time Western Europe would have to face not only a powerful and politically alien USSR, but also a group of European nations firmly fixed within the Eastern European bloc. It was felt that an exhausted and divided Europe (since the war embraced co-belligrents) presented both a power vacuum and a temptation to the USSR to fill it (see Swann 1988 and Lipgens 1992). Fourth, the ending of the war soon revealed that the wartime allies were in fact divided, with the two major powers (the USA and USSR) confronting each other in a bid for world supremacy. Hence, it should come as no surprise to learn that members of the *European Movement*, who wanted to get away from intergovernmental cooperation by creating institutions leading to a *Federal Europe*, felt the need for a third world force: 'the voice of Europe'. This force would represent the Western European viewpoint and could also act as a bridge between the Eastern and Western extremities.

Concrete Unity Efforts

The first concrete move for regional integration in Europe was made in 1947 with the establishment of the *Economic Commission for Europe* (ECE), which was set up in Geneva as a regional organisation of the United Nations (UN). Its objective was to initiate and participate in concerted measures aimed at securing the economic restructuring of *the whole* of Europe. Unfortunately, by the time the ECE started operating, the *Cold War* had become a reality. In the light of later developments in Europe, this was a turning point: economic cooperation over the whole of Europe was, for a long time, doomed. After that Western Europe followed its own path for economic and political unity, and Eastern Europe likewise pursued an independent course. This in turn led to the creation of two blocs in Europe. On the one hand was the European Community (EC) and EFTA, and on the other the Council for Mutual Economic Assistance (CEMA, or COMECON as it was generally known in the West). Any attempts to build bridges between the Western and Eastern European blocs from then on, and until recently, therefore implied trying to break down a division which began to manifest itself in 1947.

A year later, the *Brussels Treaty Organisation* (BTO) was founded by the UK, France, Belgium, the Netherlands and Luxembourg. It was designed to create a system of mutual assistance in times of attack on Europe. Obviously, the Western European nations had the USSR (and its Eastern European satellites) in mind. The BTO took an Atlantic form in 1949 when the five nations, together with the USA and Canada as well as Denmark, Norway, Portugal, Iceland and Italy (significantly, since it had been an Axis power), founded the *North Atlantic Treaty Organisation* (NATO). The aim of NATO was to provide military defence against attack on any of its members. Greece and Turkey joined NATO in 1952 and West Germany became a member in 1955 (see p. 108).

Also, in 1948 the *Organisation for European Economic Cooperation* (OEEC) was formed and was followed a year later by the *Council for Europe*. These marked the beginning of the division of Western Europe into two camps, with, on the one hand, the UK and some of the countries that later formed EFTA, and, on the other, the Six who subsequently established the EC (see p. 109). The main reason for this division was that the UK was less committed to Europe as the main policy area than the Six. This was because until the second half of the 1950s, the UK was still a world power which had been on the victorious side and a major participant in some of the fateful geopolitical decision-making at the time, and it still had the Empire to dispose of. Therefore, British policy was bound to incorporate this wider dimension: relations with Europe had to compete with Empire (later, Commonwealth) ties and with the *special relationship* with the USA. In addition, the idea of a politically united Europe (in some cases this meant a *United States of Europe*) was strongly held by the other countries, particularly by France and the BENELUX countries (Belgium, the Netherlands and Luxembourg agreed in 1944 to form a customs union, which did not become effective until 1948), but, despite the encouraging noises made by Winston Churchill (British Prime Minister at the time) both during the Second World War and after, this was not a concept that thrilled British hearts.

The different thinking between the UK and the Six about the political nature of European institutions was revealed in the discussions leading up to the establishment of the OEEC and the Council for Europe. The Second World War had left Europe devastated. The year 1947 was particularly bleak: bad harvests in the previous summer led to rising food prices; the severe winter of 1946–7 led to a fuel crisis; and the Continental countries were producing very little, and what was produced tended to be retained rather than exported, whilst imports were booming, hence foreign exchange reserves were running out. It was at this point that the USA entered upon the scene to present the *Marshall Plan*. General George Marshall proposed that the USA make aid available to help the European economy find its feet and that European governments *should get together* to decide how much assistance was needed. In short, the USA did not feel it appropriate that it should unilaterally decide on the programme necessary to achieve this result. Although it seemed possible that this aid programme could be elaborated within the ECE framework, the USSR felt otherwise. Soviet reluctance was no doubt due to the fear that if its satellites participated, this would open the door to Western influence. Therefore, a conference was convened and a *Committee for European Economic Cooperation* (CEEC) was established.

The attitude of the USA was that the CEEC should not just provide it with a list of needs. The USA perceived that the aid it was to give should be linked with progress towards European unification. This is an extremely important point since it shows that right from the very beginning, the *European Movement* enjoyed the encouragement and support of the USA. The CEEC led in turn to the creation of an aid agency: the OEEC. Here, the conflict between the UK and the Six, especially France, came to a head over the issue of *supra-nationalism.* France in particular (and it was supported by the USA) wanted to introduce a supra-national element into the new organisation. But what is supra-nationalism? It can mean a situation in which international administrative institutions exercise power over, for example, the economies of the member states; or ministerial bodies, when taking decisions (to be implemented by international organisations) work on a majority voting system rather than insisting on unanimity.

The French view was not shared by the British since they favoured a body which was to be under the control of a ministerial council in which decisions should be taken on a unanimity basis. The French, on the other hand, preferred an arrangement in which an international secretariat would be presided over by a secretary-general who would be empowered to take policy initiatives on major issues. Significantly, the organisation which emerged was substantially in line with the British wish for a unanimity rule. This was undoubtedly a reflection of the UK's relatively powerful position in the world at the time.

In the light of subsequent events it is also interesting to note that the USA encouraged the European nations to consider the creation of a customs union. Although this was of considerable interest to some Continental countries, it did not appeal to the UK. In the end the OEEC convention merely recorded the intention to continue the study of this proposal. For a variety of reasons, one of which was the opposition of the UK, the matter was not pursued further.

The creation of the Council for Europe also highlighted the fundamental differences in approach between the countries who later founded the EC, on the one hand, and the British and Scandinavians, on the other. The establishment of the Council for Europe was preceded by the *Congress of Europe* at The Hague in May 1948. This was a grand rally of 'Europeans' which was attended by leading European statesmen, including Winston Churchill. The Congress adopted a resolution which called for the giving up of some national sovereignty before the accomplishment of economic and political union in Europe. Subsequently, a proposal was put forward, with the support of the Belgian and French governments, calling for the creation of a *European Parliamentary Assembly* in which resolutions would be passed by majority vote. A *Committee of Ministers* was to prepare and implement these resolutions.

Needless to add, the UK was opposed to this form of supranationalism and in the end the British view largely prevailed. The Committee of Ministers, which was the executive organ of the Council for Europe, alone had power of decision and generally these were taken on the unanimity principle. The *Consultative Assembly* which came into existence was a forum (its critics called it a debating society), not a European legislative body. In short, the British and Scandinavian *Functionalists* (who believed that European unity, in so far as it was to be achieved, was to be attained by *inter*governmental cooperation) triumphed over the *Federalists* (who sought unity by the radical method of creating European institutions to which national governments would surrender some of their sovereignty). The final disillusionment of the federalists was almost certainly marked by the resignation of Paul-Henri Spaak (a devoted European federalist) from the presidency of the Consultative Assembly in 1951.

The next step in the economic and political unification of Western Europe was taken without the British and Scandinavians. It took the creation in 1951 of the *European Coal and Steel Community* (ECSC) by the Six, and marked the parting of ways in post-war Western Europe. The immediate factor in these developments was the revival of the West German economy. The passage of time, the efforts of the German people and the aid made available by the USA through the Marshall Plan all contributed to this recovery. Indeed, the West German *economic miracle* was about to unfold.

It was recognised that the German economy would have to be allowed to regain its position in the world, and that the Allied control of coal and steel under the *International Ruhr Authority* could not last indefinitely. The fundamental question was how the German economy in the sectors of iron, steel and coal (the basic materials of a war effort) could be allowed to regain its former powerful position without endangering the future peace of Europe. The answer was a French plan, elaborated by Jean Monnet and put forward by Robert Schuman in May 1950. The *Schuman Plan* was essentially political in character. It sought to end the historic rivalry of France and Germany by making a war between the two nations not only unthinkable but also materially impossible. This was to be achieved in a manner which ultimately would have the result of bringing about that European federation which is indispensable to peace. The answer was not to nationalise or indeed to internationalise the ownership of the means of production in coal, iron and steel, but to create, by the removal of customs duties, import quota restrictions and similar impediments on trade and factors, a common market in these products. Every participating nation in such a common market would have equal access to the products of these industries wherever they might be located, and, to reinforce this, discrimination on the grounds of nationality was to be forbidden.

The plan had a number of attractive features. First, it provided an excellent basis for solving the *Saar* problem: the handing back of the Saar region to West Germany was more likely to be acceptable to the French if Germany was firmly locked in such a coal and steel community. Second, the plan was extremely attractive to Germany since membership of the community was a passport to international respectability; it was the best way of speeding up the end of occupation and avoiding the imposition of dampers on the expansion of the German economy. Third, the plan was also attractive to the Federalists who had found the OEEC far short of their aspirations for the Council for Europe (its unanimity rule and that no powers could be delegated to an independent commission or *Commissariat* were extremely frustrating for them), and, in any case, the prospects for the OEEC were not very good since by 1952 the four-year period of the Marshall Plan would be over, and the UK attitude was that thereafter the OEEC's budget should be cut and some of its functions passed over to NATO.

As it turned out, however, the ECSC was much more to the Federalists taste since its *High Authority* (the executive body; its other institutions being a *Council of Ministers*, a *Parliamentary Assembly* and a *Court of Justice*) was given substantial direct powers which could be exercised without the prior approval of the Council of Ministers.

The plan received a favourable response from Belgium, France, Italy, West Germany, the Netherlands and Luxembourg (the Six).

The UK was invited to join but refused. Mr Clement Attlee, British Prime Minister at the time, told the House of Commons: 'We on this side [of the House] are not prepared to accept that the most vital economic forces of this country should be handed over to an authority that is utterly undemocratic and is responsible to nobody.' However, the Six were not to be deterred, and in April 1951 the *Treaty of Paris* was signed. The ECSC was born and it embarked on an experiment in limited economic integration, albeit a sectoral one, on 1 January 1952.

The next stage in the development of European unity was also concerned with Germany. When the Korean War broke out in 1950 the USA put pressure on the Western European nations to do more to defend themselves against possible attack by the USSR. This raised the issue of a military contribution from West Germany, the implication being that Germany should be rearmed. However, this proposal was opposed by France, which was equally against Germany becoming a member of NATO. This was not a purely negative attitude. Indeed, René Pleven, French Prime Minister at the time, put forward a plan which envisaged that there would be no German army as such, but that there would be a *European Army* to which each participating nation, including Germany, could contribute.

Britain was not against this idea but did not itself wish to be involved. The Six were positively enthusiastic and discussion began in 1951 with a view to creating a *European Defence Community* (EDC). It was envisaged that there would be a *Joint Defence Commission*, a *Council of Ministers*, a *Parliamentary Assembly* and a *Court of Justice*. In other words, the institutions of the EDC were to parallel those created for the ECSC. The Six made rapid progress in the negotiations and the *EDC Treaty* was signed in May 1952.

Having gone so far, there were a number of reasons for further integrative efforts. First, the pooling of both defensive and offensive capabilities inevitably reduced the possibility of independent foreign policies; it was logical to follow integration in defence with measures which serve to achieve political integration as well. Second, it was also desirable to establish a system whereby effective control could be exercised over the proposed European army. Third, there was also the Dutch desire that progress in the military field should be paralleled by more integration in the economic sphere as well. Therefore, the Foreign Ministers of the Six asked the ECSC Assembly, together with coopted members from the Consultative Assembly of the Council for Europe, to study the possibilities of creating a *European Political Authority*.

In 1953, a draft of a *European Political Community* (EPC) was produced in which it was proposed that, after a period of transition, the political institutions of the ECSC and the proposed EDC be subsumed within a new framework. There would then be a *European Executive* responsible to a *European Parliament* (which would consist of a *People's Chamber* elected by direct universal suffrage, and a *Senate* elected by national parliaments), a *Council of Ministers* and a *European Court* to replace the parallel bodies created under the ECSC and EDC treaties.

This was a watershed in the history of the European Movement. The Six had already successfully experimented in limited economic integration in the fields of iron, coal and steel; had now signed a treaty to integrate defence; and were about to proceed further by creating a community for the purposes of securing political unity. Moreover, the draft treaty proposed to push economic integration still further by calling for the establishment of a general common market based on the free movement of commodities and factors of production.

However, on this occasion the success which had attended the Six in the case of iron, coal and steel was not repeated. Five national parliaments approved the EDC Treaty, but successive French governments felt unable to guarantee success in asking the *French Assembly* to ratify. Finally, the Mendès-France government attempted to water down the treaty but failed to persuade the other five nations. The treaty as it stood was therefore submitted to the French Assembly which refused to consider it and in so doing killed the EPC too.

There were a number of reasons for the refusal of the French Assembly to consider the treaty. First, there was opposition to the supra-national elements which it contained. Second, the French 'left' refused to consider the possibility of the rearmament of Germany. Third, the French 'right' refused to have the French army placed under foreign control. Fourth, British aloofness was also a contributing factor: one of the arguments employed by those who were opposed to the treaty was that France could not participate in the formation of a European army with Germany if the UK was not a member.

It is perhaps worth noting that the failure of the EDC was followed by a British initiative also aimed at dealing with the problem of rearming Germany in a way acceptable to the French. A series of agreements was reached in 1954 between the USA, the UK, Canada and the Six under which the BTO was modified and extended: Germany and Italy were brought in and a new intergovernmental organisation was formed – the *Western European Union* (WEU).

These agreements also related to the termination of the occupation of Germany and its admission into NATO. As a counterbalance to the German army, the UK agreed to maintain specified forces on the Continent. In short, the gist of the agreements was to provide a European framework in which Germany could be rearmed and become a member of NATO, while providing also for British participation to relieve French fears that there would be no possible German predominance. It should be pointed out that the response of Eastern Europe to these agreements was a further hardening of the East–West division in the shape of the formation of the *Warsaw Pact*.

Unity via the Back Door

The year 1954 was a bad year for European unity since those advocating the creation of supra-national bodies had suffered a reverse and the establishment of the WEU, an organisation cast more in the traditional intergovernmental mould, had thereafter held the centre of the stage. However, such was the strength then of the European Movement that by 1955 new ideas were being put forward. The relaunching initiative came from the BENELUX countries. They produced a memorandum calling for the establishment of a general common market and for specific action in the fields of energy and transport.

The basic idea behind the BENELUX approach was that political unity in Europe was likely to prove difficult to achieve. It was the ultimate objective but it was one which could be realised in the longer run. In the short and medium terms the objective should be overall economic integration. Experience gained in working together would then pave the way for the achievement of political unity, i.e. political unity will be introduced through the 'back door'. The memorandum called for the creation of institutions which would enable the establishment of a *European Economic Community* (EEC).

These ideas were considered at the meeting of the Foreign Ministers of the Six at Messina in June 1955. They met with favourable response. The governments of the Six resolved that work should begin with a view to establishing a general common market and an atomic energy pool. Moreover, a committee should be formed which would not merely study the problems involved but should also prepare the texts of the treaties necessary in order to carry out the agreed objectives. An intergovernmental committee was therefore created, and significantly enough, Paul-Henri Spaak, then Foreign Minister of

Belgium, was made its president; what a triumph for members of the European Movement.

The Messina resolution recorded that since the UK was a member of the WEU and had been associated with the ECSC (the UK signed an *Agreement of Association* with the ECSC in 1954), it should be invited to participate in the work of the committee. The position of the other OEEC countries was not so clear. In fact, the question of whether they should be allowed to participate was left for later decision by the Foreign Ministers of the Six.

The *Spaak Committee* held its first meeting in July 1955. British representatives were present and then and subsequently played an active role in the committee's deliberations. However, as the committee's discussions continued, differences between the Six and the UK became evident. The UK was in favour of a free trade area arrangement, whilst the Six were agreed upon the formation of a customs union (the Messina resolution had explicitly called for this type of arrangement). Moreover, the UK felt that only a little extra machinery was needed to put the new arrangement into effect: the OEEC, perhaps somewhat strengthened, would suffice. This view was bound to anger the Federalists who put emphasis on the creation of supra-national institutions which should help achieve more than just economic integration. These differences culminated in the withdrawal of the UK representatives from the discussion in November 1955.

Meanwhile, the *Spaak Committee* forged ahead, although not without internal differences. For example, the French were worried about the transition period allowed for the dismantling of intra-member tariffs, escape clauses, the harmonisation of social charges and the height of the common external tariffs (CETs); they wanted high CETs while the BENELUX nations desired low ones.

In April 1956, the *Spaak Committee* reported and its conclusions were considered by the Foreign Ministers of the Six in Venice in May of the same year. However, the attitudes amongst the Six were not uniform. On the one hand, the French liked the idea of an atomic energy community, but were not keen on the proposition for a general common market, while, on the other, the remaining five had reverse views. Nevertheless, in the end the Six agreed that the drafting of two treaties, one to create a general common market and another to establish an atomic energy community, should begin. Treaties were subsequently signed in Rome on 25 March 1957. These were duly ratified by the national parliaments of the Six. The *EEC* and *Euratom* came into being on 1 January 1958. Thus, in 1958 the Six belonged to three separate entities: the ECSC, EEC and Euratom.

THE INITIAL AIMS

With history still in the background, one needs to ask about the initial objectives of the EEC. These are stated in Article 3 of its treaty and can be summarised as:

1. The establishment of free trade between the member nations such that *all* impediments on intra-union trade are eliminated. The EEC treaty did not simply ask for the elimination of tariffs, import quota restrictions and export subsidies, but for all measures which had an equivalent or similar effect (what are generally referred to as *non-tariff trade barriers* – NTBs). Moreover, that treaty called for the creation of *genuine* free trade and therefore specified rudiments of common competition and industrial policies.
2. The creation of an intra-union free market for all factors of production by providing the necessary prerequisites for ensuring perfect factor mobility. These include taxes on, and subsidies to, capital, labour, enterprise, etc.
3. The formation of common policies with regard to particular industries which the members deemed it necessary to single out for special treatment, namely, agriculture (hence the *Common Agricultural Policy* – CAP) and transport (hence the *Common Transport Policy* – CTP).
4. The application of procedures by which the economic policies of the member nations could be coordinated and disequilibria in their balances of payments can be remedied.
5. The creation of a *European Social Fund* (ESF) in order to improve the possibilities of employment for workers and to contribute to the raising of their standard of living.
6. The establishment of a *European Investment Bank* (EIB) to facilitate the economic expansion of the EEC by opening up fresh resources.
7. The establishment of a common commercial policy *vis-à-vis* the outside world, i.e. the creation and management of the common external tariff rates (CETs), the adoption of a common stance in multinational and multilateral trade negotiations, the granting of a *Generalised System of Preference* (GSP) treatment to imports of

certain manufactured and semi-manufactured products coming from the developing nations (LDCs) and the reaching of trade pacts with associated countries.

It should be noted that a period of transition of twelve years, divided into three four-year stages, was granted for the elimination of intra-EEC trade barriers and for the establishment of the CETs.

Since in 1957 the Six belonged to the three entities, the aims of the EEC treaty should be supplemented by those pertaining to: (8) a common market for, and equitable access to, steel and coal as expressed in the ECSC treaty; and (9) a common approach to energy as expressed in the Euratom treaty.

THE DEVELOPMENT OF THE EC

Each one of the three entities had its own institutions. These centred on a *Council of Ministers* (Council, hereafter) and a *Commission* (*High Authority* in the case of the ECSC, see above), backed by a *European Parliament* and a *Court of Justice*. Although there were some differences of legal competences, it later became convenient to consider the three entities as branches of the same whole and, in this, the EEC became the dominant partner. When the *Merger Treaty* was passed in 1965, it seemed more logical to refer to the whole structure as the European Community (EC) whose main constitutional base was the Treaty of Rome creating the EEC. The basic treaties have steadily become overlain with later texts, the most important of which are incorporated in treaties that had to be ratified by each member state in accordance with its own legal processes. In addition to the treaties, there is a host of secondary legislation resulting from the decisions taken under the treaties and the rulings of the Court of Justice and together these form the constitution of the EC. EC legislation takes precedence over national decisions in the appropriate field and not much reflection is needed to show that this is necessary for the EC to work at all; it would otherwise be impossible to create a single economic unit, to establish the confidence necessary between the member nations or to handle external economic relations.

By the 1970s, however, it was clear that the EC needed institutional strengthening. Having completed the early tasks laid down in the Treaty of Rome (see p. 124), further internal objectives had to be formulated and a way found to ensure that the EC could act more effectively on the international stage. The result was to bring national political leaders more closely into EC affairs by the introduction of summit meetings. These were formalised under the name of the *European Council* in 1974, but the first summit meeting was held in 1969 (in The Hague) when the member states agreed that they were then so interdependent that they had no choice but to continue with the EC. That decision provided the necessary political will to reach agreement on the development of the CAP, on budgetary changes, on embarking on *economic and monetary union* (EMU) and, most importantly, on the need to work for enlargement. At that time, this meant settling the teasing question of relations with the UK which, as we have seen, had vexed the EC from the very beginning.

Additionally, it was recognised that the EC needed institutional development to match its growing international stature. Its existing international responsibilities neither matched its economic weight nor allowed effective consideration of the political dimensions of its external economic relations. Individual members still conducted most of their external affairs themselves and could easily cut across EC interests, and this was apart from the issue of whether the EC should begin to move into the field of wider foreign affairs. Since the member states had very different interests and often different views on relations with the US, with the USSR and on defence, it was clear that the EC was not ready to take over full competences. However, the Foreign Ministers were asked to study the means of achieving further political integration, on the assumption of enlargement, and to present a report. As a result, the EC began, in a gingerly fashion, to move into political cooperation with an emphasis on foreign affairs. This did not lead to a common foreign policy but it did mean efforts were to be exerted to identify common aims and it led to further institutional innovation alongside the institutions of the EC rather than as part of them, although the old and the new gradually came together.

A second landmark summit was held in 1972 (in Paris) and was attended by the three new members: Denmark, Ireland and the UK. It devoted considerable attention to internal affairs and notably to the need to strengthen the social and regional aims of the EC as part of an ambitious programme designed to lead to the EMU, thus to a full 'European Union'. It also saw a continuing need to act externally to maintain a constructive dialogue with the US, Canada and Japan and for member states to make a concerted contribution to the *Conference on Security and Cooperation in Europe*. Foreign Ministers were to meet more frequently to discuss this last issue. This meeting marked the realisation that the heads of governments would have to meet more frequently than in the past. At first sight this seemed to strengthen the intergovernmental structure of the EC at the expense of the supranational element, but this was not really the case. Rather it showed that the future was a joint one, that the international climate was changing and often bleak and that if members dealt with their internal economic difficulties alone then this could undermine the efforts of the EC to strengthen its economies. Informal discussion of general issues, whether economic or political, domestic or worldwide, was a necessary preliminary to action which often seemed stronger if it were to be EC-based. Through the summit meetings and the *Political Cooperation Procedure* (ECP) the subject matter coming to the EC steadily enlarged.

Indeed, the 1969–72 period can be described as one of great activity. Apart from what has just been mentioned, in 1970, the Six reached a common position on the development of a common fisheries policy (CFP), although total agreement was not to be achieved until 1983. Also, at the Paris summit of 1973, agreement was reached on the development of new policies in relation to industry and science and research. Moreover, the summit envisaged a more active role for the EC in the area of regional policy, and decided that a *European Regional Development Fund* (ERDF) should be created to channel EC resources into the development of the backward regions. Furthermore, later in the 1970s, the relationship between the EC and its ex-colonial dependencies was significantly reshaped in the form of the *Lomé Convention* (see Chapter 6). It is obvious from all these developments that the EC needed financial resources not only to pay for the day-to-day running of the EC but also to feed the various funds that were established: the ESF, ERDF and, most important of all, the *European Guidance and Guarantee Fund* (EAGGF), to finance the CAP. In 1970, the EC took the important step of agreeing to introduce a system that would provide the EC, and specifically the EC General Budget, with its *own resources*, thus relieving it of the uncertainty of annual decisions regarding its finances as well as endorsing its political autonomy in this respect. Another step of great importance was the decision that the European Parliament (EP, discussed fully below) should be elected directly by the people, not by national parliaments. In addition, the EC decided to grant the EP certain powers over the EC General Budget, which proved to be a very significant development. Finally, but by no means least, was the development of the political cooperation mechanism. It is important not to forget that the dedicated members of the European Movement had always hoped that the habit of cooperation in the economic field would spill over into the political arena, that is, into foreign policy matters.

By the 1980s it was clear that the political and economic environment in which the EC operated was changing fast. Tumultuous events in the former USSR and the countries of the Warsaw Pact threw the institutional arrangements of Western Europe into disarray and brought the need to reassess defence requirements, the role of NATO and the continuance of the US defence presence. The unresolved issue of whether the EC needed a foreign policy, or at least some halfway house towards one, was bound to be raised once more. Meanwhile, the economic base upon which the EC has been able to develop had become much more uncertain. Recession, industrial change, higher unemployment (see Table 5.4), slow growth (see Table 5.5) and worries about European competitiveness undermined previous confidence.

The twin issues of constitutional development and institutional reform continued to exercise EC circles but little progress was possible and the EC seemed to be running out of steam. The deepening of the integrative process required action which governments found controversial, the new members, now including Greece, Spain and Portugal, inevitably made for a less cohesive group, whilst the recession hardened national attitudes towards the necessary compromise required for cooperative solutions. EC finances were constrained so that new policies could not be developed and this, in turn, led to bitter arguments about the resources devoted to the CAP. Internal divisions were compounded by fears of a lack of dynamism in the EC economy, threatening a relative decline in world terms. Such worries suggested that a significant leap forward was required to ensure a real common market, to encourage new growth and at the same time to modernise the EC institutions.

The Single Market

As the debate progressed, a major division emerged between those who were primarily interested in the political ideal of political union and who wished to develop the EC institutions accordingly and those, more pragmatic in approach, who stressed the need for new policies. It was not until 1985 that the lines of agreement could be settled.

These were brought together in the *Single European Act* (SEA) which became operative on 1 July 1987. The SEA contained policy development which was based upon the intention of creating a true single market (usually referred to as the *internal market*), by the the end of 1992, with free movement of goods, services, capital and labour (the so-called *four freedoms*) rather than the patchy arrangements of the past. The SEA also introduced, or strengthened, other policy fields. These included: responsibilities towards the environment; the encouragement of further action to promote health and safety at work; the promotion of technological research and development (R&D); work to strengthen economic and social cohesion so that weaker member nations may participate fully in the freer market; and cooperation in economic and monetary policy. In addition, the SEA brought foreign policy cooperation into scope and provided it with a more effective support than it had in the past, including its own secretariat, housed in the Council building in Brussels. Institutionally, it was agreed that the Council would take decisions on a qualified majority vote (see p. 121) in relation to the internal market, research, cohesion and improved working conditions and that, in such cases, the EP should share in decision-making. These developments were followed later by agreement regarding the control of expenditure on the CAP, which, as we have seen, has been a source of heated arguement for a number of years and, most importantly, a fundamental change in the EU General Budget.

At this juncture, it may be worthwhile to reiterate (see Chapter 3) that, according to official Commission estimates (see Cecchini 1988), the single market was expected to increase EC GDP by 2.5–7 per cent and employment by 2–5 million jobs, and Baldwin (1989) believes the former figure might be 11–35 per cent when allowance is made for the changes in the rate of economic growth implicit in the Cecchini predictions. In spite of the fact that the assumptions on which these forecasts are based leave a lot to be desired (see Chapter 3 and El-Agraa 1994c, chapter 7), nevertheless, the single market provided a goal for the next few years and the EC became preoccupied with the necessary preparations, giving evidence of its ability to work together as one unit. However, it also brought new complications. It raised the question of how much power should be held by the EC institutions, presented member states with heavy internal programmes to complete the changes necessary for the single market, and exposed the very different economic conditions in member states which were bound to affect their fortunes in the single market. Meanwhile, the unification of Germany fundamentally changed its position within the EC by giving it a more political and economic weight, but at the same time it required it to expend considerable effort eastwards.

A further challenge at the time came from new bids for membership.[1] The single market policy finally convinced the doubters in Western Europe that they should try again. This was both a triumph and an embarrassment for the EC in that it was preoccupied with its own internal changes and a belief that it had not yet fully come to terms with the southern enlargement which had brought in Greece, Portugal and Spain. An uncertain reaction was shown in that some member states wished to press on with enlargement as a priority, whilst others wished to complete the single market and tighten internal policies before opening the doors. A closer economic relationship was negotiated between the EC and the EFTA countries, except for Switzerland, to form the EEA which was widely assumed to be a preliminary step towards membership. Austria, Finland, Sweden and Switzerland all formally applied between 1989 and 1992 and Norway shortly followed them. Hungary, Poland and Czechoslovakia signed association agreements and hoped that they might join in a few years' time. Other states in Central and Eastern Europe harboured aspirations for membership at a subsequent stage. Turkey and Morocco applied in 1987, although the former application was laid aside and the latter rejected. Cyprus and Malta applied in 1990. Clearly, an organisation with such a large and varied membership would be very different from the original EEC of the Six, and the application challenged received wisdom as to its nature. This is one reason why pursuing the question of enlargement was made consequent upon the finalising of the Maastricht Treaty (see below) and agreement upon new financial and budgetary arrangements for the existing member nations. Continuing issues about defence and the appropriate reaction to conditions in Central and Eastern Europe, the Gulf War and the collapse of Yugoslavia all suggested further consideration to foreign and defence capabilities was important.

The European Union

It was, therefore, against a troubled background that the EC set up two intergovernmental conferences to prepare the way for a meeting of the European Council in Maastricht in December 1991 which produced a new blueprint for the future. It aimed to integrate the EC further through setting out a timetable for a full EMU, introduced institutional changes and developed political competences, the whole being brought together in the *Treaty on European Union* of which the EC should form a part. It is not surprising that the ratification process, for which some have argued not a great deal of time was allowed, produced furious argument across Western Europe. Although each nation had its own particular worries, a general characteristic which the treaty made obvious was the width of the gap between political elites and the voters in modern society. Even though political leaders rapidly expressed contrition that they had failed to provide adequate explanation for their moves, they seemed less able to accept that there were strong doubts about many of the proposed new arrangements as being the best way forward, and that a period of calm thinking, with less frenetic development, might in the end serve the EC and its people better (see Collins, 1994).

The Maastricht Treaty has five main sections. The first sets out the principles of the EU and the second is concerned with amendments to the EEC, ECSC and Euratom treaties. In the course of this amendment, the treaty formally endorses the title of 'European Community', hence signalling an increased importance for the non-economic functions. Thirdly, it develops EPC by introducing provisions for a common foreign and security policy and, fourthly, lays down the aims and procedures for cooperation in the fields of justice and home affairs. It is vital to draw attention to the fact that both these sections are based on the principle of intergovernmental cooperation and are not brought directly under the same procedures as those for the EU itself. This explains why the treaty is often referred to as being built on *three pillars*: the three European Communities (ECSC, EEC and Euratom); the common foreign and security policy; and cooperation in the fields of justice and home affairs. However, the last two form an integral part of the treaty; their work is coordinated by the main EU institutions, notably the Council and Commission and the possibility of drawing some judicial and home affairs functions into the main working of the EU remains open. Fifthly, there are a number of provisions dealing with miscellaneous matters. In addition, there are seventeen protocols and thirty-three declarations attached to the treaty. Although it is possible to classify the questions covered in the last two groups, some of them contain important principles as to how the 'union' will run.

The complexity of the structure itself suggests that the treaty represents a fundamental step, taking the EC significantly down the road to statehood although it has not yet arrived. It represents an uneasy balance between the two opposing views on how to organise Western Europe which have been so eloquently expressed since the end of the Second World War. It can be thought of as the penultimate step towards a federal Europe but also as a means of checking this drive by keeping certain essential functions outside the competence of the EC institutions and under the control of national governments. If one were of the opinion that the European Movement has been waning, one would state that only the future can say if one of these drives will eventually prevail or whether a stable balance between them can be found, but the above indicates otherwise. However, an intergovernmental conference (IGC) is to be called at the end of 1996 to consider further integrative moves and how to adapt the institutions to an enlarged membership.

The EU has broad objectives. One of them is the promotion of economic and social progress, an aim which includes the abolition of internal frontiers, better economic and social cohesion[2] (facilitated by a *Cohesion Fund*) and an EMU,[3] complete with a single currency to be adopted by 1997, if certain strict yet flexible criteria (on currency and price stability, budget deficits, public debt and interest rates) are met or 1999 at the very latest.[4] It wishes to assert an international identity through a common foreign and defence policy. The WEU (see p. 107), which has been dormant since it was launched in 1954, will become the equivalent of an EU defence force. Thus for the first time the EU is set to have a common defence policy with the implication that the WEU will eventually be responsible for implementing the decisions of an inevitable EU political union. Appreciation for (or is it accommodation of?) NATO was reiterated by stating that the revival of the WEU is to be linked to NATO, thus ensuring a continued alliance with the USA and Canada for the defence of Europe. It introduces a formal union citizenship and close cooperation in justice and home affairs, including an EU police force (*Europol*). It maintains, and builds upon, the *acquis communautaire* (i.e. the achievements to date). An overarching institutional framework is intended to ensure some consistency between the many different branches. The treaty modifies the balance of power between the Council of Ministers, the Commission and the Parliament as well as that between the EU and the member states in favour of the former (see p. 121). The European Council is recognised as a source of impetus and of policy guidelines but it has to report to Parliament, thus providing some check on a possible tendency to represent national, rather than EU, views.

The objectives of the EU are now more broadly defined than before, some are firmed up and some appear for the first time, although not necessarily as matters of an exclusive competence. In addition to the economic objectives relating to the single market, agriculture and transport, the aims of economic and social cohesion, of an environmental policy and of greater scope for the ESF have been added. The need for enhanced competitiveness for EU industry, the promotion of R&D, the construction of trans-European infrastructure, the attainment of a high level of health protection, better education, training and cultural development all find their place. Recognition is given to development policies, consumer protection and to measures in energy policy, consumer protection and tourism.

The enlargement of powers was bound to touch on fears of the creation of a superstate and there is a general stress in the treaty on the importance of respecting national identities and the fundamental rights of persons, as well as on the *Subsidiarity Principle*. It is obvious that as the EU increases its powers, some clarification of the respective functions of the EU and the member states is essential but a good deal more work will be needed before the principle of subsidiarity can be said to have clarified the position. Article 3b of the EU treaty asserts that, in areas which do not fall within its exclusive competence, the EU shall act only as far as it is necessary to achieve the objective, either because member states cannot do so adequately or because the scale and effects would be such that the EU can achieve the objective more effectively. Unfortunately, this leaves the field wide open for continuing argument on whether the EU would indeed do the job better, provides no protection against a move to grant the EU more powers and gives no guidance on how the EU should proceed in matters where it already possesses exclusive competence. This is not so much a legal check upon centralising tendencies as a well-intentioned effort to reassure that the EU will 'play fair'. At Edinburgh in December 1992, the European Council adopted further guidelines on the working of the principle. A declaration attached to the treaty asks that the IGC, at the end of 1996, should consider if it would be possible to classify EU acts and establish a hierarchy between them. Collins (1994) argues that should this be found, it could help to provide rules governing the use of EU powers and thus prevent an insidious slippage of power in a direction which has never been consciously agreed. Another check is that member states should be able to bring a case to the Court of Justice arguing that the EU is extending its powers unjustifiably, but it is clear that the last word has not been said on the vexed questions of the relationship between member states and the central institutions and of their respective competences.

An element in the debate about subsidiarity is doubt concerning the remoteness of decision-taking in Brussels, the need to make the EU more responsive to the needs of the general public and more sensitive to the effects of the intrusiveness that EU legislation appears to bring. A particular issue is the undermining of national parliaments, especially those that have an important legislative function and that have found it hard to find ways of exercising control over the EU. In practice, they have been limited to scrutiny of proposals which, once they are in an advanced stage, are very difficult to change. Some efforts have also been made, through scrutiny committees, to discuss general issues, thus helping to suggest policy positions for the future, whilst Denmark, in particular, has tried to define the parameters within which ministers may negotiate. The 'democratic deficit' has been discussed for many years and steps were taken at Maastricht to diminish it. The EP was given more power, a *Declaration* was attached calling for a greater involvement of national parliaments through better contact with the EP, and a conference of parliaments is to be held to discuss the main features of the EU, whilst the general decision-making function of the EU should become more open through providing the public with more information. The right of individuals to petition the EP is buttressed by the establishment of an *Ombudsman*, appointed by the EP, but independent in investigations. A further change, directly affecting individuals, is to confer the citizenship of the 'union' to the nationals of member states.

EU INSTITUTIONS

It should by now be apparent that it is extremely difficult to separate constitutional from institutional development. Lest further confusion arises, it is high time to turn to the institutions as they presently stand. Here, discussion will be confined to the main bodies; those interested in a full coverage should consult Collins (1994) and Noel (1991).

The EU treaties assign the Commission a wide range of tasks. In broad terms, the Commission's role is to act as the guardian of the EU treaties, to serve as the executive arm of the EU, to initiate EU policy, and to defend EU interests in the Council. It may prove helpful to elaborate just a little on some of these roles.

The Commission has to ensure that the provisions of the treaties are properly implemented, and for this purpose it should endeavour to maintain a climate of mutual confidence so that all concerned can carry out their obligations to the full. If any member state is in breach, the Commission, as an impartial authority, should investigate, issue an objective ruling and notify the government concerned, subject to review by the Court of Justice, of the action needed to rectify the situation. Generally, the Commission has to see to it that individuals, companies and member states do not act in ways which clearly run against the treaties or the specific policies laid down by the Council. The Commission is directly invested by the EU treaties with wide executive powers. In addition, substantial extra powers have been conferred on it by the Council to secure the implementation of legislation based on the treaties. This is normally referred to as secondary legislation. The Commission has a virtual monoploy on the right to initiate legislation. It is the job of the Commission to draft proposals which the Council has to consider.

The Commission consists of twenty members, two from each of the large member nations and one from each of the remaining ten, i.e. the number of Commissioners is determined roughly by the size of population. All Commissioners are appointed by the member governments for five-year (four-year until the end of 1994) renewable terms. They are chosen for their competence and capacity to act independently in the interest of the EU itself, not their own country's. Each Commissioner is responsible for a portfolio which in many cases is a mixture of policy areas and administrative responsibilities. However, since there are twenty-two administrative areas (called *Directorates General*, DGs), some have more than one portfolio.

The Council is the ultimate decision-making authority. Its decisions are taken by unanimous, simple or qualified majority voting (QMV),[5] a device which is meant to ensure that the large countries cannot impose their wishes on the rest. The Council consists of representatives of member governments, but representives of the Commission always attend its meetings. It is not a group of fixed individuals in the way the Commission is, for example when matters of agriculture are under consideration, it will be the Ministers of Agriculture of the member states who will constitute the Council. The presidency of the Council rotates, with each member nation holding it in turn for a period of six months.

There are three reasons why the Court of Justice is needed. First, a body of legal experts is indispensable for ensuring that the institutions act in a constitutional manner, fulfilling the obligations laid on them by the treaties. Second, the Court is necessary for seeing to it that the member states, firms and persons observe the increasing number of EU rules. Finally, it is needed to guide national courts in their interpretation of EU law. The Court comprises thirteen judges and six advocates-general. The latter are responsible for the preliminary investigation of a matter and providing a 'reasoned opinion' to the judges to help them reach a decision.

Originally, the EP was a consultative rather than a legislative body, since the Council had to consult it before deciding on a Commission proposal. However, the SEA and the EU Treaty have turned the EP into a legislative body by establishing a *codecision procedure*, and an *assessment procedure* in certain areas, and a *cooperation procedure* in others. Where the codecision procedure applies, the EP jointly decides with the Council in a wide range of matters: the management of the single market; freedom of movement of workers and establishments; research; trans-European infrastructure networks; cultural matters; public health; etc. The EP's power of assent, the first stage on the way to the codecision procedure, was conferred by the SEA in relation to applications for accession by new members and association agreements with non-members, notably in the Mediterranean. The EU Treaty extended this to include decisions affecting the right of residence for EU citizens, the organisation of EU structural funds, the establishment of the Cohesion Fund, certain institutional matters in the context of EMU, all international agreements of sufficient importance and the adoption of uniform voting procedures for EP elections. The cooperation procedure was established by the SEA; it was the testing ground for the codecision procedure. The implementation and management of the internal market was one of the main areas, but this is now under the codecision procedure. However, under the Maastricht Treaty, the cooperation procedure now includes social policy, education and training, the environment, legislation for EMU and implementing measures for the EU structural funds, the trans-European infrastructure networks, etc.

The EP had its first elections by direct universal suffrage on 7 and 10 June 1979. It has 626 members, elected for a term of five years. Once elected, members are organised in political rather than national groups although, in some cases, national identity remains very strong.[6]

The ESC has 222 members,[7] appointed by the Council (after consulting with the Commission) on the basis of national lists. Each member is appointed for four years and acts in a personal capacity. The ESC plays an important role of a general consultative and informative nature. It represents the various categories of economic and social activity such as employers, unions and the self-employed, together with representative from community and social organisations. It is usual to seek the opinion of the ESC on all major policy proposals, and the ESC itself (since 1972) will also formulate its own opinions on subjects it deems important.

The Committee of the Regions was set up by the Maastricht Treaty in response to demands by several member nations that regional and local authorities should be directly involved in deliberations at the EU level. In many countries these authorities enjoy wide-ranging powers, either because of the federal structure of the country concerned or by virtue of legislative or constitutional measures adopted over the past few decades. The Committee consists of 189 members, each with an alternate.[8]

Formally, an EU decision results in a regulation, directive, decision, recommendation or an opinion. A *regulation* is generally and directly applicable as it stands, a *directive* is binding in objective on the member states but not in the method of achievement, a *decision* is binding on those to whom it is addressed whilst *recommendations* and *opinions* have no binding force (Article 189). These formal acts, notably recommendations and directives, are constantly adding to EU law. Decisions normally emanate from the Council which resolves the issue on procedures as laid down from the particular subject matter. Before reaching this stage, however, a complex process would have been undertaken. In short, all EU institutions have a part to play in the decision-making process, depending on a *modus vivendi* existing between the units to allow the process to operate. In practice, tensions exist between the institutions leading to a power struggle between them as there is between the national governments and the EU itself. A critical example was the conflict between the *Council* and the *Commission* in 1965–6 which curbed the development of the Commission's powers, and another period of difficulty appeared in the late 1970s when the EP tried to obtain greater power, especially over the general budget. Both episodes contributed to periods of political stagnation and led to uneasy compromises. However, given the EU treaty, these may hopefully prove to be things of the past.

HAS THE EU BEEN SUCCESSFUL?

This is a question that is often being, and sometimes has to be, asked even though the coverage in this chapter would suggest that it is, to some extent, meaningless. As we have seen, the ultimate objective of those who founded the EU is to bring about the political unity of Europe. Even if the Maastricht Treaty becomes the EU reality, the EU would still not have reached this goal, and in this sense it has not been successful. However, the EU neither started with the whole of Europe nor does it presently comprise it, and it has reached its total membership of fifteen in stages through three enlargements and an accession. Each one of these additions brought with it new problems which frustrated the progress that had been achieved before it. This was compounded by tumultuous changes in the world economy over which the EC could not be held responsible (see below). Thus, the very fact that the EU is still here and has been able to achieve all the developments that have been discussed are a clear sign that it has been very successful,[9] i.e. it has survived against all odds.

If by the question one is asking whether the EU has been able to achieve the goals it set for each policy area, then the answer would require a whole book (see El-Agraa, 1994c). Here, it suffices to state that although EU progress has been variable, it has to a large extent been successful, especially in the cases of enhanced intra-EU trade (see Tables 5.2 and 5.3), the CAP and EMU. However, the enhancement of intra-EU trade may be due to trade creation, trade diversion or both; one can never rest assured which one has been its major cause (see p. 127, Chapter 3 and El-Agraa, 1989). Moreover, there are not many analysts who would condone either the CAP achievements or the methods by which they have been reached. With respect to the EMU, as we have seen, it was first adopted in the early 1970s and was to be introduced in three stages. Although important measures were subsequently introduced in order to achieve it, indeed the first stage was successfully negotiated and the second was progressing nicely, the goal of reaching this aim eventually failed. This was due to the global economic difficulties of the early 1970s (the *Nixon* and *Oil shocks*) and to the first enlargement of the EC (as just mentioned, each of the three new member nations brought with it a new set of problems), not to any lack of real effort on the part of the total membership. Nevertheless, the idea did not go away since in the late 1970s a more modest scheme for creating a 'zone of monetary stability', based on a basket of the currencies of the member states (the *European Currency Unit* – ECU, which happened to be the name of an old French coin), was introduced: the *European Monetary System* (EMS, see Mayes in El-Agraa, 1994). The centrepiece of the EMS is the *exchange rate mechanism* (ERM) which is an alarm mechanism that asks for

Table 5.2 Exports to the EC6, EC9 and EC12
(percentage share of total exports of exporting country)

Exporter	*1957*	*1974*	*1981*	*1986*	*1990*	*1991*	*1992*
Austria	na	na	na	60.1	65.2	65.7	66.1
Belgium	46.1	69.6	70.0	72.9	75.1	75.2	74.8
Denmark	32.2	43.1	46.7	46.8	52.1	54.1	54.5
Finland	na	na	na	38.3	46.9	51.2	53.2
France	25.1	53.2	48.2	57.8	62.7	63.6	63.0
Germany	29.2	53.2	46.9	50.8	53.6	53.8	54.1
Greece	52.5	50.1	43.3	63.5	64.0	63.5	64.2
Ireland	na	74.1	69.9	71.9	74.8	74.4	74.2
Italy	24.9	45.4	43.2	53.5	58.2	59.0	57.7
Netherlands	41.6	70.8	71.2	75.7	76.5	76.2	75.4
Portugal	22.2	48.2	53.7	68.0	73.5	75.1	74.6
Spain	29.8	47.4	43.0	60.9	46.9	66.4	66.3
Sweden	na	na	na	50.0	54.3	51.4	55.8
UK	14.6	33.4	41.2	47.9	52.6	56.3	55.5

Notes
1. Germany's data is that for only the former West Germany.
2. The Luxembourg data is either insignificant or is included in that of Belgium.
3. n.a. means not available.

Source: various issues of Eurostat's *Basic Statistics of the Community* (Brussels: European Union).

intervention by the monetary authorities of a member nation to reverse a trend when its currency has reached 75 per cent of the allowed divergence of 2.25 per cent (now 15 per cent) either way. Moreover, in 1989, the member nations endorsed the *Delors Report*, committing themselves to achieving the EMU, again in three stages, the first of which began on 1 July 1990, the second in 1994 and the third will start in 1997, and a single currency will be introduced if the majority of the member nations pass the five criteria (see p. 118 and note 4), otherwise in 1999 if the Maastricht Treaty becomes the reality and no further major upheavals arise during the process.

With regard to the variable progress, one should of course point out that in contrast to this somewhat rosy picture, a number of NTBs either still remain or have sprung in the process. However, as we have seen, the aim of the internal market is to abolish these either directly or indirectly via the harmonisation of technical specifications which will promote the right environment for getting rid of them. All these NTBs are fully set out in the White Paper of 1984, and comprehensively discussed in Emerson *et al.* (1988).

Table 5.3 Imports from EC6, EC9 and EC12
(percentage share of total imports of importing country)

Importer	*1957*	*1974*	*1981*	*1986*	*1990*	*1991*	*1992*
Austria	na	na	na	66.9	68.6	68.7	67.9
Belgium	43.5	66.1	59.3	66.9	70.7	70.6	71.2
Denmark	31.2	45.5	47.9	53.2	53.7	54.2	55.4
Finland	na	na	na	43.1	46.3	45.8	47.2
France	21.4	47.6	48.2	64.4	64.8	64.2	65.6
Germany	23.5	48.1	48.2	54.2	54.1	54.5	54.7
Greece	40.8	43.3	50.0	58.3	64.1	60.2	62.7
Ireland	na	68.3	74.7	73.0	70.8	69.1	71.9
Italy	21.4	42.4	40.7	55.4	57.4	57.7	58.8
Netherlands	41.1	57.4	52.4	61.0	59.9	59.0	58.8
Portugal	37.1	43.5	38.0	58.8	69.1	71.9	73.6
Spain	21.3	35.8	29.0	51.3	59.1	59.8	60.3
Sweden	na	na	na	57.2	55.3	54.7	55.5
UK	12.1	30.0	39.4	50.4	51.0	50.2	50.7

Notes
1. Germany's data is that for only the former West Germany.
2. The Luxembourg data is either insignificant or is included in that of Belgium.
3. na means not available.

Source: As Table 5.2.

If by the question one is enquiring whether the EU has been able to perform better in terms of both reduced rates of unemployment and enhanced rates of GDP growth, the answer is also mixed. As Table 5.4 shows, the unemployment rates for the EU of twelve have certainly risen and so have the absolute numbers, reaching 16.9 million in 1993. However, the member nations involved in the last enlargement have not performed any better nor have Canada, Norway or Switzerland. Moreover, although the US may appear to have been having a steady performance, the average rate for 1987–91 was actually about 5.7 per cent. If the comparator has to be Japan, then all the countries mentioned have fared badly, hence one is not much the wiser, but one should hasten to add that many analysts believe the rate for Japan does not reveal all since a number of the employed would not be classified as such if one were to standardise the system for recording the data (see El-Agraa, 1986).

With regard to the rates of GDP growth, a comparison of the data provided in Table 5.5 for 1969–70 and 1980–93 indicates that all the

Table 5.4 Unemployment rates for the EU and a selection of countries (annual averages in percentages)

Country	*1973*	*1979*	*1981*	*1985*	*1991*	*1992*	*1993*
Austria	na	na	na	na	3.5	3.6	4.4
Belgium	3.0	8.0	11.0	14.0	7.5	8.2	9.4
Denmark	1.0	5.0	9.0	12.0	8.9	9.5	10.4
Finland	na	na	na	na	7.6	13.0	17.3
France	2.0	6.0	8.0	12.0	9.5	10.0	10.8
Germany	1.0	3.0	5.0	7.0	5.6	6.4	7.2
Greece	na	na	na	8.0	7.7	na	na
Ireland	6.0	8.0	11.0	15.0	16.2	17.8	18.4
Italy	5.0	7.0	8.0	12.0	10.1	10.3	11.1
Luxembourg	*	*	*	*	1.6	1.9	2.6
Netherlands	2.0	4.0	8.0	12.0	7.1	7.2	8.8
Portugal	na	na	na	9.0	4.0	3.9	5.0
Spain	na	na	na	22.0	16.4	18.2	21.5
Sweden	na	na	na	na	2.7	4.8	7.7
UK	2.0	5.0	10.0	16.0	8.9	10.2	10.5
EC (9/12)	2.0	5.0	8.0	12.0	8.8	9.6	10.6
Canada	na	na	7.5	10.4	10.2	11.2	11.6
Japan	na	na	2.2	2.6	2.1	2.2	2.5
Norway	na	na	2.0	2.6	5.5	5.9	6.2
USA	na	na	7.5	7.1	6.6	7.3	7.2
Switzerland	na	na	na	na	1.2	2.7	4.4

Notes

1. Germany's data is that for only the former West Germany.
2. The Luxembourg data (*) is either insignificant or is included in that of Belgium.
3. na means not available.

Source: As Table 5.2.

countries concerned have experienced a consistent decline over the two periods. The inclusion of the 1970–80 period in the comparison makes a slight difference in that Ireland, Switzerland and the UK are out of line: Ireland managed to raise its rate during this middle period while both Switzerland and the UK did the opposite relative to the last period. Thus, one is left with an equally ambiguous answer.

If by the question one is asking whether or not the EU has been able to perform better in the world economy as a result of being one trading bloc, then no answer is possible. As shown elsewhere (see El-Agraa, 1989 and Chapter 3), the measurement of changes in economic variables before and after integration, a must for answering

Table 5.5 Average annual GDP growth rates for the EU and a selection of countries (percentages)

Country	*1960–70*	*1970–80*	*1980–93*
Austria	4.5	3.4	2.3
Belgium	4.8	3.0	2.1
Denmark	4.7	2.2	2.0
Finland	4.6	3.0	2.0
France	5.7	3.2	2.1
Germany	4.4	2.6	2.6
Greece	6.9	4.9	1.3
Ireland	4.2	4.9	3.8
Italy	5.3	3.8	2.2
Netherlands	5.5	2.9	2.3
Portugal	6.2	4.3	3.0
Spain	7.3	3.5	3.1
Sweden	4.4	1.9	1.7
UK	2.9	2.0	2.5
Canada	5.6	4.6	2.6
Japan	10.5	4.3	4.0
Norway	4.9	4.8	2.6
USA	4.3	2.8	2.7
Switzerland	4.3	0.5	1.9

Notes
1. Germany's data is that for only the former West Germany.
2. The Luxembourg data is either insignificant or is included in that of Belgium.

Source: various issues of the World Bank's *World Development Report*.

such a question, is so frought with difficulties, it does not matter how advanced econometric techniques may become, no such answer can ever be achieved. Some analysts have attempted an answer by simply looking at the performance of the EU relative to its major competitors in a controlled market (see Winters, 1993), but their conclusion that the EU has not been successful in this respect cannot be taken seriously, given what has just been stated and the fact that the EU has been having variable membership. In short, the appropriate question in this particular respect should have been: have the EU member nations done better as a result of membership of the EU than they would have done in isolation or in alternative blocs? However, given the above and the ultimate aspirations of the EU, this is a question that we shall never be able to answer.

CONCLUSION

One cannot escape the conclusion that if and when the Maastricht Treaty becomes the reality, the EU would still not yet have arrived, but would have gone a long way towards achieving the dream of its founding fathers: the creation of a *United States of Europe*. The long march is easily explicable in terms of the difficulties inherent in securing the necessary compromises needed for going forward and accommodating new members, and the tackling of unforseen economic and political problems, from both within and without. It does not really matter when the EU will realise its dream, since what is important is that one should never forget that that vision has been the guiding light without which disaster might have struck at any time. It behoves all those who would like to think of the EU as, or dearly want to reduce it to, a trading bloc to think twice.

Notes

1. So far there has been one withdrawal. Greenland, which joined the EC in 1973 as a territory of Denmark, voted solidly against EC membership in the ensuing referendum and, in 1984, finally unilaterally departed from the EC. However, it remains associated as an *Overseas Country or Territory* and has a special agreement to regulate mutual fishing interests.
2. Greece, Ireland, Portugal and Spain, the less developed members of the EU, will receive increased support from the remaining partners to assist them in the process of catching up with the average level of development in the EU as a whole. For this purpose, the EU created the Cohesion Fund in 1993 as agreed.
3. One should state that a three-stage timetable for EMU started on 1 July 1990 with the launching of the first phase of intensified economic cooperation, during which all the member states were to submit their currencies to the ERM of the EMS. The main target of this activity was the UK whose currency was not subject to the ERM discipline; the UK joined in 1991 while Mrs Thatcher was still in office, but withdrew in 1992. During the second stage, which started in 1994, the EU created the *European Monetary Institute* (EMI) to prepare the way for a European Central Bank which will start operating on 1 January 1997. The treaty allows Denmark and the UK to opt out of the final stage when the EU currencies will be permanently and irrevocably fixed and a single currency floated.
4. The criteria for membership of the EU are:

   (a) *Price stability*. Membership requires an inflation rate not exceeding 1.5 per cent of the average for the three EU nations with the lowest rates.

(b) *Interest rates*. Membership requires a long-term rate within two percentage points of the average for the lowest three in the EU.
(c) *Budget deficits*. Membership requires a deficit of less than 3 per cent of the member nation's GDP.
(d) *Public debt*. Membership requires a ratio not exceeding 60 per cent of the member nation's GDP.
(e) *Currency stability*. Membership requires a member nation's currency not to have been devalued in the previous two years and to have been maintained within the 2.25 per cent margin of fluctuation allowed when the ERM was initiated.

One may wonder how the twelve instigators of the EU treaty would have fared at the time of signing the treaty. The score sheet is given in Table 5.6.

Table 5.6 Scoring on the five criteria for EMU membership

	Inflation	*Long-term govt. bonds*	*Budget deficit*	*Public debt*	*Currency stability*	*Total score*
France	yes	yes	yes	yes	yes	5
Luxembourg	yes	yes	yes	yes	yes	5
Denmark	yes	yes	yes	no	yes	4
UK	yes	yes	yes	yes	no	4
Germany	no	yes	no	yes	yes	3
Belgium	yes	yes	no	no	yes	3
Ireland	yes	yes	no	no	yes	3
Netherlands	no	yes	no	no	yes	2
Italy	no	no	no	no	yes	1
Spain	no	no	no	yes	no	0
Greece	no	no	no	no	no	0
Portugal	no	no	no	no	no	0

After the 1992–3 EMS crisis, the currency stability criterion lost its meaning for a number of these nations, hence that item can be ignored in a September 1994 score sheet. As to the remaining four criteria, Luxembourg kept its perfect record, but was joined by Ireland while France failed on the budget deficit. Greece, Italy and Portugal maintained their zero score and were joined by Spain. Of the rest, only Belgium maintained its previous score. Both Denmark and the UK failed on the budget deficit, the Netherlands on inflation and Germany on public debt, but reversed its score on both inflation and budget deficit.

5. When QMV is used, each member nation is endowed with a number of votes which are weighted so that at least some of the smaller members must assent. For the EU of 12, the total number of votes was 76 (France, Germany, Italy and the UK 10 each; Spain 8; Belgium, Greece, the Netherlands and Portugal 5 each; Denmark and Ireland 3 each; and 2 for Luxembourg), with 54 votes needed for a decision; thus the large

countries cannot impose their wishes on the rest. For the EU of 15, it was agreed that 64 votes out of a total of 90 will be needed for a decision, but if 23 votes are recorded against a decision, 'reasonable time' should be allowed for further discussion; the UK suggested that it should be indefinite, but the others believe it to be no more than three months.

6. Its present membership of 626, given in national terms, is such that: Germany has 99; France, Italy and the UK have 87 each; Spain has 64; the Netherlands has 31; Belgium, Greece and Portugal have 25 each; Sweden has 22; Austria has 21; Denmark and Finland have 16 each; Ireland has 15; and Luxembourg has 6. In terms of party distribution, the EP of June 1994 consists of: 221 members of the European Socialist Party; 173 members of the European Peoples Party; 52 members of the Liberal, Democratic and Reformist Group; 31 members of the European United Left Group; 29 members of Forza Europa; 26 members of the European Democratic Alliance; 25 Greens; 19 members of the European Radical Alliance; 19 members of the Europe of Nations; and 31 Non-affiliated members.
7. The national distribution of the ESC's 222 members is as follows: France, Germany, Italy and the UK have 24 each; Spain has 21; Austria, Belgium, Greece, the Netherlands, Portugal and Sweden have 12 each; Denmark, Finland and Ireland have 9 each; and Luxembourg has 6.
8. The distribution of the members is the same as that for the ESC.
9. Let us consider one aspect of this question: the smooth, or otherwise, negotiation of the transition period by the Six, and the performance of new members in this respect. It is needless to add, one cannot discuss the progress achieved by the members involved in the latest enlargement.

   Between 1958 and 1969, when the transition period came to an end, the Six were preoccupied with the construction of the 'community' envisaged in the EEC treaty. Here, it is not necessary to describe all the measures that were undertaken during this period since these are fully discussed in El-Agraa (1994c), and space limitations precludes them. It is enough to state that the basic elements of the customs union (i.e. the removal of the internal tariffs and the creation of the CETs) were established ahead of schedule – see Tables 5.7 and 5.8. Initial steps were undertaken and measures proposed to tackle the many NTBs to the free movement of goods, services and factors of production so that by 1969 a recognisably common market could be said to exist, at least in legal terms.

   Progress was uneven in the area of common policies. Because of French demands, sometimes bordering on threats, the CAP was almost fully operational by 1969, but the CTP was slow to evolve. Moreover, the ESF and EIB were duly established and were fully operational at an early stage. Furthermore, steps were taken to create a common commercial policy and appropriate trade and aid arrangements were undertaken in respect of the colonial and increasingly ex-colonial dependencies. Also, a rudimentary system of macroeconomic policy coordination was devised.

   Although during this period progress was evident and optimism about the success of the EC was much enhanced, there were some disappointments. From a 'federalist' point of view, perhaps the greatest was the French refusal to accept the supra-national element in the treaty

Table 5.7 EC intra-area tariff reductions (percentages)

Acceleration of	*Individual reductions made on the 1.1.1957 level*	*Cumulative reduction*
1 January 1959	10	10
1 July 1960	10	20
1 January 1961	10	30
1 January 1962	10	40
1 July 1962	10	50
1 July 1963	10	60
1 January 1965	10	70
1 January 1966	10	80
1 July 1967	5	85
1 July 1968	15	100

Source: Commission of the European Communities, *First General Report of the Activities of the Communities* (Brussels: EC Commission), p. 34.

Table 5.8 The establishment of the CET (percentages)

Acceleration of	*Industrial products adjustment*	*Cumulative adjustment*	*Agricultural products adjustment*	*Cumulative adjustment*
1 January 1961	30	30		
1 January 1962			30	30
1 July 1963	30	60		
1 January 1966			30	60
1 July 1968	40	100	40	100

Source: As for Table 5.7.

decision-making system, hence the *Luxembourg compromise*. When the member nations signed the EEC Treaty, they opted for a Council which could take decisions on the basis of a majority voting system, but the Luxembourg compromise meant that any member state could insist that nothing should happen unless it agreed that it should do so, i.e. a vetoing system was adopted.

With regard to later members, Tables 5.9 and 5.10 give the timetable for the dismantling of intra-EC tariffs and the adjustments in the CETs for the three countries involved in the first enlargment: Denmark, Ireland and the UK. The tables do not cover all groups of commodities. For example, tariffs on coal imports were abolished from the day of accession, and tariffs on certain groups of commodities given in Annex III of

Table 5.9 New members' intra-tariff reductions (percentages)

Acceleration of	*Individual reductions made on 1.1.1972*	*Cumulative reduction*
1 April 1973	20	20
1 January 1974	20	40
1 January 1975	20	60
1 January 1976	20	80
1 July 1977	20	100

Source: Bulletin of the European Communities, no. 8, 1978.

the *Treaty of Accession* were abolished on 1 January 1974, etc. In the case of the CETs, those tariffs that differed by less than 15 per cent were adjusted on 1 January 1974. Import quota restrictions were also eliminated from the day of accession. Measures having equivalent effects to the import quota restrictions were removed by the deadline of 1 January 1975. All three member nations had no difficulties in achieving these changes.

In the case of Greece's adhesion to the EC, a five-year period was agreed for the progressive dismantling of residual customs duties on Greek imports of products originating in the EC and for the progressive alignment of Greek tariffs to the CETs. Customs duties on Greek imports from the EC were to be reduced in six stages commencing on 1 January 1981, with a reduction of 10 percentage points followed by a further reduction of the same percentage points on 1 January 1982 and four annual reductions of 20 percentage points, so that all customs duties on Greek intra-EC trade would be removed by 1 January 1986. Alignment of the CET was to follow the same timetable.

Quantitative restrictions between Greece and the EC were to be abolished on adhesion, except for fourteen products for which Greece has been authorised to maintain transitional quotas. These quotas were to be

Table 5.10 Approaching the CET (percentages)[a]

	Individual adjustments made on 1.1.1972	*Cumulative adjustment*
1 January 1974	40	40
1 January 1975	20	60
1 January 1976	20	80
1 July 1977	20	100

Note

[a] For products which differ by more than 15 per cent from the CET.

Source: As Table 5.9.

progressively increased during the five-year transitional period and to be completely eliminated by 31 December 1985. As a general rule, the minimum rates of increase for such quotas was 25 per cent at the beginning of each year for quotas expressed in value terms and 20 per cent at the beginning of each year for quotas expressed in volume terms. Measures having equivalent effect to quantitative restrictions were to be eliminated upon adhesion, except for the Greek system of cash payments and import deposits which were to be phased out over three years (the *Bulletin of the European Communities*, no. 5, 1969, is the best source for these and further details).

In the case of Portugal and Spain, a ten-year transitional period was agreed. For Portugal, this is divided into two equal (five-year) stages for the majority of products and a basic seven-year period for other products, although some measures will apply for the full ten years. For Spain, there are some variations, but the essentials are basically the same.

It can be stated that Greece has navigated its transition period successfully and it would seem that the Iberian member nations are having no difficulties accommodating their required changes either.

6 EU Trade and Aid Policies Towards the LDCs and CEECs

Enzo Grilli

INTRODUCTION

As mentioned in the previous chapter, the European Union (EU) is the oldest functioning trading bloc[1] and the largest in the world. The Treaty of Rome gave the EU a development mandate *vis-à-vis* 'associated countries and territories', i.e. the colonial possessions of the member states, which later became independent nations. This mandate generated direct aid relations with a group of developing countries, which expanded over the years and made the EU a significant supplier of development assistance. The aid mandate was recently extended to the Central and Eastern Europe Countries (CEECs) and to the nations of the former Soviet Union.

The EU has a leading position in world trade. Its external merchandise trade (i.e. its trade in goods with non-members, sometimes called extra-EU trade) accounts for 20 per cent of world total. This compares with the 15 per cent share of the United States and the 10 per cent share of Japan. In services, the weight of the EU is even greater, since it accounts for over a quarter of world trade. The external relations of the EU are very important to a large number of countries, both industrial and developing. In 1990, for example, it absorbed a quarter of all US exports, nearly a fifth of those of Japan and 22 per cent of the total exports of the non-oil developing countries. For reasons of size alone, the common external trade policies of the EU have a large bearing on world commercial relations. The EU is a 'pace maker' in international trade policies (GATT, 1991). Its relative importance as an export market has risen with the increase in membership, which now includes practically the whole of Western Europe.[2]

The EU has also assumed over time an important position in world economic aid. Despite the nearly complete bias in favour of Africa present at the start, given geography and the colonial heritage of several of its members, EU aid relations evolved worldwide and have become a meaningful component of its development cooperation policy. A strong preference towards Sub-Saharan Africa, however, continues to exist, as aid to this region still accounts for 55–60 per cent of the total in the early 1990s. Aid to the CEECs[3] and to the New Independent States (NIS)[4] of the former Soviet Union is instead a very recent phenomenon. It started in 1991, even though EU members extended aid to this region earlier. On the whole, CEECs and NIS now absorb about 15 per cent of total direct aid from the EU. Such aid is in effect European multilateral aid, administered directly by the Commission, and juxtaposed to the bilateral aid of the members.[5] It constitutes 5 per cent of world annual Official Development Assistance (ODA) flows,[6] but much more of the annual multilateral aid flows (over 20 per cent).

KEY TRAITS OF EU EXTERNAL TRADE AND AID POLICIES

Since its very beginning the EU has played an important (at times critical) role in shaping world trade relations, through both direct dealings with trade partners and participation in multilateral negotiations, conducted within the framework of the General Agreement on Tariff and Trade (GATT).[7] It started regional trade integration among industrial countries. It was the first to grant trade preferences to developing countries, beginning with the Treaty of Rome. Until it found a joint position on the reform of its Common Agricultural Policy (CAP) in 1992, the EU *de facto* blocked the progress of the Uruguay Round. Its single European Market (SEM) programme was, according to some, a key stimulus to the generalisation of trade regionalism in the second half of the 1980s. If a multilateral agreement on trade in services was finally reached, albeit without the United States, in mid-1995, it was largely for the leadership exerted by the EU.

Inside the EU, commercial policies are usually seen as the most complete expression of its common external relations. In no other area has communality of decision-making and harmonisation of member country behaviours reached the extent that it did in the trade field. Commercial integration, through the creation of the customs union, was at the core of the construction of the common market and of European economic integration at large. Common trade policies remained the cornerstone of the European construction and are generally regarded as its most successful dimension. Yet, EU trade polices have always been difficult to understand and to characterise precisely. This has been due in part to their complexity, in part to their evolutionary nature, and to some extent to the internal contradictions that they always carried (McAleese, 1994). Most of these difficulties are really not unexpected, if one considers that arriving at a common external policy is intrinsically difficult among countries that are not fully amalgamated politically or even economically (a key problem of all customs unions), and that in the specific case of the EU the number of member states grew over time, encompassing a progressively larger variety of interests and goals.

In terms of stated intentions, the EU always made solemn professions of liberalism in external trade relations, beginning with Article 110 of the Treaty of Rome, which set for the customs union then being established the goals of contributing, 'in the common interest, to the harmonious development of world trade' and 'to the progressive abolition of restrictions on international trade'. Official professions of liberalism have continued before and after the completion of the SEM, which some saw instead as the cornerstone of a new 'fortress Europe'. In one of its rare public review of trade policies, the European Commission recently claimed that 'the Community made clear that one of the central objectives of the single market program [was] that of [external] trade liberalization' (Commission of the European Communities, 1993a, p. 188), a concern that one does not find clearly expressed in either the White Paper on the completion of the internal market or in the Cecchini Report,[8] which focused instead on the internal effects of market unification (El-Agraa, 1994c).[9] Even more recently, the (then) Commissioner for External Affairs, Leon Brittan, emphasised that 'the first major strategic decision taken by the Union after the entry into force of the Maastricht Treaty [was] to lower barriers and to free trade (European Communities, 1994, foreword).

Even a cursory look at the evidence of EU external trade relations reveals a much more complex, and at times puzzling, picture. Uncertainties have persisted about the basic thrust of EU commercial policies, at least since the first enlargement of the EU in 1975, as shown by a number of reviews conducted since then. Some of them have emphasised the inconsistency of EU tariff and non-tariff policies, the first liberalised in successive rounds of GATT negotiations, the latter stiffened since the 1970s (Pelkmans, 1987; Hine, 1991; Hiemenz, 1993; McAleese, 1994). Others have highlighted the inward-looking bent of EU sectoral policies, aimed at protecting declining industries such as textile-clothing, shipbuilding and chemicals, or at fostering the growth of high-technology industries such as electronics and aircrafts (Xafa *et al.*, 1992; Scott, 1993; Moore, 1994). Others have reflected on the considerable differentiation of EU trade policy not only across economic sectors, but also across the countries impacted by it, and on the complex hierarchy of preferential relations (and thus discrimination) built into such policies (Hine, 1985; GATT, 1991, 1993). Finally, the strong protectionist posture maintained by the EU in agriculture through the CAP and its related trade policy measures, notwithstanding the various attempt to reform it, has been extensively highlighted (GATT, 1991; Winters, 1989, 1992). Given this complex and contradictory picture, and the diversity of trends evident in EU behaviours over time, a basic uncertainty has existed for quite some while among observers about the strategic direction of EU trade policies. Such uncertainty is clearly reflected by the neutral position taken on this issue by Hine (1985, p. 264), at the end of the most comprehensive review of EU trade policies undertaken by a single scholar.

EU aid polices have been the subject of much less attention than trade policies. The EU nearly exclusive focus on associated African countries made the subject rather specialised and of limited interest. None the less, while the regional soul of European development cooperation emerged victorious from the negotiations of the Treaty of Rome, the globalist one was not eliminated. It gradually reasserted itself over time and was clearly reflected, *inter alia*, in the progressive extension of the EU's aid to developing countries in Asia and Central America (Grilli, 1993). More recently, the extension of aid relations to CEECs and the former Soviet Union without evident cutbacks in nominal flows to most other regions, could indicate a strengthening of the globalist position on development cooperation inside the EU.[10] None the less, EU aid policies have not shined for either developmental effectiveness (Court of Auditors of the EC/EU, 1982; Hewitt, 1982) or even for their capacity to influence member countries' bilateral policies, which in terms of resources commanded vastly outstrip in importance those of the EU,[11] but are still poorly coordinated with each other and with those of the EU.[12]

STRUCTURE AND EVOLUTION OF EU TRADE POLICIES

EU trade policies towards developing countries, as a subset of overall trade policies, have attracted over time a considerable amount of attention (Mishalani *et al.*, 1981; Pelkmans, 1987; McQueen, 1992; Hiemenz, 1993; Grilli, 1993). Interest in EU trade policies towards Central and Eastern Europe is more recent, but developing fast (Pinder, 1991;[13] Hindley, 1992; Langhammer, 1992; Grilli, 1993; Messerlin, 1992, 1993; Kramer, 1993; Kaminski, 1994; Faini and Portes, 1995). Several key characteristics of these polices have long been noticed. Among them, the literature has underlined the initial reliance by the EU on trade preferences, first granted to the colonial possessions of the original members of the EC on nearly all their exports, then extended (although in different amounts) to the exports of industrial products of practically all developing countries with the Generalised System of Preferences (GSP) in 1971. The Yaoundé and Lomé Conventions, entered into effect respectively in 1963 and 1975, which succeeded the Treaty of Rome as regulatory instruments of trade relations with associated countries, ensured the continuation of preferential access for the exports of Africa, Caribbean and Pacific countries (the ACPs, sometimes characterised as the most privileged among the developing countries). Another category of developing countries, particularly those of the southern Mediterranean, were granted through individual Cooperation Agreements signed in the mid-1970s a slightly less privileged access to EU markets than the early associates, but generally better than the standard GSP treatment received by all other developing countries, thus creating a second tier of preferred beneficiaries. Finally came the rest of the developing world, whose trade preferences applied only to industrial products, were generally lower than those of the associates, and had product and quantity limitations (Table 6.1). Trade in agriculture and in textiles-clothing was generally left out of the preferential system (with the partial exception of the ACP preferences and those included in the new agreements with Mediterranean countries). The first type was unilaterally regulated by the EU under the provisions of the CAP, while the second was subject to collective management through the Multifibre Arrangements (MFAs), negotiated by most industrial countries with developing exporters.[14]

Yet, despite the evident efforts to differentiate market access across products and countries, and the complexity of the construction of the preferential pyramid, the trade enhancing effects of tariff preferences

Table 6.1 EU trade preferences towards developing countries by sector

Sector	*Agricultural and food products*	*Manufactures*			*Other provisions*
Beneficiaries (ranked in order of preferences)		*Textiles and clothing*	*Steel products*	*Other industrial products*	
ACP Countries (Lomé Conventions) 69 countries of Sub-Saharan Africa, Caribbean and Pacific regions	Free access[1] for non-CAP products; better than MFN[2] treatment for other products; guaranteed import quotas for beef and sugar; special import regime for bananas and rum.	Free access.[1]	Duty-free access, with safeguard clause.	Free access.[1]	Full ACP/EC cumulation of origin status; derogation procedures to rules of origin available.
CEEC Countries (Association Agreements) 6 countries of Central and East Europe	Near free access[1] for non-CAP products; better than MFN treatment for other products;[2] special regime for beef imports; minimum import prices for some products.	Elimination of import duties and QRs within a given period (no longer than 1/2 of the period agreed in the Uruguay Round).	Elimination of QRs from 1992 and import duties over 6 years; safeguard clause: surveillance regime.	Access[1] for most products, with tariff quotas ceilings for sensitive products (to be eliminated in 5 years).	Creation of free trade area with EU within 10 years.
Mediterranean Countries (Cooperation Agreements) 7 countries of the Maghreb and Mashreq	Free access[1] for non-CAP products; better than MFN treatment for other products since 1993.[2]	Free access[1] in principle; administrative (surveillance) agreements with Morocco, Tunisia and Egypt.	Duty-free access with safeguard clause.	Free access.[1]	Full Maghreb/EC cumulation of origin status; bilateral cumulation with each of the Maghreb countries.

GSP countries A. 130 developing countries[3] (in practice 54, i.e., 130 minus 69ACP minus 7 Mediterranean that enjoy better than GSP treatment) B. 10 CEECs and 4 NIS (in practice only 4 CEEs and 4 NIS, since 6 Central European countries enjoy better than GSP treatment)	Reduction or abolition of import duties on certain products.	Duty-free access, within tariff quotas or ceilings, for countries with which community has concluded MFA or similar agreements; special regime for jute/coir imports from India, Thailand and Sri Lanka.	Duty-free access within quantitative ceilings.	Preferential duties; duty-free entrance for a wide range of products subject to quantitative ceilings or a safeguard provision; graduation (i.e. exclusion from preference) based on objective criteria.	Cumulation of origin status granted only to members of certain regional agreements;[4] rules of origin more restrictive than for ACP and Mediterranean countries.

Countries: (in practice only NIS since CEEC enjoy a better than GSP treatment).

Notes

1 Free access means zero duty and no quantitative restrictions on imports.

2 Including reduction of variable levies (specific duties after the Uruguay Round).

3 Plus 20 dependent territories. Least developed countries enjoy better treatment than the rest.

4 Andean Pact; ASEAN; Central American Common Market (CACM).

Sources: Commission of the European Communities (1993a); GATT (1993); Grilli (1993).

for developing countries (and sub-groups of them) were generally estimated to be modest in size by both *ex-ante* and *ex-post* analyses (Baldwin and Murray, 1977; Sapir 1981; Langhammer and Sapir, 1987; Moss and Ravenhill, 1987; Brown, 1989; Grilli, 1993), even though recent studies have pointed to some specific, if limited, trade benefits coming from EC preferences granted to ACP countries (McQueen and Stevens, 1989; McQueen, 1992). Even the trade-creating impact of GSP preferences, long considered minimal in size (aside from being highly concentrated in a few higher-income beneficiaries), have also been more positively evaluated in recent years (Karsenty and Laird 1987; MacPhee and Rosenbaum, 1989).

Unlike the developing countries, the CEECs and the former Soviet Union, which were state-trading and for the most part non-members of the GATT, were not only kept for a long time outside the domain of EU preferences, but trade with them was specifically (and rather stringently) regulated. This tendency, aptly characterised as the EC's 'stubborn diplomacy' (Pinder, 1991),[15] continued until the early 1980s.

After nearly two decades of preferential trade policies and high-sounding rhetoric about interdependence and mutual advantage in trade relations especially between Europe and the ACP countries, which spanned from the Treaty of Rome to the signing of the first Lomé Convention, it was with surprise, and some delay, that the increasing use by the EU of non-tariff barriers (NTBs) against imports from developing countries was noted in the literature (Hine, 1985; Grilli, 1990a). This new form of protectionism, opaque and highly discriminatory, began somewhat hesitantly in the mid-1970s in the aftermath of the first oil crisis, when it appeared to be directed mostly towards other industrial countries and to the then state-trading countries of Eastern Europe, but gained considerable momentum in the first part of the 1980s. Then, the tendency to force upon foreign producers 'voluntary' restraints on their exports, the over-use of surveillance measures and antidumping procedures to obtain from foreign competitors 'self-limitations' of export quantities or price undertakings that would limit competition with domestic producers, became more clearly correlated with the market penetration threat emanating from newly industrialising economies (the so-called NIEs) of Asia and Latin America. Observers' attention was first focused on the direct consequences of NTBs (a tendency which was by no means limited to the EU) on developing countries' export possibilities, and then on the change of direction in overall EU trade policies that the growing use of NTBs seemed to indicate.

On the first set of effects – the direct trade consequences of the new protectionism – most observers took a pessimistic view, undoubtedly heightened by the emergence of the debt crisis in the early 1980s and by the need, strongly felt by many highly indebted developing countries, to improve their export performance in order to redress existing external imbalances and to proceed with structural reforms in the face of high external debt burdens. The most common view was that the threat posed by the new protectionism on developing countries was real and serious (Diaz-Alejandro and Helleiner, 1987). Its potential negative effects extended to a reduced capacity of many adjusting developing countries to take advantage of their increasing outward-orientation and openness imparted to their economies (World Bank, 1986). There were some notable exceptions to this view, which emphasised the continued capacity of developing countries' exports to penetrate foreign markets (Hughes and Waelbroeck, 1981), but among those who examined the ways in which developing countries actually adapted to the new protectionism in industrial countries and dealt with the new challenges that it created, clear preoccupations emerged about the costs and long-term sustainability of an adjustment largely based on price cutting (Grilli, 1990b). The lasting nature of the concern about the negative consequences of EU NTBs towards developing countries is well reflected in the first review of EU trade policies conducted by the GATT secretariat (GATT, 1991, para 72).

An EU, apparently bent on taking away through the use of NTBs in sectors of crucial interest to developing countries – from textiles to footwear, to consumer electronics – some or all the extra market opportunities supposedly granted to them through trade preferences, did not appear to have a credible and consistent overall policy. These contradictions in actual trade policies, combined with the concomitant increasing supply of aid to developing countries at both the bilateral and communal level during the 1980s, tended to make the development posture of the EU look as lacking coherence and solid internal construction (Grilli, 1993).

In addition, an EU chiefly preoccupied with the SEM and its difficult implementation, apparently stalling in the Uruguay Round negotiations because of the needs of its Agriculture Trade Policy (Secchi, 1995), whether it realised it or not, did not project in the second half of the 1980s a reassuring external image. From it emanated, instead, a sense of inwardness and of *de facto* neglect of the outside world, including the developing countries. The strong new interest demonstrated towards CEECs at the very beginning of this region's transition towards political democracy and market economies, also appeared to much of the outside world as conforming to the enhanced regional look that the EU was progressively assuming. Preoccupations regarding trade, aid and even investment diversion from developing to CEECs were voiced, both in connection with the SEM and with the trade and cooperation policies put in place *vis-à-vis* the economies in transition (Hughes-Hallett, 1992). To complicate matters, the numerous concerns voiced by outside observers were met for a long time by silence, or by contradictory answers, from inside the EU (Balassa, 1989).

The trade policy response of the EU to the plight of post-communist CEECs was swift in time and traditional in kind. The transition of Central Europe towards democracy and a market economy was followed with strong and constant attention by the EU and its constituent members. The first element of its response to it was to abolish the complex apparatus of protection against imports from that region that the EC had erected in the years of 'stubborn diplomacy' (import authorisations, quantitative restrictions, high import tariffs, etc.) and to do it unilaterally. This was done with the Trade and Cooperation Agreements concluded in the late 1980s, which also established that trade with the CEECs would be conducted right away on a MFN basis. The second, and more traditional part of the response, was to grant preferential access to exports from Central Europe, first through the extension of GSP treatment to all of them,[16] and subsequently through the concession of an even more preferential treatment within the framework of Association Agreements (the so-called Europe Agreements). These agreements foresaw the establishment of a free trade area between the EU and each of the now associated countries over a period of ten years, to be implemented in two equal stages, during which liberalisation of trade would proceed asymmetrically, with the EU going more rapidly than its associates. With this move the EU extended its time-tested associative model to relations with the neighbouring countries of Central Europe, with the possibility of a later extension to those of Eastern Europe. The NIS were only offered GSP treatment. Neither the early Trade and Cooperation Agreements nor the recently concluded Partnership and Cooperation Agreements (Table 6.2) extend any further preferential treatment to them. Here again the EU, while improving the market access of all the CEECs and NIS, was giving in time and extent a more favourable access to the former than to the latter, thus introducing another differentiation in the trade treatment of the economies in transition. Put differently, while the CEECs were placed high up in the 'pyramid of trade privileges', at roughly the same level as the Mediterranean countries, and just below the ACPs, the NIS were given a 'third-tier' status, more or less at par with the rest of the developing world (Table 6.2).

THE MIX OF INSTRUMENTS IN EU TRADE POLICIES

Given their complexity and degree of country and sector differentiation, in order to characterise with some precision and to evaluate the main tendencies of EU trade policies towards developing countries over the past ten to fifteen years, one must at a minimum analyse what protective instruments were used to conduct it, and what was their sectoral incidence and geographical focus. It would be highly desirable to be able to analyse and compare on a common basis the external trade and welfare consequences of such policies. This is unfortunately not possible here, given the extreme variety of commercial policy instrument used by the EU, and in particular the recent reliance on NTBs, whose tariff-equivalency is often very hard to calculate (Deardorff and Stern, 1985). One should also allow for the possibility of the EU using the various trade policy tools in a complementary or substitutive way. This too is very difficult. The analysis presented here, will be less rigorous and largely based on the frequency in the use of instruments aimed at influencing trade between the EU and its non-industrial partners and on their reach, measured by the trade that they affect.

A matrix of the EU's main trade policy instruments, by main type and sector of application, is presented in Table 6.3. It indicates quite clearly that the EU has practised a protection of its domestic markets using a multiplicity of devices such as fixed tariffs, variable tariffs and NTBs, and has concentrated them on commodity sectors which clearly betray a special focus on developing countries.

Beginning with pre-Uruguay Round import tariffs, despite low average levels, especially on manufactures, and the existence of numerous (and in some cases generous) preferences in favour of developing countries, the distribution of burdens was such that much above-average rates were applied on imports of agricultural and food products, textiles, articles of clothing, footwear and electrical equipment, large portions of which are supplied by non-associated developing countries. CEECs and NIS were similarly affected by above-average tariffs in food and chemicals. The concentration effect

Table 6.2 EU major trade policy actions *vis-à-vis* Central and Eastern Europe

Countries / *Actions*	*Poland*	*Hungary*	*Check and Slovak Republics*	*Bulgaria*	*Romania*	*Albania*	*Baltic states*
Trade and Cooperation Agreements[1]	1989	1988	1989–90	1990	1991	1992	1993
Extension of GSP treatment[1]	Jan. 1990	Jan. 1990	Jan. 1991	Jan. 1991	1974	Jan. 1992	Feb.–Mar. 1993
Free Trade Agreements						Dec. 1992	Jan. 1995[3]
Associations (Europe) Agreements	Feb. 1994	Feb. 1994	Feb. 1995	Feb. 1995	Feb. 1995		
(Interim agreements)[2]	(March 1992)	(March 1992)	(March 1992)	(Dec. 1993)	(May 1993)		
Countries:	Russia	Ukraine	Moldova	Belarus			
Actions:							
Trade and Cooperation Agreements[1]	1990	1990	1990	1990			
Extension of GSP treatment	Jan. 1993	Jan. 1993					
Partnership and Cooperation Agreements	June 1995[3]	June 1995[3]	Nov. 1994[3]	March 1995[3]			

Notes
[1] Entry into force
[2] Entry into force of interim agreement, later superseded by the entry into force of the Association Agreements
[3] Signature date
Source: Communication of the European Countries, Directorate General I, External Economic Relations (information hand-outs).

Table 6.3 Utilisation of EU trade policy instruments by most affected sectors, 1980–90

Sector / *Instrument*	*Agricultural & food products*	*Textiles & clothing*	*Footwear*	*Automobiles & transport equipment*	*Electronics*	*Steel*	*Chemicals*
High tariff*	X[1]	X	X	X	X		X
Variable import levies	X[2]						
Quotas (national and EU-wide)	X	X	X	X	X	X	X
VERs[3]	X	X	X	X[4]	X	X	
Authorisations to restrict trade ex. art. 115	X	X		X	X		
Antidumping actions		X			X	X	X

Notes

* At least 30–40% higher than the average tariff (i.e. > 8%)

1 Sensitive agricultural and food products (including fisheries).

2 Applied to such products as cereals, rice, sugar, meat, dairy products and olive oil.

3 Including surveillance measures under Reg. 283/82.

4 Industry-to-industry agreements to limit exports to France, United Kingdom and Portugal (not recognised by the Commission and not enforced through art. 115 authorisations) which remained in force until 1991, when an EU-wide VER with Japan was negotiated.

Sources: GATT Tariff Study as in GATT (1991); Xafa *et al.* (1992) for safeguard actions ex. art. 115 of the treaty; Commission of the European Communities (1993d) for antidumping actions; Xafa *et al.* (1992), Grilli (1990a) for VER (period covered is 1986–90); Rosenblatt *et al.* (1988) for variable import levies and quotas under the CAP; Grilli (1990a) and Commission of the European Communities (1993a) for quotas under the MFA.

of EU tariffs is confirmed by more detailed analysis of the frequency distribution of rates applied in the late 1980s on imports from developing countries: 9 per cent of them were subject to duties ranging between 5 and 10 per cent, and another 11.7 per cent to tariffs higher than 10 per cent. In the case of textiles the share of imports from developing countries subject to duties higher than 10 per cent reached 26 per cent of the total (UNCTAD, 1990).

The same conclusion of a differentiated, and sometimes product-discriminatory, use of tariffs by the EU can be reached by looking specifically at the duties that were charged on the main categories of imports of special interest to developing countries in 1988. This is shown in Table 6.4, using again pre-Uruguay Round tariff information. Food and agricultural products that compete with those produced in the EU were all subject to higher than average tariffs (10–15 per cent), which reached peaks of 20 per cent in the cases of vegetable oils and prepared fish, and of 60 per cent in that of manufactured tobacco. Imports of minerals, fuels and industrial raw materials, which do not compete with EU productions, or do so only weakly, faced instead less-than-average tariffs. Manufactures such as textiles and clothing, footwear, electrical machinery (and within it electrical equipment) and motor vehicles all faced tariffs in the neighborhood of 10 per cent, with upper ranges of 20 per cent. After the Uruguay Round of trade negotiations concluded in 1994, average EU tariff rates on industrial products imported from developing countries declined by 21 per cent. Average tariff rates on the imports of the same products from transition economies declined by 40 per cent (De Paiva Abreu, 1995). A comparison of pre- and post-Uruguay Round tariff rates charged by all industrial countries seems to indicate that sizeable tariff discrimination against products largely imported from developing countries still exists only for textiles and clothing and (less so) for footwear.

If the new structure of EU tariffs turns out to reflect closely that of other industrial countries, the Uruguay Round changes will represent a significant change in the pre-existing bias against developing countries. The same tentative conclusion can be drawn, under the same assumption of close correspondence between tariff structures of industrial countries, by looking at the percentage of imports affected by different tariff ranges by main product categories, before and after the Uruguay Round: only in the case of textiles and clothing has the distribution remained unchanged across tariff brackets. Considerable improvements in the distribution (from the point of view of developing countries) are instead noticeable in the case of electrical

Table 6.4 EU tariff levels on selected categories of imports, 1988 (percentages)

	Average Tariff		*Tariff range*
	Simple	*Weighted*	
A. *Competing food and agricultural product*			
Foodstuffs	14.5	9.8	0–30
Oil seeds, oils and fats	6.9	0.3	0–18
of which: vegetable oils	(10.4)	(9.8)	0–15
Fish and products	12.3	10.1	(0–30)
of which: prepared fish	(20.1)	(11.6)	(5.5–30)
Tobacco	26.6	9.4	26–117
of which: manufactured tobacco	(66.6)	(30.9)	(26–117)
B. *Minerals and fuels*			
Petroleum	3.1	0.5	0–7
Mineral ores	0	0	0
Coal and gas	2.2	4.0	0–16
C. *Other raw materials*			
Raw hides and skins	3.1	2.5	0–10
Rubber	3.1	4.0	0–10
Wood and cork	4.4	2.0	0–10
D. *Manufactures*			
Textiles and Clothing	10.1	7.6	0–17
Chemicals	7.3	6.7	0–17.6
Non-electrical machinery	4.1	4.4	0–12
Electrical machinery	5.8	8.3	0–15
of which: electrical equipment	(7.2)	(10.6)	(0–15)
Motor vehicles	9.5	9.4	4.4–22
Footwear	11.7	13.5	4.6–20
Toys	6.7	6.8	0–10.5
Memorandum items:			
All industrial products	6.4	5.6	
Raw materials (excl. petroleum)	1.1	1.2	

Source: GATT tariff study as quoted in GATT (1991).

machinery and chemicals, and small improvements in the case of textile-clothing products (GATT, 1994).

Nominal rates on finished products, however, have been shown to underestimate badly the real protective effect of the tariffs used. Given the much lower rates applied to imports of raw materials (and intermediates), effective tariff rates on the imports of finished products by the EU are typically double in value or more (Hine, 1991). The restrictive impact of EU effective rates of protection is strongly emphasised in Hiemenz (1993) and in GATT (1993).

In addition to above-average (fixed) *ad valorem* tariffs, the import of many agricultural products covered by the CAP are subject to variable levies, which reflect the difference between the minimum domestic prices ensured to farmers and the lower international market prices (plus *ad valorem* tariffs, where applicable).[17] These tariffs are thus designed to insulate the domestic markets from outside competition, and when applied to homogenous products are virtually prohibitive.[18] They therefore render the EU market almost impermeable to imports, affording domestic producers the strongest type of protection possible, short of outright bans on imports. Moreover, variable levies exert their protective effects *vis-à-vis* the exports of all developing countries. The preferences that are granted even to the most favoured of them (the ACPs) do not extend to variable levies. They apply only to the *ad valorem* tariffs charged simultaneously on some of these imports. The same is true for transition economies in Central and Eastern Europe. EU variable levies are not eliminated by the Europe Agreements, but only reduced to a predetermined percentage. Preferences are restricted by quotas and ceilings, increased by 35 per cent with respect to the pre-agreement levels, but still from very small bases (Messerlin, 1992).

Aside from tariffs, the EU has used in the 1980s and early 1990s a variety of NTBs to protect domestic productions: import quotas, restrictions on exports applied 'voluntarily' by foreign producers (the so-called voluntary export restraints or VERs), surveillance measures set at both the level of the EU and of single member states, antidumping and (a few) antisubsidy actions, plus a variety of administrative rules, health, packaging and other standards at least in part designed to make domestic markets less easily penetrable by imports. The more observable and identifiable NTBs used by the EU are shown by category of products to which they were applied during the 1980s and by most affected countries in Table 6.5. The major sectors of concentration, as in the case of above-average tariffs, appear again to be agricultural and food products, textile and clothing products, automobiles and electronics. In the last decade, steel and footwear have been subject to numerous VERs, which affected mostly the NIEs and the CEECs. Antidumping actions were instead most numerous against steel and chemical imports from the same countries, followed by actions on electronics and textile fibres, the first affecting the Asian countries and the second all of the developing countries and CEECs. The geographical reach of this group of NTBs (VERs

Table 6.5 Utilisation of EU non-tariff barriers by most affected sectors and countries*, 1980–90

Sector *Instrument*	*Agricultural & food products*	*Textiles & clothing*	*Footwear*	*Automobiles & transport equipment*	*Electronics*	*Steel*	*Chemicals and fertilisers*
Surveillance measures		Mediterranean countries Central and East Europe	Korea Taiwan All third countries	Japan	Japan Korea Taiwan	Central and East Europe	Central and East Europe
Quotas[1]	Industrial countries Developing countries	Non-ACP developing countries Central and East Europe	Korea Taiwan China	Japan Korea	Korea Taiwan	Central and East Europe	Central and East Europe
VERs	Industrial countries Developing countries Central and East Europe		Korea Other developing countries Japan	Japan	Japan Korea Other Developing countries Central and East Europe	Japan Korea Brazil Central and East Europe	
Antidumping actions		Developing countries Eastern Europe			Japan Asian NICs	Mexico Brazil Other developing countries Central and East Europe	Central and East Europe Asia NICs Industrial countries

Notes

* Coverage is indicative only of most frequently affected countries or groups.

[1] The country coverage of natural quotas cannot be ascertained with precision outside the motor-vehicle and the textile-clothing sectors. The row is therefore incomplete.

Sources: See Table 6.3 and GATT (1991 and 1993).

and antidumping) was thus quite varied. The rest of NTBs (mostly surveillance and import quotas) used by the EU applied prevalently to textile and clothing imports from non-associated developing countries and to steel and chemicals from CEECs and NIS[19]

The qualitative conclusion of a trade protectionism (both tariff and non-tariff) largely directed at keeping out of EU markets products originating from non-associated developing countries, and in some cases in transition economies, is therefore hard to avoid when looking at the extensive overlapping (and sometimes cumulation) of restrictions on imports of such commodities as food, textiles, clothing, consumer electronics and footwear.

Also quite apparent from both Tables 6.4 and 6.5 are the key characteristics of the sectors most frequently targeted by EU protection: outside agriculture, they are with few exceptions those in which productions are most labour-intensive (which generally means also those in which value added per person is lower than average), and where competitive advantages of established EU producers, stemming from technological progress and market size, were generally on the wane relative to new entrants from outside the EU. By and large, these are technologically mature sectors, capable of obtaining protection because of their importance as generators of employment, sometimes for especially vulnerable categories of workers.

Trade protectionism in the 1970s and 1980s went hand in hand with continued preferential treatment for developing countries, and with the enlargement of the reach of the tariff preferences on imports granted to them by the EU. Not only were more countries added to the list of the beneficiaries of Lomé preferences in both the 1970s and 1980s, but import preferences granted to Mediterranean countries were also expanded in scope during the 1980s. In the early 1990s GSP treatment was extended to the CEECs, and subsequently to the NIS as well. A revised standard system of GSPs was introduced by the EU in 1995. The new system abolished all quotas and ceiling previously limiting the extent of tariff preferences, and substituted them with a system of tariffs modulated according to the 'sensitivity' of the imports. Country graduation from the preferences will now take place sector by sector on the basis of objective criteria (Commission of the European Communities, 1994). These trade policy decisions eased the access to market of their beneficiaries outside the specific areas of agriculture and textiles-clothing, even though the value of the preferences will continue to decline in the 1990s, with the progressive reduction of MFN rates to which they apply. On imports of agricultural and textile-clothing products only ACPs and, to a lower extent, the Mediterranean countries obtained some preferential advantages. To be noted, however, is that the ACP countries produce and export few agricultural products that compete with CAP-protected ones (apart from tobacco, vegetable oils, animal feeds, beef and sugar, whose exports to the EU take place under special import regimes). Their capacity to export textiles (with the most notable exception of Mauritius) is also quite limited. Typically, instead, even privileged developing countries such as those of the Maghreb and Mashreq, which have a much greater export supply capacity in textiles and clothing than the ACPs, are subject to a surveillance regime in these product categories, despite the free entry for *all* their exports of manufactures into the EU that the Cooperation Agreements granted them. Rules of origin, moreover, differentially applied depending on the source, can further restrict the entry of manufactured exports of developing countries into EU markets.

EU TRADE POLICIES AND THE URUGUAY ROUND

After the tariff adjustments negotiated in the Tokyo Round of trade liberalisation were completed in the early 1980s, the EU kept roughly constant its tariff treatment of imports from non-associated developing countries, at both the MFN and GSP levels. Under Lomé III and IV the preferences granted to ACP countries also remained practically unchanged.[20] Much of the changes in trade policies can be detected in the field of NTB, even if clear trends during the 1980s are difficult to discern. An increase in the frequency of use of all NTBs (against all trade partners) seems to have occurred in the first half, followed by a decline in the second. In the 1990s, on the contrary, evidence is mounting that the utilisation of some of them (such as quantitative import restrictions and certain types of surveillance measures) has abated. Yet, the evidence available is not only incomplete (in the case of VERs, for example), but also difficult to interpret. NTBs are notoriously difficult to evaluate in terms of their restrictive effects on trade. They are also vastly different in their product and country reach. Being non-homogeneous in terms of effects and used, in addition, in a highly discriminatory fashion, i.e. to restrict the imports of specific products from specific countries, they do not easily lend themselves even to simple aggregate coverage analysis. Tracking NTBs by countries of destination is also very difficult in some cases.

Keeping these caveats in mind, one can look at the trends in the utilisation of NTBs by the EU.

Import quotas, national and EU-wide,[21] still constituted in the 1980s an important, if declining, segment of NTBs in the EU. Most of the national quotas represented the residuals of measures not eliminated by member states, or harmonised at the EU level, when they originally joined it. They affected mostly agricultural, textiles and clothing products and transport equipment, but also extended to footwear, electronics, steel and machinery. In 1987 there were quantitative restrictions applied by member countries on 519 4-digit trade categories. By 1992 this number had fallen to 283, 82 per cent of which enforced by Spain and Portugal. This tendency clearly reflected the requirements of internal market unification and the impossibility of enforcing national quotas in a single market (Grilli, 1995). Correspondingly, one can therefore notice in the same years a sharp drop in the number of restrictions to free entry authorised under Art. 115 (from 112 in 1990 to 19 in 1992), as well as in the number of surveillance measures authorised for the purpose of preventing trade deflection inside the EU (from 185 to 58 over the same period).[22]

EU-wide import quotas reflected the special import regimes in place for textiles and clothing and for steel, including imports coming from the state-trading countries of Europe, and a few other products such as footwear. They have traditionally been most numerous, within the context of the MFAs. Import quotas have declined in number and product coverage since 1985. This tendency was given a further boost by the conclusion of the Europe Agreements and the consequent elimination of all quotas on imports from the CEECs.[23] The decision taken with the Uruguay Round to dismantle the MFAs over the next ten years will most likely strengthen the ongoing trend towards the complete elimination of import quotas (which were always GATT-illegal).

There is ample evidence that the EU and its member states forced foreign competitors to adopt various types of VERs in order to protect domestic markets during both the 1970s and 1980s. But the very informality of VERs, some of which are negotiated directly by national industry concerns, makes it very difficult to document and track them on an ongoing basis. About 200 VERs were in force in the EU in the mid-1980s, covering a variety of products in the agriculture and food sectors, textiles and clothing, automobiles and electronics (ibid.). These measures mostly affected exports from Japan and other industrial countries, but non-associated developing countries (especially the NIEs of Asia) were also an important, if secondary target. By the end of the 1980s the number of VERs on exports to the EU was apparently declining, even if product and country coverage appear to have undergone only limited changes from previous years. The geographical reach of these measures was also shrinking at the start of the 1990s. EU-imposed VERs involved 69 countries in 1990, but only 47 in 1992, reinforcing the notion of a decline in the use of these trade-restricting measures by the EU. In terms of sectors, textiles (including clothing) and steel were the most affected by VERs (11 each), followed by electronics (8), machinery (6) and motor vehicles (5).

The most important factors behind the reduction in the number of VERs imposed by the EU on its trade partners was its near abandonment in early 1991 of the special import regime for steel (whose imports from all non-EFTA countries are, none the less, still subject to surveillance), and the consolidation into EU-wide arrangements of the import restraints enforced by single member states in footwear and motor vehicles.[24] The first consolidation affected the exports of Korea and Taiwan, while the second concerned only Japan. Japan, however, is still the country most frequently targeted by EU VERs: in machinery all measures apply to it; in electrical equipment half of them concern exports from this country, while the remainder applies to exports from South Korea; in motor vehicles all measures in force are still directed at restraining imports from Japan. South Korea and Taiwan have been and remain the most frequently targeted among developing countries, followed by Latin American nations in steel and by the CEECs in food, steel and electronics.

Antidumping procedures initiated in the EU have attracted a lot of attention in the 1980s because they appeared to be the instrument of choice for discouraging imports from specific sources. The number of complaints received by the Commission, as well as that of investigative actions initiated by it, did in fact increase substantially in the first part of the decade, fuelled by the economic recession in Europe, rising unemployment and persistent fluctuations in exchange rates. The surge in the number of complaints consolidated the suspicion that these legal procedures were being used to intimidate competitors. Both the number of actions initiated and of measures actually taken under the antidumping regulations of the EU, however, tapered off substantially in the second half of the 1980s. In the initial years of the 1990s there has been some resurgence of initiated antidumping cases, and of cases terminating with the imposition of antidumping measures (which in the past few years have practically become limited to import duties). Again, low economic activity and high unemployment seem to explain this trend. The stock of measures in force in the EU from the mid-1980s to the early 1990s has none the less declined from the peak of 207 in 1986 to 149 in 1992 (ibid.).

Over the 1980–92 period, the most affected imports were chemicals, electronics and steel, followed by textiles, mechanical and engineering products and by non-ferrous metal manufactures. In terms of targeted countries, between 1981 and 1985 actions initiated against non-associated developing countries were 48 per cent of the total. Between 1986 and 1990 they became 67 per cent of the total, followed by actions initiated against industrial countries (16 per cent) and CEECs (13 per cent). For this reason the antidumping practices of the EU became a matter of considerable concern not only for industrial countries like Japan, but also for many NIEs and other semi-industrialised developing countries. This also explains why all these countries were so keen on tightening antidumping procedures in the Uruguay Round of trade negotiations under GATT, a result that was only very partially achieved (Secchi, 1995).

Numbers of actions *per se* would mean little, without some idea of their trade effects, considering above all that EU antidumping actions have apparently affected no more than 2–3 per cent of its total imports. But the actions taken by the EU in this field during the first half of the 1980s, in addition to having an intimidatory effect on exporters, were shown to have been severe in intensity (with average antidumping duties of 23 per cent *ad valorem* charged on imports) and to have resulted in substantive and sustained reductions of imports (three years after the initiation of the investigations the quantity of imports of the products to which they applied was found to have fallen by 40 per cent). They were also shown to have caused trade diversion in the case of developing countries, both NIEs and non-NIEs (Messerlin, 1989).

Systematic inventories of frequencies in the use of NTBs by the EU conducted on both the number of tariff lines and the value of imports actually affected, show a similar picture of slowly declining incidence of NTBs. According to the available data, from 1981 to 1988 the percentage of trade covered by NTBs measures (broad definition) increased by nearly 3 percentage points (UNCTAD, 1990).[25] The increment in coverage that occurred was common to both agricultural and industrial products. It represented a continuation of the longer-term trend documented by Laird and Yeats (1990). Between 1988 and 1990 the trend shown by this indicator of coverage was substantially

Table 6.6 Frequency and import coverage ratios of non-tariff measures[1] applied by the EU, 1988–93 (percentages)

SITC categories	*1988*	*1990*	*1991*	*1992*	*1993*
Frequency ratios					
All items	19.1	18.8	18.6	17.8	17.7
Food	37.4	37.4	37.3	37.0	35.9
Agricultural raw materials	3.4	3.3	3.3	3.2	3.1
Ores and metals	28.9	28.7	27.2	26.7	26.5
Fuels	11.4	9.8	9.8	9.8	9.8
Chemicals	4.9	4.6	4.3	4.1	4.1
Manufactures (excluding chemicals)	18.8	18.4	18.3	17.4	17.3
Import coverage ratios					
All items	19.0	19.9	19.7	19.0	18.3
Food	33.1	33.8	33.3	32.3	30.0
Agricultural raw materials	2.0	2.1	2.1	2.0	1.9
Ores and metals	22.4	22.4	21.4	21.0	21.2
Fuels	21.2	21.2	21.2	21.2	21.2
Chemicals	4.7	5.3	4.4	4.4	4.3
Manufactures (excluding chemicals)	18.8	20.4	20.5	19.3	18.6

Note

[1] Broad definition, including variable levies, quantitative restrictions, surveillance measures, antidumping and countervailing duties, para-tariff measures, surcharges, automatic licensing and price control measures.

Sources: UNCTAD data base on control measures.

flat. From 1990 to 1993, however, both the frequency and the import coverage ratios of EU NTBs (considered on the same 'broad' basis) showed a gradual, if small, decline, somewhat more pronounced in food and manufactured products. The import coverage ratio in food declined from 33.8 to 30 per cent. In manufactures it fell from 20.4 to 18.6 per cent. Similar declines are shown in the case of food also by the frequency ratio (Table 6.6).

Whether the moderate decline in the coverage of NTBs since the late 1980s constitutes a significant change in the direction of EU trade polices towards non-associated developing countries, or simply a single step adjustment largely brought about by the implementation of the SEM and by the requirements of the Uruguay Round negotiations (such as the gradual dismantling of the MFAs), is still unclear. Less difficult to characterise is the change in the direction of EU trade policies towards the CEECs. Notwithstanding the fine print of the Europe Agreements and the safeguard clauses built into them, trade protectionism against the CEECs was strongly and willingly lowered from the end of the 1980s.

According to recent estimates (Kaminski, 1994), the industrial product provisions of the Europe Agreements cover about 80 per cent of the signatory countries' exports to the EU and improve significantly access to its market. In 1992, their first year of application to Hungary, Poland and the former Czechoslovakia, the Agreements freed about 50 per cent of the exports of these countries to the EU. The equivalent share for Bulgaria and Romania in 1993 is estimated at 54 per cent and 39 per cent respectively. Over the first five-year period of their application the Agreements are expected to let free trade with the EU increase to 80 per cent in the case of the former Czechoslovakia, to 60 per cent for Hungary and 70 per cent for Poland.

Trade with the countries of the former Soviet Union was also liberalised and GSP treatment extended to them. The average weighted EU tariff on imports from Russia, for example, is now about 1 per cent and the EU has become the largest trading partner for Russia, accounting in 1994 for about 35 per cent of its total trade (and for about a quarter of that of the other NIS).

PROTECTIONISM AND TRADE PERFORMANCE OF THE LDCS AND CEECS

The review of available evidence does not, therefore, support the presumption often stated, or the conclusion otherwise arrived at, of steadily increasing non-tariff protectionism in the EU during the 1980s. *Prime facie*, our analysis of trends in the use of NTBs during the past ten to fifteen years tends to support, if weakly, the notion of a change in the opposite direction since the late 1980s. Yet, because of the intrinsic weakness of the direct evidence, a review of the trade performance of developing countries and CEECs during this period assumes particular importance, because it can either yield additional, if indirect, evidence in support of the inference that a change in an established tendency of EU trade policies may have occurred, or cast additional doubts on the meaning of NTBs coverage indices, and thus on the real direction of trade policies in Europe. Naturally, *ex-post* results concerning trade flows or market shares cannot *per se* either prove or disprove the direction of EU trade policies towards developing countries, given that actual outcomes are determined by a variety of market factors, among which changes in trade regimes may be important, but not necessarily dominant. Presumably changes in other determinants such as incomes, relative prices of imports and market structures might also be relevant. This is certainly the case for much of CEECs, whose trade was forcibly reoriented towards the West by the collapse of previous trade arrangements within COMECON and whose performance was strongly affected by large changes in domestic incomes and in the relative prices of traded and non-traded goods. Export outcomes can, however, either be found consistent or inconsistent with the presumption of increasing NTBs in the markets of destination.

Analysis of the shares held by non-oil developing countries in EU markets by main import sectors (i.e. by main SITC product categories) highlights a composite picture, but indicates that developing countries' gains, in addition to being geographically widespread, also spanned across a wide range of products exported to the EU. In fact, aside from agricultural and food commodities, which compete with those produced in the EU and are subject to (often prohibitive) CAP-type protection, and non-ferrous metals and fuels, where developing countries' exports were in part displaced by domestic EU supplies, the share of extra-EU imports coming from developing countries increased in almost all other product categories (Table 6.7).

Yet, the evidence that can be derived from import data pertaining to fairly wide product categories cannot be taken as strongly indicative of the insulating power of protective regimes. Imports from developing countries could in fact be increasing in a falling total market because of displacement of imports from other sources. Moreover, as already noted, market access is only one of the factors influencing import shares. The large size of the import categories considered here leaves considerable scope to intra-category product switching by exporters, which can help them circumvent specific protection, such as non-tariff protection generally is. Most importantly, evidence derived from import shares is partial because it has to do with only one component of EU demand: the part that is met from outside. Only if it can be shown that extra-EU imports maintained at least a constant share of EU domestic consumption, do rising shares of developing countries' imports also signify a gain in overall market presence. This correspondence can be verified, at least for the 1980s, by looking first at the shares of all extra-EU imports in total apparent consumption of different categories of products (Commission of the European Communities, 1993a, table 89).

Table 6.7 Share of imports from developing countries in EU imports by sector[1] (percentages)

SITC categories	*1969–71*	*1979–81*	*1989–91*
Competing food and agricultural products	39.1	40.0	38.3
Non-competing tropical beverages	95.0	96.6	93.9
Oils and fats	49.0	66.5	45.4
Fuels	38.9	33.5	33.3
Chemicals	9.6	13.0	11.1
Footwear and leather goods	49.4	44.6	53.0
Rubber, cork and paper products	4.3	7.7	9.1
Iron and steel	6.5	5.6	12.6
Non-ferrous metals	52.9	39.5	40.2
Metal manufactures	5.4	11.1	19.1
Electrical machinery	4.7	16.0	22.6
Non-electrical machinery	1.6	2.4	8.6
Instruments	3.0	12.0	11.2
Furniture	25.5	28.1	32.0
Textiles	37.2	41.8	43.5
Clothing	59.1	68.5	76.5
Other manufacturers	15.0	19.3	27.5

Note
[1] Total imports exclude intra-EC Trade.
Source: COMTRADE data bank.

Analysis of import-consumption shares from the EU or the UNCTAD data base (UNCTAD, 1987, 1992) shows that, apart from food and chemicals, increasing penetration of EU markets by imports was general in the past decade. Given this tendency, growing shares of extra-EU imports from non-oil developing countries should have translated for the most part also in increasing shares of total consumption of the same products.

The picture of a favourable performance by developing countries' exports – in EU markets since the early 1980s – that uniformly emerges from trade and consumption data is more consistent with the notion of a stable or declining trend in trade protectionism by the EU, as it emerges from our survey of trade policies actually followed during this period, than with the presumption, or the opposite inference, of rising non-tariff protectionism inside it. Put more directly, if non-tariff protectionism increased in the EU during the 1980s, this tendency was not sufficient to stem the export market performance of non-oil developing countries, which outside agricultural and fuel sectors were generally able to increase their share of both extra-EU imports and of EU apparent consumption. EU markets thus remained permeable to exports by developing countries, despite the existence of numerous NTBs.

The trade performance of the CEEs,[26] lackluster for many years, began to improve in the aggregate at the very end of the 1980s, in concomitance with the generally improving access of their exports to European markets. The overall share of these countries in extra-EU imports, which had fallen to about 2 per cent by the end of the 1970s, remained unchanged at such a low level until 1989. Since then it rose steadily to over 4 per cent in just three years. In EU markets these countries did better as exporters in practically all product categories, both directly competing (food products and manufactures) and non-competing (crude materials, non-ferrous metals) with EU domestic productions. The only exception was fuels, where their market shares remained unchanged. Liberalisation of imports by the EU appears to have helped particularly in textiles, clothing, footwear, furniture, steel and metal manufactures (Table 6.8). These are mostly labour-intensive export products on which the labour cost advantages

Table 6.8 Share of imports from Central and Eastern Europe in EU imports by sector[1] (percentages)

SITC categories	*1976*	*1980*	*1988*	*1990*	*1992*
Competing food and agricultural products	3.0	4.4	4.8	6.5	6.1
Crude materials (excl.fuels)	2.5	2.1	2.5	2.8	4.2
Fuels	5.8	1.0	1.3	1.1	1.2
Chemicals	6.0	3.4	3.0	3.8	4.4
Footwear and leather goods	4.1	4.3	3.0	3.9	6.5
Rubber, cork and paper products	1.5	1.9	1.6	2.3	4.3
Iron and steel	15.4	9.2	7.0	9.5	12.5
Non-ferrous metals	3.9	3.6	3.4	3.5	6.7
Metal manufactures	4.2	3.3	2.9	4.2	8.3
Electrical machinery	2.6	2.0	1.1	2.1	3.0
Non-electrical machinery	5.7	2.7	1.5	1.9	2.7
Transport equipment	1.0	2.1	1.3	0.8	2.5
Furniture	3.3	11.1	8.9	10.7	17.4
Textiles	6.8	3.4	3.0	3.3	4.7
Clothing	4.8	7.2	4.4	5.1	7.9
Other manufactures	3.2	1.3	0.8	0.8	1.4

Note
[1] Total imports exclude intra EC-trade.
Source: As Table 6.7.

enjoyed by Central European countries weighed very strongly, once access to market became less encumbered. For these countries, broad-based improvements in market positions correspond in time and product composition to broad-based liberalisation of imports implemented by the EU since 1990.

STRUCTURE AND EVOLUTION OF EU AID POLICIES

The external aid policies of the EU began in 1958 with the first European Development Fund (EDF), contributed by the member states. The Implementing Convention attached to the Treaty of Rome had defined the terms and extent of the EU's involvement in development aid (Cosgrove-Twitchett, 1978). Like trade preferences, aid from the Community had from the start, and maintained through time, a strong regional bias. It was concentrated on the former colonial possessions of the member states in Africa. For nearly twenty years, the expansion of beneficiaries remained strictly in the domain of former colonies, first those of France, Belgium and Italy and subsequently those of the United Kingdom.

Again, like trade preferences, EU aid was first unilaterally granted, then negotiated with the beneficiaries in the context of the Conventions of Yaoundé (of 1963 and 1969) and Lomé (of 1975, 1980, 1985 and 1990), even though in practice it was the EU that made 'a final offer', which was then accepted by the counterparts. It was not until 1976–8 that development assistance in the form of aid was extended to the low-income countries of Asia and Latin America and to the countries of the Mediterranean (the ALAMED countries).[27] Aid transfers to the countries of CEECs started in the early 1990s. The 'transcendence' of purely regional cooperation took a long time and was never complete. Africa still absorbs well over half of the total EU aid disbursed annually, a share about the same as that held in the bilateral aid of EU member countries. History evidently still matters a good deal in EU development cooperation.

Together with trade preferences, economic aid was to foster 'the economic and social development' of the associated countries and territories (Art. 131 of the Treaty of Rome), an objective that was solemnly reaffirmed and generalised after Maastricht. The generalisation has to do with the extension of the basic goal of EU development cooperation to the promotion of 'the sustainable economic and social development' of all developing countries, and particularly of the most disadvantaged ones, and with the addition of another objective, namely the contribution to 'a smooth and gradual integration of [all] developing countries in the world economy' (Art. 130u of the amended treaty). The balance in EU development cooperation policy between social and economic objectives was further emphasised in the same article of the treaty by making the fight against poverty in developing countries a specific priority. In a potentially major innovation, the development cooperation policy of the EU was then specifically singled out for its expected contribution to the development and consolidation 'of democracy, of the rule of law', and the respect of 'human rights and of fundamental freedoms' (ibid.).

The EU always emphasised some key aspects of its aid policies: the additionality of its aid with respect to the bilateral assistance supplied by member states, the contractual nature of most of its aid, the participation of recipients in its administration ('cogestion'), and the partnership between the EU and the recipients that aid contributed to form. Particularly important was the EU-African partnership, from which Africa was supposed to gain accelerated development and the EU security of supply for raw materials. Before the Maastricht Treaty, the EU had also strongly emphasised the neutral nature of its development cooperation, intended sometimes as respect of recipients' development choices, sometimes as lack of conditionality attached to aid, and other times as absence of political aims in the EU's aid transfers (Cosgrove Twitchett, 1978; Lister, 1988; Grilli, 1991, 1993). The claim of additionality, very strong at the start of EU aid cooperation with associated countries and always hard to prove, was in time quietly dropped. Stronger than average participation of the recipients in the management of EU aid flows has not yielded better than average project implementation, with respect to either (good) bilateral aid or other multilateral aid. What it seems to have ensured is somewhat more certain aid flows, a much more modest objective, especially if compared to that of enhanced aid effectiveness (Grilli, 1993). Conditionality was introduced explicitly in development aid to ACP countries starting in the mid-1980s, when aid for structural adjustment started to be extended within the framework of the third Lomé Convention. Any pretence of a lack of political goals in EU development cooperation was dropped after the Maastricht Treaty, which introduced a clear-cut ideological and political dimension in the supply of aid from the EU. Respect of individual country development strategies and policies, a sensitive issue in the 1960s and 1970s, had, however, become progressively less contentious in the 1980s, with the gradual acceptance (or tolerance) by developing countries of the open-economy paradigm favoured and sponsored by the major international organizations.

Recent EU pronouncements on development cooperation have emphasised the needs for economic restructuring in Sub-Saharan Africa, and thus the role of aid in support of structural adjustment. They have also stressed the importance of enhanced local participation in project design and implementation (e.g. in Lomé IV) and of regional cooperation, to transcend what the Commission calls 'purely geographical considerations' in the programming of aid (Commission of the European Communities, 1992, 1993b). Finally, depending on the recipient countries, they also stressed the goals of private sector development and of protection of the environment (in both North Africa and Latin America), and of poverty alleviation (in the least developed countries of Asia).

For reasons of history, expediency and politics, the EU's aid has always been unevenly spread among different regions, quite independently of their respective needs, however measured. South and central Asian countries, for example, where the bulk of world poverty was always located, received a share of EU aid inferior to that of the Mediterranean region, where average incomes were much greater and poverty much less prominent. In per capita terms, interregional differences in aid receipts were even wider. Africa was always the privileged recipient of EU aid, even though its relative share of the total declined in the 1970s and early 1980s. The Commission, in reassessing EU development cooperation policy in 'the run-up to 2000', recognized that the volume of EU ODA is unequally spread amongst the different regions of the world, but also indicated that 'it is likely to remain so' in the future (Commission of the European Communities, 1993c, p. 16). A further rebalancing of EU aid on a geographical or need basis does not seem, therefore, to be in store even after the emergence of CEECs as an important new claimant. This position of the Commission is reflected in the results of the recent negotiations among EU members over the replenishment of the EDF for the remainder of Lomé IV (from 1995 to 2000). The financial endowment of the fund was increased by over ECU 2 billion (with respect to the previous five years of operation of the convention), which seems to keep its real value constant, but with nearly one half of the increment coming from the new EU members. This outcome can be interpreted as a demonstration of the influence over the entire membership that the regionalist inside the EU still holds, although one could also expect that its influence will be diluted in time by the enlarged presence among the members of countries that have a globalist perspective in aid policies.

EU aid has, however, been concentrated not only regionally but also intra-regionally. This aspect of the geographical–political distribution of aid from the EU is best exemplified by Sub-Saharan Africa, whose ten largest recipients (out of a total of 47) have obtained nearly 49 per cent of all discretionary aid under the first three Lomé Conventions, with the next five accounting for another 17 per cent of the total. STABEX transfers, which constitute compensatory payments to eligible countries for shortfalls in export earnings from specified primary products, and which make up for the bulk of non-discretionary aid to Sub-Saharan Africa, are distributed even more unevenly than discretionary (or programme) aid: the first ten largest recipients had nearly 70 per cent of these transfers during the first three Lomé Conventions. In Lomé IV the country concentration of STABEX transfers has increased even further. From the commodity standpoint, coffee and cocoa account for about 80 per cent of all compensatory payments (Court of Auditors of the EC/EU, 1995).

Even when receipts are corrected for population in the recipient countries, and the very small and very large countries are excluded from the sample,[28] EU discretionary aid to Sub-Saharan Africa still looks unevenly spread, with flows ranging on average from ECU 10 to ECU 30 per capita during Lomé III, without any apparent strong correlation with either the structural characteristics or the economic performance of the recipient countries. There seemed to be a clear preference for francophone Africa in the first two Lomé Conventions, which was substantially corrected in the third.

A more systematic analysis of the geographical distribution of EU aid to ACP countries (thus including the associated ones in the Caribbean and Pacific) indicates that both donor interests and recipient needs have a bearing on it. The country distribution (measured on a per capita basis) is related to the human development level (measured by the United Nations Development Programme Index) of the recipients, as well as to their relative importance as export markets for the members of the EU: the lower the level of the index of development in a recipient country and the higher are the member countries' exports to it, the more is the EU aid that it receives. There is also a bias against large countries present in the distribution. In the 1980s there was one in favour of highly indebted recipients (Grilli and Riess, 1992). This pattern of 'determinants' of the country distribution of

EU aid is quite similar to that shown by the bilateral aid of EU member countries, indicating that the EU did not exercise leadership in aid distribution. The explanatory value of these models, however, is comparatively low, which indicates that other factors, relevant in the distribution of development aid, are possibly left out. Among them, some authors have emphasised the importance of political–colonial linkages of the recipients with important EU members or, by inference, the value of previous connections with the EU (Anyadike-Danes and Anyadike-Danes, 1992).

Aid by the EU to the CEECs, and to some of the countries of the former Soviet Union (so far mostly Russia and the Ukraine), started in 1991, with new commitments in excess of ECU 1 billion for financial aid and ECU 350 million in food aid, equivalent to one-third of total aid committed that year (here including the exceptional assistance to countries most affected by the Gulf crisis). It remained at about 30 per cent of total aid commitments in the next three years. Despite the substantial increment in budgetary aid decided by the EU in the early 1990s, the accommodation of the foreign assistance needs of the CEECs and NIS, plus the substantial increment of aid to the Mediterranean countries previously approved, represented a challenge of such magnitude that could only be met without some redistribution among beneficiaries. The EU, however, made a strong effort to keep at least constant, in nominal terms, aid disbursements to most of the traditional recipients. Aid payments to two regions (South-Central Asia and Latin America) came down slightly, while Sub-Saharan Africa held its own in absolute terms. Clearly, the percentage distribution had to change appreciably, with gains in shares posted by Europe, and losses by practically all other regions (Table 6.9).

Since disbursements are influenced by past commitments and by delays in making payments for reasons often outside the control of the donor, new commitments of aid should give a better picture of the changes in intentions that might have occurred in the distribution of EU aid in the early 1990s. The geographical distribution of EU aid commitments, however, is only partially known. What can be reconstructed over time are the commitments of financial aid of the EU, with the major exception of the special aid programmes. Food aid distributions, moreover, are not regularly reported and are thus known only with approximation and long time lags. In addition, one must consider that financial aid committed in 1991 was strongly affected by the amount (over ECU 500 million) directed that year (and only that year) to compensate countries for the negative effects

Table 6.9 European Union aid and regional distribution, 1987–94

	1987–9 (average)	*1990*	*1991*	*1992*	*1993*	*1994*
A. ODA disbursed (million $)	2207	2563	3478	4170	3637	4330
B. ODA distribution (% of total)						
Sub-Saharan Africa	59.1	64.8	53.4	60.5	53.1	na
South and Central Africa	10.4	10.6	6.6	4.9	4.2	na
Other Asia and Oceania	8.2	5.2	4.5	2.2	5.3	na
North Africa and Middle East	10.6	7.6	18.1	14.0	13.6	na
Latin America	11.7	11.8	9.3	8.2	6.7	na
CEECs and NIS	0.0	0.0	8.1	10.3	17.1	na
Total	100.0	100.0	100.0	100.0	100.0	
C. Aid committed[1] *(million ECU)*						
	1912[2]	1469	3013	4074	4109	4405
D. Distribution of commitments (% of total)						
Asia and Latin America	19.3	25.8	15.5	10.7	15.4	11.8
Mediterranean region	10.5	14.9	3.7[3]	9.5	9.7	9.8
ACP countries (Lomé)	70.2	59.3	41.0[3]	50.4	39.0	45.0
CEEC's and CIS	0.0	0.0	39.8	29.4	35.8	33.3
Total	100.0	100.0	100.0	100.0	100.0	100.0

Notes

1 Financial aid only, excluding 'other cooperation measures' and Gulf-related aid in 1991 and 1992.

2 The figures are for 1989.

3 Figures do not include aid committed by the EU to the countries affected by the Gulf War.

Sources: OECD, Annual Reports on Development Cooperation, various years, Paris, (for lines A and B); Court of Auditors of the EC/EU (1994); and Commission of the European Union (1995a, 1995b) (for lines C and D).

of the Gulf crisis. With these caveats in mind, the distribution of financial commitments to 1994 that can be reconstructed from regularly published data seems to indicate that large changes have occurred in the shares of aid destined to Europe, compared to those going to all other regions (Table 6.9). Some have seen in this redistribution of EU aid (in relative terms) a response to both the need of sustaining the transition to democracy and market economy of an area holding considerable strategic value for Western Europe, and to that of preventing socially disruptive migrations from it in case of failure of economic and political reforms. Such interpretation seems to find support also in the special attention paid by the EU in terms of aid (and trade policies) to North Africa, another region from which large migrations to Europe could occur.

While a common trade policy towards developing countries was a direct and automatic result of the decision made by the original EU members to establish a customs union among themselves, a common aid policy was not required by it. Such policy developed largely as the result of circumstances facing key members at the time of the Treaty of Rome and from the desire felt by some of them to maintain over time a special relationship with their former colonies. Aid was almost certainly one of the elements that cemented European associationism with Africa (Lister, 1988), and perhaps a key one. This factor may help explain why member countries of the EU agreed on a common aid policy at the start, but kept it separate from their own. There is in fact a paradox in EU aid: it was a common policy that was not mandated by the establishment of the customs union and one that lasted for a long time, but which did not foster integration of member countries' national policies. In this sense one can see in it a failure to create shared goals and common practices, which could in time have been translated into coherent and common behaviours at the national level. But one can see in it also the strength of the limits to the aid-sharing compromise reached in Rome in 1957 that were maintained by some EU members. That compromise might have been judged necessary to launch European economic integration in the 1950s, but was certainly not considered appropriate to shape uniform aid policies for the whole of Europe.

EU aid policies did not even lead to a *de facto* convergence of national policies. Dutch and Scandinavian national aid remained strongly oriented towards the needs of the recipients and was global in reach. French, and for a long time UK, aid policies continued to be largely driven by national interests (commercial and political) and regionally focused, while Italian and German policies straddled across the principal motivations and geographical aims of the others (Grilli and Daveri, 1993). The Commission, after an earnest effort made in the early 1970s at improving aid coordination with member states, practically abandoned even this modest goal, except for having the Council sanction in the early 1980s the non-policy of 'a la carte', voluntary coordination. Since then, it took another ten years for the Commission to revisit the issue of coordination of aid policies with its member countries, even after the Maastricht Treaty had enshrined this goal in Art. 130x. The Commission made some modest and sensible proposals to the Council about priorities and procedures (Commission of the European Communities, 1993e, 1993f), but got only a mixed response from it. Even policy coordination is proceeding very slowly within the EU. The formulation of a common aid policy, required to improve both the economic effectiveness and the political reach of the aid disbursed, in a situation of severe scarcity of resources, is nowhere in sight within the EU.

CONCLUSIONS

There is an apparent paradox between a rather widespread perception of rising EU protectionism, of greater inwardness in the EU's trade outlook, of deflection of interest towards those nations lying on the boundaries of Europe, of possible trade diversion due to the progressive enlargement of the Continental European free-trade area, on the one hand, and the reality of continued, wide-ranging penetration of EU markets by manufactures exported by a growing number of developing and CEECs, on the other. The explanation may have to do with the lags normally encountered in adjusting to a changed reality. It may also have been due to the difficulty faced by outsiders in assessing EU trade policy, and in part to outside preconceptions, or fears, generated at a time when EU policies appeared to be focused on the strengthening of the domestic market. The reality of continued market penetration of EU markets by manufactures originating in developing and transition economies, almost irrespective of trade preferences, and in some cases despite NTBs, may well signify that supply conditions matter the most in ensuring export success. The poor export performance of ACP countries tends to support the same conclusion (Agarwal, Dippl and Langhammer, 1985), and the ancillary notion that preferential access to the market *per se* does not make much difference. Such access must be accompanied by the expansion of export capacity at home.

In the area of aid policies, the extension of the EU mandate to the CEECs and the nations of the former Soviet Union also generated fears of aid diversion among the associated developing countries, at a time, moreover, when aid-giving capacity was under strain. Despite some redistribution of aid to the new European claimants in the early 1990s, the EU has made a substantial effort to sustain aid flows to the ACPs and to increase those going to the Mediterranean countries.

Even if EU trade and aid policies since the mid-1980s appear to have been more benign, in both intentions and results, than anticipated by some (most?), recent trends have not yet changed significantly the overall posture of the EU *vis-à-vis* developing countries. Nor do the changes that have intervened so far mean that a new and stable trend in trade policies started in the late 1980s. EU cooperation policies with developing countries are still highly fragmented, going in opposite directions, and subject to considerable risk of change. EU trade policies, moreover, are more protectionist *vis-à-vis* the NIEs (of both the first and second generation) than the rest of the developing world, and more protective of certain sectors than others. This reflects a variety of domestic situations, but also betrays a persistent mercantilistic posture, characterised by fear of competition and by an ingrained penchant for managed trade relations.

As for the durability of the recent trends in EU trade and aid policies, the factors that have a bearing on it are many and contrasting in their respective effects. On the side of continuity in trade policy militate both the results of the Uruguay Round and the likely durability of the SEM. The Uruguay Round will further reduce tariffs on imports (and the value of tariff preferences, making the overall tariff regime more uniform) and progressively dismantle the MFA regulations of trade in textiles, making the EU markets more accessible to exports from developing countries. As a result of the Uruguay Round, the access to EU markets for exports of temperate-zone agricultural products will not be significantly improved (except for the substitution of variable levies with specific duties), but a fairly fundamental reform of the CAP was none the less set in motion by the Round and future relaxation of import regimes for competing agriculture was made more probable. The virtual elimination of national import restrictions and the harmonisation of technical standards that occurred within the EU as a result of the SEM should also improve the entry of developing countries' exports. Finally, depending on how the antidumping regime negotiated in the Uruguay Round evolves, the ease with which this category of measures can be used against imports from developing countries may be reduced. The single market, moreover, is a reality and was achieved without any evident backlash inside the EU.

On the negative side, it is puzzling that Art. 115 was kept in the treaty even after the full unification of the internal market, which should have made it totally redundant. The Europe Agreements with the CEECs contain numerous protectionist escape clauses. There are safeguard provisions built into them, which can be invoked in case of either serious injury to EU producers or serious sectoral difficulties leading to a significant deterioration of economic conditions in any region of the EU. There are specific safeguard clauses concerning textiles and the possibility of a return to managed trade in specific sectors (such as steel) is in no way diminished by the content of the Agreements. Contingent protectionism seems to be still alive and well in the EU. There will also remain within it a strong propensity to strengthen the existing 'new commercial policy instrument', the seldom used capacity, established in 1984, to combat third countries' illicit trade practices, at least as long as US trade policies will continue to be aggressive and prone towards bilateralism. Moreover, exchange rate fluctuations, if pronounced and long-lasting, will affect the propensity to use NTBs inside the EU. Finally, internal economic conditions will also matter. The direction of EU trade policy has been shown to be responsive to them. The persistence of very high unemployment rates does not augur well for liberal trade policies in Europe. The spreading to the old continent of the aggressive bilateralism now practised in the new cannot, therefore, be excluded.

Aid in general is also being increasingly questioned in Europe, and while both transfers to North Africa and Central Europe, and improved market access for their exports seem to be accepted by the general public in part as substitutes for migration, the strength and stability of these relationships is uncertain at best. Recent changes in the direction of EU trade policies and aid policies, though positive and encouraging for developing countries and economies in transition, are still modest in size, young in age and reversible in direction.

Notes

1. The size of the European trading bloc varied over time, and quite substantially due to its changing membership (see the previous chapter). These changes had a bearing on trade (and aid) flows, and must therefore be taken into consideration in any quantitative analysis of these phenomena. Throughout this chapter, unless otherwise specified, we will refer to the EU in its EC(12) configuration.
2. The Western European countries outside the EU are Switzerland, Norway, Iceland and Liechtenstein. The last three, however, are part of the European Economic Area (EEA) which came into being at the beginning of 1994 (see the previous and following chapters). This means

in practice that the single market of the EU is fully open to them as far as goods, services, capital and people. They retain, however, control of their trade relations with non-EU countries.

3. These are Albania, Bulgaria, the Czech Republic, Estonia, Hungary, Latvia, Lithuania, Poland, Romania, Slovakia and Slovenia.
4. Armenia, Azerbaijan, Belarus, Georgia, Kazakhstan, Kyrghyzstan, Moldova, Russia, Turkmenistan, Ukraine and Uzbekistan.
5. The largest part of the aid resources administered by the EU has none the less come from direct contributions of member states to the European Development Fund (EDF), utilised to fund transfers to associated developing countries in the context of the conventions governing relations with them. Aid to non-associated developing countries, and more recently, to CEECS and NIS has instead come from the EU General Budget.
6. This is the definition of aid used by the development Assistance Committee (DAC) of the Organisation for Economic Cooperation and Development (OECD).
7. GATT has now been succeeded by the World Trade Organisation (WTO).
8. The White Paper of the Commission listed three objectives for the single market: (i) enlargement of the effective size of the European market, (ii) ensuring its growth; and (iii) ensuring its flexibility to realise optimal distribution of resources (Commission of the European Communities, 1985, p. 5). Openness was nowhere mentioned.
9. Actually, the failure of the EU to focus upon and clarify the external trade effects of the SEM may have contributed to the raising of outside fears of a more protectionist turn in its trade policies (Hine, 1991, p. 80). Balassa (1989) shows how public statements of European leaders over policy intentions were quite varied, but on the whole not reassuring to outsiders.
10. This obviously implied some redistribution of aid among recipients, about which more will be said in the section on ‘Structure and evolution of EU aid policies’.
11. EU multilateral aid is about 15 per cent of bilateral aid. This share has not changed even after the emergence of the CEECs and the NIS as aid recipients.
12. See, for example, Commission of the European Communities (1993b). Until the mid-1990s the underlying principles of coordination between the EU and its member states in the field of aid were those set out by the Council in June 1984 and November 1985, the most important of which was ‘à la carte’ coordination on a voluntary basis.
13. Pinder has long been a distinguished student of European policies towards Eastern Europe.
14. Only the ACPs came to enjoy early on some special preferences for competing agricultural exports to the EU (but the range of this competition was largely limited to a few products such as sugar and meat), while both ACPs and North African countries tied to the EU by the special cooperation agreements were exempted from the MFA import regime. However, the North African countries undertook in practice to

limit their exports of textiles and clothing to the EU so as not to create market disruptions. The new agreements with the Mediterranean countries eliminated the normal duties on imports of CAP products charged by the EU.

15. See also Grilli (1993) for a history and review of the trade policies of the EU towards CEECs, including the period up to the 'Europe Agreements'.
16. Romania had already been granted GSP status in 1974.
17. In mid-1992 EU imports of milk, veal, beef, cereals, olive oil and sugar were subject to variable levies.
18. The complement to variable levies on imports are the export subsidies that the EU must extend to its farmers to help them dispose in international markets of the surplus they accumulate because of internal price support (see the previous chapter). These subsidised exports naturally exert a downward pressure on international market prices of the products in question, creating gains for importers and losses from competing exporters.
19. The exports of steel from Central and Eastern Europe were subjected in the late 1980s to minimum prices. These remain in the Europe Agreements, while all the export quotas that they were obliged to enforce were eliminated.
20. Apart from some minor improvements in those applicable to agricultural imports.
21. Examples of EU-level quantitative restrictions were the quotas imposed on textiles and clothing imports within and outside the MFAs, plus the informal export restraints on footwear and steel. In addition, some of the members, above all France and Italy among the original members, had maintained residual national restrictions on the basis of Regulation 288/82. Typical in this respect was the national quota on imports of automobiles from Japan kept by Italy. In addition there were numerous import quotas on specific products coming from state-trading countries under regulation 3420/83.
22. No new authorisations to restrict trade inside the EU under Art. 115 of the treaty was granted by the Commission in 1993 and 1994.
23. Imports of steel from the NIS, however, are still quantitatively limited.
24. In these cases, however, consolidation does not necessarily mean a reduction of protection, but only in the number of VERs in operation.
25. The broad definition of NTMs used by UNCTAD included, in addition to those considered in this chapter, certain para-tariff measures, import surcharges and deposits.
26. The aggregate is here defined as the summation of Poland, Hungary, the Czech and Slovak Republics, Bulgaria and Romania.
27. We refer here to financial aid or ODA flows. The EU has long extended also food aid to developing countries (associated and non-associated). The aid terminology of the EU can be confusing. The Union refers to the (financial) aid to the associated countries of Africa, the Caribbean and Pacific as the summation of 'programme aid' and 'non-programme aid'; to the (financial) aid to the rest of the developing countries as 'financial aid' and to aid to the CEECs and of the former Soviet Union

simply as 'aid'. Food aid is referred to as such. In addition, (financial) aid granted in relief situations is called 'emergency aid'. In addition, the EU refers to 'humanitarian' aid as aid granted to finance priority emergency and post-emergency operations for disaster victims in non-EU countries. This included both financial and emergency food aid. This form of aid is now administered by the newly created EU Humanitarian Office, under the special responsibility of one of the Vice-Presidents of the Commission. Aid to the ACPs has long been administered by the Commission's Directorate General for Development Cooperation (DG VIII); aid to Asia, Latin America and the Mediterranean countries (ALAMED) has, instead, fallen in the purview of the Directorate for External Economic Relations (DG I). Aid to the CEECs and NIS is administered by the Directorate of External Political relations (DG IA) for the Phare and Tacis components and by the Directorate for Economic and Financial Affairs (DG II) for the balance of payments support component. Presumably for this reason, regular and systematic information on total EU ODA to developing and CEEC/NIS countries cannot be found anywhere in the publications of the Commission. The Commission reports regularly on the administration of aid to ACPs. Aid to the rest of the beneficiaries is reported in the Budget, but without information on its distribution, which can be gathered only at irregular intervals from specific reports of the Commission on aid to ALAMED countries and the CEECs/NIS. Finally, the country distribution of food aid and of special aid programme is even more difficult to gather. As a result, piecing together the EU aid picture can be quite a difficult task for any outside observer. Information on EU aid (and its country distribution) is available from reports of the Development Assistance Committee (DAC) of the OECD, which cover the developing countries quite well, but not yet the CEEC and NISs, which were for a long time aid donors and have only recently become recipients. The DAC has started in recent years to cover aid received by the latter group, but still does it with difficulty when it comes to EU aid to them.

28. There is in all aid distributions a strong bias in favour of small countries and a large bias against large countries, the result perhaps of misplaced concreteness in allocating aid, as its effects are much more visible in small than large recipient countries. The aid distribution of the EU suffers from the same problem.

7 The European Free Trade Association

Victoria Curzon Price

The European Free Trade Association (EFTA) celebrated its 35th anniversary in 1995. During this time, it had gone through three main phases. The first (EFTA-I, 1960–72), now part of distant history (see Price, 1974; and EFTA Secretariat 1980a, 1980b), forms the introductory part of this chapter. The second (EFTA-II, 1972–84), during which free trade in industrial products was forged with the EC forms the central part. The third (EFTA-III, 1985–95), during which the 'second generation' of integration problems was explored with the EC (now EU), forms the concluding section. Each of these periods reflects a change in the attitude of the EC/EU to the 'problem' of integrating a set of countries which, for one reason or another, had refused to join the Treaty of Rome at its inception.

EFTA-I: THE FREE TRADE AREA PROTOTYPE

EFTA-I was founded in 1960 by seven countries which, at the time, did not wish to join the EC. These countries were Austria and Switzerland in the centre of Europe, Denmark, Norway and Sweden in the north, Portugal to the south and the UK to the west; Finland joined as an Associate Member in 1961 – a more geographically dispersed group of countries would have been difficult to find! This was a classical reaction on the part of a set of countries severely threatened with the prospect of trade diversion caused by the newly created EC. However, because EFTA was much smaller than the EC, and its individual members smaller still and extremely dependent on their relationship with the nascent Common Market, this retaliatory aspect was played down. In fact, from the start the basic objective of EFTA's members, hence of EFTA itself, was to reach a mutually satisfactory understanding with the EC.

Barely twelve months after EFTA-I began functioning, its largest member, the UK, decided to apply for full membership of the EC. It was followed by Denmark and Norway, two EFTA members which had already decided that they would follow their principal export market wherever it went. EFTA looked dead before it was born. The remaining members considered the British move to be a severe blow to their prospects of reaching a satisfactory agreement with the EC. Interestingly enough, however, they managed to extract from a reluctant UK (which thought it had signed a mere free trade area – FTA – treaty, with no limits on its right to conduct an independent foreign policy) the then-famous 'London Declaration' of June 1961. By this, the British government bound itself with a solemn promise not to join the EC until 'satisfactory arrangements' had been worked out to 'meet the various legitimate interests of all members of EFTA' (EFTA Secretariat, 1966, pp. 22–3). In the event, General de Gaulle's January 1963 veto cut short the negotiations, but the feeling lingered that the London Declaration had helped the General to reach his decision, confirming the worst suspicions of the smaller EFTA countries, namely, that the EC was not prepared to meet their 'various legitimate interests'.

These small neutral countries – Austria, Finland, Sweden and Switzerland – all had overriding political reasons for not joining the EC, the most obvious being that the Soviet Union would no longer have recognised at best their neutrality or at worst their very right to existence as sovereign states (which could have led to the reoccupation of Austria and Finland by Soviet troops). Switzerland, in addition, had strong domestic political reasons for abstaining from membership of the EC, connected with its finely balanced federal structure designed to accommodate a multicultural society.

EFTA-II AND THE FREE TRADE AREA ARRANGEMENTS: FROM PROTOTYPE TO MASS PRODUCTION

For the rest of the decade EFTA and the EC trod separate paths. EFTA's members concentrated on demonstrating that intra-area tariffs could be dismantled, that non-tariff barriers could be kept under control, that origin rules could be devised and administered satisfactorily and that both sides of industry could shoulder the inevitable burden of structural adjustment without difficulty.

This they did, and when General de Gaulle's departure from the centre of Europe's political stage reopened the question of Britain's accession to the EC in December 1969, the FTA as a model of economic integration was no longer a disputed blueprint, but a successful operational prototype. This time, the EC Council of Ministers itself announced that the interests of the non-applicant neutral countries would be taken into account during the process of enlargement, and that, in particular, existing free trade would not be compromised in the process.

The form in which the EC was to honour its promise was, however, left undefined. A customs union, a FTA, partial preference zone or what? In view of the very sceptical attitude of the EC towards FTAs, it is interesting that this formula should have been chosen for the EFTA–EC trade links.

That the FTA formula should have suited the neutrals' purposes was self-evident. They obtained access to the EC for their industrial products in exchange for eliminating their own already low tariffs on manufactured goods. They did not have to participate in the costly Common Agricultural Policy (CAP), and they remained free to determine their own commercial policy *vis-à-vis*, for example, developing countries, Japan, Eastern Europe and Hong Kong. On the other hand, they had to forego the privilege of helping to shape EC policies with respect to industrial policy, free movement of labour, transport, energy, services, and a host of other 'second generation' issues. This was no problem since the EC showed no signs of tackling these issues either.

But what of the EC? Right up to and during the 1971–2 negotiations, both the EC Commission and France viewed the FTA formula with deep distaste. On the straightforward technical level there was the problem of policing the origin system. Surely origin rules would be avoided by hordes of unscrupulous traders, requiring equally large armies of zealous customs officials to track them down? EFTA's empirical demonstration to the contrary was partly discounted on the grounds that in such a geographically dispersed grouping, the incentive for circumventing origin rules was much diminished by high intra-area transport costs. This would no longer be the case if, say, France and Switzerland were linked in a FTA. This scepticism has not died with time and lies behind the very much stricter origin rules established for the 1972 FTAs and the 1995 European Economic Area (EEA) arrangement (see Binswanger and Mayrzedt, 1972, pp. 63–6, and Price, 1974, pp. 234–9).

On the more complex and elevated level of policy and principle the European hawks (proponents of 'l'Europe pure et dure') were very worried that FTAs represented a soft option – integration without tears – which might prove an attractive alternative to some faint-hearted European doves *within* the EC, as well as to potential members, such as Greece or Spain. In fact, the FTA option *did* provide an alternative to Norway which, after vacillating, took it up in preference to joining the EC, in 1972 and again in 1994. In short, the European hawks were loath to relinquish the use of the economic threat of trade diversion to further their longer range political objectives. Ironically, as we shall see, in 1989 the EC wanted to stave off new applications and offered a new FTA-based deal (the EEA) instead.

Back in 1971, however, the advantages of the FTA formula began to dawn on even its sternest opponents. How could the EC agree to tie its own hands in a stronger link (say via a customs union) with a non-member? This would be tantamount to giving Sweden, for instance, veto power over any changes in the EC's common external tariff (CET), a privilege which only fully paid-up members ought to enjoy. A weaker link, for instance via a preferential trading zone stopping short of full free trade, would not only fall foul of GATT's Article 24, but would also renege on the European Summit's promise not to allow trade barriers to reappear between the new EC members and their old EFTA partners. In the end, the FTA formula proved to be the only one which satisfied everybody's interests at minimal cost and without transgressing international obligations. Negotiations were brought to a successful conclusion in July 1972 with the signature of six bilateral Free Trade Agreements (FTAs) between the EC and the neutrals (plus Portugal and – a relative newcomer to the European integration scene – Iceland). The picture was completed with the signature of the Norway–EC FTA in May 1973, making seven in all.

COVERAGE

One of the reasons why the EFTA-I prototype proved so successful was that it made no attempt to cover agriculture. This sector has not been exposed to market forces for at least a century in most European countries, including those of EFTA, and any attempt to free trade on a regional basis would either have been meaningless (public policy would have continued to govern trade, prices and production) or highly distorting unless a 'common' policy could be developed (à la CAP).

On the other hand, by concentrating their efforts in the industrial field alone, the members of EFTA achieved a maximum of real integration, in terms of intra-area specialisation, for a minimum of integrative effort, in terms of achieving a public policy consensus among several countries. The reason for this high payoff was that the mere act of removing tariffs (slightingly referred to as 'negative integration' by some authors – see Chapter 1) in sectors of industry governed by market forces is enough to bring about intra-area specialisation, without the need for further government action. In particular, it is not necessary to achieve painful, delicate and unstable consensi at government level, admiringly termed 'positive integration' by those who tend to confuse effort with results. Because EFTA governments sat back and let market forces do the job of integrating, the EFTA Secretariat functioned with no more than seventy people; for the same reason, EFTA's history was remarkably uneventful because the really important things (namely market-induced specialisation) happened at such a microeconomic level that they escaped the commentator's eye.

IMPACT OF INTEGRATION, DISINTEGRATION AND REINTEGRATION

Doubts that mere 'negative' integration can have startling effects on patterns of trade and production, even in such a dispersed FTA as EFTA, can be laid to rest by consulting the evidence – see Table 7.1.

From 1959 to 1972 intra-EFTA trade as a proportion of total trade rose from 11 to 19 per cent, and the annual rate of growth of intra-area trade was consistently higher than the rate of growth of EFTA's trade in general: 15 per cent (as compared with 9.2 per cent) from 1959 to 1967, and 17.4 per cent (as compared with 14.3 per cent) from 1967 to 1972 – see EFTA Secretariat 1980a. Whether this substantial degree of intra-area specialisation was on balance trade-creating or trade-diverting is, of course, another matter – see Chapter 4. On the EFTA secretariat's own estimate, trade creation amounted to 721 millions US dollars by 1967, and trade diversion to 592 million US dollars (EFTA Secretariat, 1980a – the figures refer to those countries given in Table 7.1 minus Iceland). Most of the trade diversion, however, was thought to have arisen within Europe, as EFTA-based industrialists, as a result of the area preference, sought to replace marginally cheaper EC sources of supply by slightly more expensive EFTA ones.[1] The 1972 FTAs removed this source of trade diversion, besides establishing conditions for further trade creation and trade diversion in their own right. Only the roughest estimates of the effects of the FTAs will be made here, but trade figures suggest that the principal impact was

Table 7.1 EFTA exports by areas, 1959–93 (percentage shares in total)

	1959	*1967*	*1972*	*1978*	*1984*	*1993*†
Intra-EFTA*	11.1	16.6	19.0	15.1	13.6	11.2
Denmark/UK	16.2	18.2	18.4	16.9	17.7	—
EC 6	34.0	29.7	29.3	31.5	33.6	—
EC 9	50.5	48.2	48.1	48.8	51.7	—
EC 10	—	—	—	—	52.2	—
EC 12†	—	—	—	—	53.5	57.4
USA	8.7	7.8	7.3	5.9	8.5	7.2
Japan	0.6	1.2	1.4	1.7	1.8	2.4
Eastern Europe	7.7	7.2	6.0	7.5	5.9	4.9
OPEC	2.4	1.9	2.1	5.4	4.6	2.6
NIC‡	2.6	—	2.5	—	2.3	4.5

Notes

* Figures refer to EFTA-II (Austria, Finland, Iceland, Norway, Portugal, Sweden and Switzerland). Portugal left EFTA to join EC 12 on 1 January 1986.

† EFTA-III (EFTA-II minus Portugal) trade with EC 12 (EC 10 plus Spain and Portugal).

‡ Varying definitions (see Source).

Source: EFTA Secretariat, *EFTA Trade* (Geneva), various issues.

to eliminate the intra-European trade diversion inherent in the preceding integration arrangements. Thus, the original six members of the EC took 34 per cent of EFTA's exports in 1959 (the last year before the Treaties of Rome and Stockholm took effect) and 29 per cent in 1972 (when the division of Western Europe was at its zenith). However, this ratio had virtually returned to its 1959 level by 1984. The economic rift appeared to have been mended.

However, in all matters relating to free trade areas and customs unions we are in the uncertain domain of the second-best. In this instance, one needs to study whether the rift between EFTA and the EC was not mended at the expense of creating another. After all, the six bilateral FTAs could be expected to generate trade-creating and trade-diverting effects in their own right.

We in fact note that the intensification of trade between the EFTA countries and the EC between 1972 and 1993 took place largely at the expense of intra-EFTA trade. Indeed, intra-EFTA trade as a proportion of the total trade of its members fell steadily from 19 per cent in 1972 to 11.2 per cent in 1993 back to 1959 levels. This is not, of course, to imply that the whole exercise has been in vain – quite the

Table 7.2 EFTA imports by areas, 1959–93 (percentage shares in total)

	1959	*1967*	*1972*	*1978*	*1984*	*1993*
Intra-EFTA	9.3	13.8	16.6	13.8	13.2	11.6
Denmark/UK	13.4	15.4	14.1	12.0	11.4	—
EC 6	45.6	41.8	42.8	43.7	42.0	—
EC 9	58.9	57.3	57.0	55.9	53.8	—
EC 10	—	—	—	—	54.0	—
EC 12	—	—	—	—	55.3	61.8
USA	8.7	7.3	6.2	6.6	7.0	6.8
Japan	0.8	2.4	2.8	3.2	4.2	4.9
Eastern Europe	6.9	5.6	5.2	6.6	7.8	4.2
OPEC	2.5	2.6	2.5	4.5	3.7	1.4
NICs	1.7	—	1.7	—	2.9	3.3

Note
See Table 7.1 for source, notes and definitions.

contrary. It was the aim of the EFTA countries to neutralise the effect of the creation of the EC – by far their largest single export market – and in this they succeeded.

The picture is much the same if one looks at EFTA trade from the import side (see Table 7.2). While intra-EFTA shares fell sharply from 1972 to 1993, and imports from the EC(12) rose correspondingly, the United States, Japan and the NIEs all increased their share of EFTA imports, suggesting that 'external' trade diversion effects were swamped by numerous other factors and that the main effect of the FTAs was to correct the distortion of trade patterns that took place from 1960 to 1972. A more detailed statistical analysis by the UN Economic Commission for Europe (1995) comes to a similar conclusion. The fact that third-country suppliers do not appear to have suffered from substantial trade diversion since the implementation of the 1972 FTAs might seem paradoxical, but for the fact that there are good theoretical reasons for thinking that free trade areas, especially between low-tariff countries, not only tend to minimise trade diversion, but may, under certain conditions, actually *increase* trade with non-members, a point to which we now turn.

THE DISCREET CHARM OF FREE TRADE AREAS

From a theoretical point of view, FTAs produce roughly the same effects as customs unions (Balassa, 1962; Shibata, 1971; Price, 1974 and El-Agraa in El-Agraa and Jones, 1981). However, they do differ in detail, and in particular, tend to cause rather more trade creation and less trade diversion than a tariff-averaging customs union – a detail which has not received much attention in the literature.

In order to demonstrate this point, we must start by making all the conventional assumptions of microeconomic analysis (perfect competition, no transport costs, short-run rising marginal cost curves, free entry and exit, and constant or gently rising long-term costs as interfactoral substitution and technological advance permit escape from diminishing returns in the long run). We must add the assumptions common to trade theory (perfectly elastic world supply, tariffs being the only instrument of trade policy) and an extra assumption particular to free trade area theory, namely, the frictionless operation of a 'perfect' origin system which prevents trade deflection (i.e. goods manufactured outside the FTA entering at the lowest point in the non-harmonised tariff wall, and proceeding free of duty to more protected markets), without distorting side-effects.

Using the notation of Shibata (*H* for the high-tariff, relatively inefficient producer, *L* for the low-tariff, relatively efficient producer) and a simple partial equilibrium model, we can proceed as in Figure 7.1, which illustrates the position before union. With tariff *TH* in operation, country *H* produces *0A*, consumes *0B* and imports *AB* from the lowest-cost world supplier at world prices (*WP*). Turning to the left-hand side of Figure 7.1, with tariff *TL* in use, country *L* produces *0C*, consumes *0D* and imports *CD*.

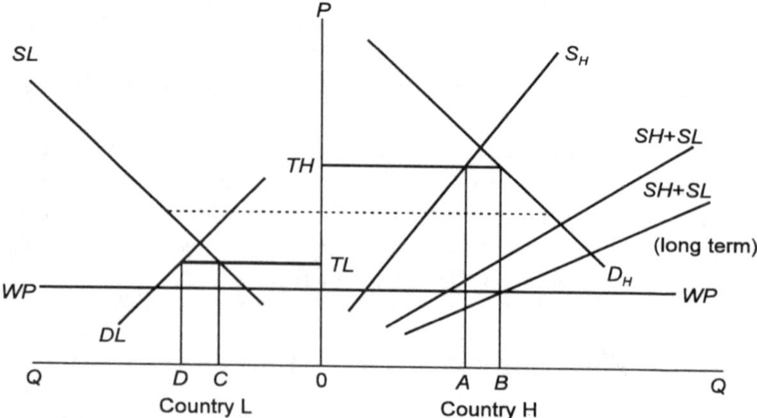

Figure 7.1 The short-term economic effects of free trade areas

After the FTA is established, producers in *L* gain access to the high-price market in *H* and will serve that market in preference to their own, gradually bringing down the price in *H*. Consumers in *L* need not fear for supplies, however, for world producers will always be prepared to export to *L* at *WP* plus the tariff *TL*, in infinite quantities if need be. Theoretically, the entire production of *L* could be freed for export to *H*. This is the 'shifting' effect described by Shibata: it is supposedly a unique feature of FTAs (for a fundamental criticism of this notion see El-Agraa in El-Agraa and Jones, 1981, ch. 3).

It is important to ask: in this situation what happens to country *H*? According to Shibata, if we accept his analysis, the final price in country *H* is indeterminate, and depends on (i) the relative size and/or elasticity of supply in *L* and (ii) on the size and/or elasticity of demand in *H*. In the gloomiest of cases, if *L*'s supply is relatively small and inelastic, and *H*'s demand relatively large and elastic, it is clear that the price in *H* will not fall much, if at all. In this case, the FTA would cause less trade creation and more trade diversion than a tariff-averaging customs union. The reverse holds true in the most optimistic case, the price in *H* falling to or close to the level in *L*. Shibata accordingly concludes that 'there are no a priori grounds for making a general statement as to which of these two systems (a customs union or a FTA is better, even from the point of view of the world as a whole' (Shibata, 1971, p. 83).

In my view, a more positive conclusion can be reached. The analysis must be carried further, out of the short-term span, in which producers cannot increase production significantly without incurring rapidly increasing marginal costs, and into the longer term, during which they can increase or decrease capacity according to whether the price they face in the market covers their long-term average costs or not.

Returning to Figure 7.1, it is clear that it represents a short-run situation. If the two supply curves are added together on the right-hand side (*SH* + *SL*), and applied to *H*'s demand curve, the short-run equilibrium price turns out to be higher than the long-run equilibrium price in *L*(*TL*). However, as long as this situation persists, entrepreneurs in *L* will be encouraged to expand capacity, since they were presumably meeting their long-run average costs at price *TL* before union, and are now making excess profits in *H*. This will cause the supply curve in *L* to shift bodily to the left until the combined *H* + *L* supply curves wipe out the price difference between *L* and *H*, representing the end of the opportunity for producers in *L* to make excess profits in *H*. Unlike Shibata, I therefore conclude that price differences cannot persist in a FTA for goods of area origin (for an alternative explanation of this, see El-Agraa in El-Agraa and Jones, 1981, ch. 3) and that the price level of the most efficient area producer will prevail – under the conventional assumptions, of course.

It follows from this conclusion that a FTA is more trade-creating and less trade-diverting than a tariff-averaging customs union – see Chapter 3. It also tends to be less detrimental to non-member interests, since exports to *L* need not diminish and may well expand in the short run, allowing world producers to gain a foothold from which it may be difficult to dislodge them at a later date once producers in *L* have expanded capacity. Finally, returning to Figure 7.1, if a horizontal line is drawn mid-way between *TL* and *TH*, representing the CET of a tariff-averaging customs union, it is clear that the FTA avoids an oft-neglected cost to customs union, namely, the increased level of protection in *L*. This is fine for producers, of course, since marginal capacity can be brought into use and efficient plants will make excess profits, but the economy as a whole suffers from misallocation and consumers suffer a direct consumption loss. This does not occur in the case of FTAs, and is one reason why low tariff countries tend to prefer them to customs unions.

TOO GOOD TO BE TRUE?

Against all these (static) advantages two drawbacks must be pointed out.

Distortion in Resource Allocation

It is commonly objected that because the FTA offers different levels of effective protection (EP), allocation distortions will occur. Two comments need to be made in this connection. First, if we maintain our initial assumptions (especially with regard to our 'perfect' origin system) it can be shown that intra-area free trade sets a natural limit to distortions arising from this source. Secondly, the amount of misallocation will depend on whether the origin rules are strict or generous.

Let us consider the following example (Figure 7.2): Sweden[2] imports man-made fibres (cost = 25), spins them (adding another 25 to the value of the fibres) and weaves them into cloth (adding another 50), giving a total cost for cloth in Sweden of 100. The Swedish tariffs

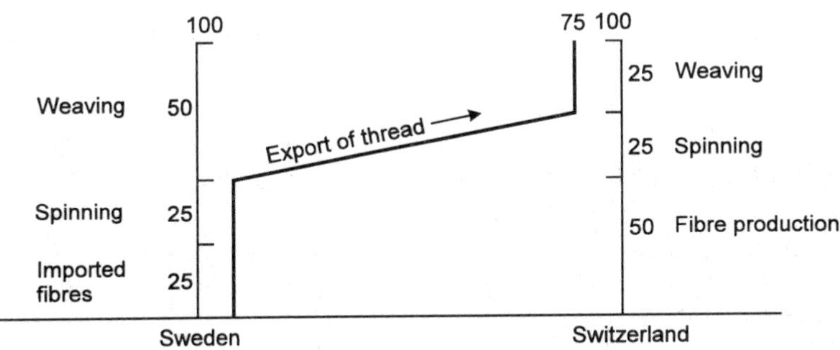

Figure 7.2 The long-term economic effects of free trade areas

on fibres, thread and cloth are designed to ensure that the inefficient weaving function is given a high level of EP.

In Switzerland, on the other hand, a different tariff structure obtains, designed to ensure that fibres are produced locally. Spinning and weaving enjoy low or possibly negative levels of EP, and are therefore highly efficient.

If trade is freed for goods of area origin, without tariff harmonisation taking place, the Swedish spinning industry will displace the Swiss (Swedish thread costing 50 instead of 75), but Swiss weavers will displace the Swedes (their costs being 25 instead of 50). The total cost of making cloth will be 75 [25 (fibre imported into Sweden) + 25 (spinning in Sweden) + 25 (weaving in Switzerland). People will simply stop making fibres in Switzerland, and weaving in Sweden]. Neither the high level of EP in Sweden for weaving nor the high level of explicit protection in Switzerland for fibres will attract investment. Both have become redundant because of free trade with a more efficient partner. In terms of efficiency of resource allocation, the efficient segments have been encouraged to expand and the inefficient ones to contract.

From this example, it can be seen that the danger of misallocation arises not from *high* levels of EP, but from *low or even negative* rates of protection. The latter is a rare but by no means unheard of phenomenon. Returning to our numerical example, it is illustrated by the hypothetical Swiss spinning industry which is indeed discriminated against: it is as efficient as the Swedish, but burdened by negative EP. If negative as well as positive EP is embedded in the tariff structure we shall be in a familiar second-best situation, where a move towards improved efficiency coexists with conditions favouring inefficiency. If positive EP exceeds negative EP (the more common situation) then movements towards improved efficiency may outweigh those towards inefficiency.

Many authors have suggested that FTAs would generate spontaneous pressure towards a harmonisation of EP rates, in order to prevent efficient activities from being penalised by negative EP. Indeed, there is some merit in the argument. Returning to our hypothetical example, we see that Swiss fibre producers will be unable to sell their goods, even to their own efficient down-stream local spinners (since the FTA price for thread is 50). They will either strive to become more competitive or go out of business. In the first case, Swiss spinners may be able to survive; in the second, they will go the same way as the fibre producers – out – unless the Swiss government notices in time that it is unnecessarily throwing away a perfectly healthy industry along with the inevitable loss of a dud one, and that a reduction of the redundant tariff would save it.[3]

This discussion raises the question why governments would discriminate against the activity in the first place. In fact, most tariff structures are progressive, namely, levying nil or negligible rates of duty on imported raw materials and semi-processed manufactures, intermediate rates of duty on competent and industrial inputs, and high rates of duty on finished goods. Both governments and industry are well aware that raising the cost of intermediate goods penalises all downstream sectors, and tariff structures are on the whole designed to favour the higher value-added downstream segments. However, if EP rates are positive, no distortions arise in a FTA from the lack of harmonisation, as noted above. Perhaps it is for this reason that there is little evidence of conscious tariff alignment in EFTA or the FTAs, although the low (and generally declining) absolute levels of protection anyway limit the scope for large negative EP rates.

Rules of Origin

Returning to our hypothetical numerical example, it can be seen that the ability of the Swiss to displace Swedish weavers depends on free intra-area trade in thread, half of whose value consists of non-area fibres. Were origin rules to specify that, say, 60 per cent of the value had to be produced in Sweden, then Swiss weavers would not have access to cheap thread and would not be able to displace the Swedes.

However, if the area preference were worthwhile and the differences in efficiency were large enough, entrepreneurs would soon find a way of adding the required extra amount of area content and shipping thread to Switzerland at a slightly higher cost.

From these remarks it should be clear that rules of origin may fulfil more than one purpose. The obvious one is to stop non-member goods from enjoying the area preference: this can be accomplished by specifying some 'reasonable' uniform level of area content (50 per cent being the benchmark actually used in EFTA-I). A less apparent function is to use the origin system to concentrate the demand for intermediate goods on area producers. The reason for the assumption concerning a 'perfect' non-distorting origin system above should now be clear. Indeed, the origin system is the key to the nature of the FTA: if it is generous, it will encourage trade creation; if it is restrictive, it will foster trade diversion.

This holds true irrespective of the height of the individual country tariffs. Thus a group of high-tariff countries forming a FTA with generous origin rules would still tend to be more trade-creating than a tariff-averaging customs union (since the highest tariffs would become redundant, and prices within the area would be governed by the lowest of the high tariffs): conversely, a group of low-tariff countries forming a FTA with strict origin rules might well turn out to be more trade-diverting than a tariff-averaging customs union. Of course, this does not alter one of the basic conclusions of customs union theory, namely, that a high level of protection *vis-à-vis* third countries will tend to cause an excess of trade diversion over trade creation.

In practice, this means that the analysis of a FTA's origin rules, though not perhaps the most fascinating of tasks, is most revealing. The rules of origin of EFTA-I, though generally considered to be a model of liberalism, contained a couple of darker areas (textiles and chemicals) – see Price, 1974, pp. 158–60, 162–7 – while the rules of origin imposed by the EC in the FTAs were visibly less generous (ibid., pp. 234–5). Very briefly, whereas EFTA-I rules of origin offered two alternative methods of acquiring origin status (50 per cent value-added within the area or fulfilment of a 'process' criterion), EC-FTA rules specified only one method (a *combination* of a value *and* a process criterion); also, whereas the EFTA 50 per cent criterion was softened by a 'basic materials list' (some 200 imported basic materials which, if transformed or incorporated in the area, counted towards the area content, irrespective of where they came from) the EC rules of origin contained no such list; also, by using the fob export price as the denominator, EFTA producers could add to the area content the cost of handling from the factory to the port of exit, whereas the EC value-added criteria were based on the ex-factory price; also most of the EC's value-added criteria required more than 50 per cent local value-added whereas in practice EFTA's implied considerably less; finally, whereas EFTA created a group of seven countries within which origin status could be accumulated multilaterally, the FTAs, being bilateral treaties between the EC and each individual EFTA country, did not permit multilateral cumulation across EFTA for the purposes of EFTA–EC trade.

This last point is important, if read in conjunction with the generally stricter origin requirements outlined earlier. It implied that whereas the whole of the EC was treated as a single 'country' within the bilateral FTAs, each EFTA country was considered separately. This made it harder for EFTA industrialists to comply with the rather strict origin requirements embedded in the FTA treaties than for EC industrialists. EFTA industrialists had every reason to concentrate a maximum of their purchases of industrial inputs, components and raw materials in the EC area, rather than to buy from their EFTA partners or third-country suppliers.

The EFTA countries fought this lack of 'multilateral cumulation' from the outset. They obtained a minimal concession from the EC during the FTA negotiations themselves: the right to so-called 'diagonal' cumulation. This arcane term allows goods *which have acquired* origin status under the *one* FTA to be incorporated or transformed into a new product in a parallel FTA without losing their origin status under the *first* FTA. On the other hand, they were merely counted as 'neutral' in the calculation of local origin, and could not be *added* to the amount of area origin of the final product unless they accounted for less than 5 per cent of its value – the so-called 'bagatelle' provision. This was not considered to be a substantial concession on the part of the EC, and the EFTA countries continued to strive both for a reduction of the complexity of the rules themselves, and for straightforward 'multilateral cumulation'. For this they had to wait for the EEA negotiations (see p. 191).

There is indeed some evidence that the FTAs did cause an unusual shift of trade flows in favour of the EC and to the detriment of EFTA and third-country suppliers in certain sectors, especially in semi-manufactures – as expected (see Table 7.3).

The EC raised its share of EFTA imports of industrial raw materials and semi-manufactured goods in all categories except for chemicals, where its share – already very large since the EC supplies

Table 7.3 Impact of rules of origin on the structure of EFTA trade (percentage share of designated trading partner in EFTA imports)

	EC		*EFTA*		*LDCs*		*USA*	
	1973	*1984*	*1973*	*1984*	*1973*	*1984*	*1973*	*1984*
Raw materials	34.0	36.0	17.6	16.8	21.0	18.3	6.2	7.5
Chemicals	69.0	68.5	13.0	11.3	3.4	2.4	8.7	7.6
Other semi-manufactures	55.7	60.0	26.7	22.0	7.0	6.8	6.8	4.1
Textiles	56.8	63.7	27.5	18.6	4.3	8.5	4.6	2.0
Steel	65.0	69.0	18.2	17.0	1.3	1.9	1.7	1.0

Source: GATT, *International Trade*, 1976–7 and 1984–5.

70 per cent of EFTA's imported chemicals – remained virtually stable. The largest relative increase was recorded in textiles, which was to be expected, since this was a relatively protected sector, as were its principal down-stream user industries. Proof of origin for the purpose of enjoying tariff-free treatment was therefore correspondingly valuable.

Apart from negative allocation effects of bilateral cumulation between individual EFTA countries and the EC, just referred to, the origin rules themselves were irksome and costly to comply with, in a way the old EFTA rules were not. This deadweight administrative cost was compounded by the fact that the EFTA countries had to relinquish their own liberal origin system and adopt the FTA origin system for the purpose of intra-EFTA trade. They could not face the thought of having to administer two different origin systems – one was bad enough.

Whereas producers and exporters were reported to have been 'broadly satisfied' with the old EFTA-I origin rules as they stood and EFTA-I goods used to clear customs 'with no greater formalities than apply to other goods',[4] the same cannot be said of the FTA or EEA rules of origin. The administrative costs alone were judged 'quite significant' for both enterprises and for customs authorities.[5] A Finnish study quoted in a report issued by the Economic Affairs Department of the EFTA Secretariat, which added both firms' and customs authorities' costs of handling the paperwork concluded that total documentation costs amounted to between 1.4 and 5.7 per cent of the value of imports in 1982.[6] Other studies put the costs even higher, if one includes the cost of delays at the border. The EFTA study just referred to thus concludes, in sharp contrast to views of the old system, that 'it is quite clear that documentation and the administration of origin rules impose heavy costs on exporters and could cause delays and discourage trade'.[7]

Be this as it may, the Economic Affairs Department of the EFTA Secretariat estimated that the total costs for the European economy of rules of origin 'are in the range of some 3 to 5 per cent of the value of the goods involved' – *if* a conservative estimate is applied.[8] This amounted to a not-insignificant $26–43 billion annually (1984 figures).

The constant complaints on the part of EFTA countries relating to the FTA origin rules did lead to a partial victory in 1982, when the EC agreed to apply an *alternative percentage system* for a three-year trial period. This reform did not tackle the cumulation problem, but tried to make it simpler from an administrative point of view for a firm to prove the origin of its products. Instead of having to comply with a single origin requirement, firms were given the choice of two methods (as in the old EFTA system): the original combination of process and value criteria established in the FTA agreements, or a simple percentage rule, limiting non-area parts and materials to between 25 and 40 per cent of the value of the finished product. This simplification became permanent in 1986 after it had been shown to be harmless.

The EC's deep reluctance to multilateralise the FTA origin system stemmed from a fear that it would cause important trade deflections: EFTA countries having, on the whole, lower duties on most industrial products than the EC's CET, it was felt, especially in France, that non-European parts and components would gain access to the EC market via the FTAs, thus undermining the structure of the CET, upsetting the competitive position of firms within the EC and putting them at a disadvantage compared with firms in the EFTA area. Were multilateral cumulation permitted, it was thought that the 'hidden' non-European content of goods would rise. Components made, say, partly from Swiss and partly from Japanese inputs, but qualifying as 'European', would enter yet another product as wholly 'European' and the Japanese element would be neglected in the final calculation. It was not until the 1990s and the EEA negotiations that these old fears were laid to rest.

THE COST FOR THE NEUTRALS OF REMAINING OUTSIDE THE EC

The cost for the neutrals of remaining outside the EC was insignificant as long as the EC was making no progress towards real integration. All this changed the day the EC decided to tackle the 'second generation' of integration issues (see Chapter 4). In the field of industrial trade, this implied that the EC would finally come to grips with all the major non-tariff barriers which had, hitherto, prevented the emergence of a real customs union. In the field of services, capital movements and free movement of labour, it implied that the EC would evolve from a customs union to a much more ambitious economic union. Finally, if the EC ever took the plunge to a single currency, then it would develop into a fully fledged economic and monetary union. Each one of these steps became official EC policy in the short period from 1985 to 1990. Even if only half the programme was implemented, it was quite enough to create a gap between operating from an EFTA base and operating from within the EC. The cost for the EFTA countries of remaining outside the EC suddenly increased substantially.

One of the concessions which the EC made in the 1972 negotiations, on which the EFTA countries pinned much hope for the future, was the so-called 'evolutionary clause'. This permitted either party in a bilateral FTA to raise a question in any field not covered by the arrangement, which it considered would be in the interests of their respective economies to develop. We shall now see how this 'evolutionary clause' fared in practice.

EFTA-III: FROM THE LUXEMBOURG MEETING TO THE EEA

April 1984 was an important milestone in EFTA's history. For the first time ever the EC and EFTA met at ministerial level. The occasion ostensibly marked the final dismantling of tariffs on industrial trade between the two groups, but much more importantly and symbolically the final communiqué expressly included EFTA in the EC's new concept of a 'dynamic European economic space'.[10] This suggested not only that 'second generation issues' would be addressed in the future (building on the 'evolutionary clause'), but also that EFTA had achieved some kind of formal status with the EC, which had studiously ignored it for a quarter of a century.

This vague promise became crucially important a year later when, in June 1985, the EC committed itself to creating a single European market. This qualitative leap in economic integration (in which, to begin with, no one believed) contained the potential to discriminate most painfully against the EFTA countries – *unless* they could be included in the process.

The 'Luxembourg Process' in Practice

EC–EFTA relations were still based on a *bilateral* approach and each EFTA country raised issues with the EC Commission individually, as and when they occurred. The result was a network of *bilateral* side-agreements covering such matters as cheese, fish or trade marks, depending on the intensity with which the problem was perceived from the EFTA country's point of view and the willingness of the EC to respond to it.

This process was variously described as 'the bottom-up approach of the Luxembourg process', 'picking the cherries from the cake', 'à la carte' integration and other such metaphors, all suggesting that the EFTA countries were in the privileged position of choosing from the EC menu only those dishes which they liked (Kleppe, 1991, pp. 70–2).

This was clearly problematic for the EC. First, the case-by-case, country-by-country approach meant that the agenda was determined by the EFTA states. Secondly, the potential for diversity (six or seven EFTA countries, negotiating perhaps hundreds of different mini-agreements) was worrying for the EC, much concerned with maintaining *homogeneity* within its own borders and in its external relations. Thirdly, the EFTA countries naturally avoided areas of cooperation that they considered sensitive (such as agriculture, labour migration or foreign direct investment in natural resources). Finally, because of the minimalist, bilateral approach, it was difficult for the EC to broaden the scope of the negotiations and to insist on trade-offs involving precisely these sensitive areas.

The Greek, Spanish and Portuguese governments, in particular, did not see why Switzerland should be allowed to negotiate an agreement on insurance without a corresponding improvement in the status of immigrant workers. The Spanish government argued that the formal reciprocity contained, for instance, in the non-life insurance agreement did not constitute 'real' reciprocity, since Switzerland gained access to a huge market, twenty times the size of its own, while the EC gained access to only a tiny market, correspondingly small in relative terms.[11] This 'maxi reciprocity' argument was new to the EFTAns and signalled the beginning of the end of the 'Luxembourg process'.

In 1987, at the Interlaken EC–EFTA Ministerial Meeting, this inevitable development became official policy. The EC announced three principles which were, from then on, to govern negotiations between itself and the EFTA countries:

(a) the EC would from now on be giving priority to its own internal integration process;
(b) the EC would accept no external obligations which might hamper its internal decision-making process; and
(c) the EC would expect a reasonable balance of advantages and obligations.[12]

The further development of EC–EFTA relations was effectively placed on a back burner. Far from being able to negotiate 'in parallel' with the EC on achieving market access on roughly the same terms as member states of the EC, the EFTAns were basically being told to wait until the single market was in place. Although the 'Luxembourg process' continued until the end of 1988, it had entered the phase of diminishing returns and, in the words of one EFTA insider, had become 'a rather exhausting and exhausted exercise' (Wijkman, 1995, p. 173).

In the meantime, the single market programme was forging ahead according to schedule, much to the surprise (and, doubtless, dismay) of the EFTAns.

The Delors Initiative

The stage was therefore set for a new approach, dramatically proposed by Jacques Delors, then President of the European Commission, in a speech to the European Parliament on 17 January 1989.[13] In this speech, Jacques Delors proposed 'a new form of association' based on 'a more structured partnership with common administrative and decision-making institutions'.

The EFTA countries were being offered two alternatives: to continue with the Luxembourg process, now blocked until the end of 1992; or to join the single market process in the making, *as a whole*. The EFTAns were being offered no less than a package deal intended to cover all relevant aspects of the 'four freedoms' upon which the single market process was based. But there were strings attached: they had to 'speak with one voice' and there was to be no more 'picking and choosing'.

A common interpretation, on the EFTA side, of the Delors initiative was that the EC 'wished to concentrate its energies on completing its internal market – the "1992 Programme" – and to this end wished to stave off applications for EC membership' (ibid., p. 172) by offering an acceptable economic alternative. If this was one of the unstated objectives of the Delors initiative – and there is of course no evidence that it was – it was singularly unsuccessful, for in July 1989 Austria submitted its application for membership, followed by Cyprus and Malta in 1990, Sweden in 1991 and Finland, Switzerland and Norway in 1992.

Of course, the single most important fact governing the course of these events was completely external to the EEA initiative – the fall of the Berlin wall, the collapse of the USSR and the removal of the external political constraint on neutral countries joining the EC. At the time of the Delors initiative, in January 1989, it was still unthinkable that Austria, Finland, Sweden or Switzerland could join the EC without provoking a strongly negative reaction on the part of the USSR.[14] while the EC itself was divided on the question of whether neutral countries should be admitted.[15] Six months later Austria submitted its application, a step which met with thunderous silence on the part of the Kremlin.

Yet despite these 'defections' from the EEA process (suggesting that all was not well with the negotiations), the talks continued. In the end, their main effect may simply have been to create a fast-track to EU membership for Austria, Finland and Sweden, since the problems inherent in the EEA approach remain for the others, and at the time of writing it is not clear whether the EEA will be successful in constructing a permanent economic alternative to full membership.

Institutional Difficulties

The challenge inherent in the Delors proposal was to construct an economic union between EFTA and the EC, permitting the EFTA countries to participate fully in the single market without being members of the Community. It sounded easy enough in principle, but it turned out to be virtually impossible in practice. The reason, in a nutshell, was that the EU was an *unfinished union*. Even at the time of writing (1995) the relevant 'acquis communautaire'[16] is still growing. The future agenda of the EU still contains much unfinished business relating to establishing and maintaining the four freedoms and the single market.

The EFTA countries were, in effect, being asked to accept not only the existing 'acquis' on a take-it-or-leave-it basis at the time of signature, but all the future relevant 'acquis' as well. The EC did its best to square the circle by offering EFTA countries 'as wide a participation as possible... in the preparatory stage of draft measures' (Art. 100,

EEA). Although this process was bravely referred to in EFTA circles as 'decision-shaping' (as opposed to 'decision-making') it was difficult to avoid the impression that the EFTA input in the EU's future 'acquis' would be very small indeed.

'Homogeneity' and Surveillance

If the lack of any real EFTA influence over the shape of the future 'acquis' was a bitter pill to swallow, the problem of ensuring the *uniform application and interpretation* of this 'acquis' gave rise to a similar type of problem.

On the EU side, in this regard, the Commission plays the part of watch-dog and the European Court of Justice (ECJ) remains the final arbiter in all matters of application and interpretation pertaining to the Union. The EU legal order represents genuine supra-nationality in that member states (and their institutions and citizens) *must* comply with the resulting decisions. Most importantly, *individuals* possess direct rights under the EU legal system and can, through their complaints, initiate proceedings against any EU government, or Community institution, which they consider is not acting according to the law.

Thus Community law is constantly interpreted, developed, applied and in all logic, one cannot have more than one source of interpretation for this law. So what was one to do with the EFTA countries? Were they to be allowed to interpret the relevant 'acquis' as they wished? Certainly not. Should they therefore submit to the relevant judgments of the ECJ? Not either. The EFTA countries would not be represented in the Commission or the ECJ, which would be in no way accountable to them (as they are to member states of the Union). In the end a compromise was hammered out whereby a joint EC–EFTA court was to be established to adjudicate issues arising from the application of the 'acquis' to the EFTA countries. But this compromise turned out to be unacceptable to the ECJ itself, which deemed it incompatible with the Treaty of Rome.[17] Finally a compromise was worked out whereby the EFTA countries agreed to create an EFTA Court of Justice and an EFTA Surveillance Authority which would undertake, within their delineated sphere of competence, the same type of work as the Commission and the ECJ in the EU.[18]

Inevitably, this sphere of competence was very, very small. In the realm of competition policy, it would apply to 'individual cases where *only trade between EFTA States is affected*' (Article 56.1(a) EEA, emphasis supplied). The Commission and ECJ would decide on 'the other cases', i.e. on cases involving EU–EFTA relations. In fact, despite the dressing-up, this was a fairly total capitulation on the part of the EFTAns.

Negotiations on the Substance of the EEA

From the start, it was agreed that the EEA would not cover agriculture and fisheries, the common external tariff and the common commercial policy, the common fiscal policy, common monetary policy and monetary union, common foreign policy and the acquis communautaire with respect to regional policy. The remainder of the EC's common policies constituted the 'relevant acquis' for the EEA negotiations.

In the early phases of the EEA negotiations, in 1989, just after the Delors initiative, the EC was reportedly prepared to make adjustments to the existing 'acquis' in cases where EFTA countries might experience difficulties: (i) for political reasons ('what the Russians would not allow an EFTA country to do' (ibid., p. 174); (ii) for reasons of 'vital national interests' justifying permanent exceptions.

The EFTAns accordingly drew up long lists of exceptions to the existing 'acquis', only to be told a year later that 'the Russians now appeared to allow anything', and as for 'vital national interests', if EC members had accepted the 'acquis' why should EFTA countries refuse it? In short, in view of the sea change which had occurred in the global strategic picture, no permanent exception to the 'acquis' would be permitted. Derogations justified by serious economic or social difficulties would have to be dealt with by not too lengthy transition periods.

This was very tough for the EFTAns. It meant that the negotiations were no longer about which parts of the relevant 'acquis' the EFTAns would accept, but how long they would take to pass the entire relevant 'acquis' into their own legislation. The negotiations thus centred on transition periods and safeguard clauses, rather than substance, since that substance was already given by the 'acquis'.

Again, the logic from the EC side was inescapable. The change in the geopolitical situation had, in effect, eliminated the political justification for the EEA, since no barriers to full membership remained for the neutral countries. Indeed, with the exception of Iceland, they drew the inevitable conclusion and successively submitted their applications to join as full members. Anything was better than the EEA satellisation process...

The spate of applications did not, however, stop the EEA talks from reaching a conclusion, but rather altered their character, turning them into pre-accession negotiations.

From an initial starting point where each EFTA country submitted its own list of 'sensitive' issues, requesting either permanent exemptions from the 'acquis' or long transition periods, the EC successfully narrowed the field by insisting (i) that transition periods should not last longer than two years, (ii) that the same transition period should apply to all EFTA countries, and (iii) that the EC would not allow access to its own market until the end of the longest transition period requested by any one country (ibid., pp. 176–81). This last condition was, of course, designed to make EFTA countries put pressure on their slowest member(s).

In short, the EC negotiated so uncompromisingly, from a position of total strength, that the final agreement failed to muster sufficient political support in most EFTA countries.

The 'Financial Mechanism'

Nor was this all. The EFTA countries, being notoriously wealthy, were to pay a tribute to the EC for the privilege of accepting the 'acquis' and obtaining access to a market far, far larger than theirs. The 'maxi-reciprocity' argument of Spain, used with great effect to stop the Luxembourg process in the latter 1980s, reappeared. This time, because the EFTAns were taking on all the relevant 'acquis', it was couched in different terms. Spain argued that since its economy would suffer from the extra competition coming from the small, rich EFTA countries, it (and other southern members) deserved financial compensation for this threat.[19] EFTA states agreed to supply 500 million ECU over five years in outright grants and 1500 million ECU in soft loans. All these arrangements have since fallen by the wayside and the residual amounts to be contributed by Iceland, Finland and Norway are, of course, much smaller. But the fact remains that the 'financial mechanism' was conceived as a straightforward pay-off to the poorer members of the EU.

Rules of Origin in the EEA

As far as tariffs were concerned, EFTAns retained their treaty-making power, since at no time did the EC seriously consider offering them full customs-union treatment (although Austria and Norway would reportedly have been prepared to go that route as a preliminary step to full membership (see Schwamm, 1990).

It is interesting in this regard to note that the EC's concern with 'homogeneity' stopped short of insisting that EFTAns should align themselves unilaterally on the common external tariff and EC common commercial policy (as it had insisted upon for the rest of the 'relevant acquis'). But in fact, enough experience had been accumulated in running the bilateral FTAs, with the help of strict rules of origin, to lay fears of unacceptable trade distortions to rest.

The EEA rules of origin take over the essential characteristics of the old FTA rules with the important change that the EEA is 'considered as a single territory'.[20] Thus at last, in the dying days of EFTA, did EFTA countries finally achieve their long-standing objective of 'full cumulation' of origin.

They also obtained the right, long asked for but never accorded, for goods sent outside the EC–EFTA area (for instance to Eastern Europe or North Africa) for so-called 'outward processing' not to lose their EEA-origin status – on condition that the outward processing constituted no more than 10 per cent of the final value of the product. Unfortunately, this concession (already very restrictive) was not extended to textiles and clothing, the principal area where outward processing is so useful to EU producers.

Agriculture

Another part of the 'acquis' which the EFTA countries were not asked to absorb related to the Common Agricultural Policy. However, the EEA agreement provides for the inclusion of industrial materials of agricultural origin and for free trade in agro-industrial products such as yogurt, frozen foods, pasta, etc.

In the course of the negotiations, the southern EC members insisted that EFTA countries should open their frontiers to specifically 'Mediterranean' agricultural products, such as flowers, vegetables, fruit and olive oil. This was viewed by the EFTA governments as additional arm-twisting, since they had already extracted 'payment' in the form of the above-mentioned 'financial mechanism'. The *bilateral* agreements on Mediterranean goods that resulted did not form part of the EEA itself, and are typical 'managed trade' arrangements. In other words, although consumers in Iceland or Norway presumably have much to gain from free access to delicious fresh out-of-season fruit and vegetables, this is definitely not what they have got. For instance, the EC–

Sweden bilateral agreement opened zero-tariff quotas for (*inter alia*) fresh asparagus (100 tons), frozen beans (700 tons), frozen spinach (500 tons), lettuce (from 1 November to 29 February), cherries (from 16 June to 31 July), strawberries (from 1 September to 7 June) and so on.

The purpose of these bilateral agricultural agreements was to meet specific Spanish demands. They had nothing to do with promoting free trade. Their principal effect (and intention) was to divert trade from non-EC Mediterranean producers like Morocco or Israel (see Price, 1995).

Third Countries

A common EEA policy towards third countries was, by definition, not aimed at as far as commercial policy was concerned, as we have just seen. But what of the remaining 'acquis'? How free would the EFTA countries be to negotiate in such areas as services or capital movements with other countries? The answer is – not free at all.

One can scan the Main Agreement in vain for a reference to third countries, apart from the usual reference, in the Preamble, to the Contracting Parties' devotion to 'worldwide trade liberalization and cooperation'. Embedded in the Protocols, however, one can find a few references to third countries. For instance, concerning the negotiation of third-country agreements in respect of mutual recognition of conformity assessment, Protocol 12 states that: 'The Community will negotiate on this basis that the third countries concerned will conclude with the EFTA states parallel mutual recognition agreements equivalent to those to be concluded with the Community.' There is no doubt as to which side takes the initiative in relations with third countries, nor what is expected of the EFTA states! They must not stray from the path marked out for them by the EU.

In fact, to the extent that the 'acquis' itself contains provisions regarding third countries (for example, the audio-visual sector, banking and financial services, public procurement, etc.), the EFTA countries must simply take over the external aspects of the relevant 'acquis' as well as the internal ones. To the extent that the future 'acquis' will involve international negotiations, for example within the context of the WTO, the EFTAns must simply negotiate 'parallel' agreements 'equivalent to those to be concluded with the Community', as the phrase goes. A moment's reflection will soon convince one that the EC, in the name of homogeneity, could not in fact tolerate any independent action on the part of the EFTAns.

CONCLUSION

The EEA may have started out well enough, and possibly, under different conditions, might have borne fruit. But the EC gained so much political weight and self-confidence during the very years which were devoted to negotiating the agreement, that it rode roughshod over the little EFTA countries. The hardest condition for the EFTAns was doubtless the agreement to integrate the unknown future 'acquis' into the EEA, without any exceptions and without any control over its content. Yet from the EU's point of view, it was out of the question to open its own, already complex, decision-making procedures, to a group of non-member states. It was so suspicious of diversity that it simply imposed the past, present and future 'acquis' without exceptions, as we have seen.

But nothing is without a cost. So complete was the success of the EC in the EEA negotiations that no wonder the EFTAns rushed to join their tormentors! No wonder Switzerland rejected the agreement in December 1992. No wonder only peripheral Iceland, with its economy entirely based on fish, and Norway with its huge oil reserves, could 'afford' to put up with the EEA. Only little Liechtenstein's acceptance of the EEA (including – amazingly – the 'acquis' on money laundering) remains a mystery – one of those quirks in the ongoing story of European integration which reminds us that the process is inscrutable and far from linear.

On 1 January 1995, Austria, Finland and Sweden duly joined the EU as members, leaving Iceland, Liechtenstein and Norway as the only EFTA signatories of the EEA agreement, and reducing EFTA itself to a membership of only four – the above three plus Switzerland. Intra-EFTA trade fell to negligible proportions (less than 1 per cent), while EFTAns' trade dependence on the EU rose to 70 per cent. The sky, however, did not fall on their heads. Virtually simultaneously the Final Act of the Uruguay Round came into force, the WTO was created and the 'second generation' of integration issues was sketched into the multilateral system itself. The EFTA 'orphans' had found a shelter.

Notes

1. EFTA MFN tariffs on manufactured goods being on the whole rather low (with the exception of Austria and Portugal), there was not much scope for sizeable trade diversion.

2. Any resemblance to a real country is purely accidental and unintentional.
3. Note that 'drawback' (namely, the restitution of import duties paid on intermediate goods which are transformed or incorporated in another product and subsequently exported) is not permitted on intra-EFTA or intra-FTA trade. This constitutes an added incentive to members to ensure that viable activities are not penalised by redundant tariffs.
4. See Price (1974), pp. 171–2.
5. See Herin (1986), p. 7.
6. See Koskinen (1983), p. 7.
7. See Herin (1986), p. 8.
8. Ibid., p. 11.
9. See Binswanger and Mayrzedt (1972), pp. 84–7 for a discussion on what the evolutionary clause seemed to imply in 1972. It has come up to expectations as far as scientific cooperation is concerned, but not in respect of monetary cooperation or industrial policy.
10. The full text of the joint declaration issued after the Luxembourg meeting, 9 April 1984, is to be found as an appendix to the *Twenty-fourth Annual Report of the European Free Trade Association*, Geneva, March 1985, pp. 53–5.
11. International commercial diplomacy, for instance in GATT or WTO, is generally based on formal reciprocity only, since 'size of market' arguments would constitute an all too blatant exercise of power on the part of large countries or units, and would in the long run prove unacceptable to smaller ones. However, it would be naive to think that such arguments are not sometimes used. From an economic point of view, it is not clear that they have any validity. Reciprocal agreements to liberalise commerce open up new opportunities to be seized upon by alert entrepreneurs. There is no knowing in advance where these alert people live (or where their counterparts, the sleepy non-entrepreneurial managers of established firms, are situated). 'Access to markets' can be turned into 'fearsome competition', depending on the quality, or ineptitude, of a country's entrepreneurs. Put another way, 'access to markets' does not imply property rights over such markets. Markets, to be 'possessed', must be won every day by producers persuading customers that their product is competitive. This is why 'size of market' arguments in commercial diplomacy are false in economic terms and are more akin to the neo-mercantilist 'managed-market' view of trade than one based on free market processes.
12. *Bulletin of the European Communities*, no. 5, 1987, point 2.2.14.
13. Text of speech to be found in *Bulletin of the European Communities*, supplement 1/89, pp. 1–27.
14. See René Schwok (1989). Although, already by 1988, the Austrian government seems to have reached the conclusion that Gorbachev would not object too strongly to Austrian membership of the EC, and that it was therefore urgent to take advantage of this window of opportunity before a change of power took place in the USSR.
15. The worry was, at the time, that admitting 'too many' neutral countries would make it impossible for the EC to proceed from economic to

political union. See Willy De Clercq (1988). In the event, these concerns have fallen quickly away with the end of the Cold War; even such a venerable institution as neutrality seems to have lost its relevance in the post-communist world.

16. The term 'acquis communautaire' covers all relevant EC directives and regulations, plus all relevant decisions by the European Court of Justice, forming the vast body of EC law which underpins the single European market. As we shall see below, the EEA does not cover *all* aspects of EU life, so there are parts of the 'acquis' which are not 'relevant'.
17. Opinion 1/91 of the ECJ, 16 December 1991.
18. For EFTA citizens this implied a right of direct access to a legal system similar to the rights enjoyed by EU citizens with regard to the 'acquis'. It should be emphasised that this 'direct applicability' of international trade law does not constitute a loss of sovereignty of one state *vis-à-vis* another, but rather gives individuals legal rights *vis-à-vis* their own governments, which thereby lose their discretionary powers to act as they please in the relevant field. See Ernst-Ulrich Petersmann (1994). Of course, GATT–WTO law is not directly applicable in the EEA, and consequently EEA citizens have no legal rights in this regard.
19. This argument has, of course, no more standing in economics than the 'size of market' argument used previously. The Spanish economy *benefits* from extra competition, since this improves the conditions for alert entrepreneurs (of which there are many in Spain) to take reasonably correct decisions based on market realities. Neo-mercantilism, however, still holds great sway over policy-makers.
20. Protocol 4, Title II, Article 2.

8 The North American Free Trade Agreement

Sidney Weintraub

The North American Free Trade Agreement (NAFTA) went into effect on 1 January 1994. Three aspects of the agreement should be highlighted:

1. NAFTA reinforces an emphasis on regionalism by the United States, which, earlier – before the Canada–US Free Trade Agreement (CUFTA) of 1989 – had been the bulwark of multilateralism.[1]
2. NAFTA is an integration arrangement between one dominant economic power, the United States, with two other countries which are much smaller economically, Canada and Mexico.
3. NAFTA brings together two countries with high per capita incomes, Canada and the United States, with a low income country, Mexico.

The first of these elements has shaped international trade discussions – indeed, international economic and even geopolitical debate – ever since. This was inevitable because the United States is the world's leading trading nation. The second was decisive in shaping the form of the agreement as a free trade area as opposed to a customs union. And the third stimulated what was the most vitriolic trade debate in the United States since the Second World War. In addition, because the economic disparities between Mexico and the two other NAFTA members are greater than between the highest and lowest income countries in the European Union (EU) as now constituted, the experiment can influence EU decisions with respect to the inclusion of countries in Eastern Europe and the former Soviet Union.

The discussion that follows, after some groundwork is laid, will elaborate on each of these points. The next section will set forth the motivations of each of the three countries in entering NAFTA. This will be followed by a description of developments within the NAFTA area since it has been in effect. The content of the agreement will then be sketched in broad outline. The analysis will then focus in the final section on the three points mentioned above.

MOTIVATIONS OF THE NAFTA COUNTRIES

The United States

The US shift from near exclusive reliance on multilateralism to adding regionalism as another trade policy option had two major stimuli. The first was dissatisfaction with the progress of trade liberalisation in negotiations in the General Agreement on Tariffs and Trade (GATT), now the World Trade Organisation (WTO). This was especially true in areas in which GATT had no real track record, such as trade in services, protection of intellectual property, and investment matters, and in those sectors in which GATT had been singularly ineffective, such as liberalising agricultural trade.[2] There was a conviction that more rapid progress could be made in regional negotiations than in the multilateral framework.[3]

US supporters of the dual track of regionalism and multilateralism also justified their position – their advocacy of departure from the most-favoured-nation principle (MFN) – by asserting that regional agreements on difficult and new themes would encourage progress in GATT negotiations as well. This, in fact, occurred in the Uruguay Round, but there was no assurance at the time of the CUFTA that it would, nor does it necessarily follow that US regionalism was the main impetus for the GATT progress in these areas.

Table 8.1 Economic and demographic data: NAFTA and western hemisphere

	Mexico	*Canada*	*United States*	*NAFTA*	*ROH**
GDP (billion $, 1993)	343	477	6,260	7,080	1,063
GNP per capita ($, 1993)	3,610	19,970	24,740	16,107	2,834
Exports (billion $, 1993)	30	145	465	640	105
Imports (billion $, 1993)	50	132	603	785	114
Population (million, 1993)	90	29	258	377	375

Note
* Rest of hemisphere.
Source: World Bank, *World Development Report, 1995*.

A second argument supporting US regionalism was the existence of the expanding European Community (today's EU). It was becoming increasingly difficult to persuade the US Congress that the United States should not itself embark on regional trade agreements because of their inherent discrimination against non-members in the face of the discrimination exporters from the United States faced in Western Europe. It had become evident that regionalism in Europe would not disappear; if anything, it was expanding to additional countries. Preferential regionalism in Europe, so the argument went, could not be purged by US insistence on multilateralism. This was the ideal context in which to argue that regionalism in Europe is best dealt with by regionalism in North America and that one day – some day – the two regionalisms can come together.[4]

Canada was the logical country with which to make the significant change in US trade policy. Canada, which normally is the destination of about 20 per cent of US merchandise exports, is by far the largest US trading partner.[5] Beyond this, the investment and production links between the two countries are extensive. US foreign direct investment (FDI) is greater in Canada than in any other country, save the United Kingdom, where the high level is the result of large US investments in banking and finance. About half of US investment in Canada is in manufacturing.[6]

Perhaps even more germane is the reinforcement that US FDI gives to merchandise and service trade with Canada. Some 70 per cent of Canadian exports are not conducted at arm's length; about 40 per cent is intra-firm and another 30 per cent the result of licensing and strategic alliances between Canadian and foreign corporations (Hart, 1994, p. 20). The US Department of Commerce estimates that about half of US manufactured exports to Canada is to affiliated companies. The degree of economic integration between Canada and the United States was extensive even before the negotiation of the CUFTA. The agreement provided a legal framework for assuring investors of the continuity of this close relationship.

The coproduction inherent in intra-firm trade requires low border barriers because much of the interchange is in intermediate products that require further elaboration, rather than in final products. It was no accident that the most important supporters of CUFTA were large multinational corporations who produce in both countries and trade extensively with each other. These are led by the big three automobile producers – General Motors, Ford and Chrysler – but not exclusively by them.[7]

The motivation for US support of free trade with Mexico was more complex than with Canada, but the underlying rationale of reinforcing the growing coproduction arrangements was the same. In 1992, about 40 per cent of manufactured imports from Mexico were intra-firm and the proportion has grown since then.[8] This figure does not include trade resulting from strategic alliances between US and Mexican firms. Here, too, as with Canada, multinational corporations wished to obtain, under the protection of an international agreement, the security of low border barriers to stimulate FDI and facilitate coproduction by affiliated firms located in both countries. Coproduction had become particularly important in the border area in *maquiladora* plants, but NAFTA facilitates the extension of this practice more widely in Mexico.[9]

Two other US motives for entering into free trade with Mexico were important. The first was to lock in the extensive policy changes that had occurred in Mexico following that country's entry into GATT in 1986. This proved to be important at the end of 1994, when Mexico suffered a deep financial and economic crisis. After the previous crisis of similar proportions, in 1982, Mexico reacted by raising import barriers. NAFTA foreclosed this option for imports from the United States and Canada and Mexican adjustment this time took the form of restrictive macroeconomic policy.

The second reason was political. Mexico took the initiative for free trade with the United States in 1990. This was a remarkable shift in bilateral relations which earlier had been what one widely read book called 'distant' (Riding, 1985, p. 21). The proposal for free trade signified that Mexico instead wished relations to be close. It would have been hard for any responsible US leader to spurn this initiative of a populous neighbouring country and George Bush, then president of the United States, did not.

Canada

Canada, among the industrial countries, was a latecomer to liberalising its import regime. This did not really take place until the Tokyo Round, which was completed in 1979. Even now, Canadian tariffs, on average, are about 8 to 9 per cent, double those of the United States. While there was considerable US FDI in Canada, much of this took the form of what in Canada were called branch plants, that is, operations protected against imports and which produced primarily for the Canadian market. Productivity in Canada lagged behind that in the United States by some 25 per cent (Hart, 1994, p. 21).

In addition, Canada did not succeed in diversifying its export markets. In the early 1970s, Canada adopted what was called the 'third-option' policy, essentially a programme to diversify markets. In the period since, Canadian export dependency on the United States has grown from about 70 per cent of the total to more than 80 per cent today (Figure 8.1). Consequently, when there were indications during the 1980s that US trade policy might become more protectionist, the Canadian authorities, buttressed by big businesses in the country, looked for a way to insulate Canadian exports to the United States from increased barriers.[10] A free trade agreement was the logical technique.

Canada thus had two major motives for requesting free trade negotiations. These were to attract investment in plants of sufficient size to achieve economies of scale, and to obtain insurance against an expected increase in US protectionism. The first, in fact, is being achieved. Canadian firms are increasingly looking south, whereas the branch plant mentality forced them to look primarily east and west within Canada. The second objective was only partly achieved in that while US tariffs will disappear, US use of antidumping (AD) and countervailing duty (CVD) procedures were not altered by CUFTA. Under NAFTA as well, each member country retains its own AD and CVD laws and procedures despite the existence of free trade.[11] The most serious trade disputes between the two countries generally arise over the application of these trade remedy laws. The most spectacular case, potentially involving billions of dollars of Canadian exports, concerned softwood lumber.[12]

The use of AD and CVD protection can be costly for the exporting firms involved, but they generally do not affect more than 1 to 2 per cent of trade in either direction. CUFTA did include a dispute settlement mechanism for these cases under which binational panels can be empowered at the request of the aggrieved party to determine whether the country imposing AD or CVD measures correctly followed its own national laws and regulations. The system has worked well in the sense that a number of administrative actions have been reversed. This dispute resolution mechanism has been carried over into NAFTA.

When the United States made known its intention to enter into free trade negotiations with Mexico, Canada was confronted with a decision of its own. Should it enter into these negotiations as well? The argument against entering into the negotiations was the same as that

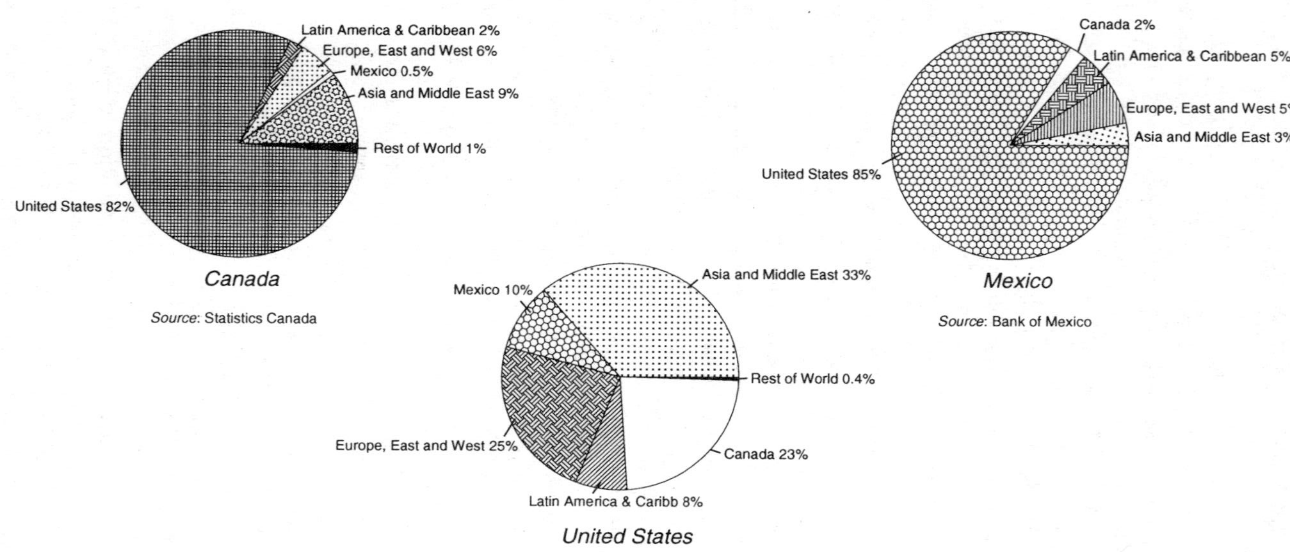

Figure 8.1 Merchandise exports of NAFTA countries, 1994

of US opponents, namely, concern over free trade with a developing country whose wages were, at most, one-seventh of those in Canada. Canada, in addition, had little direct trade with Mexico. The case for joining the negotiations was that if the United States and Mexico concluded a free trade agreement, a hub-and-spoke arrangement would result – the United States would be the hub and Canada and Mexico the spokes and only the United States would have free trade across North America (Wonnacott, 1991).[13] In the end, Canada entered into the three-way negotiations, although as a 'reluctant' partner.[14]

Mexico

The decision to seek free trade was a more momentous decision for Mexico than for either the United States or Canada. Mexico had an emerging industrial structure, but it had been sheltered from practically all international competition until just a few years before the free trade decision was taken. Prevailing economic thinking of trade experts was that integration would lead to polarisation favouring the stronger partner at the expense of the weaker. In addition, Mexico was coming out of a Latin American tradition which believed in the dependency theory, that open markets inexorably led to exploitation by the stronger countries. In Mexico's case, this was buttressed by a long-standing sentiment, rooted in history, of suspicion of US motives and therefore of seeking as much independence of action as feasible. Mexico's philosophy of development from within (it is worth recalling that Mexico did not even accede to GATT until 1986) and limits on FDI were designed primarily as defensive measures against ingrained concern about US power dominating internal Mexican affairs.

Nevertheless, once Mexico shifted policy from emphasis on import substitution towards export promotion, the logic as seen by its leaders was to assure access to its main market, the United States. This way of thinking was similar to that of Canada. Each country relied overwhelmingly on the US market for its exports (70 to 85 per cent in each case – see Figure 8.1) and each was concerned about what it feared was nascent US protectionism. Carlos Salinas de Gortari, the Mexican president after 1988, decided to take the plunge into free trade after he was convinced that Mexico could expect little FDI from Europe and that Europe was unlikely to be a major destination for Mexican manufactured exports in any reasonable time period. This assessment also paralleled that of Canadian policy-makers when they opted for free trade with the United States.

One final philosophical consideration was important in the Mexico decision. This was the make-up of Mexico's economic cabinet. The senior officials and many of their most important subordinates received their doctorates in economics from leading US universities. They also were believers in an open market and the importance of export promotion. This led Mexico into a sharp and unilateral reduction of import barriers before the free trade initiative was taken. Their concern, and that of President Salinas as well, was to lock in these market-opening reforms to make it difficult for any future government to reverse course. This locking-in desire also motivated US policy-makers.

Public opinion polls showed greater support for NAFTA in Mexico than in the United States, but the figures were unreliable. There was not deep knowledge of the proposed agreement in either country, but surely less in Mexico than in the United States. The authoritarian nature of the Mexican political structure also served to limit the debate that took place. Thus, the government chose to hold hearings on NAFTA in the Mexican Senate, which it thoroughly dominated, and not in the Chamber of Deputies, where the opposition voices were more numerous. Most of the media, especially television, supported the NAFTA initiative. Thus, while it is relatively easy to analyse the motives of the Mexican authorities, it is more problematic to be certain about public views of entry into NAFTA and the economic–political accommodation with the United States that this step represented.

NAFTA IN OPERATION

NAFTA, despite its wordiness, is like the frame of a house, a design of what must be constructed, and not a finished product. An economic integration arrangement among countries cannot be static but must deepen as circumstances change. Failing that, it will atrophy and die. Consequently, it is most unwise to reach any definitive conclusions about the success or failure of NAFTA from the short period it has been in operation. It is possible to state what happened since 1 January 1994, in trade, economic relations and overall interaction between the three countries, but it is impossible to conclude that what has occurred is the result solely or even mainly of NAFTA's existence – see Chapter 4. Every new student of economics is taught to beware of the *post hoc, ergo propter hoc* fallacy.

In addition, a preferential arrangement involving the most important country and the largest market for exports in the western hemisphere must act as a magnet for other, would-be, adherents. The present EU attracted new members once it was clear that the intent was serious and the results beneficial for the member countries. This was not a continuous process, but an accretion that proceeded in fits and starts. The enlargement in Europe is still going on – Poland soon, other countries in Eastern Europe later, and perhaps after that the republics of the former Soviet Union (see Chapters 5 and 6 for more on this).

When President George Bush suggested the enlargement of NAFTA to include the rest of the western hemisphere, to construct what is now called a Free Trade Area of the Americas (FTAA), this was seen as a most positive step by most countries of the hemisphere (Weintraub, 1993, 1994). There is now agreement among these countries to conclude negotiations for an FTAA by the year 2005.

These introductory words are to warn the reader that NAFTA is very much an agreement in formation, that even if all goes as anticipated over time there will be setbacks along the way, and that one or two years is an inadequate period from which to judge what is intended to be a long-term arrangement. This goes against the grain of many politicians in the United States for whom there is only the here and now – whether favourable or not – but must not be forgotten by students of NAFTA or by the governments involved.

During NAFTA's first year of life, 1994, trade among the three member countries flourished. For example, US–Mexico trade grew by more than 20 per cent in each direction. Because NAFTA was sold to the American public on mercantilistic grounds – that the United States would have a trade surplus with Mexico – the 1994 trade results were hailed by NAFTA supporters. Following the financial and economic crisis that erupted in Mexico at the end of December 1994 and the consequent devaluation of the peso and slowdown in the economy, there was a Mexican trade surplus in 1995. The opponents are seizing this outcome as proof of NAFTA failure.

Both arguments are faulty. A bilateral merchandise trade surplus or deficit in a global trading structure is not normally a significant fact. The growth in two-way trade is the more relevant measure. What is intended to be a long-term relationship cannot be judged by year-to-year outcomes, to laud the agreement when it is mercantilistically favourable and then deplore it when the bilateral trade balance shifts.

For many years after CUFTA came into effect, Canada had low economic growth and high unemployment. The primary reason for this was Canada's tight monetary policy, which raised interest rates and led to capital inflows and appreciation of the Canadian dollar.

Canadian opponents of CUFTA, however, blamed the poor economic performance on the free trade agreement. Even in those years, an analysis of Canadian trade with the United States showed that trade in both directions increased most in those sectors liberalised by CUFTA. The Canadian export increase was particularly great in non-resource-based manufacturing industry (Schwanen, 1993). Merchandise exports of each country to the other two NAFTA members increased substantially in 1994.

NAFTA differs from the EU and most other economic integration arrangements in that it did not create a central executive arm, such as the Commission of the EU. This was deliberate. The framers wanted to minimise the political content of the agreement. There is a NAFTA commission, with headquarters in Mexico City, but it is not a body that meets continuously, nor does it have independent authority to originate proposals. It is intended much more to help resolve disputes between the three member countries and to serve as a forum for discussions among them. It resembles the EU Council much more than the Commission.

NAFTA also differs from the EU in that there are no provisions for the transfer of resources from the economically stronger countries to Mexico. Had aid of this type been included, it is certain that NAFTA would not have been approved. Nevertheless, when Mexico needed support to overcome the financial difficulties of late 1994 and early 1995, massive resources were made available. As will be noted below, NAFTA made a big difference in both Mexican and US–Canadian behaviour during this financial crisis.

One other difference between NAFTA and the EU should be noted. NAFTA is a free trade area; it was never intended to be a common market that permitted the free movement of labour across the three countries. Many critics of the agreement, in Mexico as well as the other two countries, criticised this omission. They argued that there would be free movement of capital; why not free movement of the other mobile factor of production, labour? This, however, was never more than a rhetorical position because it was clear that there could be no approval either in the United States or Canada if low income, low wage, generally low skill Mexicans were given legal authority to enter the United States at will. This is a practical reality of economic integration between a low income and two high income countries. Nevertheless, there is probably more movement of labour, open and clandestine, to the United States from Mexico than there is among the countries of the EU.[15]

NAFTA's Institutional Structure

The lack of a sizeable and powerful central executive body does not mean that NAFTA has no institutional depth. Two commissions were established under the parallel agreements approved simultaneously with NAFTA, the Commission for Environmental Cooperation located in Montreal, and the Commission for Labour Cooperation with headquarters in Dallas. A North American Development Bank was established, with headquarters in San Antonio, to provide funding for border infrastructure and this institution works cooperatively with the Border Environmental Cooperation Commission between Mexico and the United States.

The NAFTA document establishes many working groups dealing with salient issues for the operation of the agreement. These groups include those seeking harmonisation or compatibility of industrial standards; of safety and other standards for trucks and buses which over a number of years will have the right to traverse the territory of the three countries; sanitary standards for foodstuffs; simplifying rules of origin; accelerating customs clearances; facilitating trade in a number of sectors, such as agriculture, textiles and clothing, and telecommunications; and working out procedures for financial relations among the three countries.

NAFTA has a number of dispute-resolution mechanisms, those dealing with trade generally, AD and CVD cases, agriculture, and financial issues. Rosters of panellists have been created for the arbitral proceedings necessary for resolving many of these disputes. As noted earlier, the technique for dealing with AD and CVD disputes is highly innovative in that it substitutes an arbitration process that operates more rapidly than the normal judicial procedure.

The United States, outside the purview of NAFTA as such, has separate arrangements with Canada and Mexico for annual meetings between cabinet level officials. There are long-standing interparliamentary meetings between the United States and each of the other two countries.

Mexico's 1995 Economic Crisis

NAFTA was severely tested after Mexico devalued the peso on 20 December 1994. The background to this action has been widely discussed in the media and needs only a brief description here to set the context for the actions that followed.[16] Mexico, during 1994, had a number of concurrent developments that weakened confidence in the peso and in the management of economic policy. These included a large deficit in the current account of the balance of payments amounting to around $30 billion, or 8 per cent of GDP; political shocks of major dimensions, such as the assassination of the presidential candidate of the Institutional Revolutionary Party (PRI), the party that has dominated the Mexican political scene since 1929, and then later the murder of the number two officer of the PRI; and a presidential campaign that stimulated charges of irregularities and which also apparently encouraged relatively lax monetary policy so as not to damage the chances of the PRI candidate. In addition, the US Federal Reserve Board raised interest rates repeatedly during 1994 and this forced up interest rates in Mexico to enable the country to attract the large volume of portfolio capital needed to finance the current account deficit.

Mexico's foreign exchange reserves declined from a level of $29 billion at the start of 1994 to a low of about $5 billion in mid-December. Under these circumstances, the Mexican authorities felt they had no choice other than to devalue the peso, which they did on 20 December from 3.50 to 4.00 to the dollar. The action, rather than calm international investors, stimulated panic. The 4.00 peso to the dollar rate did not hold and Mexico lacked reserves to protect it. At one point, the peso was trading at more than 8.00 to the dollar. But the most dire outcome was that holders of Mexican government debt, particularly that indexed to the dollar, were unwilling to roll over this debt at an acceptable interest rate and the country immediately faced a liquidity problem of major proportions.[17]

The choices theoretically open to Mexico were to default on payment of its notes, impose exchange controls, or increase import restrictions. Neither the first nor the second option – really, the same option phrased differently – was chosen. The third choice, to raise import tariffs, would have ruptured Mexico's commitment in NAFTA and Mexico did not do so. It did raise import tariffs on many consumer goods coming from countries with which there were no free trade agreements.

Mexico was spared the default/exchange control option by the rescue package stimulated by the United States, involving $20 billion of funds from the US Exchange Stabilisation Fund (ESF), a potential $17.8 billion from the International Monetary Fund, $10 billion from a number of central banks operating through the Bank for

International Settlements, plus commitments from the World Bank and the Inter-American Development Bank. These credits were designed primarily to provide assurance to money markets that funds would be available for Mexico to meet its obligations.

The rescue package worked in the sense of stabilising the peso and permitting Mexico to meet its obligations. The conditions accompanying the package for tight fiscal and monetary policy were quite strong and, consequently, Mexico in 1995 faced a declining economy and a substantial rise in unemployment.

The rescue package was highly controversial and led to a renewed debate in the United States on the wisdom of NAFTA. Yet, the more salient matter was that difficult measures were taken by Mexico and the United States that arguably would not have been adopted had NAFTA not been in existence. When President Clinton's proposal for legislation to provide a credit of $40 billion for Mexico ran into congressional opposition, he shifted instead to the ESF, which was under the jurisdiction of the Treasury Department, to provide funds without legislative approval. Much pressure was exerted on the IMF for its standby agreement with Mexico. The US $20 billion and the IMF $17.8 billion were the largest credits of their type ever granted to any country. While the United States had provided financial assistance during previous Mexican crises, for example in 1982, it is doubtful that the size of the 1995 effort would have been as great had NAFTA not been in place. Even in the absence of a formal structure within NAFTA for resource transfers, financial assistance was forthcoming in the emergency Mexico faced.

In previous crises, such as 1982, when Mexico faced a balance of payments crisis, the remedy included increased import restrictions. This solution undoubtedly would have been used again in 1994–5, absent NAFTA. NAFTA, in other words, did have the effect of deepening the relationship (Weintraub, 1995b).

Crisis Causation

Did NAFTA bring on Mexico's financial crisis, as many critics assert? The short answer is 'no', but some elaboration is needed. Much confidence had been built up outside Mexico about the correctness of its economic programme. The programme consisted of many linked policies, such as the trade opening, the shift to greater reliance on the private sector epitomised by the substantial privatisation of government-owned enterprises, the welcome to FDI, the reduction of the public sector deficit, and the sustained anti-inflation programme. These policies antedated NAFTA. There was concern both inside and outside Mexico about the increasingly overvalued exchange rate and the large current account deficit, but this did not impede inflows of capital, both direct and portfolio, until the catastrophic political events of 1994.

This confidence in the abilities of Mexico's key economic officials, coupled with approbation of the broad elements of economic policy, certainly stimulated the inflow of capital. The establishment of NAFTA surely reinforced this confidence by providing some assurance against backsliding on trade and economic policy. NAFTA, in this sense, encouraged capital inflows. But foreign capital was seeking out many emerging markets, not just Mexico, so the motivation was not just NAFTA, but rather the promise of high returns with what was thought to be moderate risk.

Another line of reasoning of NAFTA opponents is that the agreement was the major cause of Mexico's large current account deficit in 1994. This argument does not stand up to scrutiny either. Mexico, in 1994, had a merchandise trade deficit of $18.5 billion. Of that, $3 billion was with Mexico's NAFTA partners, almost all of this with the United States. The remainder, more than $15 billion, was with Europe and Asia, almost equally divided between the two. It was not intra-NAFTA merchandise trade that aggravated the current account deficit, but Mexico's inability to penetrate non-NAFTA markets. Mexico's exports to the United States grew by 20 per cent in 1994 over 1993, while its exports to the rest of the world grew by only 4.3 per cent.[18]

Despite its comprehensiveness, the NAFTA document did not deal with the one area that turned out to be critical – namely, Mexico's macroeconomic policy. The exchange rate was allowed to become overvalued due to its use as the anchor of the anti-inflation policy. Mexico allowed itself to become highly vulnerable to shocks by excessive reliance on portfolio capital to finance its large current account deficit. Monetary policy did not tighten in the face of declining foreign exchange reserves. Government debt became shorter and shorter in maturity and much of it was indexed to the dollar.

In the aftermath of the crisis, it is possible to argue that these issues should have been part of the agreement, but that would have entailed a political commitment that none of the three countries wanted. It is now possible that the earlier imperative of an agreement with minimum political content will be re-examined. An alert and more independent secretariat might have signalled danger signs. This will certainly be an issue for the future, especially if and as NAFTA is enlarged. In that case, the preference for minimal bureaucracy may have to give way to more organisational sophistication.

CONTENT OF NAFTA AS WRITTEN

NAFTA is a lengthy document, but much of the space is taken up with transition arrangements until the free trade area is in effect, generally in ten years but up to fifteen (even more for used cars) for products considered sensitive.[19] The form the agreement takes is a core document, quite straightforward as these things go, with special features, generally contained in annexes to the main chapters, dealing with different arrangements for the member countries. Thus annex 2106 (that is, an annex to chapter 21) continues the exclusion Canada obtained in the CUFTA from free trade in cultural industries.[20] Neither of the other two countries felt it necessary to obtain this exception. Annexes 602.3, 603.6 and 605 provide exceptions for Mexico on energy exploration, exploitation and trade. In effect, this means there are two distinct agreements in this sector, one between the United States and Canada and the other between these two countries and Mexico. There are also, in practice, two separate agreements on trade in agriculture, a transition over fifteen years for free trade between Mexico and the United States and a less comprehensive commitment between Canada and the other two countries.

The structure of the agreement, by placing transition arrangements in annexes, was designed in part to facilitate negotiation with other applicant countries. They, presumably, would be expected to accept the core document but could seek their own transitional arrangements. The first test of how well this works is the expected negotiation for Chilean accession. The accession clause, which is in the main text of the agreement, is quite brief – two sentences – and requires consent of all member countries, although a country can permit accession to NAFTA without allowing the agreement to apply between it and the acceding country.

Although NAFTA represents 'integration of a lesser kind' as compared with the EU, it is quite comprehensive in its coverage.[21] It comprises the usual things, such as the transition to free trade in goods, reducing technical barriers to trade in such areas as setting industrial and sanitary standards, opening up government procurement, and providing national and most-favoured-nation treatment for foreign investment. On this last point, it was common for Mexican critics of the agreement to argue that it was primarily an investment, not a trade agreement.[22] This, in its way, was an appeal to nationalism. NAFTA most certainly is an investment agreement, but the thinking of the framers was that trade and investment are not separable, particularly in this age of growing coproduction and trade between affiliated firms in intermediate products.

The agreement also has chapters on trade in services, telecommunications, finance, competition policy and intellectual property. Many of these themes are precisely those the United States emphasised in the Uruguay Round. The financial sector liberalisation called for in the agreement was accelerated in the aftermath of the crisis in Mexico's banking industry. The agreement permitted gradual entry of foreign banks into Mexico until the year 2000 for individual firms and 2007 for Mexican use of temporary safeguards to protect the national industry. As a result of the financial crisis, foreign banking investment was opened much more widely and, in fact, more than half a dozen foreign banks have opened new operations in Mexico.

There have also been frustrations on both sides with lingering protectionism for various sectors.[23] These showed up in onerous labelling requirements imposed by the Mexicans for the entry of machinery and equipment and on denial of national treatment to United Parcel Service on the size of trucks it could use for delivery of packages in Mexico; and in continuing restrictions by the United States on the entry of Mexican avocados, allegedly on sanitary grounds. Each of these has either been resolved or is being negotiated.

The more serious shortcomings of the agreement, because they are intended to be durable, are the protectionism inherent in the rules of origin, particularly for automotive products and the textile and clothing trade. The rules for these two products are complex and occupy many pages of text in the agreement. For automobiles, the basic rule is that to be eligible for free trade, North American content must reach at least 62.5 per cent. The percentage is 60 per cent for some vehicles and parts. The actual percentage will be determined only after what is known as deep tracing, that is, tracking the North American content in key components. The process is laborious and expensive, perhaps more so than paying the 2.5 per cent import duty for entry of autos into the United States. The rule in the textile and clothing sector has been called the triple transformation test; this requires that in order for clothing products to be eligible for free trade, they must be made from fabric spun from North American fibres.

Rules of origin are obviously necessary in a free trade area to prevent shipment of products into a low tariff member country for trans-shipment into another country with higher tariffs. Yet, they can be converted easily from a practical necessity into a protective device. Protection exists as well in a customs union, as the EU's common agricultural policy demonstrates, but the manipulation of rules of origin is too arcane for the general consumer to appreciate. There is much to the argument that a customs union in North America, with a common external tariff (CET), would have been preferable from a trade viewpoint, but this was politically impossible at the time.

The other major shortcoming is the lack of NAFTA-wide rules for AD and CVD actions. Petitions for such duties have become the protective device of choice for producers to exclude competitive products.[24] Canada, which is a heavy user of AD actions, has stated its desire to make North America more of a 'free trade' area rather than three separate countries with respect to these actions. The United States has been unwilling to deal with its restrictive laws and procedures for AD and CVD actions – or more likely, unable to do so in the current atmosphere of trade politics. US law requires no evidence of predation when petitions are presented to impose duties on foreign goods allegedly dumped in the United States, whereas domestic anti-competition law does have such a requirement. Thus, the same product, produced under the same circumstances in, say, Detroit, Michigan and Windsor, and Ontario, just across the border, and shipped to the same destination in the United States, would be treated differently from a dumping viewpoint despite the existence of a free trade area between Canada and the United States.

Mexico, which did not employ these so-called unfair trade measures before NAFTA, has since become an avid user. Perhaps progress on a less protectionist structure will come as each country calculates that its producers are being hurt as much as they are being protected.

Despite these shortcomings, reaching agreement on NAFTA in the three countries was a significant accomplishment. Trade, for the most part, will be made much freer. As NAFTA matures, as the transition gives way to the free trade area and as the voids in the agreement are filled in by the many working groups and commissions that exist, many of the current shortcomings are likely to diminish. The three countries will also gain experience in dealing with environment and labour market issues related to trade. As NAFTA is enlarged, its institutional structure will have to become more elaborate.

IMPLICATIONS

Trading Blocs

The EU, under its various names, has been in existence for more than thirty-five years, but there was little talk of the world dividing into three major trading blocs before CUFTA and NAFTA were concluded. This division has since become a major theme of international trade and geopolitical debate.

It is technically arguable whether North America is a trading 'bloc' in the absence of a common external tariff or a common commercial policy. NAFTA, however, is clearly a preferential trading area. Moreover, there are pretensions for enlarging the preferential region to the entire western hemisphere. The MFN principle, in that case, will be eroded further.

An even stronger technical argument can be made that there is no trading bloc in East Asia in the absence of even a preferential arrangement, particularly one including Japan, the region's dominant economic and trading nation. Yet there is no doubt that intra-regional trade has been growing rapidly in East Asia. While there is no formal bloc, there is de facto regional trade growth.

The evidence is indisputable that intra-regional trade is growing rapidly in each of the three geographic areas – Western Europe defined as the EU, North America defined as NAFTA, and East Asia. The change in intra-regional and interregional trade between 1980 and 1990 is shown graphically in Figure 8.2. The proportion of North America's interregional trade with the other two regions has declined over this period. Whether or not 'bloc' is the appropriate word to describe what is happening in the three major regions, the facts speak for themselves – a tripolar trading world is emerging.

This surely has political as well as economic implications. In its long-running trade conflict over Japanese imports of automobiles and parts, the United States was prepared to go to the brink of a trade war that was averted only at the eleventh hour in mid-1995. Whatever one thinks of US tactics and the Japanese response, this was a sign that security relationships no longer dictate US policy and that trade issues have a high profile.

As recently as thirty years ago, the United States specifically rejected the idea of limiting trade preferences to Latin America and chose instead a general system of preferences for developing countries, on the grounds that regionalism would distort global political

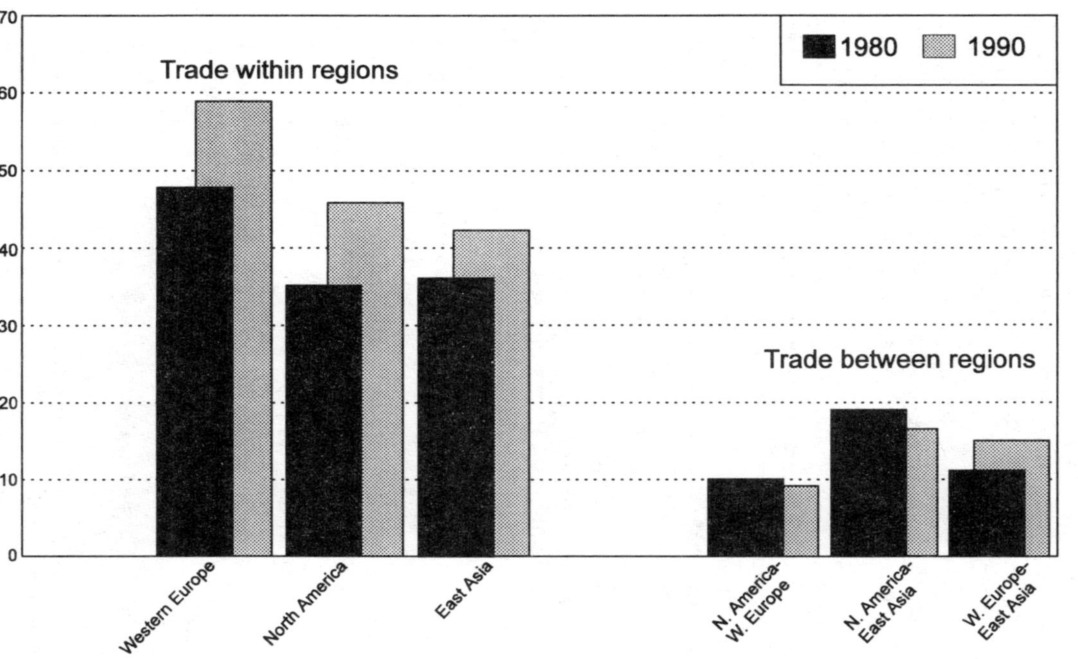

Source: Weintraub (1994).

Figure 8.2 Trade within and between three world regions, 1980 and 1990 (percentage merchandise imports, current values).

relations. Now the United States proudly trumpets its free trade concentration on the Americas. All the countries in the hemisphere, save Cuba, endorsed the concept and put a specific date – 2005 – on completion of the negotiations.

The political ramifications of trade regionalism go beyond the western hemisphere. The countries of the Asia-Pacific Economic Cooperation (APEC) grouping have endorsed the idea of starting to implement an APEC-wide free trade area by the year 2000, for full achievement by 2020.[25] Each of the NAFTA countries participates in APEC.

The key concern raised in the United States in earlier years, when regionalism in trade policy was explicitly rejected, was that this would encourage emphasis on regional political policy as well, and would cast into doubt the US role as a worldwide political actor. The more recent double regionalism in economic integration, first the Americas and then the Pacific, has in fact stimulated discussion as to whether the United States was withdrawing or downgrading European relations, economically and then inevitably politically. This concern, as much as any other consideration, has led to the speculation about potential free trade between North America and Western Europe.

One can only guess about where the growing regionalism in trade matters will take the multilateral trading system. The successful conclusion of the Uruguay Round has shown the importance of the multilateral structure. The key argument of the partisans of regionalism is not that this should replace multilateralism, but that the two can coexist – indeed, must coexist because both strands are in existence – and that each accelerates liberalisation in the other. It is possible that the various regional groupings will come together. The APEC and transatlantic free trade proposals point in this direction. But this is not a foreordained outcome.

NAFTA, whatever its merits and defects, surely has opened a worldwide debate about a tripolar trading world and its implications for global trade and political relationships.

Regionalism with a Single Dominant Partner

As Table 8.1 shows, the US economy is substantially larger than that of either of the other two NAFTA partners, and of both together. Figure 8.1 shows that while Canada and Mexico are important markets for US exports, the United States is far and away the leading destination for their exports. The United States is a world trader; neither Canada nor Mexico is.

The contest in Canada on approval of the CUFTA had a number of themes, but the most emotional was the issue of sovereignty. In a debate before the national parliamentary election of 1988, in which the central issue was free trade with the United States, John Turner, the Liberal Party leader, made the following comments in opposing the agreement: 'one signature of the pen ... will reduce us I am sure to a colony of the United States, because when the economic levers go ... political independence is sure to follow'.[26]

There is a long history of Canadian–US efforts to reach free trade agreements, or reciprocity agreements as they were called in the nineteenth century. Each failed until CUFTA and their unacceptability in Canada was based on the fear of US economic and, consequently, political domination. When the decision was made to go ahead with the CUFTA negotiations, the only acceptable form of economic integration was a free trade area because this involved less political content than a customs union and a common market that would permit free movement of people. A customs union would have involved a CET and common commercial policy. Canada feared both.

The Canadian concern was that the CET would almost certainly lean towards US tariffs, which were lower than those of Canada, because of the greater economic power of the United States. In addition, there undoubtedly would have been complaints in GATT had a simple average of the two tariffs been chosen, as was done at the time when the European Economic Community established its CET. A simple average would have entailed raising US tariffs. Because the bulk of imports from outside the free trade area would go to the United States, this would have stimulated questions under GATT Article XXIV about raising average tariffs against outsiders – see Appendix to Chapter 1. In any event, sovereignty demanded that the Canadians maintain their own higher tariff.

Canadians were even more fearful that a common commercial policy would require adoption of US commercial actions that were based on political considerations, such as trade embargoes against Cuba and other countries or import restrictions to protect clamouring US industries. Canada had its own import restrictions but they were geared to the Canadian and not the US scene.

For Canada, it was really a free trade area or nothing. This was acceptable to the United States, which for its own internal reasons did not want too much political content in the agreement. When the CUFTA was transformed into NAFTA, the free trade format was carried over. Mexico might have accepted negotiation for a customs union, if that is all it had been offered, but the issue never arose. Mexico, for its own internal reasons, also preferred the free trade format.

This initial requirement – to minimise the political content as economic integration proceeded – has led to some of the defects that now exist in the construction of rules of origin. However, now that NAFTA is in effect, the tariff implications of retaining its own external tariff are not substantial for Canada. The natural pressure is for Canadian and US import tariffs to converge, especially for intermediate and capital goods imports, because higher Canadian tariffs would make Canada a less attractive place for locating production facilities for export throughout North America. Vastly different tariffs are not tenable even for consumer goods. Canada discovered this when it taxed cigarettes at a significantly higher rate than in the United States and was forced to backtrack after a black market in smuggled cigarettes emerged.[27]

For Mexico, at the moment, a CET would not be feasible because Mexico, in the aftermath of its financial–economic crisis, raised many of its tariffs against countries with which it does not have free trade agreements. It could not have done this had there been a CET. Once the crisis has been overcome, the Mexican situation with respect to establishing a CET will be similar to that of Canada. The United States now has the lowest tariff level of the three against non-NAFTA countries, Canada is intermediate, and Mexico has the highest tariffs.

The choice of a free trade area for NAFTA will have its effect on NAFTA enlargement. If this takes the form of new accessions to NAFTA, the entry will be into a free trade area. If economic integration in the Americas takes the form of agreements between the different sub-regional groupings, such as between the Common Market of the South (MERCOSUR, consisting of Argentina, Brazil, Paraguay and Uruguay) and NAFTA, these would be free trade agreements (see Chapter 10). Thus the integration pattern set by the initial disparity in economic power between Canada and the United States is now built into the genetic structure of potential hemispheric integration.

Integration between High and Low Income Countries

The debate on free trade with Mexico in the United States resembled that of Canada on its economic integration with the United States. Emotional arguments played a large role in both cases. The phrase used by Ross Perot in opposing the agreement, that there would be a giant 'sucking sound' of investment being pulled out of the United States into Mexico, was widely quoted. Other opponents, like Ralph Nader, drew a picture of the United States being overwhelmed by imports from Mexico.[28] The Republican Pat Buchanan, an aspirant for nomination as president in 1992 and again in 1996, said on the political stump and in many newspaper columns that 'NAFTA ... is about a loss of American sovereignty'.[29]

The concern at the heart of the opposition to NAFTA was that low Mexican wages would attract much investment in productive activities and then lead to growing exports to the United States based on this runaway investment. When NAFTA supporters argued that low wages reflected low productivity, this was countered by citing isolated examples of Mexican factories that had high productivity coupled with low wages, particularly in the automotive sector. NAFTA, in the end, was approved by the US Congress, but the debate was fierce.

Then a little more than a year later, when Mexico was confronted by its financial–economic crisis, NAFTA opponents raised the same issues. The cry this time was that even if US exports to Mexico were large in 1994, their predictions about the bilateral relationship were turning out to be correct. Mexico, they argued, was a corrupt, non-democratic country unable to manage its affairs and not a suitable partner for free trade.

When President Clinton proposed legislation to provide Mexico with a $40 billion rescue credit, it was opposed in the Congress on economic grounds, but many political conditions were also suggested. These, among other things, called for Mexico to break diplomatic relations with Cuba, to take steps to prevent would-be undocumented immigrants from leaving Mexico, and to privatise Pémex, the national oil company. It was clear that no Mexican government could accept these conditions and survive politically. The motivation for suggesting them, therefore, seemed to be either to kill the loan package or to use Mexico's rejection as a tool to destroy NAFTA. President Clinton, in the end, withdrew the legislative proposal and used funds at his disposal to provide the rescue credit.

National sentiment in the United States on NAFTA was mixed, but generally favourable towards Mexico in late 1994, before the Mexican crisis. The Chicago Council on Foreign Relations included questions on NAFTA and Mexico in a 1994 poll of foreign affairs leaders and the general public, and two of the more salient findings were the following:[30]

1. 86 per cent of leaders thought that NAFTA was mostly good for the US economy, compared with 13 per cent who thought it was mostly bad. The general public attitudes were 50 per cent mostly good, 31 per cent mostly bad, and 13 per cent who didn't know.
2. 98 per cent of the leaders and 76 per cent of the public thought that the United States has a vital interest in Mexico. Mexico was tied with Russia for first place among the most important countries in the poll of the leaders, and was tied with Canada for fifth place among the public.

NAFTA represents an emphasis on neighbourhood for all three countries. The CUFTA was non-controversial in the United States; indeed, it was hardly noticed by the general public. NAFTA was controversial because of Mexico's less developed economic status, and this controversy existed despite the high importance accorded US relations with Mexico by both leaders and the general public.

Comparable circumstances exist in Europe. The countries of Eastern Europe are neighbours of the EU countries. What happens in Eastern Europe obviously affects interests of EU members. And the differences in wages between countries in Eastern Europe and the EU are as great as between the United States (and Canada) and Mexico.

NAFTA thus provides an experiment that will surely be observed closely in Europe. If, when the experiment has gone on long enough to make some judgement about its effect on the Mexican economy and trade with the other NAFTA partners, when there is sufficient evidence about its impact on wages in Mexico and the other two countries, the outcome is likely to affect EU behaviour towards Eastern Europe.

CONCLUSION

NAFTA is very much an agreement in formation. Because of economic developments in Mexico less than a year after it went into effect, the agreement came under severe strain. Its existence proved to be important at that moment of crisis. It determined Mexican behaviour not to resort to trade measures against the United States using a balance of payments justification, as it had done several times in the past. The agreement was also critical in persuading President Clinton to undertake a financial rescue of unprecedented size. For Mexico, openness of the US market became a critical element in surmounting its economic problems given the lack of sufficient capital inflows to sustain a large current account deficit in 1995.

NAFTA will evolve, as must all economic integration arrangements if they are to survive. The deepening process has already begun, as has the institutionalisation of trade and associated relationships between the countries.

Finally, to return to the ideas with which this chapter began, when the United States adopted regionalism as an explicit element of trade policy, this set up a counterpart to the integration process in Europe. The nature of the world trading system, the interplay between regionalism and multilateralism, then became an active and significant issue.

Beyond this, NAFTA is a new phenomenon in that it is comprised of one dominant country allied with two others that are less powerful economically; and it combines two high income, high wage countries with a much poorer one. These two elements have set in motion an important experiment worthy of international scrutiny and careful analysis.

Notes

1. The United States did conclude a free trade agreement with Israel in 1987, before the agreement with Canada, but the global trade policy implications were not significant.
2. Low (1993, p. 31) makes this point as follows: 'While the United States has maintained that regional arrangements complement its multilateral trade interests, the policy change is doubtless a reflection of frustration with the GATT and uncertainty about its future.'
3. This is a point made by Hufbauer (1989).
4. The two may never come together, but it is interesting that precisely such proposals were being made on both sides of the Atlantic in 1995. They were not prevalent in 1989, when the CUFTA came into effect, or in 1994, when NAFTA entered into force.
5. Preliminary unpublished data from the US Department of Commerce are that US merchandise exports to Canada were 22 per cent of total exports in 1994.
6. Data are from the *Survey of Current Business*, a monthly publication of the US Department of Commerce (various issues).
7. There has been a separate free trade agreement between the two countries in the automotive sector since 1965.
8. Bureau of Economic Analysis (1993), tables II.H.5 and II.H.22.
9. Maquiladoras are plants established within Mexico, mostly along the border, under which semi-finished products can be imported into Mexico in bond, that is, without payment of import duties, for further

elaboration there and then reshipment back to the United States with payment of the US import duty only on the value added in Mexico. The maquiladora system will gradually disappear for US firms under NAFTA, but the coproduction inherent in this system will extend throughout Mexico. The major stimuli for maquiladora plants were proximity to the United States and low Mexican wages.

10. Hart (1994, p. 20) points out that fewer than 100 firms are responsible for the preponderance of Canadian exports.
11. At the insistence of Canadian Prime Minister Jean Chrétien, shortly after he took office in 1994, a trilateral working group of the NAFTA countries has been exploring ways to change the AD–CVD procedures in North America. The prospects for success are not great because the US side has insisted that these changes cannot include alteration of US law.
12. This dispute has dragged on for years, although was in remission in 1995.
13. The irony is that, today, Mexico has converted itself into a hub by concluding separate free trade agreements with Chile, Costa Rica, Bolivia, and with Colombia and Venezuela in what is known as the Group of Three.
14. This description comes from Hufbauer and Schott (1992, p. 19).
15. Mexico is the leading source of legal immigrants to the United States, averaging about 70 000 a year in recent years. Following passage of the Immigration Reform and Control Act of 1986, the status of about 3 million Mexicans living illegally in the United States was regularised. There is now a backlog approaching 1 million family members of these legalised Mexicans seeking entry into the United States or regularisation in their own right. Apprehension of Mexicans entering the United States without documents has exceeded one million a year in recent years and many other Mexicans overstay visas to live illegally in the United States.
16. Weintraub (1995a) contains a description of the financial crisis while it was developing.
17. There were $30 billion of these dollar-indexed notes, or *tesobonos* as they were called, at the time.
18. The data in this paragraph come from Banco de México (1995).
19. Discussion of the content of the agreement can be found in Hufbauer and Schott (1993).
20. The definition of a 'cultural' industry is imprecise and has been the subject of much dispute between Canada and the United States.
21. The quoted phrase is from Hufbauer and Schott (1993, p. 6).
22. Adolfo Aguilar Zinser, an academic at the National Autonomous University of Mexico (UNAM), the spokesman for the presidential campaign of Cuauhtémoc Cárdenas in 1994 and a deputy in Mexico's Chamber of Deputies, made this point in many conferences on NAFTA.
23. Gruben and Welch (1994) point out that the agreement is much like a Hegelian dialectical approach to free trade, incorporating compromises that will require some new synthesis in the years to come. This is hardly

an original insight. Hufbauer and Schott (1993) point out at the beginning of their book (p. 9) that 'FTAs [free-trade agreements] result in freer trade, not free trade'.

24. *The Wall Street Journal*, 3 July 1995, p. A18, has an editorial entitled 'Cement', which mocks the 60 per cent CVD on cement imports from Cemex, Mexico's largest producer, and which effectively prevents Cemex from exporting to the United States.
25. Eminent Persons Group (1994). The eminent persons group consisted of representatives from Australia, Brunei, Canada, China, Hong Kong, Indonesia, Japan, South Korea, Malaysia, Mexico, New Zealand, the Philippines, Singapore, Taiwan, Thailand, and the United States.
26. Television debate of 25 October 1988, between John Turner, Liberal Party leader, and Prime Minister Brian Mulroney, leader of Canada's Progressive Conservative Party. When the Conservatives won the election, the Canadian Parliament shortly afterwards approved CUFTA.
27. To deal with the rules of origin horror if NAFTA is widened to other countries, there have been suggestions of having a hybrid between a free trade area and a customs union, that is, a CET but without a common commercial policy. NAFTA made a modest start on this when the three countries agreed to harmonise their external tariffs on computers.
28. US direct investment in Mexico was less than 1 per cent of gross domestic investment in the United States. US imports from Mexico were a fraction of 1 per cent of US GDP.
29. The column from which this quotation was taken appeared in the *Washington Times*, 22 September 1993.
30. Rielly (1955). The polls were carried out by the Gallup Organisation, using a sample of 1492 persons aged 18 or more. In addition, 383 interviews were conducted between October and December 1994 with individuals identified as leaders with knowledge of foreign affairs. This was the sixth such public opinion survey and analysis by the Chicago Council since 1984.

9 Regional Integration in Latin America Before the Debt Crisis: LAFTA, CACM and the Andean Pact

Victor Bulmer-Thomas

The integration of the Latin American subcontinent, following the withdrawal in the 1820s of Spain and Portugal as colonial powers, is an old dream that has inspired numerous visions. Simón Bolívar, the Liberator of South America, launched his plan for a Latin American Union at Panama in 1826; Justo Rufino Barrios, ruler of Guatemala, invaded neighbouring El Salvador in 1876 under the banner of Central American unity; Víctor Raúl Haya de la Torre, charismatic leader of Peru's Alianza para la Revolución Americana (APRA), proclaimed an anti-imperialist rhetoric designed to unite all Latin America in the 1920s.

All such dreams were thwarted by a combination of economic, geographic and political constraints. With the centralising influence of the Iberian powers absent, the centripetal tendencies latent in the demanding geography of the subcontinent exercised a decisive influence. Even an apparently homogeneous creation such as Gran Colombia, forged by Bolívar in the 1820s, had fallen apart in less than ten years into Colombia, Ecuador and Venezuela. Mexico, although gaining Chiapas from Guatemala early on, fought a losing battle to preserve its territorial integrity. Argentina had to wait almost fifty years after independence before a secure federation of Argentine states could be established.

In the last analysis it was the absence of economic ties that undermined early attempts at regional integration in Latin America. As colonies, some intra-regional trade had taken place under the watchful eye of crown representatives, but the overriding need for government revenue by the fledgling states led to the adoption of high nominal tariffs restricting imports from both extra- and intra-regional sources. The political will to adjust these tariffs to offer special concessions to neighbouring countries was almost always absent. At the same time, the colonial legacy – coupled with the post-independence emphasis on export-led growth based on primary products – left each Latin American country pursuing integration with the world economy on the back of commodities for which there was little intra-regional demand. As late as 1929 only 6.9 per cent of Latin American exports and 9.2 per cent of imports were intra-regional.[1]

The situation only began to change with the Second World War. Faced with a drastic reduction in imports from traditional sources (Europe and the United States), Latin American countries looked to their neighbours to satisfy a level of domestic demand that held up well as a result of the expansion in the value of wartime exports to the United States. By 1945, at the end of the war, no less than 25.6 per cent of all imports were intra-regional (a figure that has still not been surpassed) while 16.6 per cent of exports were sold to other Latin American countries (see Table 9.1).[2]

The growth of intra-regional trade in the war years did not affect all countries equally. Only those countries that had established a modern manufacturing base (Argentina, Brazil, Chile, Colombia and Mexico) were in a position to benefit from the trade diversion implied by the decline in imports from traditional sources. Smaller countries had less opportunity to expand their intra-regional exports as demand was primarily for manufactured goods. For such countries, the absence

Table 9.1 Intra-regional trade in Latin America, 1945–60

Year	*Total Exports ($m)*	*Intra-Regional Exports ($m)*	*Intra-Regional Exports (%)*[a]	*Intra-Regional Imports (%)*[b]
1938	1856	114	6.1	8.3
1945	3254	540	16.6	25.6
1948	6666	609	9.9	11.4
1952	7000	601	9.1	9.7
1956	8395	653	7.8	9.9
1960	8660	689	8.0	9.9

Notes
[a] As a percentage of total exports.
[b] As a percentage of total imports.
Sources: Horn and Bice (1949), table 7, p. 112; Baerresen, Carnoy and Grunwald (1965), p. 75

of capital goods imports made it impossible to begin industrialisation in the war years.

Two instances of wartime economic cooperation proved to be particularly important in terms of strengthening western hemisphere integration. Mexico, its tense relationship with the United States caused by oil nationalisation in 1938 now resolved,[3] increased sharply its exports of agricultural, mineral and manufactured goods to its northern neighbour; Mexico's strategic importance for the US also made it a privileged recipient of scarce capital goods so that the industrialisation programme made huge strides in the war years. By the end of the war 83.5 per cent of Mexico's exports were destined for the US[4] and wartime cooperation had led to a flow of capital southwards and labour northwards.

The second instance involved Argentina and Brazil. Despite a long history of hemispheric rivalry, the war brought these two countries closer together than ever before. An ambitious plan for regional economic cooperation, embracing a customs union, was laid before the Argentine Congress by the Minister of Finance, Federico Pinedo, in November 1940. His Brazilian counterpart, Osvaldo Aranha, was equally enthusiastic. Although the Pinedo Plan was not adopted (domestic political considerations intervened), economic cooperation went ahead and was boosted by a bilateral agreement between Argentina and Brazil in 1941 that led to a substantial rise in trade between the two countries.[5] Indeed, by 1945 11.9 per cent of Brazil's exports were destined for Argentina with no less than 43 per cent represented by manufactured goods.[6]

The return to normal trading conditions after the war undermined regional cooperation. Much of the increase in intra-regional trade had been trade diversion and the opportunity once again to buy from the cheapest source led to a decline in its importance (see Table 9.1). Furthermore, the post-war emphasis on import-substituting industrialisation (ISI) increased the tariff and non-tariff barriers faced by imports from all sources, including other Latin American countries, so that regional economic cooperation through intra-regional imports became prohibitively expensive. The trade barriers were particularly severe in the case of the new dynamic branches of industry (e.g. automobiles) being established in the larger countries in the 1950s.

Frustration at the loss of regional markets was one factor behind the movement in favour of economic integration at the end of the 1950s. However, a key role was also played by the United Nations Economic Commission for Latin America (ECLA or CEPAL in its

Spanish acronym) that had been established in 1948. Under the dynamic leadership of Raúl Prebisch, CEPAL had promoted ISI as a policy response to the alleged secular decline in the net barter terms of trade of primary product exporting countries. The welfare losses associated with ISI were all too apparent, but CEPAL remained unconvinced that manufactured exports from Latin America were a viable option even with a unilateral reform of commercial trade policy.

The solution to this dilemma was seen by CEPAL to lie in regional integration. Intra-regional trade liberalisation would allow for exports of manufactured goods to neighbouring countries while extra-regional trade barriers would continue to provide a stimulus to ISI. Thus, in the CEPAL vision regional integration was an instrument for promoting industrialisation rather than a mechanism for enhancing welfare through net trade creation. Indeed, by emphasising the replacement of cheaper (dollar) initial imports from third countries by more expensive (dollar) imports from partners, the Cepalino version of regional integration was almost certain to lead to net trade diversion.[7]

THE LATIN AMERICAN FREE TRADE ASSOCIATION

The momentum in favour of economic integration in Latin America gathered pace in the second half of the 1950s. The Treaty of Rome, giving birth to the European Economic Community (EEC), had been signed in 1957 (see Chapter 5) and a General Agreement on Tariffs and Trade (GATT) waiver had been granted to permit this deviation from most favoured nation (MFN) treatment of international trade flows. Although most members of Latin America were not yet in GATT, Brazil was a founder member and an economic integration scheme designed to promote industrialisation without the participation of Brazil was clearly unrealistic. The US under President Eisenhower, conscious of the deterioration in its relations with Latin America since the end of the Second World War, dropped its initial objections to Latin American integration and, as in Europe, came to see it as an opportunity for US multinational companies (MNCs) rather than a threat to US exporters.

The efforts to establish a regional integration scheme were rewarded in February 1960 with the signing of the Treaty of Montevideo, leading to the creation of the Latin American Free Trade Association (LAFTA).[8] Membership was at first confined to Argentina, Brazil,

Chile, Mexico, Paraguay, Peru and Uruguay, but Colombia and Ecuador joined in 1961, Venezuela in 1966 and Bolivia in 1967. Thus, membership eventually embraced all of the Latin American republics in South America together with Mexico. The excluded republics of Central America and the Caribbean accounted for less than 10 per cent of total Latin American population and 7 per cent of total GDP.[9]

The creation of LAFTA was a major achievement, but it could not disguise the fact that the initial conditions were almost the opposite of those predicted by economic theory to yield net welfare benefits. First, as already mentioned, the emphasis on industrialisation made each country enthusiastic about the opportunities for the expansion of manufacturing output through trade diversion, but there was little interest in the possible benefits to be obtained for consumers from trade creation. Net trade diversion could therefore be expected – particularly as external tariffs were often raised in anticipation of the loss of tariff revenue from intra-regional trade liberalisation.

Secondly, the imbalance in terms of industrialisation of the members of LAFTA made it extremely unlikely that the gains from the liberalisation of trade in manufactured goods would be equally distributed. On the contrary, industrially weak countries such as Bolivia, Ecuador and Paraguay could expect to replace cheaper manufactured imports from the rest of the world with more expensive imports from neighbouring countries, while their own primary product exports to neighbouring countries would remain subject to trade restrictions.

Thirdly, the low initial base for intra-regional trade (see Table 9.1) meant that extra-regional trade would dominate the balance of payments for the foreseeable future. With ISI leading to overvalued currencies and anti-export bias (at least as far as third countries were concerned) and with the net barter terms of trade deteriorating,[10] a severe balance of payments constraint haunted most LAFTA countries from the beginning. This discouraged a radical approach to intra-regional trade liberalisation, ruled out the harmonisation of macroeconomic policies and made countries suffering net trade diversion particularly vulnerable.

These initial conditions were reflected in the legal instruments adopted by the Treaty of Montevideo to achieve a free trade area. Intra-regional trade liberalisation was promoted through an annual round of tariff negotiations on national schedules and a triennial round of tariff negotiations on common schedules. The former listed commodities on which the member countries separately made concessions applicable to other countries and the target was to make 'tariff concessions to other members annually on commodities traded in the previous three-year period, by an amount equivalent to 8 per cent of the weighted average tariff applicable to non-member countries' (see Finch 1988, p. 241). The latter listed commodities on which free trade was to be established in four rounds of negotiations and the target was to agree a list of commodities on which tariffs would be eliminated immediately and which represented 25 per cent of the aggregate value of regional trade.

The imbalance in size and industrial strength of the LAFTA members was reflected in the special status given to Bolivia, Ecuador and Paraguay allowing these countries additional time to implement intra-regional trade liberalisation. These three republics accounted for a mere 3.9 per cent of intra-zonal exports in 1961–3 so that the concession did not appear to undermine substantially the commitment to regional free trade. The balance of payments constraint was acknowledged by the adoption, in 1965, of a multilateral clearing house to reduce the need for hard currency in intra-regional trade, while the signing of the Santo Domingo Agreement in 1969 provided multilateral support to countries in balance of payments difficulties.

The national tariff schedules at first appeared to be a great success. The first round in 1961 achieved an estimated average tariff reduction of 25 per cent and the second 15 per cent compared with the target of 8 per cent. In these two years 7593 tariff concessions were granted. However, in the next four years only 1800 tariff concessions were made under the national schedule and a further 1625 by the end of the decade. Facing almost insuperable obstacles to trade liberalisation, the LAFTA countries adopted the Caracas Protocol in 1969, slowing down the timetable for regional integration. Not surprisingly, the decade of the 1970s saw only 224 additional tariff concessions under the national schedule.

The national schedules were aimed at annual tariff concessions. Many of these were redundant as the goods on which tariffs had been reduced played little or no part in intra-regional trade. Far more significant, therefore, were the triennial common schedules with the first taking place in 1964. After months of negotiations a list of mainly agricultural commodities, including bananas, cocao, coffee and cotton, was agreed with free trade to commence in 1973. These products did at least represent 23 per cent of intra-regional trade in the base period (compared with the target of 25 per cent).

By the time of the second set of negotiations in 1967, however, resistance to trade liberalisation had hardened and no progress was made. Under the Caracas Protocol in 1969 the common schedule negotiations were suspended for five years (they were never restarted), and even the date for implementing free trade in the products agreed in the first common schedule was left undecided.

The inability of LAFTA countries to meet the targets for intra-regional trade liberalisation under the Treaty of Montevideo was a big disappointment. Despite this, intra-regional trade grew in both absolute and relative terms (see Table 9.2). Indeed, the share of intra-regional exports in total exports rose from 7.7 per cent in 1960 to 9.9 per cent in 1970 and 13.6 per cent in 1980, before falling to 8.3 per cent in 1985.[11] In a few cases (e.g. Argentina, Bolivia, Chile, Paraguay and Uruguay), intra-regional trade came to occupy a significant (greater than 20 per cent) share of total trade (see Table 9.2).

Part of the above proportional growth in intra-regional trade in the first LAFTA decade could be attributed to tariff concessions. However, much of the growth in trade took place in products not covered by trade liberalisation, while tariff concessions under the national schedules could not explain the growth in trade in the 1970s. Thus, additional explanations must be sought.

Table 9.2 Intra-regional exports of LAFTA/LAIA countries (in $US million and as percentage of total exports)

	1960		*1970*		*1980*		*1985*	
Country	*$m*	*%*	*$m*	*%*	*$m*	*%*	*$m*	*%*
Argentina	170.3	15.8	365.8	20.6	1,850.5	23.1	1,485.5	17.7
Bolivia	8.3	12.2	20.3	8.9	380.4	36.7	403.0	60.0
Brazil	88.5	7.0	304.0	11.1	3,459.0	17.2	2,233.0	8.7
Chile	33.0	6.7	152.0	12.2	1,117.0	23.0	546.9	14.1
Colombia	6.2	1.3	54.5	7.5	551.3	14.0	288.3	8.1
Ecuador	8.1	7.7	20.2	9.6	439.7	17.7	132.6	4.6
Mexico	8.1	1.1	92.7	7.1	608.0	4.0	596.0	2.7
Paraguay	8.9	33.0	24.5	33.1	140.6	45.3	83.4	27.4
Peru	36.8	8.5	63.6	6.1	590.9	15.1	357.8	12.0
Uruguay	3.3	2.5	29.2	12.5	393.4	37.2	237.8	28.0
Venezuela	195.7	7.8	137.3	4.3	1,396.0	7.3	761.0	5.4
Total	567.2	7.7	1,264.1	9.9	10,926.8	13.6	7,125.3	8.3

Source: ECLAC (1992), tables 276, 277, 279, 284.

The external shocks of the 1970s – the collapse of the post-war Bretton Woods system, the first oil crisis and the commodity price boom – were by no means all unfavourable for Latin America. The improvement in the terms of trade of most republics (oil exporters and importers), coupled with the spectacular growth in syndicated bank lending to Latin America, brought to a temporary end the balance of payments constraint that had overshadowed LAFTA in its first decade. At the same time, the recession in OECD countries for many years in the 1970s encouraged a search for new trade partners in Latin America.

The new rules adopted for LAFTA after the Caracas Protocol also helped. While tariff concessions under both the national and common schedules ground to a halt, industrial complementarity agreements accelerated. Tariff concessions under this scheme did not have to be extended to all LAFTA countries, so that it was ideally suited to MNCs seeking to liberalise trade among their subsidiaries in different Latin American countries. By 1979 over 3500 tariff concessions had been negotiated under the industrial complementarity regime – mainly in sectors with a large MNC presence.

The spread of industrial complementarity agreements helps to account for another notable feature of LAFTA – the rising share of manufactured goods in intra-regional trade (see Table 9.3). The share of manufactured exports in intra-regional trade rose from around a quarter to a half between 1960 and 1975. This was much

Table 9.3 Intra-regional manufactured exports by product group 1965, 1970 and 1975 (as percentages of total exports by product group)

Product group	*1965*	*1970*	*1975*
1. Chemical elements and compounds	36.1	48.2	53.9
	(5.6)	(7.4)	(8.2)
2. Manufactured goods classified by	15.6	18.0	27.1
material	(13.3)	(19.6)	(16.3)
3. Machinery and transport equipment	70.2	51.0	52.6
	(4.1)	(9.2)	(15.4)
4. Miscellaneous manufactured articles	70.0	55.2	38.5
	(3.7)	(5.5)	(5.3)
Total manufactured products	(26.7)	(41.7)	(45.2)

Note
Figures in parentheses refer to the composition of intra-regional exports in percentages.
Source: Bulmer-Thomas (1994), table 9.3, p. 305.

higher than the corresponding ratio for extra-regional exports, which continued to be dominated by primary products.[12] Thus, CEPAL could draw some comfort from the fact that LAFTA had apparently contributed to the growth of manufactured exports even if much of the growth could not be attributed to tariff concessions under the national or common schedules. Furthermore, the importance of intra-industry trade (IIT) was far higher in intra-regional trade among LAFTA members than in extra-regional trade with Europe, Japan or the US.[13]

These achievements notwithstanding, LAFTA failed to live up to its expectations. The original aim of achieving intra-regional free trade by 1973 was not remotely met and the postponement to 1980 made little difference. The strategy of trade liberalisation was both cumbersome and inefficient. The fact that intra-regional trade could grow as fast or even faster in products excluded from trade liberalisation as in products included was a damning indictment of the LAFTA approach. Despite the rapid rise in intra-regional manufactured exports, no major country – not even Brazil – had been able to overcome the bias against exports and increase its share of world trade.

As the difficulties facing LAFTA became more and more apparent, new efforts were made to breathe life into the integration process. A Mexican initiative led to the creation in 1975 of the Sistema Económico Latinoamericano (SELA). Embracing all of Latin America and much of the Caribbean, SELA explored new approaches to intra-regional trade liberalisation as well as new concepts of integration itself. The new ideas emanating from SELA, however, found little support among LAFTA countries. By 1980, as the Treaty of Montevideo expired, most of the LAFTA countries had fallen under military rule with governments showing no enthusiasm for any form of regional cooperation that could be construed as a diminution of national sovereignty.

The 1980 Treaty of Montevideo that replaced its 1960 predecessor captured the new mood of scepticism towards regional integration. The Asociación Latinoamericana de Integración (ALADI – LAIA in English) that replaced LAFTA abandoned all quantitative and temporal targets for achieving intra-regional free trade. Instead, a loose association was promoted in which countries were free to offer trade privileges to each other without the need to extend these to all ALADI countries. If a Latin American Common Market remained the long-term ambition, no strategy was offered as to how the member states would achieve it. Furthermore, after two decades of integration efforts

ALADI had still made no provision for the new regional institutional arrangements that were to prove so decisive in turning the EEC of six countries into the European Community (EC) of 12 and eventually the European Union (EU) of 15 members (see Chapter 5).

It is very doubtful if ALADI could have worked. However, within a few months of coming into existence both ALADI and the dream of regional integration had been overwhelmed by the Latin American debt crisis (see p. 246). This crisis crushed all integration schemes in Latin America – not merely LAFTA/ALADI. Thus, we need to examine two other Latin American economic integration schemes that were adopted in the 1960s and 1970s – the Central American Common Market and the Andean Pact – before proceeding to explore the impact of the debt crisis on Latin American integration in the 1980s. Although this impact was highly negative, the solution to the debt crisis ironically provided the basis for a renewed attempt at integration in Latin America in the 1990s (see next chapter).

THE CENTRAL AMERICAN COMMON MARKET

Although LAFTA embraced Mexico as a founder member, it was in essence a South American project whose roots could be traced to the earlier efforts at wartime regional cooperation among countries of the Southern Cone. Incorporation of the small republics in the Caribbean Basin, including the Central American ones, was never considered.

The Central American countries – Costa Rica, El Salvador, Guatemala, Honduras and Nicaragua – as late as the 1950s were still linked to the world economy on the basis of a handful of primary product exports that provided the foreign exchange needed to purchase a wide array of manufactured imports. ISI was still in its infancy and the tariff was used primarily for its revenue function, providing nearly 50 per cent of government income. Although each republic was relatively open in trade terms, these trade flows took place primarily with the developed countries of Europe and North America; intra-regional trade was negligible since each country was largely self-sufficient in foodstuffs and no country as yet had an important manufacturing base.[14]

As the net barter terms of trade of the five republics deteriorated in the second half of the 1950s, interest in industrial policy and a programme of industrialisation began to grow. This interest was strongly encouraged by the staff of CEPAL, who were quick to point out the limitations of an industrial strategy limited to the national market in small republics such as those in Central America. CEPAL, therefore, actively promoted a regional integration project for Central America with its efforts coordinated through its office in Mexico City.

Regional integration had, and still has, special significance in Central America because of the existence of a Central American Federation from independence until 1838. The knowledge that the five republics had once been united provided a strong incentive for integration, although previous attempts had always collapsed under the weight of sub-regional fear of supra-national sovereignty in general and Guatemalan hegemony in particular. Economic integration, as proposed by CEPAL, at least offered the chance of regional cooperation without the need to surrender national sovereignty.

Numerous sub-regional schemes of regional integration were attempted in the 1950s. The success of these schemes was hampered in part by US opposition since the US was not persuaded that a regional integration scheme designed to foster industrialisation would be in her interests. US opposition, however, was gradually overcome and the General Treaty on Economic Integration was signed in December 1960 by El Salvador, Guatemala, Honduras and Nicaragua with Costa Rica joining in 1963.[15]

The General Treaty established the Central American Common Market (CACM). Despite its name and the accompanying rhetoric, it was never the intention to permit the free movement of factors of production – at least not labour – so that the CACM was not, and was never intended to be, a common market. However, unlike LAFTA, it was the intention to create a customs union and the five republics moved swiftly towards the harmonisation of external tariffs. This had been largely achieved by 1965, by which time intra-regional trade in manufactured (but not agricultural) goods had been almost entirely liberalised.[16]

This early success in establishing a common external tariff (CET) and removing restrictions on internal trade was translated into a rapid rise in intra-regional imports. As Table 9.4 shows, their share of total imports rose rapidly from 7.0 per cent in 1960 to 26.0 per cent in 1970 at a time when total imports themselves were also rising very fast. Even the disastrous war between El Salvador and Honduras in 1969 failed to stop the increase in intra-regional trade, although it did lead to a complete halt to bilateral trade between the two countries until 1980.[17]

The first decade of the CACM was hailed as a remarkable achievement both inside and outside the region. By 1970 intra-regional

Table 9.4 Central American intra-regional exports in $ million (as percentage of total exports)

	1950	*1960*	*1970*	*1980*	*1985*
Costa Rica	0.3	2.5	45.2	260.1	137.6
	(0.6)	(2.9)	(19.8)	(26.8)	(14.8)
El Salvador	2.2	12.9	73.7	295.8	157.2
	(3.3)	(11.0)	(32.3)	(27.6)	(25.7)
Guatemala	1.3	5.0	102.3	440.8	205.0
	(1.7)	(4.3)	(35.3)	(29.0)	(20.7)
Honduras	4.0	8.1	18.0	91.4	19.9
	(6.2)	(12.9)	(10.6)	(11.0)	(2.8)
Nicaragua	0.5	2.8	46.0	75.4	24.1
	(2.0)	(4.5)	(25.8)	(18.2)	(8.8)
Central America	8.3	31.3	285.2	1163.5	543.8
	(2.8)	(7.0)	(26.0)	(24.2)	(15.5)

Sources: Bulmer-Thomas (1988), table 13.2, p. 292; ECLAC (1994a), tables 281, 282 and 284.

exports had reached almost $300 million – a ninefold increase in one decade – with El Salvador and Guatemala selling more than 30 per cent of their total exports in the regional market (see Table 9.4). Intra-regional trade, as CEPAL had hoped, was almost entirely concentrated in manufactured goods and the region had begun to develop for the first time a modern industrial sector with MNCs strongly represented in the most dynamic sectors. Regional institutions were established to oversee the process of regional development and the new Banco Centroamericano de Integración Económica (BCIE) gave special attention to the needs of the weaker countries (Honduras and Nicaragua). Yet many problems had begun to surface and these deprived the CACM of much of its dynamism in its second decade (1970–80).

The first problem was the scale of net trade diversion. With a very small manufacturing base in 1960, the scope for trade creation was strictly limited unless intra-regional trade liberalisation covered all activities. Agricultural products, however, were largely excluded from the terms of reference of the CACM. Meanwhile, trade diversion occurred on a large scale as the newly established industries replaced cheaper imports from the rest of the world.

That the CACM was net trade diverting was demonstrated in numerous empirical studies.[18] Under certain circumstances net trade diversion can be welfare-improving and these conditions may have applied in Central America: economies of scale, a shadow price of foreign exchange different from the official rate, less than full employment, etc.[19] However, net trade diversion placed a particular burden on those countries subject to a structural deficit in intra-regional trade. Such countries were expected to pay each year an additional foreign exchange cost equivalent to the difference between the dollar price of intra- and extra-regional imports, without necessarily being able to increase dollar earnings through intra-regional exports.

The country most seriously affected by net trade diversion was Honduras. Unable to expand her sales of agricultural products to Central America as a result of continuing trade restrictions, Honduras also failed to attract much new investment into the small manufacturing sector. The result was a widening deficit in intra-zonal trade that had to be settled in hard currency twice a year. Moreover, the deterioration in the net barter terms of trade in the 1960s made it difficult for Honduras to generate an extra-regional trade surplus to finance the intra-regional trade deficit. As a result, following her failure to negotiate special treatment from her CACM partners, Honduras withdrew from the regional integration scheme at the end of 1970.[20]

The second problem was fiscal. Since the tariff had traditionally had a revenue function, the rapid growth of duty free intra-regional imports had serious fiscal consequences. Furthermore, in order to attract new investment into the manufacturing sector, the government of each country offered attractive tax holidays for a maximum of ten years. Finally, in order to increase the profitability of consumer goods production, the CET was restructured with low tariffs on intermediate and capital goods. The result was a sharp drop in the relative importance of the tariff as a source of government revenue that led in 1968 to the San José Protocol raising the CET by 30 per cent. This increased still further the effective rate of protection (ERP) for consumer goods production, while at the same time adding to anti-export bias.

The third problem was the size of the market. With a population in 1960 of less than 11 million, and many of these effectively excluded from the market economy by their poverty, the Central American region could not provide the level of demand needed to support the optimal scale of production needed in most industries. An attempt to circumnavigate this problem through the creation of regional monopolies subject to regulation had collapsed in the face of opposition from both the US government and the Central American private sector.[21] As a result, the market was quickly saturated and it became increasingly difficult to attract new investment into the manufacturing sector. All attempts to encourage regional producers to export manufactured goods were undermined by the high levels of anti-export bias and this was made worse by the San José Protocol.

As a consequence of these problems, the CACM lost dynamism in its second decade. Honduras signed bilateral trade agreements with all republics other than El Salvador and intra-regional trade continued to expand, but its share of total trade fell (see Table 9.4) with traditional primary product exports to the rest of the world now providing the engine of growth. Intra-regional trade in agricultural products continued to be subject to restrictions and non-tariff barriers remained a formidable obstacle for the expansion of manufactured exports. Indeed, non- tariff barriers go a long way to explain an observed inverse relationship between the importance of a manufacturing sector in gross production and its importance in intra-regional trade.[22]

Many efforts were made in the 1970s to revive the CACM, but these efforts never commanded the highest priority among the political élites. Furthermore, regional suspicions were accentuated towards the end of the 1970s as the Somoza regime in Nicaragua began to crumble and as the left gained in popularity in El Salvador. Ironically, however, the Sandinista victory in Nicaragua in 1979 provided the conditions for a boom in intra-regional trade the following year, with Nicaraguan imports soaring on the back of economic reconstruction.

The boom in intra-regional trade in 1980 was short-lived with Nicaragua unable to service her debts through the multilateral clearing house. With the advent of the debt crisis in 1982, Central America entered into a downward spiral of import restrictions, balance of payments crisis and debt default. Intra-regional trade – concentrated in non-essential consumer goods – was the first casualty and intra-regional trade fell in both absolute and relative terms. By 1985 (see Table 9.4) the dollar value of intra-regional exports had fallen by more than half, its importance had declined to 15.5 per cent of total trade and the Central American political crisis ruled out any attempts to revive the integration process.

THE ANDEAN PACT

Frustration at the lack of progress in LAFTA persuaded a group of member countries to adopt a parallel integration scheme with wider scope and greater ambition. This was the Andean Pact (AP), established in 1969 by Bolivia, Chile, Colombia, Ecuador and Peru with Venezuela joining in 1973.[23]

The goal of the AP was a customs union with a CET. Unlike the case of the CACM, the CET was never achieved. However, the stated goal was one of the factors that persuaded Chile to withdraw in 1976 since a major objective of the military dictatorship led by General Pinochet was trade liberalisation and tariff reductions – a goal that was inconsistent with the high CET desired by other members of the AP.

The ambitions of the AP were not limited to the creation of a customs union. One of the reasons for the frustration of AP members with LAFTA was the lack of progress in terms of industrialisation so that the Cartagena Agreement establishing the AP put great stress on industrial development through joint programming of activities, so that all members would benefit from intra-regional trade expansion.

In LAFTA and the CACM a high share of new industrial capacity was controlled by MNCs. The Cartagena Agreement coincided with the high point of hostility in Latin America towards MNCs and this was reflected in the Treaty itself. The now notorious Decision 24 placed severe restrictions on MNCs, limiting the proportion of profits remitted abroad to a maximum of 14 per cent (later raised to 20 per cent) and obliging them to sell equity to local partners within a specified time period, so as to ensure local majority shareholdings. Decision 24 also banned foreign investment from banking and insurance, the media, marketing, transport and public services.

Although there were a number of qualifications to the application of Decision 24, there is no doubt that the ethos of the AP was very different from that prevailing in the CACM or LAFTA. Nationalist regimes, in some cases under military control, saw the AP not only as an instrument of industrial development but also as a counterweight to the power of foreign capital. Similarly, the Cartagena Agreement gave special treatment to Bolivia and Ecuador, the least developed members of the AP, in the hope that the benefits of membership would be equitably shared. Market forces were not trusted to achieve a satisfactory division of the gains from trade.

Despite – or perhaps because of – its ambitions, the AP was not very successful at achieving its stated goals. Intra-regional trade was not completely liberated and the CET was never achieved. By 1980, when the CET was supposed to be in place, Ecuador and Venezuela – both oil exporters – were arguing for a rate of 80 per cent, while Colombia was prepared to settle for a 'modest' 60 per cent and Peru, where neo-liberal policies enjoyed a brief vogue after 1978, pushed for 40 per cent.

Intra-regional trade certainly increased and its share of total trade at first rose (see Table 9.5). However, the base in 1969 was so low that this expansion was hardly surprising. As late as 1980 intra-regional trade among AP countries still only accounted for 3.7 per cent of total trade. Furthermore, this trade was heavily concentrated between Colombia and Venezuela with their exports to each other representing nearly 50 per cent of intra-regional exports. By contrast, Bolivia and Ecuador (after 1975)[24] played a very marginal role in the expansion of AP trade. Bolivia threatened to withdraw in 1980, its military government was subsequently not recognised by the other members and Ecuador announced in 1981 that its long-standing border dispute with Peru put its own membership in jeopardy.

The biggest disappointment for the architects of the AP was the failure of industrial programming. The Sectoral Programme of Industrial Development (SPID), like the Integration Industries Scheme in Central America (see note 21), was designed to distribute new

Table 9.5 Andean Pact intra-zonal exports in $ million (as percentage of total exports)

Country	*1970*	*1975*	*1980*	*1985*
Bolivia	8.5 (3.7)	28.1 (5.4)	48.5 (4.7)	16.8 (2.5)
Chile[a]	18.8 (1.5)	106.4 (6.4)		
Colombia	34.8 (4.8)	189.8 (12.9)	387.9 (9.8)	217.9 (6.1)
Ecuador	14.6 (6.9)	209.3 (22.4)	124.0 (5.0)	73.8 (2.5)
Peru	21.1 (2.0)	123.4 (9.9)	260.9 (6.7)	205.1 (6.9)
Venezuela[b]		147.0 (1.7)	316.0 (1.6)	254.0 (1.8)
Total	97.8 (3.4)	804.0 (5.5)	1137.3 (3.7)	767.6 (3.2)

Notes

[a] Chile withdrew from the Andean Pact in 1976 and is therefore excluded from the statistics in 1980 and 1985.

[b] Venezuela did not join the Andean Pact until 1973 and is therefore excluded from the statistics in 1970.

Source: ECLAC (1992), tables 277, 278, 279 and 284.

industrial capacity among the member countries in such a way as to exploit economies of scale and ensure the participation of all countries. What actually happened is that in key sectors, such as car and metal working, 'production was allocated to member countries where production facilities were already in existence' (see El-Agraa and Hojman, 1988, p. 264). Allocations were easier to agree for industries that had not yet come into existence, but the hostility to foreign capital made it very difficult to attract the new investment needed into these kinds of activities. Domestic private capital may have been favoured, but it lacked the technological capacity to establish the new industries without foreign partners.

Like LAFTA and the CACM, the AP limped into the 1980s before being crippled by the 1982 debt crisis. The most serious casualty was trade between Colombia and Venezuela. Although Colombia never rescheduled its external public debt, Venezuela used devaluation and exchange rate controls to reduce its imports sharply from all sources. Bilateral trade between the two countries entered into a downward spiral and this largely explains the 32.5 per cent decline in AP intra-regional exports between 1980 and 1985 (see Table 9.5). As in the CACM, intra-regional AP trade contained a high proportion of non-essential consumer goods – an obvious target at a time of severe balance of payments constraints.

The AP reflected the prevailing ideology among the member states at the end of the 1960s. This ideology favoured state-directed industrialisation, hostility towards foreign capital and a complete disregard for the interests of the consumer. Market forces were tolerated rather than encouraged and public ownership of the 'commanding heights' of the economy was widely practised. AP countries, with the partial exception of Colombia, combined the promotion of intra-regional exports with high levels of extra-regional anti-export bias. This inconsistent treatment of exports made it almost inevitable that the AP would fail. As the prevailing ideology in Latin America began to change in favour of market forces, foreign investment and trade liberalisation, few mourned the passing of the AP in its first incarnation.

THE DEBT CRISIS AND REGIONAL INTEGRATION

The regional integration model in Latin America had a number of common elements across the different schemes. Designed to promote industrialisation, it was an import-intensive model in which most capital goods and many intermediate inputs were only available from extra-regional sources. With exports of manufactured goods outside the region undermined by anti-export bias, this left a negative balance on extra-regional trade in industrial products.[25]

The foreign exchange needed to pay for these net imports of manufactured goods was at first provided by primary product exports. Thus, the new integration model promoted by CEPAL did not remove the dependence on primary products that had provided the justification for CEPAL's original emphasis on industrialisation. Only if alternative sources of foreign exchange were available could Latin America hope to avoid the balance of payments difficulties traditionally associated with primary product exports.

An alternative source began to emerge at the end of the 1960s in the form of commercial bank debt. As a result of two changes – syndicated lending and flexible interest rates – foreign banks began to take an interest in a region they had traditionally neglected. For the borrowers, mainly governments and state-owned enterprises, the new loans had numerous advantages: low or zero conditionality and high flexibility with regard to final use.[26]

Bank lending to Latin America expanded rapidly at the beginning of the 1970s, allowing modest current account deficits to be financed with ease. However, the first (1973–4) and second (1978–9) oil crises produced an explosion in bank lending as 'petro-dollars' were recycled through the Euro-currency markets to Latin America. This new source of foreign exchange not only produced a positive net flow of capital to the region, but also a positive transfer of resources as the net capital inflow easily exceeded the outflow of interest payments and profit remittances.

By 1981, the last 'normal' year before the debt crisis, the net transfer of resources reached $10.4 billion (see Table 9.6) – equivalent to 2 per cent of regional GDP.[27] The value of imports from all sources had risen from $42 billion in 1975 to $101 billion in 1981. Intra-regional imports had risen to $16.8 billion and were nearly 25 times greater than their level in 1960 (see Table 9.1). Their share of total imports had almost doubled from 9.9 per cent in 1960 (see Table 9.1) to 16.7 per cent in 1981 (see Table 9.6).

The threat by Mexico to default in August 1982, the event that finally triggered the Latin American debt crisis, reversed the net transfer of resources to Latin America. The net flow of capital (*K*) fell sharply and was exceeded by net payments of interest and profits

Table 9.6 Latin America's balance of payments, 1980–5 ($ billion)

	1980	*1981*	*1982*	*1983*	*1984*	*1985*
1. Net capital inflow	29.7	37.6	20.2	2.9	10.0	2.5
2. Net payment of profits and interest	18.1	27.2	38.8	34.4	36.7	35.3
3. Transfer of resources (3) = (1) – (2)	+11.6	+10.4	–18.6	–31.5	–26.7	–32.8
4. Exports of goods	91.4	98.6	89.5	89.9	100.2	94.3
5. Imports of goods	93.5	100.9	82.2	60.3	61.8	61.1
6. Intra-regional imports	15.6	16.8	14.0	10.9	12.0	10.3
7. Intra-regional imports (%) (7) = (6)/(5)	16.7	16.7	17.0	18.1	19.4	16.7

Sources: ECLAC (1989), table 15, p. 25; Inter-American Development Bank (1990), tables D-3 and D-4; ECLAC (1992), tables 280, 282 and 283; ECLAC (1994a), tables 282, 283 and 284.

(*F*). The implications of this change can be best understood by reference to the balance of payments presented as follows:

Credits	*Debits*
Exports of goods/services (*E*)	Imports of goods/services (*M*)
Net transfer receipts (*T*)	Net factor payments (*F*)
Net capital receipts (*K*)	Current account deficit (*B*)
	Net fall in reserves (*R*)

The equality between total incomings and outgoings means:

$$E + T + K = M + F + R \tag{9.1}$$

Assuming that external adjustment cannot be financed in the long run by falls in international reserves, *R* can be set to zero. Thus, equation (9.1) can be rearranged as:

$$(F - K) = (E + T) - M \tag{9.2}$$

The left-hand side of equation (9.2) represents the transfer of resources from Latin America to the rest of the world consequent on the debt crisis. The right-hand side shows that this required a comparable trade surplus, assuming that net transfer receipts (*T*) were of minor importance.

One year after the debt crisis, in 1983, the net transfer of resources ($F - K$) had reached $31.5 billion (see Table 9.6). Latin America, therefore, was forced to move swiftly from a positive transfer of resources in 1981 equivalent to 2 per cent of GDP to a negative transfer of resources from 1983 onwards equivalent to 6 per cent of GDP. This adjustment – 8 per cent of GDP – was one of the largest the region had ever had to undertake and it required drastic measures to be taken to turn a trade deficit into a trade surplus. Since export promotion takes time and since the net barter terms of trade deteriorated sharply after 1980, the full burden of adjustment had to be carried by imports. Indeed, these fell by 40 per cent in the four years after 1981 (see Table 9.6).

Latin America was no stranger to import suppression. Indeed, in the fifty years since the Great Depression a formidable arsenal of instruments had been forged to control imports: tariffs, non-tariff barriers, multiple exchange rates, prior deposit schemes, etc. However, no mechanism had been developed for discriminating between intra- and extra-regional imports. Thus, import suppression (see Table 9.6) was indiscriminate with intra-regional imports falling as fast as extra-regional imports after 1981.

The fall in intra-regional imports had an immediate effect on intra-regional exports since one country's imports were another country's exports. However, the need to give priority to servicing the external public debt led to difficulties in the multilateral clearing schemes established by ALADI, CACM and the AP. Those countries with intra-regional net exports found that intra-regional debts were accumulating through non-payment of outstanding balances. Some countries therefore began to impose restrictions on intra-regional exports in addition to those that operated on intra-regional imports. Intra-regional trade then entered into a downward spiral.

The multilateral clearing schemes had minimised the need for hard currency, but outstanding balances still had to be settled twice a year in US dollars. Technocrats responsible for regional integration experimented with the use of soft currencies to settle regional imbalances, drawing upon the experience of the European Payments Union in the 1950s. Such efforts, however, were doomed to failure; only hard currency could satisfy the needs of intra-regional net exporters as they searched for resources to service their external debts.

The decline in new lending by commercial banks therefore provoked a crisis in regional integration. As it became clear that the debt crisis was not a short-term liquidity problem, Latin American countries began to re-evaluate the inward-looking model. Import supression had been effective, but it had brought stagnation or recession. If the trade surplus was required for the foreseeable future to service the external debt, an alternative – less damaging – approach was required.

This approach was found in export promotion (EP). One by one the Latin American countries committed themselves to a version of export-led growth that hoped to use non-traditional exports as the engine of development. Export promotion would permit imports to recover and would lead to modest GDP growth while still preserving a trade surplus. The new ideology began in Chile,[28] Costa Rica and Ecuador in 1984, spread to Bolivia and Mexico in 1985 and had reached Argentina and Brazil by 1990.

This sea-change in Latin American thinking led to a chain reaction. Market access for exports required a reconsideration of the international trade regime. Those countries that had not already done so joined the General Agreement on Tariffs and Trade (GATT now WTO) and participated actively in the Uruguay Round of trade negotations beginning in 1986. Export promotion, however, obliged governments to remove the barriers against exports and this could only be done through trade liberalisation. Tariff and non-tariff barriers tumbled throughout Latin America as firms sought to place their export firms on an equal footing with competitors elsewhere.

At first, trade liberalisation was unilateral. Latin American countries did not seek reciprocity and instead dismantled their trade barriers without demanding compensatory action by trade partners. As export volumes from Chile, Costa Rica and Mexico soared, other countries followed suit. However, market access remained a problem and protectionism in the European Union, Japan and the US became a sensitive issue, while the continued weakness of the net barter terms of trade deprived many countries of the chance to convert an increase in export volumes into an increase in export values.

Regional integration was deeply affected by these changes. The initial reaction after 1982 was one of deep hostility. Integration schemes were seen as part and parcel of the inward-looking model of import-substituting industrialisation that had rendered Latin America so vulnerable to the reversal of capital flows. The subsequent reaction was one of indifference as the new policies of export promotion and trade liberalisation were assumed not to require any discrimination between intra- and extra-regional trade.

By the end of the 1980s the mood was again changing. After the initial enthusiasm for unilateral trade liberalisation, a preference began to emerge in favour of bilateral or multilateral trade concessions. As protectionism in the north became a bigger issue, the prospect of increasing *intra*-regional trade once again became attractive. Finally, the growth of imports after 1986 made possible by reduced debt service payments permitted a disproportionately rapid recovery in intra-regional trade.[29]

All these factors led to a new approach to regional integration. Rather than being interpreted as a scheme for regional ISI, integration was now seen as a natural stepping stone towards the promotion of extra-regional exports. The emphasis shifted from the demand side (the captive market) to the supply side (the reduction of costs). Even the international financial agencies, previously hostile or lukewarm at best to regional integration schemes, began to re-evaluate their position. The emergence of new schemes of regional integration alongside the revival of old schemes forms the subject matter of the next chapter.

Notes

1. See Pan-American Union (1952), pp. 25, 26, 29 and 30.
2. Intra-regional imports and exports in any given year should be equal, but extra-regional imports in 1945 were much lower than extra-regional exports as a result of wartime problems of supply from Europe and the US. This explains why intra-regional trade represented a much higher proportion of total imports than exports at the end of the war.
3. The confrontation with the US administration as a result of the expropriation of US oil companies was brought swiftly to a close once Mexico and the US entered the Second World War in December 1941.
4. See Pan-American Union (1952), pp. 164–5.
5. See Meirelles (1995), chapter 3.
6. See Pan-American Union (1952), pp. 72–3 and Meirelles (1995), table III. 6.
7. See, for example, ECLA (1959).
8. For further details, see Finch (1988).
9. See Inter-American Development Bank (1981), pp. 305, 400.
10. The net barter terms of trade began to deteriorate after 1954, following a sharp rise during the Korean War (1950–4). The index (1963 = 100) fell from 135 in 1954 to 99 in 1962. See CEPAL (1976), p. 25.
11. The data in Table 9.2 refer to exports to other LAFTA countries. They do not include exports to Latin American countries that were not members of LAFTA.
12. See Thoumi (1989).

13. See Inter-American Development Bank (1992), p. 191ff.
14. See Bulmer-Thomas (1987b), chapters 8, 9.
15. The reluctance of Costa Rica at first to sign the treaty has both an economic and political explanation. Some of the country's industrialists believed that they would be unable to compete successfully with El Salvador and Guatemala if trade barriers were lowered, while a vocal section of the National Assembly was reluctant to enter a scheme that was expected to be dominated by Guatemala.
16. For further details, see Bulmer-Thomas (1988).
17. The war between El Salvador and Honduras was due to the expulsion of Salvadorean migrants from Honduras in order to help provide the land for agrarian reform needed by the Honduran military government. See Durham (1979).
18. See, for example, Willmore (1976).
19. Cline (1978) demonstrated both theoretically and empirically that net trade diversion in Central America could be welfare-increasing.
20. The withdrawal of Honduras took place eighteen months after the war with El Salvador. Although this dispute was a factor in the Honduran decision, it was less significant than the widespread view that the republic was not benefiting from membership of the CACM.
21. The scheme, known as the Regime for Central American Integration Industries, provided for the creation of regional monopolies in those industries subject to major economies of scale. The intention was that each country would receive an equal number of these regional monopolies. Three regional monopolies were created before the scheme collapsed in 1962. See Ramsett (1969).
22. See Bulmer-Thomas *et al.* (1992), table 4.
23. For further details, see El-Agraa and Hojman (1988).
24. Ecuador became a major exporter of oil in the 1970s and this led to a shift of exports away from the AP even before the debt crisis.
25. In the area of intermediate manufactured goods, the deficit was $40 966 million in 1980. See ECLAC (1992), tables 274, 275.
26. See Griffith-Jones (1984).
27. Regional GDP in 1980 was just in excess of $500 billion. See Inter-American Development Bank (1981), p. 400.
28. Chile had begun the process of export promotion after 1973 with a radical programme of trade liberalisation measures. These were temporarily reversed after 1981 in order to protect the balance of payments from the full impact of the debt crisis. The process of trade liberalisation was restarted in 1984. See Scott (1996).
29. The reduction in debt service payments was at first due to the moratorium declared by a number of Latin American governments on the external public debt. With the launch of the Brady Plan in 1989, Latin American countries were finally able to exploit the difference between the par value and the market value of their commercial bank debt, leading to a substantial saving in debt service payments. See Felix and Caskey (1990).

10 Regional Integration in Latin America since 1985: Open Regionalism and Globalisation

Victor Bulmer-Thomas

By the mid-1980s the integration schemes in Latin America that had been founded in the 1960s were in a state of deep crisis. The weaknesses identified before 1980 had not been corrected and the debt crisis had exposed the vulnerability of each scheme to external shocks and balance of payments crises. The prevailing ideology inside and outside Latin America had changed sharply with a rejection of inward-looking development in general and import-substituting industrialisation (ISI) in particular; regional integration was seen as a manifestation of the old ideology and was assigned responsibility for much that had gone wrong in the process of industrialisation. International financial agencies (IFIs) were deeply hostile towards any suggestion of reviving regional integration with the World Bank leading the way in promoting export-led growth as the only realistic alternative to ISI.

Within ten years the situation had changed completely. By the mid-1990s old integration schemes had been revived, new ones created and the IFIs had become enthusiastic supporters of regional cooperation. Even the US, for so long lukewarm or even hostile towards regional integration schemes, became a proponent of free trade areas and led the way with the establishment of the Canada–US Free Trade Area (CUFTA) in 1989 – see Chapter 8. The European Community (EC), renamed the European Union (EU) in 1994 (see Chapter 5), for its part saw an opportunity in Latin America to promote integration as a solution to many of the region's long-standing problems.[1]

This chapter explores the new integration project in Latin America developed since the mid-1980s. Yet the transformation of the theory and practice of regional integration in Latin America is simply part of a bigger story in which countries have undergone a sea-change in their attitude to trade policies, export-led growth and international cooperation. It is impossible to understand the changes in regional cooperation – often described as 'open regionalism'[2] – without understanding these other changes.

First, the debt crisis finally killed off any lingering hopes that ISI could be used to maintain rapid economic growth. The deep recession in Latin America after 1982, provoked by the need to generate a trade surplus to service the public external debt, had emphasised the need to promote exports. Cuts in imports after fifty years of ISI were deeply damaging as most imports consisted of intermediate and capital goods whose reduction had an immediate impact on production and capacity. Only by promoting exports could Latin America hope to generate a trade surplus without the need for stagflation. The contrast with South-East Asia, where heavily indebted countries such as South Korea had avoided recession through export promotion, was frequently made.[3]

Latin American countries, however, were not interested in export promotion based on traditional primary products alone.[4] The message of CEPAL with regard to the net barter terms of trade appeared to be confirmed by the deterioration in the real price of primary products after 1980, making it exceedingly difficult to increase the value of exports through an increase in the volume of traditional primary products. Thus, export promotion implied a new emphasis on non-traditional products in general and manufactured goods in particular.

Export promotion had been used sporadically by Latin American countries before 1980. Almost invariably, however, these efforts had sought to avoid a reduction in the effective rate of protection (ERP), leaving firms to enjoy high protection in the domestic market. Thus, export promotion had typically relied on subsidies with the most inefficient firms enjoying the highest support. This policy could be quite effective, but it was fiscally irresponsible, inconsistent with membership of the General Agreement on Tariffs and Trade (GATT now WTO) and earned the wrath of many governments in developed countries.

Export promotion therefore obliged Latin American countries to bring domestic costs and prices closer into line with international costs and prices. A necessary condition for this was a reduction in tariff and non-tariff barriers, so that export promotion implied trade liberalisation. Throughout Latin America, therefore, the elaborate quantitative barriers constructed over more than half a century were dismantled, while tariff barriers fell to an average of 10–15 per cent.[5]

Trade liberalisation transformed the prospects for regional integration. The risk of trade diversion was reduced as a result of the change in trade barriers towards third countries. Meanwhile, the scope for trade creation increased as each country had built up high cost manufacturing production behind a wall of protection before 1980. However, net trade creation still ran the risk of being welfare-reducing unless the factors of production released by additional imports could find employment in alternative activities. This suggested a much broader vision of integration than in the past, one that no longer limited intra-zonal trade liberalisation to manufactured goods.

The idea of an integration scheme embracing agriculture and services as well as industrial products also appealed to the new supply-side approach. If export promotion required policies to increase the efficiency of firms so that they could compete on a more equal footing with firms outside the region, then regional integration needed to operate in such a way as to enhance the prospects for cost reductions. This could only happen if firms were permitted to buy all their inputs from the cheapest source within the region. Thus, the ideology of regional integration changed from a demand-side emphasis on the captive market, stressing manufactured products, to a supply-side emphasis on cost reduction, stressing trade liberalisation in all areas.

By the mid-1990s integration was seen not so much as an instrument for promoting industrialisation, but as a stepping stone towards export promotion and export-led growth. It did not matter, therefore, if intra-regional trade remained as a relatively small share of the total as long as total exports expanded rapidly and became the engine of growth of the economy. This meant, however, that the vector of intra-regional exports for each country needed to correspond more closely to the vector of extra-regional exports; firms needed to use the regional market as a first step towards exports to the rest of the world.

The revival of regional integration in Latin America was at first fraught with difficulty. Regional suspicions remained severe and the debt crisis continued to cast a shadow over any attempts to increase imports. However, debt reduction schemes – including default – from the mid-1980s onwards freed resources that could be used to increase imports. The growth of imports accelerated further as exports started to expand and net capital flows to Latin America soared in the first half of the 1990s.[6] Intra-regional trade grew more rapidly than extra-regional trade and by the mid-1990s the region had overtaken the levels of intra-regional trade recorded before the debt crisis began.

MERCOSUR

The new approach towards regional integration has been nowhere more apparent than in the southern part of Latin America. After many years of military rule, in which industrialisation acquired special significance because of its alleged 'strategic' role, the new civilian administrations of Argentina under President Alfonsín and Brazil under President Sarney signed a cooperation agreement in 1986. This agreement was to lead to the creation of MERCOSUR in 1991 with the participation also of Paraguay and Uruguay.

The cooperation agreement was signed at a time when both Argentina and Brazil were subject to intense balance of payments constraints. At the same time, as Table 10.1 makes clear, both economies had large industrial sectors facing little competition from imports. The cooperation agreement therefore opened the possibility of balanced trade expansion in key industrial sectors. Agricultural trade and services were not excluded from the cooperation agreement.

The legal framework for bilateral cooperation was provided by a series of protocols. The first referred to capital goods and provided for the elimination of trade barriers on a common list of products. Inevitably, the list included many more products of interest to Brazil, since the Brazilian capital goods industry was much more developed than in Argentina. However, Protocols 2 and 3 established quotas for wheat exports from Argentina and allowed for complementary food exports in case of a supply crisis in either country. Protocol 8 established the conditions for cooperation in energy supply between the two countries, while Protocol 9 created a joint Centre of Biotechnology. Altogether, there were more than twenty protocols and the next step came in November 1988 with the signing of the Argentina–Brazil

Table 10.1 Basic data for MERCOSUR countries for 1990 (1988 prices)

	Argentina	*Brazil*	*Paraguay*	*Uruguay*	*Total*
GDP ($bn)	121.4	332.8	6.7	8.6	469.5
Population (millions)	32.3	149.0	4.3	3.1	188.7
GDP per head ($)	3755	2233	1557	2791	2488
Manufacturing/GDP (%)	28.3	26.4	16.6	27.3	26.8
Imports/GDP (%)	5.0	7.2	28.4	17.2	7.1
Exports/GDP (%)	11.6	10.8	25.7	25.3	11.5

Source: Inter-American Development Bank (1994), Statistical Appendix.

Treaty of Integration, Development and Cooperation, setting out a specific timetable for the elimination of all trade barriers.[7]

The cooperation agreement had begun as a defensive strategy consistent with managed trade and avoiding the need for major restructuring by either country. Progress was substantial, however, and presidential elections in 1989 led to the formation of administrations committed to a more radical approach to trade liberalisation. For both President Menem in Argentina (1989–) and President Collor de Mello in Brazil (1990–3) trade liberalisation was an essential part of their strategies to modernise their respective economies, as well as to curb chronic inflation. Thus, the Buenos Aires Act was signed in July 1990 committing both countries to the creation of a customs union by the end of 1994 with the abolition of all intra-zonal trade barriers.

The Buenos Aires Act raised deep concerns in Paraguay and Uruguay. Unlike in Argentina and Brazil, with which Paraguay and Uruguay shared frontiers, intra-regional trade had reached a high share of total trade in these two small countries and both feared that the proposed customs union would lead to trade and investment diversion. Although the combined GDP of both countries was minute in relation to that of Argentina and Brazil (see Table 10.1), the larger countries agreed to reopen negotations and the result was the Treaty of Asunción in March 1991 creating MERCOSUR (in Portuguese MERCOSUL).

The Treaty of Asunción committed Argentina, Brazil, Paraguay and Uruguay to the creation of a customs union by 1 January 1995. Although widely regarded as far too ambitious, the target was in fact met – albeit with some qualifications. Thus, MERCOSUR established a common external tariff (CET) at the beginning of 1995 for approximately 80 per cent of extra-regional imports. The main exceptions were capital goods and computers, where Brazil wished to retain a much higher degree of protection than Argentina, and automobiles. In these cases, as in the case of free trade zones, a date in the twenty-first century was set by which external trade policies had to be harmonised among the four countries.[8] Intra-zonal trade was almost entirely freed with each country allowed to maintain protection only for a limited number of products.

Much of the credit for the establishment of the customs union can be attributed to the speed with which intra-regional trade expanded after 1990. As Table 10.2 shows, intra-regional imports increased from $4 billion in 1990 to nearly $12 billion in 1994. This increase was much

Table 10.2 MERCOSUR: intra-zonal exports in $ million (as percentage of total exports)

	1990	*1991*	*1992*	*1993*	*1994*
Argentina	1833	1978	2327	3684	4740
	(14.8)	(16.5)	(19.0)	(28.1)	(30.0)
Brazil	1320	2309	4098	5394	5918
	(4.2)	(7.3)	(11.4)	(13.9)	(13.6)
Paraguay	379	259	246	276	377
	(27.4)	(23.1)	(22.7)	(16.7)	(21.7)
Uruguay	712	679	689	1019	716
	(42.1)	(42.3)	(38.3)	(58.8)	(37.4)
Total	4244	5225	7360	10,373	11,751
	(9.1)	(11.3)	(14.5)	(18.8)	(18.6)

Sources: Inter-American Development Bank (1995) and data provided by MERCOSUR embassies in London (September, 1995).

faster than the increase in total imports despite the fact that total imports were themselves growing very rapidly. For the region as a whole intra-regional exports had risen from 9.1 per cent of total exports in 1990 to 18.6 per cent in 1994 (see Table 10.2).

The increase in intra-regional trade was widely attributed to trade liberalisation within MERCOSUR. This was indeed partially correct. However, other – less benign – forces were at work. The birth of MERCOSUR coincided with the rise in capital flows to Latin America, permitting a big increase in imports and current account deficits. At the same time, the stabilisation programme launched in Argentina in March 1991 may have led to a sharp reduction in inflation, but it left as its legacy an overvalued currency from which Brazilian exporters were quick to benefit.[9] Thus, Brazil ran a large trade surplus on its bilateral trade with Argentina, a surplus that began to be eroded following the adoption of the Brazilian stabilisation programme in the middle of 1994.

In the new integration theory in Latin America, the customs union is seen as a mechanism for promoting exports to the rest of the world. It is still too early to evaluate MERCOSUR from this perspective. Brazil has had considerable success in expanding non-traditional exports in both intra- and extra-regional markets with a high correlation between the two vectors. However, Brazil's export performance was due more to currency undervaluation in the late 1980s and domestic recession in the early 1990s than to cost reductions as a result of trade liberalisation within MERCOSUR. Argentina, on the other hand, has remained dependent on traditional agro-industrial products for its extra-regional exports with intra-regional exports (including manufactured goods) benefiting from trade diversion in Brazil and enjoying only a low correlation with extra-regional exports.

For Paraguay and Uruguay, the creation of MERCOSUR has created a different set of problems. Paraguay's intra-regional exports expanded rapidly after 1985 as the giant hydroelectric schemes constructed jointly with Brazil (Itaipú) and Argentina (Yacyreta) came on stream. This expansion, however, had nothing to do with MERCOSUR. Meanwhile, the CET agreed at the beginning of 1995 placed in jeopardy the lucrative contraband trade located in Ciudad del Este near the border with Argentina and Brazil. Uruguay, on the other hand, after a period of fast export growth in the 1980s before the creation of MERCOSUR, saw the ratio of exports to GDP decline in the first half of the 1990s as a result of a sharp real appreciation of the currency.

MERCOSUR, therefore, has yet to fulfil the role indicated by the new theory of regional integration. It has certainly contributed to a rapid increase in intra-regional trade, but part of this was simply a recovery of the trade lost as a result of the debt crisis, while part has been due to the growth of imports made possible by net capital inflows at the beginning of the 1990s. As these two factors pushing intra-regional trade decline in importance, it will become harder for MERCOSUR to sustain its early dynamism.

An additional problem is provided by the economic size of Brazil in relation to the other countries. The low ratio of intra-regional exports to total exports for MERCOSUR as a whole (see Table 10.2) is above all a reflection of the low ratio in Brazil (still only 13.6 per cent in 1994). While the size of the Brazilian market makes it possible for other countries to increase the ratio of their intra-regional exports to total exports without a major adjustment problem on the part of Brazil, it is very difficult for Brazil to do the same. If Brazil were to sell 25 per cent of her exports in the regional market, it would require additional imports of $6 billion by her three partners – an increase of more than 100 per cent on their estimated 1995 level and implying a ratio of intra-regional imports to total imports in each country in excess of 50 per cent. Unless her partners are able to absorb this increase, the trade ratio for MERCOSUR as a whole will remain at approximately 20 per cent because of the dominant position of Brazil in the regional economy (see Table 10.1).

Like the EU, MERCOSUR has been a successful club that others have wanted to join. By mid-1995 Bolivia and Chile had reached agreement in principle on associate status, paving the way for abolition of intra-zonal trade barriers while keeping differential external tariffs. The participation of Chile, the model Latin American economy in the decade after 1985, was particularly welcome as the Chilean policy-makers had argued for years that the country did not need to participate in regional integration schemes. Similarly, the EU entered into negotations with MERCOSUR in 1995 for the creation of a free trade agreement between the two trading blocks. Although agriculture – at the insistence of the EU – will not be included in the first stage, there were reasonable prospects at the time of writing of an agreement covering most manufactured goods and services.

No discussion of MERCOSUR would be complete without mentioning the integration project favoured by its largest member (Brazil). As the North American Free Trade Agreement (NAFTA) came into existence on 1 January 1994 (see Chapter 8), Brazil launched its own project for a South American Free Trade Area (SAFTA) as a geopolitical counterweight. At first greeted with scepticism and even fear by Brazil's neighbours, SAFTA gradually found more favour as an expansion of NAFTA to other Latin American countries became less likely. The associate membership of MERCOSUR by Bolivia and Chile was seen by Brazil as simply the first step towards the creation of SAFTA – a regional bloc that would effectively be the same as the 1980 Latin American Integration Association (LAIA – see previous chapter) without Mexico.

THE CENTRAL AMERICAN COMMON MARKET AND THE ANDEAN PACT

The Central American Common Market (CACM), once hailed as the most successful example of integration among developing countries, virtually collapsed after 1980 as the debt crisis combined with the regional political crisis to drive down intra-regional trade despite the resumption of bilateral trade between El Salvador and Honduras in 1980. By 1985, the nominal value of trade was less than half the level in 1980 and intra-regional exports had fallen from 24.2 per cent of total exports in 1980 to 15.5 per cent in 1985.[10]

Efforts to revive the CACM started in the mid-1980s, but they were overwhelmed by several factors. First, the tension between the

Sandinista government in Nicaragua and other governments in Central America made any major restructuring of the CACM impossible. Secondly, the IFIs had become strongly opposed to regional integration as at best a distraction from the need to promote non-traditional exports to the rest of the world and at worst a return to regional ISI. Thirdly, the Reagan administration in the US, whose support was essential for a revival of regional integration, resisted any move in Central America that could be interpreted as throwing a lifeline to the Sandinistas. Finally, the non-payment of debts through the multilateral clearing house provided a strong disincentive for an increase in intra-regional exports.

An imaginative scheme, supported by the EU, was launched in 1989 to circumvent the payments problem. Known as the Derecho de Importación Centroamericana (DICA), the new financial instrument was in effect a soft currency issued by central banks to intra-regional exporters that could be used to buy intra-regional imports or sold to others interested in buying such imports. It did not remove the debt overhang, but it did provide a mechanism under which trade could expand without the need for further debt arrears. Sadly, however, the DICA did not catch on as exporters in general insisted on payment in dollars.

With the defeat of the Sandinistas in free elections in February 1990, the path was cleared for a new attempt to revive the integration scheme building on the success of the Arias Plan in ending the civil war in Nicaragua.[11] The summit of Central American presidents held in Antigua, Guatemala, in June 1990 outlined a new integration scheme in which Honduras would return as a full member, the CET would be re-established (at much lower levels), intra-zonal non-tariff barriers would be swept away, and trade liberalisation within the region would embrace agricultural products for the first time.

The last provision was the most radical. As Table 10.3 shows, a significant gap in living standards had emerged between the strongest (Costa Rica) and the weakest (Honduras and Nicaragua) economies with El Salvador and Guatemala in an intermediate position.[12] With trade liberalisation limited to manufactured goods (as happened in the 1960s), the benefits of regional integration would flow disproportionately to the stronger countries. With the liberalisation of agriculture, however, factors of production in the weaker countries might be expected to gain from the expansion of regional trade.

Agriculture in Central America is bimodal. Large farms dominate the market for export agriculture (bananas, coffee, beef, sugar and

Table 10.3 Basic data for the AP and CACM countries for 1990 (1988 prices)

	GDP ($bn)	*Population (mn)*	*GDP per head ($)*	*Manu/ GDP (%)*	*Imports/ GDP (%)*	*Exports/ GDP (%)*
Andean Pact						
Bolivia	6.4	6.8	947	16.0	12.0	14.0
Colombia	47.1	32.3	1457	21.7	13.7	18.0
Ecuador	13.3	10.3	1298	19.9	16.5	21.5
Peru	28.9	21.6	1339	28.6	12.0	12.9
Venezuela	65.7	19.3	3400	19.8	14.2	20.3
Total	161.4	90.3	1787	21.8	13.7	18.1
CACM						
Costa Rica	5.1	3.0	1688	20.8	42.9	40.0
El Salvador	5.5	5.2	1059	17.6	25.3	21.3
Guatemala	8.4	9.2	910	15.0	21.7	18.2
Honduras	3.9	4.9	798	13.5	28.7	27.8
Nicaragua	2.1	3.7	568	17.0	30.0	20.3
Total	25.0	26.0	962	16.7	28.6	25.0

Source: Inter-American Development Bank (1994), Statistical Appendix.

cotton), while small farms are concentrated in agriculture for the domestic market. Trade liberalisation could therefore lead to a major adjustment problem for those countries with a comparative disadvantage in agricultural trade. In order to avoid this, the Central American countries committed themselves to a system of price bands for the main agricultural products modelled on Chile. In this scheme variable tariffs would be used to provide domestic producers with a modicum of protection from international competition and ensure that some small farmers in all republics could still survive.[13]

Intra-regional trade recovered slowly after 1985, but remained a very small proportion of total trade. Only after 1990 (see Table 10.4) did the pace of intra-regional trade growth accelerate with the value of intra-regional exports surpassing the previous 1980 peak in 1993. Agreement was reached on a CET with a maximum of 20 per cent and the price bands for agricultural products began to function as planned. By 1994 El Salvador, Guatemala and Honduras felt sufficiently confident to launch a further stage in the integration process with the creation of the *Triangulo del Norte* to which Nicaragua later attached herself.

Table 10.4 Central American intra-zonal exports in $ million (as percentage of total exports)

	1990	*1991*	*1992*	*1993*	*1994*
Costa Rica	134.6	177.8	246.0	315.5	342.1
	(9.9)	(11.9)	(13.3)	(16.2)	(15.8)
El Salvador	176.7	197.3	270.5	310.0	339.1
	(30.4)	(33.6)	(45.3)	(41.8)	(41.5)
Guatemala	288.2	323.6	395.4	418.5	465.8
	(24.8)	(26.9)	(30.5)	(30.9)	(30.5)
Honduras	26.0	32.1	44.6	48.7	59.4
	(4.4)	(5.3)	(6.5)	(6.0)	(7.1)
Nicaragua	47.5	51.4	41.7	57.0	67.1
	(17.4)	(19.3)	(17.6)	(21.3)	(19.5)
TOTAL	673.0	782.2	998.2	1149.7	1273.5
	(16.9)	(18.8)	(21.4)	(22.4)	(22.4)

Sources: SIECA (1995) for 1990–2; CEPAL (1995) for 1993–4.

The regional integration scheme, however, was far from healthy. The revival of intra-regional trade in the decade after 1985 amounted to little more than a recovery of the trade lost between 1980 and 1985. The composition of intra-regional exports did not alter significantly and continued to bear little resemblance to the pattern of extra-regional exports. Non-tariff barriers remained formidable and no mechanism was found for eliminating them, placing severe limits on the scope for intra-regional trade expansion. The regional institutions, crippled in the 1980s, remained extremely weak and the preferred 'solution' was the creation of a new framework rather than the reform of existing institutions.

A particular source of concern was the reluctance of Costa Rica, the region's most successful economy, to enter fully into the new scheme. Having lowered its tariffs unilaterally in the 1980s, Costa Rica felt under no obligation to join in creating a CET in the 1990s. Unwilling to contemplate free movement of labour, Costa Rica also stayed outside the *Triangulo del Norte* whose stated aim was the creation of a (true) common market. Furthermore, Costa Rica made no secret of its desire to enter into bilateral agreements with countries outside the region and signed in 1994 a free trade agreement with Mexico. This complicated even further the prospects for a customs union in Central America.[14]

The new CACM is unlikely, therefore, to be more than a free trade area at best. Other countries, notably El Salvador, have already indicated their desire to lower tariffs unilaterally and the CET now looks like a distant goal. Trade within the CACM has grown, but remains highly concentrated with bilateral exchanges between El Salvador and Guatemala responsible for nearly 35 per cent of the total (see Table 10.5). The two weakest economies, Honduras and Nicaragua, have remained on the margin of trade expansion so that the CACM – despite some novel features – has largely reproduced the pattern of the 1960s and 1970s.

Like the CACM, the Andean Pact (AP) was effectively destroyed by the debt crisis. Although regional tensions were much less severe than in Central America, attempts to revive the scheme had to wait until 1987 when the Quito Modifying Protocol was adopted by the member countries, committing them once again to a customs union.[15] Subsequent meetings rescinded Decision 24 (see previous chapter), reversing the hostility to foreign capital, and steps were taken to

Table 10.5 Country shares of total intra-regional exports, 1992 (percentages)

Part A. Andean Pact

Exports >	*Bolivia*	*Colombia*	*Ecuador*	*Peru*	*Venezuela*	*Total*
Bolivia		1.1	0.2	2.7	0.4	4.4
Colombia	0.7		6.9	11.1	26.5	45.2
Ecuador	0.1	2.7		4.5	0.6	7.9
Peru	1.7	3.7	2.6		4.3	12.3
Venezuela	0.1	22.4	2.2	5.4		30.1

Part B. Central American Common Market

Exports >	*Costa Rica*	*El Sal.*	*Guatemala*	*Honduras*	*Nicaragua*	*Total*
Costa Rica		6.0	8.0	1.4	5.4	20.8
El Salvador	5.6		13.7	1.9	2.9	24.1
Guatemala	10.3	21.0		7.0	7.1	45.4
Honduras	0.5	2.7	1.4		1.0	5.6
Nicaragua	1.2	1.9	0.6	0.4		4.1

Part C. MERCOSUR

Exports >	*Argentina*	*Brazil*	*Paraguay*	*Uruguay*	*Total*
Argentina		23.2	3.8	5.3	32.3
Brazil	42.1		7.5	7.1	56.7
Paraguay	0.9	2.4		0.1	3.4
Uruguay	3.5	3.9	0.1		7.5

Source: ECLAC (1994a).

eliminate tariffs on internal trade and harmonise tariffs on external trade.

The development of AP members remains very uneven (see Table 10.3). Colombia and Venezuela continue to dominate in terms of GDP, total trade and intra-regional trade while Bolivia and Ecuador – like Honduras and Nicaragua in the CACM – are very marginal to the whole process. Regional suspicions have increased rather than decreased since the relaunch of the AP, with Peru suspending membership in 1992 and Ecuador reconsidering her position following the border war with Peru in 1995.

The AP has suffered from the pull of two alternative integration projects: NAFTA and SAFTA. With the combined market of AP countries only a fraction of US or even Brazilian GDP, each country has felt tempted to pursue a unilateral path leading to other associations. The political will to create a customs union has simply been absent for most of the time and national rivalries have been intense. The greater attraction of the alternatives became clear when Bolivia began discussions in 1995 on associate membership of MERCOSUR.

Intra-regional trade barriers have come down, the CET – yet to be fully implemented – has been set at a maximum of 15 per cent[16] and trade among AP countries has increased (see Table 10.6). However, it still constitutes a very small part of their total trade. The ratio of intra-regional exports to total exports rose from 4.1 per

Table 10.6 Andean Pact intra-zonal exports in $ milion (as percentage of total exports)

	1990	*1991*	*1992*	*1993*	*1994*
Bolivia	59.9	89.8	99.4	125.0	195.8
	(6.5)	(10.0)	(13.0)	(15.5)	(17.4)
Colombia	372.7	778.5	1002.2	1169.0	1275.6
	(5.5)	(10.7)	(14.5)	(15.7)	(14.8)
Ecuador	188.5	203.7	176.0	325.0	352.3
	(6.9)	(7.1)	(5.8)	(9.3)	(7.9)
Peru	214.1	214.8	273.2	270.0	302.7
	(6.5)	(8.6)	(8.1)	(7.8)	(6.7)
Venezuela	429.3	443.8	665.8	1049.0	1140.0
	(2.5)	(3.0)	(4.8)	(6.2)	(7.0)
Total	1264.5	1730.6	2216.6	2938.0	3266.4
	(4.1)	(6.1)	(7.9)	(9.1)	(9.3)

Sources: ECLAC (1994), tables 289–91; International Monetary Fund (1995).

cent in 1990 to 9.3 per cent in 1994 with only Bolivia and Colombia reaching a ratio in double figures. Exports between Colombia and Venezuela constitute almost 50 per cent of total intra-regional exports (see Table 10.5) with many bilateral links of negligible importance.

The AP has therefore once again been reduced effectively to a bilateral relationship between Colombia and Venezuela. This relationship was formalised in 1994 with the formation of the G-3 linking the two countries with Mexico in a free trade area. Trade between the two countries has increased rapidly, but problems began to multiply after 1993. The banking crisis suffered by Venezuela in February 1994 forced the new Caldera administration (1994–) to take emergency action to defend the balance of payments and Colombian exports inevitably suffered. Maritime border disputes between the two countries, as well as guerrilla incursions and drug-related problems, compounded the difficulties.

The AP was originally created in response to frustration at the lack of progress in the Latin American Free Trade Area (LAFTA – see previous chapter). The collapse of LAFTA left a vacuum that has effectively been filled by MERCOSUR. If the latter continues to progress, adding more members until it becomes in effect SAFTA, there will be no space left for the AP. If, however, MERCOSUR fails, it is difficult to see the AP overcoming its inherited problems. The political will is still absent and there is no consensus in favour of institutional reform and the transfer of national sovereignty to supranational organisations. This, of course, does not rule out the possibility of a deepening of the integration process between Colombia and Venezuela where the dynamic in favour of regional integration is much more firmly rooted. There is also evidence that Colombia in particular has been able to use the regional market to export products which have later entered into extra-regional trade.

MEXICO, NAFTA AND WESTERN HEMISPHERE INTEGRATION

NAFTA, embracing Canada, Mexico and the United States, was established on 1 January 1994. It is the subject of Chapter 8 and will not be considered in detail here. However, it is impossible to understand the dynamics of regional integration in Latin America in the 1990s without some appreciation of NAFTA and the logic of the Mexican position.

Trade liberalisation had begun in Mexico in 1985 under President Miguel de la Madrid (1982–8). Since Mexico has traditionally done more than 70 per cent of its foreign trade with the US, the question of market access to its northern neighbour became critical following the expansion of exports under trade liberalisation. President Carlos Salinas de Gortari (1988–94) therefore chose to make the process irreversible by seeking a free trade agreement with the US in 1990. The previous year, however, the Canada–US Free Trade Agreement (CUFTA) had been implemented so that the Canadian position was also relevant. Although trade between Canada and Mexico was negligible, the decision was taken to make the negotiations tripartite. These concluded in 1992 and NAFTA was ratified in 1993.[17]

The logic of NAFTA for Mexico was very strong and domestic resistance was surprisingly modest. However, NAFTA presented the rest of Latin America with a series of challenges. The first was the fear of trade diversion. The trade privileges extended to the three members of NAFTA could lead to some Latin American exports being lost to a less efficient source. Textile producers in the Caribbean Basin were particularly concerned as the rules of origin for clothing in NAFTA are very demanding; the fear was that NAFTA firms would replace textile imports from outside NAFTA with NAFTA inputs in order to qualify for duty-free status for their own NAFTA exports.

Studies by the World Bank and other organisations suggested that trade diversion was unlikely to be a very serious threat for the rest of Latin America. The main NAFTA importer, the US, had low average tariffs so that trade diversion to Mexico from the cheapest source elsewhere was likely to be small. Attention therefore shifted to investment diversion – seen by many as much more serious. Thus, the rest of Latin America feared both that existing investment in their countries might be relocated to take advantage of Mexico's unique access to the US and that future investment might be diverted for the same reason.

The third challenge was related to the second. All Latin American countries, including Mexico, had seen it as one of their highest international trade policy priorities to gain preferential access to the US market. Like the EU, therefore, the US had constructed a pyramid of privilege with Puerto Rico at the top and Cuba at the bottom. In the middle were the beneficiaries of numerous US import quotas as well as the small countries of Central America and the Caribbean for whom the Reagan Administration had created the Caribbean Basin Initiative (CBI) in 1984. The launch of NAFTA effectively eroded the margin of preference enjoyed by the rest of Latin America under the pyramid of privilege. The inclusion of sugar in NAFTA raised a question over the ability of the US to maintain its import quotas from the rest of Latin America, while the trade privileges enjoyed by the CBI countries in the US market were undermined by Mexican membership of NAFTA.

The formation of NAFTA therefore triggered a response from all Latin American countries with implications for regional integration in the subcontinent. Mexico herself was not immune since NAFTA created an extraordinary opportunity for Mexico to redefine her economic relationship with the rest of Latin America. Thus, it is appropriate to begin with the Mexican response before turning to other parts of the region.

Before NAFTA the only Latin American country to have duty free access to the US was Puerto Rico. The Caribbean island had exploited this advantage through a series of initiatives designed to attract trade and investment from elsewhere in joint ventures with Puerto Rican companies, leading ultimately to duty free access to the US. The strategy had been very successful, contributing to a standard of living in Puerto Rico far higher than in the rest of Latin America.

Mexico's membership of NAFTA provided a similar opportunity. At the same time, the rules of NAFTA worked against the *maquiladoras* (assembly plants) that had mushroomed on Mexico's northern border. Thus, assembly plants were no longer to be allowed to purchase all imports free of duty – only those from NAFTA partners. In effect, the whole of Mexican territory was now subject to the same regime: duty-free imports from Canada and the US and no restrictions on exports complying with the complex rules of origin.[18]

Mexico therefore chose to market herself in the rest of Latin America as the bridge to the US. A series of free trade agreements were signed providing for duty free treatment on a broad range of goods. The partners in these bilateral agreements are Bolivia, Chile, Costa Rica and Ecuador, while a trilateral agreement – the G-3 (see above) – was signed with Colombia and Venezuela. Although initial trade with each of these countries was small in both absolute and relative terms, the free trade agreements did have the effect of stimulating a rapid increase in intra-regional exports and imports.

Mexico's free trade ambitions were not limited to the western hemisphere. She was the only Latin American country to participate fully in the first meeting of the Asia-Pacific Economic Cooperation (APEC) forum and fully endorsed the decision of APEC to establish a free trade agreement by the year 2020.[19] Mexico also became a member of the Organisation for Economic Cooperation and Development (OECD) after joining NAFTA, despite the huge gap in income per head between herself and the other members. The network (present and planned) linking Mexico to the rest of the world is shown in Table 10.7.

The rest of Latin America had to confront both NAFTA and the Mexican trade strategy. At the same time, the situation was rendered even more complex by the US proposal for a western hemisphere free trade zone. Launched by President Bush in 1990 as the Enterprise for the Americas Initiative (EAI), it was always long on rhetoric and short on detail. Yet it re-emerged at various moments, including the Summit of the Americas held in Miami in December 1994 and the subsequent meeting of trade ministers in Denver in July 1995. Thus, each Latin American country had to evaluate the prospects for a free trade agreement with the US, Mexico and Canada through NAFTA membership, as well as for bilateral free trade agreements with each of the NAFTA countries and sub-regional agreements in Latin America itself (see Table 10.7).

Table 10.7 Free trade in the Americas: integration schemes in place and under consideration

Part A

	Argentina	*Bolivia*	*Brazil*	*Chile*	*Colombia*	*Costa Rica*	*Cuba*
Argentina		M(e)	M	M(e)			
Bolivia	M(e)		M(e)	M(e)	AP		
Brazil	M	M(e)		M(e)			
Chile	M(e)	M(e)	M(e)		FTA		
Colombia		AP		FTA			
Costa Rica							
Cuba							
Dom. Rep.							
Ecuador		AP			AP		
El Salvador						CACM	
Guatemala						CACM	
Haiti							
Honduras						CACM	
Mexico		FTA		FTA	G-3	FTA	
Nicaragua						CACM	
Panama		AP(e)			AP(e)	FTA	
Paraguay	M	M(e)	M	M(e)			
Peru		AP			AP		
Uruguay	M	M(e)	M	M(e)			
Venezuela		AP	FTA	FTA	G-3/AP	SJ	

Part B

	Dom. Rep.	*Ecuador*	*El Salvador*	*Guatemala*	*Haiti*	*Honduras*	*Mexico*	*Nicaragua*
Argentina								
Bolivia		AP					FTA	
Brazil								
Chile							FTA	
Colombia		AP					G-3	
Costa Rica			CACM	CACM		CACM	SJ/FTA	CACM
Cuba								
Dom. Rep							SJ	
Ecuador							FTA	
El Salvador				CACM		CACM	SJ/FTA(e)	CACM
Guatemala			CACM			CACM	SJ/FTA(e)	CACM
Haiti							SJ	
Honduras			CACM	CACM			SJ/FTA(e)	CACM
Mexico	SJ	FTA	SJ/FTA(e)	SJ/FTA(e)	SJ	SJ/FTA(e)		SJ/FTA(e)
Nicaragua			CACM	CACM		CACM	SJ/FTA(e)	
Panama		AP(e)					SJ	
Paraguay								
Peru		AP						
Uruguay								
Venezuela	SJ	AP	SJ	SJ	SJ	SJ	G-3	SJ

Part C

	Panama	*Paraguay*	*Peru*	*Uruguay*	*Venezuela*	*CARICOM*	*EU*	*USA/Can.*	*Asia*
Argentian		M		M			FTA(e)		
Bolivia	AP(e)	M(e)	AP	M(e)	AP		CA		
Brazil		M		M	FTA		FTA(e)		
Chile		M(e)		M(e)	FTA		FTA(e)	(a)	APEC
Colombia	AP(e)		AP		G-3/AP		CA		
Costa Rica	FTA				SJ		CA	CBI	
Cuba						FTA(e)	CA(e)		
Dom. Rep.					SJ	FTA(e)	Lomé	CBI	
Ecuador	AP(e)		AP		AP		CA		
El Salvador					SJ		CA	CBI	
Guatemala					SJ		CA	CBI	
Haiti					SJ	FTA(e)	Lomé	CBI	
Honduras					SJ		CA	CBI	
Mexico	SJ				G-3		FTA(e)	NAFTA	APEC
Nicaragua					SJ		CA	CBI	
Panama			AP(e)		SJ/AP(e)		CA	CBI	
Peraguay				M			FTA(e)		
Peru	AP(e)				AP		CA		
Uruguay		M					FTA(e)		
Venezuela	SJ/AP(e)		AP				CA		

Notes
M = Mercosur member; M(e) = expected Mercosur associate member; AP = Andean Pact member; AP(e) = expected Andean Pact member; FTA = bilateral Free Trade Agreement; FTA(e) = expected bilateral FTA; CACM = Central American Common Market member; G-3 = Group of Three.
Source: Hufbauer and Schott (1995), Appendix C.

SJ = San José energy agreement participant; APEC = Asia-Pacific Economic Cooperation forum; CA = Cooperation Agreement; CBI = Caribbean Basin Initiative; NAFTA = North American Free Trade Agreement; Lomé = participant in Lomé Convention.

(a) Chile began negotiations for membership of NAFTA in 1995.

NAFTA membership was for many the greatest prize.[20] Chile in particular made it clear that she wished to join NAFTA at the earliest opportunity, and the announcement by President Clinton at the Miami summit that negotiations would begin with Chile in 1995 was considered a triumph of Chilean diplomacy. However, although Chile was widely perceived as the Latin American country most likely to meet the conditions for NAFTA entry, there was no certainty of membership.[21] Indeed, Chile suspended negotiations on NAFTA membership in 1995 until such time as the US Congress should grant the US administration 'fast-track' authority.[22]

For the small countries of Central America and the Caribbean, the prospect of NAFTA membership appeared ever more distant once the rhetoric of western hemisphere integration had subsided. With the possible exception of Costa Rica, these countries fell far short of the rigorous conditions for entry likely to be imposed by the US and no US administration relished the possibility of small countries joining one by one. Thus, the strategy of these countries became defensive rather than offensive – reforming the CBI to provide parity of treatment with Mexico in order to minimise trade and investment diversion. These efforts appeared to come to fruition when a bill was drafted by the Clinton Administration providing for 'NAFTA parity' in the case of CBI countries. The bill was dropped, however, in order to ensure the ratification of the Uruguay Round by the US Congress.

While most Latin American countries looked favourably on the possibility of NAFTA membership, however remote the chances, the Brazilian reaction was quite different. Brazil had little or no interest in joining NAFTA since it was unlikely to meet the conditions for membership and would in any case expect to run up against US congressional opposition. Thus, the entry of Mexico into NAFTA in 1994 encouraged Brazil to revive an old geopolitical project of South American as opposed to Latin American integration. Brazil therefore saw MERCOSUR as the first step towards the creation of a SAFTA that would have political as well as economic dimensions. In effect, Brazil promoted a concept of ALADI without Mexico – a scheme that would be free of US interference and in which the hegemonic role would inevitably be played by Brazil.

The options open to each Latin American country were therefore extremely complex (see Table 10.7). Chile, for example, in 1995 was simultaneously pursuing membership of NAFTA, associate membership of MERCOSUR, full participation in APEC and new bilateral free trade agreements, while implementing existing free trade agreements with several Latin American countries and observing closely developments in the AP. The position for Chile and other Latin American countries was complicated still further, however, by the initiatives taken by the EU.

The EU, while still the EEC, had signed trade and economic co-operation agreements with a number of Latin American countries. None of these had prevented a relative decline in the importance of trade between the two regions, although the EU remained an important market for Latin American exports and a major source of imports.

As the most important regional trading bloc in the world, the EU has always felt a special empathy for regional integration schemes in Latin America. This was reflected, for example, in the agreement reached with the AP in 1990 giving special Generalised System of Preferences (GSP) treatment to a wide range of non-traditional exports with the explicit aim of encouraging Andean countries to replace illegal narcotics exports destined in part for Europe (see Chapter 6). This was followed by a similar agreement with the Central American countries designed to provide support for the consolidation of democracy in the region.

The agreements with the AP and the CACM were unilateral gestures designed to underpin non-economic goals favoured by the EU. The entry of Mexico into NAFTA, however, led to a renewed focus on South America in general and MERCOSUR in particular. Approximately 50 per cent of the EU's trade and 70 per cent of direct foreign investment with Latin America is done with the members of MERCOSUR. Thus, the EU was concerned to protect its economic links with these countries and offered in 1994 to negotiate a free trade agreement. This meant that countries considering membership of MERCOSUR now also had the prospect of duty free access for many goods and services into the European market.

CONCLUSIONS

The new regional integration schemes in Latin America have been widely and correctly perceived as very different from their predecessors in the 1960s and 1970s. While regional integration remains an instrument, the goal has shifted from import-substituting industrialisation to export-led growth. As part of this shift trade liberalisation has been implemented by all countries with a huge reduction in external tariffs. This has altered the context in which regional integration schemes develop. Domestic prices are no longer so far out of line with foreign prices and the margin of preference available to be extended to partner countries is now much smaller.

The new regional integration schemes have brought some successes. Since the mid-1980s intra-regional trade has been growing faster than total trade so that its importance has been increasing in relative terms. Yet even in 1994, after a decade of recovery in intra-regional trade, the ratio of intra-regional exports to total exports was only 18.6 per cent in MERCOSUR (see Table 10.2), 22.4 per cent in CACM (see Table 10.4) and 9.3 per cent in the AP (see Table 10.6).

Since the goal of regional integration is now the promotion of export-led growth, the share of intra-regional exports in total trade may no longer be so significant. What matters is the ability of each integration scheme to contribute to the international competitiveness of firms through cost reductions, increased marketing skills, enhanced bargaining power, etc. However, the growth in intra-zonal commodity trade has led to new investments in regional energy and transport projects with the prospect of further investments to come. Examples are the proposed road bridge between Argentina and Uruguay over the Río de la Plata and the ambitious scheme, known as the hidrovía, to improve navigation from the port of Buenos Aires to river ports in Bolivia, Brazil, Paraguay and Uruguay.

Financial links between Latin American countries, aided by the abolition of capital controls, have been vastly improved and cross-border investment has become much more important. In many cases, e.g. between Argentina and Chile, or Chile and Peru, these investments have taken place without the existence of a formal regional integration scheme. Joint ventures between Latin American countries have become more common and even national airlines – those symbols of national pride – have succumbed to the economic logic of transnational competition.

The existence of high cost manufacturing in each country at the beginning of the process has increased the chances of trade creation, while external tariff reductions have reduced the risk of trade diversion. Thus, the prospects for net trade creating regional integration schemes in Latin America is much greater in the 1990s than in the 1960s. Whether net trade creation is welfare-improving depends in part on the ability of factors of production to shift out of high-cost inefficient manufacturing into other activities. This prospect has been enhanced by the willingness of Latin American countries to include agriculture and services in the framework of their integration schemes as well as industrial products.[23]

Despite these successes, regional integration in Latin America is still subject to numerous limitations. The first decade after 1985 amounted in many cases to little more than a recovery of the levels of intra-regional trade lost as a result of the debt crisis. The 1980 level of intra-zonal trade in the CACM, for example, was only surpassed in 1993 and the share of intra- regional exports is still lower today than in 1980. Intra-regional trade (see Table 10.5) remains dominated by a small number of bilateral exchanges: Argentina–Brazil in MERCOSUR (nearly 70 per cent of the total); El Salvador–Guatemala in Central America (nearly 40 per cent of the total) and Colombia–Venezuela in the AP (nearly 50 per cent of the total).

The second problem is that extra-regional trade continues to dominate the total in virtually all countries, so that economic policy cannot realistically give priority to intra-regional trade. This means that, where conflicts arise, policy cannot be assumed to favour regional integration. Thus, inflation stabilisation – with or without an agreement with the IMF – may require the adoption of measures that are inconsistent with the promotion of intra-regional trade.

A third problem arises from the virtual impossibility of reconciling all possible integration schemes open to each country. Costa Rica, for example, is a member of the CACM whose stated goal is a customs union. Costa Rica, however, wishes to join NAFTA (a free trade area) and as a first step signed a free trade agreement with Mexico in 1994 (see Table 10.7). This agreement makes it virtually impossible for the CACM to achieve a CET and the problem was compounded when El Salvador threatened to lower external tariffs unilaterally as part of its efforts to promote extra-regional exports and lower inflation. Much the same problem is faced by members of the AP. Colombia, for example, is committed to a customs union as a member of the AP, but none the less chose to join the G-3 with Mexico and Venezuela despite the fact that the tariff concessions extended to Mexico undermine the possibility of a CET for the AP as a whole.[24]

A fourth problem arises from the weakness of the institutional framework. The idea of a regional secretariat staffed by civil servants not representing their own countries is still not accepted in Latin America. The funding of regional institutions is far from adequate and such institutions as do exist lack the powers to remove the obstacles in the path of further integration. Numerous studies have shown, for example, that the principle obstacle to regional integration in Central America is non-tariff barriers, yet no regional mechanism exists for removing such barriers. There is no redress against national measures that blatantly conflict with the obligations of regional integration treaties since there is no system of community law. NAFTA is in this respect an exception, since – despite its institutional weakness – it does allow for binding arbitration in the case of trade disputes.[25]

These limitations raise doubts over whether the new integration schemes in Latin America will be able to achieve the high hopes vested in them. There is little chance, for example, of intra-regional trade in Latin America coming to play the role it does in the EU where it accounts for nearly 70 per cent of total trade. However, the new integration schemes are more solidly based than their predecessors with much less risk of price distortions and misallocation of resources. It is therefore quite possible that the new schemes will come to play their part in the promotion of export-led growth in Latin America provided that other necessary steps are also taken. Thus, with the notable exception of Mexico, whose trade is overwhelmingly with its NAFTA partners, Latin American countries cannot expect to secure their reintegration into the world economy through intra-regional trade expansion alone.

Without additional measures to promote exports, export-led growth will fail and regional integration schemes are then likely to decline in importance. If, however, the necessary additional measures are taken, building on the success of Chile and the South-East Asian countries, there are grounds for optimism with regard to the future of regional integration in Latin America. The conflict between intra- and extra-regional exports, so apparent in the 1960s and 1970s as a result of import-substituting industrialisation, is no longer so acute. Lower tariff and non-tariff barriers on extra-regional imports have increased the prospects for net trade creation and changes in legislation have encouraged foreign investment. Regional integration will never be a panacea, but it can play a supportive role in the transformation of Latin American countries from inward- to outward-looking growth.

Notes

1. By the end of 1995, the EU was involved in free trade negotations with Chile, the four republics of MERCOSUR (Argentina, Brazil, Paraguay and Uruguay) and Mexico. Cooperation agreements were in place with the Andean Pact countries as well as the republics of Central America (including Panama), while negotiations were under way with Cuba. See Chapter 6.

2. See ECLAC (1994b).
3. See, for example, Fishlow (1991).
4. While the policies of the United Nations Economic Commission for Latin America and the Caribbean (ECLAC – CEPAL in Spanish) in favour of ISI had been discredited by the mid-1980s, there was still some support for the original CEPAL hypothesis on the alleged secular deterioration in the net barter terms of trade of primary product exporters.
5. See FitzGerald (1996), table 2.
6. See Ffrench-Davies and Griffith-Jones (1995).
7. See Meirelles (1995), pp. 416–26.
8. The final date is the year 2013, at which time the CET must be finalised on all goods and the free trade zones in cities such as Manaus will have to be phased out.
9. The rise in Brazil's intra-regional exports after 1990 (see Table 10.2) is almost entirely explained by exports to Argentina. Since mid-1994, however, the Brazilian currency has appreciated against the Argentine peso leading to a sharp rise in Argentine exports to Brazil.
10. See Table 9.4 in the previous chapter.
11. The Arias Plan, sometimes known as the Esquipulas Plan, was named after Oscar Arias Sánchez, President of Costa Rica from 1986 to 1990. The plan's contribution to the resolution of the regional crisis led to the award of the Nobel Peace Prize to President Arias.
12. Both Belize and Panama had observer status in the meetings leading to a reconstitution of the regional integration scheme, but neither chose to participate as full members.
13. See Bulmer-Thomas (1992).
14. In 1994 fiscal problems obliged Costa Rica to raise tariffs on extra-regional imports, while an initiative of the executive in El Salvador to lower tariffs unilaterally in 1995 was only dropped after congress declared its opposition.
15. See Bywater (1990), pp. 10–13.
16. Bolivia, where trade liberalisation is more advanced, has been allowed to apply a CET of 10 per cent. See Hufbauer and Schott (1995), p. 237.
17. Implementation was only assured following a close vote in the US Congress in November 1993.
18. See Ten Kate (1994).
19. Chile was later admitted as a full member of APEC.
20. Hufbauer and Schott (1995) is devoted to an evaluation of the prospects for membership of NAFTA of the Latin American countries.
21. Any expansion of the membership of NAFTA became much less probable following the Mexican devaluation of December 1994 and the subsequent financial package mounted by the Clinton Administration. An inward-looking US Congress, dominated by Republicans after mid-term elections in November 1994, became disenchanted with the concept of western hemisphere economic integration after the costs of the Mexican rescue package had been quantified.
22. 'Fast-track', used by the Clinton Administration in the case of both NAFTA and the Uruguay Round, is the mechanism under which the

US Congress denies itself the right to make amendments to trade treaties proposed by the executive while preserving the right to reject the treaty as a whole. All attempts by the Clinton Administration to reintroduce fast-track after the passage of NAFTA have failed.

23. This progress was thrown into doubt by the sharp rise in the rate of unemployment in 1995 in a number of countries (it reached 20 per cent in Argentina, for example). The increase in unemployment made government less willing to contemplate policy changes that implied a major adjustment problem.
24. The problem of consistency in free trade agreements in Latin America has proved so problematic that both CEPAL and the Inter-American Development Bank have given it priority in their research agendas.
25. On institutional weakness in MERCOSUR, see Haines-Ferrari (1993). The situation improved with the ratification of the Protocol on MERCOSUR's Institutional Structure in December 1995.

11 The Caribbean Community and Common Market

Ali M. El-Agraa and Shelton M. A. Nicholls

INTRODUCTION

Contrary to popular perception, the Caribbean region does not just comprise the archipelagic group of islands stretching from the Yucatan and Florida peninsulas towards the north-eastern coast of Latin America. It also includes the Central American territory of Belize and the mainland territories of Guyana, Suriname and French Guiana which share similar historical and cultural ties. The member countries of the Caribbean Community and Common Market (CARICOM) form a subset of this wider grouping. CARICOM consists of Antigua and Barbuda, the Bahamas, Barbados, Belize, Dominica, Grenada, Guyana, Jamaica, Montserrat, St Kitts and Nevis, St Lucia, St Vincent and the Grenadines, Trinidad and Tobago and most recently Suriname. Other Caribbean countries such as, Cuba and Haiti participate on an *ad hoc* basis in specific CARICOM areas.

The Eastern Caribbean States of Antigua and Barbuda, Dominica, Grenada, Montserrat, St Kitts and Nevis, St Lucia and St Vincent and The Grenadines formed the Organisation of Eastern Caribbean States (OECS) in June 1981 to promote closer forms of cooperation amongst themselves.

Although it has recently been decided to transform the organisation by incorporating an economic and monetary union, the Treaty of Chaguaramas establishing CARICOM in 1973 is the most recent stage of a long history of efforts to promote political unity, economic integration and other forms of cooperation between the member nations. In the past, two broad categories of effort were made. The first, which was aimed primarily at political unity and pursued by the British government since the early period of settlement in the seventeenth century, culminated in the West Indies Federation in 1958. The Federation lasted only four years, collapsing in 1962 (Mordecai, 1968b; Wallace, 1977). One of the main aims of the Federation was the creation of an infrastructure which was thought at the time to be the essential prerequisite of independence as it was felt that none of the islands individually had the capability of assuming the responsibilities of independence unilaterally (Proctor, 1956). With the collapse of the Federation, however, all these countries became independent, starting with Jamaica and Trinidad in 1962 and most of the rest thereafter.

FROM POLITICAL TO ECONOMIC UNITY

The collapse of the Federation did not end the efforts at cooperation but inaugurated a new thrust with the Caribbean governments themselves taking the initiative. This stage was dominated by issues regarding economic integration since it was felt that political unification without the support of vital economic and social arrangements would inevitably invite disaster. On 1 December 1965, the Heads of Government of Antigua, Barbados and Guyana signed an accord which culminated in the formation of the Caribbean Free Trade Association (CARIFTA). The agreement was not immediately implemented since it was felt at the time that a more complete representation of regional governments needed to be involved in the integration efforts. This did not happen until a new CARIFTA agreement signed by Antigua, Barbados and Guyana became effective on 1 May 1968. Dominica, Grenada, Trinidad and Tobago, St Kitts-Nevis-Anguilla, St Lucia and St Vincent joined on 1 July; Jamaica and Montserrat in August; and Belize in May of the same year.

CARIFTA aimed:

(a) to promote the expansion and diversification of trade in the region;
(b) to ensure that trade between the member countries was conducted under conditions of fair competition;
(c) to encourage the progressive development of the economies in the region; and
(d) to foster the harmonious development of Caribbean trade and its liberalisation through the removal of barriers.

Thus CARIFTA was established to promote free trade amongst the member nations (McIntyre, 1965; Brewster and Thomas, 1967; CARICOM Secretariat, 1971; Demas, 1976). Although it was relatively successful in freeing trade between the member countries and stimulating a greater volume of exports especially in manufactured products, by 1972 CARIFTA was generally seen as inadequate to meet the needs of economic integration amongst the member nations. This is because it was a very limited form of integration and had two major deficiencies: (i) it had no explicit rules for formulating the joint and coordinated development of the productive resources of the region nor for any joint actions and common policies with regard to the rest of the world; and (ii) it made insufficient provisions for an equitable distribution of the benefits of integration between the member nations. It was then decided that a more comprehensive scheme of economic integration was essential if the economic development of the region were to become a reality (CARICOM Secretariat, 1972).

CARICOM then is an outgrowth of this long period of cooperation and to that extent it reflects the legacies of those efforts (Hall and Blake, 1978). Like its predecessors, CARICOM is intended to overcome the specific limitations of small developing island states (Demas, 1974a). In general, the Caribbean region is characterised by underdevelopment, fragmentation and a high degree of external dependence. CARICOM is a very small area with a population of just over 5 million people and a total GDP of about 11 billion $US. In specific economic terms, these countries have high rates of unemployment ranging from 20 to 30 per cent in the late 1970s and 14 to 35 per cent in the late 1980s, and a high concentration of export commodities with petroleum, bauxite, alumina and sugar accounting for 87 per cent of CARICOM's export earnings. Furthermore, there are few linkages within and between the different national economies, with foreign ownership and control playing a dominant role in sectors such as manufacturing and tourism (Girvan and Jefferson, 1971; Beckford, 1976).

Although all the member countries share these characteristics there is a considerable disparity in resource endowments and stages of economic development between them. For this reason CARICOM is divided into two groups, the more developed countries (MDCs) of Barbados, Guyana, Jamaica and Trinidad and Tobago and the less developed countries (LDCs) comprising the other nations. Together, the MDCs have over 90 per cent of the land area, account for over 87 per cent of the population and labour force and 90 per cent of the technical and managerial skills. They also have all the known significant mineral resources such as oil, gas and bauxite as well as the best of the agricultural land. The economic rationale of CARICOM has therefore had to pay special attention to the traditional gains of economic integration but has also placed priority on developmental objectives as well as on the equitable distribution of the gains (CARICOM Secretariat, 1973; Blake, 1976).

The objectives of CARICOM and the areas in which it pursues activities therefore reflect both the historical traditions of close co-operation in economic and non-economic areas, as well as a desire to promote development through a strategy of economic integration. It pursues activities in three broad areas: economic integration, functional cooperation and coordination of foreign policies. Its specific objectives, as stated in Article 4 of the Treaty of Chaguaramas, are:

1. The strengthening, coordination and regulation of the economic and trade relations among member states in order to promote their accelerated, harmonious and balanced development.
2. The sustained expansion and continuing integration of economic activities, the benefits of which shall be equitably shared taking into account the need to provide special opportunities for the less developed countries.
3. The achievement of a greater measure of economic independence and effectiveness by its member states in dealing with third countries, groups of states and entities of whatever description.
4. The coordination of the foreign policies of the member states.
5. Functional cooperation, including: (a) the efficient operation of certain common services and activities for the benefits of its people; (b) the promotion of greater understanding among its people and the advancement of their social, cultural and technological development; and (c) activities in fields specified in Article 8 of the Treaty.

The political and functional aims generally fall under the jurisdiction of the Community while those dealing with economic integration fall under the auspices of the Common Market.

To carry out these objectives it has set up a number of institutions such as the Conference of Heads of Government, the Common Market Council, the Administrative and Technical Secretariat and a number of ministerial institutions as well as some associate institutions such as the Caribbean Development Bank (CDB) and the University of the West Indies (Geiser *et al.*, 1976; Pollard, 1976; Hall and Blake, 1978).

MARKET INTEGRATION

Market integration has been the most emphasised aspect of CARICOM. Its pursuit has largely been undertaken by the removal of intra-regional trade impediments. The treaty envisaged the removal of all tariff and non-tariff barriers and the imposition of a CET, the main principles behind which were to charge low rates on the capital goods and raw materials needed by CARICOM, high rates on consumer goods, higher rates on products deemed adequately supplied regionally, rates within the range of the national tariffs, and very high rates on major revenue earning items (see World Bank, 1990, for a synopsis of the CET). All members were granted a specified time frame within which to phase in the new tariff schedule. Guyana, Jamaica and Trinidad and Tobago implemented the CET in 1976 while Barbados, Belize and the countries of the Eastern Caribbean Common Market were expected to do likewise by 1981. Montserrat was granted a period until 1985 to harmonise its tariff structures. Since 1981, however, some member countries have still to implement the CET. Further revisions of the tariff schedules occurred in the 1980s but these were also not uniformly carried out in all the member nations.

On account of the different tariff schedules in the member countries, trade in CARICOM needed to be based on very clear principles in respect of the origin of goods. The rules of origin were initially implemented with the establishment of CARIFTA in 1968 and revised in 1981. To pass the rule, a good had to be consigned directly to the importing member state from another member nation and had either to be 'wholly produced' within the Common Market or to have undergone 'substantial transformation' in the case of imported materials used in the production of these goods. With regard to the latter, a first group of 187 commodities, mostly food and chemicals, were deemed to be of Common Market status if they were produced from specific regional materials, or if they were produced from materials specified by tariff heading, or if they were produced using a specified production method or process, or if the value of extra-regional material used was below a specified percentage of the export price of the finished product. A second group of 142 commodities, chiefly from assembly-type industries, was deemed to pass the condition if the value of the extra-regional materials used in production was below 65 per cent in the MDCs or below 70 per cent in the LDCs, or if in the process of transformation changed from one tariff classification to the next. Also, a series of concessions were granted to the LDCs.

Intra-regional Trade Performance

Since the formation of CARICOM in 1973, total regional trade has displayed considerable fluctuation – see Table 11.1. As the table

Table 11.1 Intra-CARICOM trade (EC$000)

Year	*Regional Imports (1)*	*Total Imports (2)*	*Regional Exports (3)*	*Total Exports (4)*	*(1)/(2) (%)*	*(3)/(4) (%)*
1960	67.50	1209.70	65.40	984.80	5.58	6.64
1961	70.00	1288.80	68.30	1137.90	5.43	6.00
1962	74.80	1322.80	77.90	1166.60	5.65	6.68
1963	67.40	1378.70	69.00	1300.20	4.89	5.31
1964	83.40	1634.30	73.00	1369.70	5.10	5.33
1965	84.90	1776.90	78.40	1365.40	4.78	5.74
1966	88.70	1862.00	88.30	1456.50	4.76	6.06
1967	95.70	1884.20	89.70	1503.10	5.08	5.97
1968	108.80	2235.80	107.70	1797.80	4.87	5.99
1969	136.40	2531.80	137.90	1887.80	5.39	7.30
1970	163.80	2973.90	180.00	2111.20	5.51	8.53
1971	182.90	3324.10	171.90	2217.80	5.50	7.75
1972	236.10	3586.00	237.00	2299.40	6.58	10.31
1973	296.50	3950.00	290.50	2709.80	7.51	10.72
1974	508.10	7180.70	486.50	6660.40	7.08	7.30
1975	649.20	7552.20	599.20	7020.50	8.60	8.54
1976	741.20	7871.70	778.70	8701.70	7.51	8.95
1977	723.20	9623.70	775.80	9281.90	7.51	8.36
1978	798.40	10399.40	827.40	9405.40	7.68	8.80
1979	1001.00	11063.00	998.00	10715.40	9.05	9.31
1980	1411.60	15976.20	1416.60	16002.00	8.84	8.85
1981	1615.40	16931.60	1493.00	15119.70	9.54	9.87
1982	1540.60	17646.80	1482.60	12470.70	8.73	11.89
1983	1349.50	14315.70	1315.00	10359.70	9.43	12.69
1984	1207.30	12461.60	1232.20	10250.60	9.69	12.02
1985	1154.90	11357.90	1242.70	9653.00	10.17	12.87
1986	796.70	10706.90	840.90	7660.80	7.44	10.98
1987	862.70	11229.60	868.90	8017.80	7.68	10.84
1988	986.40	11891.90	1036.70	8449.00	8.29	12.27
1989	1216.70	13856.50	1265.80	9283.60	8.78	13.63
1990	1314.40	13920.10	1373.80	11262.40	9.44	12.20
60–72*	112.34	2077.62	111.12	1584.48	5.32	6.74
73–90*	1009.66	11663.08	1018.02	9612.47	8.50	10.56
73–80*	766.15	9452.11	771.59	8812.14	7.97	8.85
81–90*	1204.46	13431.86	1215.16	10252.73	8.92	11.93

Note
* average for the period.
Source: CARICOM Secretariat, Statistical Worksheets.

clearly shows, both intra-regional imports and exports grew from an annual average of about EC$0.1 million (where EC stands for East Caribbean) during 1960–72 to one of EC$0.8 million during the early CARICOM period of 1973–80. This was equivalent to an average rate of growth of 26.5 per cent for the period from 1973 to 1980, more than double the rate during 1960–72. Nevertheless, this growth was smaller than that experienced by extra-area exports during the same period due to the boost given to them by the opportune rise in oil prices. Over the second decade of CARICOM, 1981–90, total exports fell on average by 2.6 per cent whilst intra-regional exports increased marginally by 0.9 per cent. This could be attributed to the collapse of oil prices during the early 1980s, especially since much of the deceleration occurred between 1982 and 1986. Intra-regional imports grew by only 0.6 per cent, showing a decline in the rate relative to the early CARICOM period of about 26 per cent. However, by 1987 intra-regional trade started to recover and is now gradually approaching its 1973–80 levels. Incidentally, the 1982–6 period witnessed the collapse of the trade financing mechanism: the CARICOM Multilateral Clearing Facility (CMCF) – see p. 288.

Although the share of intra-regional trade in total trade increased with the formation of CARICOM, from about 5.6 and 6.6 per cent in 1960 to about 7.5 and 10.7 per cent during 1973 for, respectively, imports and exports, the increase has obviously not been substantial and, more importantly, the overall percentages have remained a small fraction of total trade. Moreover, they have remained relatively constant, averaging 8.5 and about 10.6 per cent, during 1973–90.

Table 11.2 presents data on the country distribution of intra-regional trade. The table shows the dominance of the MDCs, but their share in exports and imports has declined from, respectively, about 95 and 67 per cent in 1970 to 82 and 61 per cent in 1990. At the same time, the share of the LDCs improved from, respectively, about 5 and 33 per cent to about 19 and 39 per cent. Note that amongst the MDCs, Guyana provided the largest regional market in 1970, accounting for 23 per cent of regional imports.

The onset of the oil boom changed this pattern quite substantially, and by 1980 Trinindad and Tobago emerged as the largest single market with a share in intra-regional imports of 21.4 per cent. Severe economic crises in Guyana, together with the impact of the oil price crash on Trinidad in the early 1980s, forced both to reduce substantially their imports from the regional market. By the end of 1990, Guyana accounted for a mere 4.2 per cent of intra-regional imports while Trinidad and Tobago's share fell to 16.3 per cent. In the process,

Table 11.2 Country distribution of intra-CARICOM trade (percentages)

	1970		*1980*		*1990*	
Country	*Imports*	*Exports*	*Imports*	*Exports*	*Imports*	*Exports*
Barbados	16.2	7.0	19.1	10.2	22.5	13.0
Guyana	23.0	19.9	18.0	10.2	4.2	2.6
Jamaica	11.7	15.7	16.4	10.9	18.0	14.0
Trinidad & Tobago	16.4	52.5	21.4	58.6	16.3	52.0
MDCs	67.3	95.1	74.9	89.9	61.0	81.6
Antigua & Barbuda	5.4	0.5	8.2	2.2	5.2	2.2
Dominica	3.7	0.6	2.4	1.2	5.2	2.7
Grenada	6.0	0.2	3.2	0.4	5.3	1.4
Montserrat	1.2	—	0.8	0.1	1.6	0.0
St Kitts-Nevis	2.2	0.4	1.8	0.8	3.3	0.7
St Lucia	6.2	1.5	5.1	2.9	10.0	4.3
St Vincent	4.8	0.2	3.2	1.3	5.8	5.6
Belize	3.0	1.0	0.5	1.1	2.7	1.7
OECS*	29.5	3.4	24.7	8.9	36.4	16.9
LDCs	32.5	4.4	25.2	10.0	39.1	18.6

Note
Exports refer to domestic exports.
* OECS – Organisation of Eastern Caribbean States.
Source: CARICOM Secretariat.

Barbados emerged as the largest regional importer with a share of about 23 per cent in 1990.

With regard to intra-regional exports, Trinidad and Tobago had a share of 52.5 per cent in 1970. This increased to about 59 per cent in 1980, largely due to petroleum exports to CARICOM members (see Table 11.3 which provides data on the composition of intra-CARICOM trade by broad SITC one-digit categories), but declined to just below its 1970 level by 1990. Barbados, Guyana and Jamaica had the relatively smaller share of about 10 per cent in 1980. Despite the sharp contractions in economic activity during the 1980s, the MDCs, with the exception of Guyana, were able to maintain their level of regional exports. Guyana's share fell to 2.6 per cent in 1990.

In terms of overall performance, the balance of intra-regional trade has been in persistent decline for the economies of Barbados, Guyana and Jamaica which had cumulative deficits of, respectively, US$300m, US$185m and US$283m over the 1973–89 period (Nicholls, 1995).

Table 11.3 Composition of intra-CARICOM trade (EC$000)

SITC group	*1970*	*1973*	*1980*	*1985*	*1990*
0. Food	40.5	64.6	282.8	220.3	252.4
	(24.7)	(21.8)	(20.0)	(19.1)	(19.2)
1. Beverages & tobacco	4.3	9.4	38.0	41.7	94.3
	(2.6)	(3.2)	(2.7)	(3.7)	(7.2)
2. Crude materials	4.9	8.2	24.4	22.1	18.6
	(3.0)	(2.8)	(1.7)	(1.8)	(1.4)
3. Petroleum products	37.9	80.1	578.9	545.2	262.3
	(23.1)	(27.0)	(41.0)	(46.9)	(20.8)
4. Oils & fats	3.8	5.5	12.3	4.5	20.1
	(2.3)	(1.9)	(0.9)	(0.4)	(1.7)
5. Chemicals	22.4	40.1	150.9	114.7	209.7
	(13.7)	(13.5)	(10.7)	(10.1)	(14.5)
6. Manufactured goods	23.7	34.7	125.3	120.9	291.4
	(14.7)	(11.1)	(8.9)	(10.6)	(23.7)
7. Machinery & transport	3.1	10.1	52.8	16.8	51.2
	(1.9)	(3.4)	(3.7)	(1.5)	(4.1)
8. Miscellaneous manufactures	22.5	43.1	145.0	67.3	112.9
	(13.7)	(14.5)	(10.3)	(5.8)	(7.7)
9. Other	0.7	0.5	1.1	1.4	1.5
	(0.4)	(0.2)	(0.0)	(0.1)	(0.1)
Total	163.8	296.3	1411.6	1154.9	1314.4

Note
The data in brackets stands for percentages.
Source: CARICOM Secretariat, Statistical Worksheets.

Amongst the MDCs, only Trinidad and Tobago had a surplus on this account throughout the period, largely because of its petroleum exports. It should be added that the worsening performance of intra-regional trade was also accompanied by poor external trade performance especially in the MDC territories.

In short, CARICOM trade has four characteristics: (i) regional trade is largely dominated by the MDCs; (ii) intra-regional trade remains, contrary to CARICOM expectations, insignificant in relation to total trade; (iii) the bulk of trade is in a few commodity groups; and (iv) chemicals and manufacturing have recently increased their regional importance while petroleum and agricultural products have declined.

PROBLEMS

The contribution of CARICOM to the stability and prosperity of the various island territories was mixed during 1973–90. Whereas the

1973–80 phase of the integration period was characterised by relative stability, the 1981–90 decade, constituting the second phase, was one of severely deteriorating conditions in all the MDCs. Although it has been difficult to advance unique and simple reasons for this, two broad categories of factors have been suggested. The first is concerned with international developments: falling bauxite, oil and sugar prices played havoc with CARICOM's foreign exchange earnings while recessions in the major industrial countries exacerbated protectionist policies *vis-à-vis* CARICOM. The second is concerned with specific regional issues, including the bureaucratic inertia of Caribbean politicians and institutions; indeed, lack of a viable and stable commitment by member countries to meaningful integration and sweeping changes in political leadership, coupled with ideological pluralism, affected the commitment to and continuity of regional economic goals and policies.

Perhaps the most important challenges confronting CARICOM during 1980–90 were the intensification of regional protectionism, the collapse of the CMCF, the lack of commitment to exchange rate stability and the controversy over the rules of origin. A brief elaboration on these points may be in order.

With the worsening economic position of the MDCs, severe pressures were brought to bear on the viability of the CARICOM trading arrangement. Both Guyana and Jamaica, who were experiencing severe and persistent balance of payments and foreign exchange crises, invoked Article 28 of the Annex to the treaty, allowing governments to impose quantitative restrictions under the circumstances. In January 1983, therefore, Jamaica introduced a parallel exchange rate and quota system (Bennett, 1983; Witter, 1983). This move brought about strong retaliatory responses from both Barbados and Trinidad and Tobago. For instance, in the following month, the Central Bank of Barbados ceased all provisions for foreign exchange cover for transactions with Jamaica, and in May the central bank of Trinidad and Tobago placed all CARICOM imports under licence (Williams, 1985; Griffith, 1990). Other countries also took action to protect their interests with the consequence that the MDCs' intra-regional exports declined by 31.5 per cent (from US$413.6 million in 1984 to US$283.4 million in 1988), while their intra-regional imports declined by a similar margin (29.2 per cent). Intra-regional trade was then being conducted amidst strident accusation and counter-accusation of unfair practice and was more 'honoured in the breach than the observance' (Blackman, 1989, p. 52).

The persistent balance of payments crisis in Guyana was perhaps one of the central catalytic forces causing the demise of the CMCF, a key element for the success of which was the prompt settlement of outstanding debt. In particular, an annual period running from 15 June to 15 December was instituted by which time member countries had to settle one half of their deficits. Acute foreign exchange shortages in Guyana resulted in an excess of its receipts over its payments into the CMCF, with the result of increased indebtedness to the CMCF over 1977–82 – see Table 11.4 and Williams (1985). The inability of Guyana to clear its deficit together with the fact that the legal credit limit of US$100 million was greatly exceeded, led to the collapse of the facility in March 1983, forcing the member countries to return once more to the bilateral settlement scheme which had existed hitherto.

The collapse of the CMCF was a severe blow to monetary cooperation and virtually isolated Guyana from accessing credit arrangements from its CARICOM partners, who demanded that Guyana should settle in hard currency. This issue served to further undermine the regional trading arrangement. Needless to add, it also forced the MDCs, especially Guyana and Jamaica, to seek assistance from the IMF and World Bank.

The CET and rules of origin were initially outlined in Article 14 of the treaty which delineated particular guidelines for qualification to Common Market status. These pertained to interpretative provisions relating to transport, producers and materials; specification of goods wholly produced within the Common Market; application of the percentage criterion; unit of classification; segregation of materials; treatment of mixtures; treatment of packaging; documentary evidence; verification of evidence of origin; and sanctions. Critical to the implementation of the rules was the design of a series of lists (for

Table 11.4 Guyana's indebtedness to CMCF (G$m)

Year	*Payments*	*Receipts*
1977	54.2	44.8
1978	85.0	148.1
1979	180.1	95.9
1980	245.7	118.4
1981	284.6	164.3
1982	298.1	125.8

Source: Danns (1990).

example, the Basic Materials List and Reserve List) outlining specific criteria for the eventual designation of a good as being of Common Market origin. These rules were revised somewhat in 1981 (see CARICOM Secretariat, 1981), when new guidelines were issued. However, major difficulties arose regarding the operation and administration of the rules, in the light of the numerous approved departures, relating to special arrangements for the OECS, Belize and Montserrat.

As already mentioned, the basic principle underlying the CET structure was to charge very low rates of duty on capital goods and raw materials which were needed by CARICOM countries and higher rates of foreign goods which competed with regional products. However, individual member countries were still allowed the unchallenged right to fix and change the structures in their own customs tariffs and also to prescribe other kinds of restrictive mechanisms that were appropriate to their own circumstances. Large differences in national quota arrangements therefore militated against reaching any genuine consensus on common rates.

THE NEXT PHASE

The dismal performance of the Caribbean economies during a period in which the European Community (now the European Union, EU) undertook its 'Single European Market' initiative (see Chapter 5) and North America created NAFTA (see Chapter 8) engendered much pessimism about the viability of CARICOM's own integration efforts. Consequently, the Heads of Government, instilled by a recommendation by A. N. R. Robinson, then Prime Minister of Trinidad and Tobago, mandated the establishment of a West Indian Commission, under the Chairmanship of Sir Shridath Ramphal, with the task of developing plans and proposals for preparing the West Indian society for the twenty-first century. Following a series of region-wide consultations, the Commission presented its final report (West Indian Commission, 1992a, 1992b, 1992c) in May 1992 covering diverse issues ranging from politics and economics to cricket and human resource development.

Of particular relevance were the proposals made, and later endorsed by the CARICOM Secretariat, regarding the deepening of the structure of CARICOM in terms of the creation of a single market and movement towards a closer monetary union (Field-Ridley, 1991; CARICOM Secretariat, 1992). The major proposals related to the free movement of goods, services, capital and labour, and to designing an effective structure for the CET to reflect the trade and production policies of the region. To ensure free movement of goods and services, the proposals call for:

1. The elimination of all tariffs, quantitative restrictions and other non-tariff trade barriers.
2. The development of appropriate 'rules of origin'.
3. The development of uniform customs laws and the simplification and harmonisation of customs documentation and procedures.
4. The harmonisation of standards for goods and services.
5. The introduction of rules applicable throughout the single market to ensure genuine intra-regional competition.

To promote the free movement of labour, they ask for:

1. The introduction of mechanisms for accreditation and equivalency certification for professional and technical workers.
2. The making of provisions for the transfer of remittances and pensions.
3. The harmonisation of social security measures.

To encourage the free movement of capital, they call for:

1. The abolition of intra-regional exchange controls and the introduction of a common regime of exchange controls and practices with respect to transactions from third countries.
2. The reaching of agreement on the level of the exchange rate which would allow free convertibility between a regional currency or a single currency.
3. The coordination of monetary and fiscal policies with a view to encouraging intra-regional capital mobility, avoiding major payment imbalances amongst the member states and promoting the development of a regional capital market.

To promote monetary integration, the major proposals relate to:

1. The establishment of a common currency as an essential feature of the single market and economy.
2. The establishment of a CARICOM monetary authority to issue and manage the new currency.

A brief evaluation of these proposals is now in order.

Trade Integration

As just mentioned, the trade integration proposals centre on intra-regional trade liberalisation through the CET mechanism and the modified rules of origin. In designing the CET, the Common Market Council agreed on a set of objectives which, *inter alia*, included:

(a) that the CET should be designed to protect regional, agricultural and industrial production of finished goods, raw materials and capital goods and its structure should support the development of internally competitive production in the common market;
(b) that the tariff structures should be simplified as much as possible so as to make it operationally feasible and the wide range of tariff rates had to be reduced;
(c) that special regard had to be made for the reserve needs of particular countries especially the smaller states; and
(d) that unrestricted intra-regional competition should prevail where producers in the common market enjoy the benefit of the protective tariff.

Based on these criteria, a new structure for the CET was proposed (CARICOM Secretariat, 1991a, 1991b) which differentiated between inputs and final goods. Inputs were identified according to their use as primary, intermediate or capital goods, while in the case of final goods a distinction was made between basic and non-basic goods. In addition, the new structure distinguished between goods which were in regional production and those which were not, assigning labels of 'competing' to the former and 'non-competing' to the latter. Competing goods were defined as those for which regional production or intermediate production potential from existing capacity amounted to over 75 per cent of regional demand or consumption. The rates developed for the new structure are illustrated in Table 11.5.

All member states were expected to implement the new CET between 1 January 1993 and 31 December 1994. However, the structure had problems regarding complementary policy initiatives, the global trading environment and relations with international institutions.

With regard to complementary policy initiatives, Blades (1993) argues that the CET would be implemented in an environment which takes very little cognisance of complementary fiscal initiatives,

Table 11.5 CARICOM tariff structure (percentages)

Inputs	*Group A (Non-competing)*	*Group B (Competing)*	*Group C (Non-basic competing)*	*Group D (Non-basic non-competing)*
Primary	5	20	—	—
Intermediate	10	30	—	—
Capital	10	20	—	—
Final goods	10	30	45	30

Source: CARICOM Secretariat (1991b).

monetary and exchange rate regimes, common customs legislation and systems and arrangements for production integration, including the free movement of factors of production. The CET, therefore, was singled out for immediate action in advance of effective planning for the remaining instruments mentioned above.

It is likely that developments in the external trading environment, particularly the conclusion of the Uruguay Round of GATT (now WTO) negotiations and arrangements in NAFTA may, in the short term, impact adversely on the operation of the CET. The arrangements in the global trading environment suggest a much slower liberalisation timetable for 'sensitive' products, particularly in the areas of agriculture, textiles and clothing which may affect competitive factors in individual member countries and lead to demands for tariff concessions to meet emerging global conditions. This could serve in the longer run to undermine the effectiveness of the CET.

Finally, CARICOM envisages the CET to be managed as a 'dynamic and flexible' instrument responding to economic development in the region and the international economy. Notwithstanding the possible benefits from the very dynamic nature of the tariff, it is likely to be highly demanding in respect of practical monitoring of the changes relating to exchange rate movements, trade commitments under structural adjustment programmes and so forth. A thorough and comprehensive coverage of all trade related issues may not be fully realised unless participating countries are willing to divert extra resources to effect this undertaking.

Monetary Integration

The proposals for monetary integration have initiated a series of discussions on the feasibility of a common currency and the best way to design the currency unit. A number of suggestions have been forthcoming on the best direction to take on these matters. Worrell (1991) makes a strong case for a Caribbean dollar which would be pegged to the US dollar and which would circulate alongside national currencies. The currency would be administered by an independent central bank which would be debarred from financing fiscal deficits and would thus contribute to improved fiscal discipline in the member states. Improved fiscal discipline should eventually ensure exchange rate and price stability and enhance economic growth prospects. With regard to involvement in the common currency arrangement, Worrell suggests certain eligibility criteria for the participating countries, involving foreign exchange reserves equivalent of three months' import cover or 80 per cent of central bank liabilities, as well as an invariant US dollar parity for at least three consecutive years.

Following closely the slant of Worrell's proposals are the options suggested by Hilaire *et al.* (1991) in their technical report to the Council of Central Bank Governors. After reviewing several proposals and options for monetary integration, including the replacement of national currencies by a Caribbean currency, the use of a Caribbean currency which circulates in parallel with national currencies, the use of a Caribbean Unit of Account but with the retention of national currencies and the retention of national currencies subject to limits on cross-currency realignments, Hilaire *et al.* opted for the replacement of national currencies as the best available strategy. A key element of their suggestion was also the maintenance of a fixed Caribbean–US dollar parity at a rate of 1:1. Like Worrell, Hilaire *et al.* also emphasised certain eligibility criteria: ample foreign exchange reserves; a long and unbroken record of exchange rate stability; and a sustainable debt service ratio.

Based largely on the recommendations by these two studies, CARICOM Heads of Government agreed on a two-tier staged approach to monetary union (Codrington, 1992). During the first stage, Jamaica and Guyana would sustain policies to stabilise their exchange rate parities, while a Council of CARICOM Central Bank Governors would be set up to coordinate exchange rate, monetary and fiscal policies in the states. During the second, a Caribbean Monetary Authority with the power to issue currency would be established and the stage would be set for the common currency to replace the currencies of the OECS, Barbados and Trinidad and Tobago. Currency area eligibility would depend critically on: (i) the maintenance of three months' import cover in foreign exchange reserves for at least one year; (ii) a stable exchange rate for three years; and (iii) a sustainable debt service ratio not exceeding 15 per cent.

While this discussion was in progress, very little detailed investigation was carried out on the conditions required for successful monetary integration and the extent to which the various individual CARICOM countries would satisfy these conditions. In fact, monetary union requires a high level of intra-regional capital and labour mobility as well as significant trade linkages between the various members. Obviously, these conditions are far from adequately satisfied in the Caribbean, especially where 70 per cent of export reserves are derived from external currency areas and capital and labour flows are quite insignificant. For instance, Brewster (1992) argues that the objective conditions do not provide a compelling rationale for monetary union. However, although the percentage of intra-European Union (EU) trade is very high and EU capital mobility is relatively high, monetary integration attempts by the EU have neither been painless nor free of problems (see Chapter 5).

Furthermore, although the Hilaire *et al.* report is right in assuming that monetary integration can play a dynamic role in deepening regional integration, stabilising exchange rates, inflation and the balance of payments and lowering the cost of exchange transactions (see Chapter 3), no empirical work has been attempted to demonstrate the validity of these theoretical considerations for CARICOM. For example, the stages approach recommended by CARICOM governments is based on the premise that economic convergence should precede monetary integration. However, this assumption raises at least three serious problems. First, the recent experience of the MDCs indicates that highly divergent performances in respect of the key economic indicators of inflation, fiscal deficits, external debt and GDP growth are likely to be continuing features of Caribbean econom ies for the forseeable future. Second, there is still little consensus on what the most appropriate indicators should be to measure economic performance in the context of economies which have traditionally displayed, and most likely would continue to display, highly volatile performances. Finally, decisions need to be concluded in respect of realistic targets to be achieved by each of the member countries to effect meaningful currency union. However, there have been few objective discussions on how these targets should be defined and whether they would be appropriate for the CARICOM economies. In this respect, the adoption of the convergence rates used in the EU is not likely to be of substantial value in the context of CARICOM.

With regard to the details relating to how the value of the CARICOM currency should be determined, Bennett (1985, 1990) suggests that this should be set as the weighted average of exchange rates of individual currencies in the region in terms of the US dollar. Bennett's analysis assigns the largest weights to the currencies of those countries which have been most stable, and in his hypothetical illustration he suggests certain weights for the determination of the CARICOM Unit of Account (CUA).

However, the suggestion by Bennett has a major problem concerning the determination of the weighting pattern. Bandawe and Glen (1991) have examined the feasibility of the common currency and have found specifically that the CUA numeraire is not likely to moderate the amplitude or frequency of exchange rate changes in the MDCs.

The issue of how the CUA should be constituted and the appropriate choice of the weighting mechanism therefore raises a number of important questions. Paramount among these is whether or not the weights should be immutably fixed or flexible, thus consistently adjusting to the changing circumstances in the individual member countries.

CONCLUSION

Although the initial attempts at integration in the English-speaking Caribbean before and during the Federation were largely unsuccessful exercises mainly in political, constitutional and governmental linkages, they paved the way for greater emphasis on economic considerations, culminating in the creation of CARIFTA and CARICOM. However, economic integration itself has neither been a great success nor generated the prosperity and growth that were initially envisaged. Indeed, CARICOM's main achievements have been in areas concerned with functional cooperation and external policy coordination. Nevertheless, the recent crises in the international economy have once again strengthened the case for economic integration and all efforts seem to be directed once more towards deepening this process, with the proposals for trade liberalisation and monetary and financial integration, undertaken by the West Indian Commission (1992c), Worrell (1991) and Hilaire *et al.* (1991), occupying the centre stage. The proponents see Caribbean integration as a process which is important for accelerating industrial growth; enabling a stronger bargaining position *vis-à-vis* the larger powers; facilitating the pooling of natural, financial and human resources; and creating a wider economic space.

The future of CARICOM will depend ultimately on its ability to find a policy mix in which trade and monetary integration can be combined with an outward orientation geared in the longer term to multilateral free trade. Integration must not be seen as an end in itself but rather as a means towards an end. Consequently, the integration mechanism must be targeted towards organising the production of goods and services for export so that sufficient foreign exchange reserves could be earned to sustain the economic development and growth of CARICOM.

12 The Association of South-East Asian Nations

Richard Pomfret*

The Association of South-East Asian Nations (ASEAN) is an economic enigma. South-East Asia contrasts with north-east Asia where there have been no formal regional integration schemes among market-oriented economies since 1945. ASEAN's longevity also contrasts with the many regional integration schemes initiated elsewhere in the Third World during the 1960s only to lapse. Yet ASEAN's survival is something of a puzzle in so far as its economic achievements have been minimal. Indeed, ASEAN has appeared perpetually to policy-makers and commentators to be at a crossroads, where something needs to be done to vitalise the integration process.[1]

The 1967 Bangkok Declaration established ASEAN with Indonesia, Malaysia, the Philippines, Singapore and Thailand as founding members.[2] Brunei joined in 1984 and Vietnam in July 1995. Table 12.1 presents some basic economic indicators for the six pre-1995 ASEAN members. The six countries vary greatly in population and income levels; Indonesia accounted for over half of the population, but the distribution of GNP was less skewed (Figure 12.1).

Table 12.1 Economic indicators for ASEAN countries, 1992

	Indonesia	*Malaysia*	*Philippines*	*Singapore*	*Thailand*	*Brunei*
Population (million)	184	19	64	3	58	0.3
GNP per capita ($)	670	2 790	770	15 730	1 840	13 160
– avg growth 1980–92	4%	3%	–1%	5%	6%	na
Life expectancy	60	71	65	75	69	74
Adult illiteracy (%)[b]	23	22	10	na	7	na
Exports/GDP (%)	29	78	29	174	36	61[a]

Notes
[a] 1990 data from East Asia Analytical Unit (1994, p. 58).
[b] 1990 data.
Source: World Bank (1994), *World Development Report*.

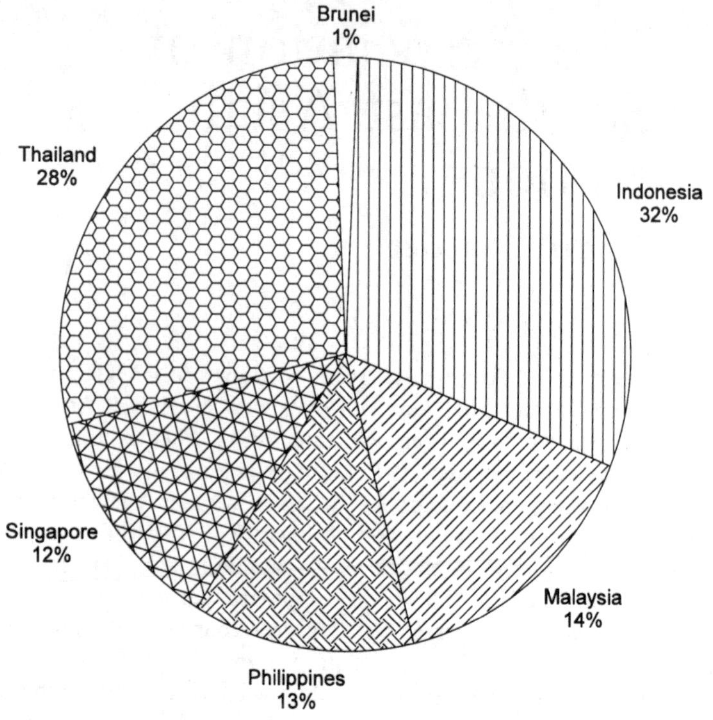

Source: As Table 12.1.

Figure 12.1 Distribution of GNP in ASEAN, 1992

In the international economy the ASEAN countries rank as medium or small trading nations (Table 12.2), and because they are all open economies they generally have higher trade/output ratios than similarly sized countries. Despite their openness, trade among the ASEAN countries has been small, with only the flows between Singapore and Malaysia being of any importance (Table 12.3 and Figure 12.2). Intra-ASEAN trade has been a small part of each member's total trade, and consists largely of entrepôt trade through Singapore (Tan, 1995, chs 7–8).[3]

This chapter describes the evolution of ASEAN from 1967 until the early 1990s and analyses why the economic integration schemes of the late 1970s and 1980s made little headway. It then discusses the issues where ASEAN is at crossroads in the 1990s: the attempt to create a free trade area; the regional integration due to private sector activity without governmental direction; the prospect of new members; and finding a role within broader Asia-Pacific organisations.

Table 12.2 Leading exporters and importers, merchandise trade, 1993 (US$ billion)

	Exports	*Imports*
1. European Union (12)	568	571
2. United States	465	603
3. Japan	362	242
4. Canada	145	139
5. Hong Kong	135	141
6. China	92	104
7. South Korea	82	84
8. Taiwan	85	77
9. **Singapore**	**74**	**85**
10. Switzerland	65	52
11. Mexico	52	67
12. **Malaysia**	**47**	**46**
13. Sweden	50	43
14. Austria	40	49
15. Australia	43	46
16. **Thailand**	**37**	**46**
17. Saudi Arabia	42	31
18. Brazil	39	28
19. **Indonesia**	**37**	**28**
20. Russia	38	23
30. **Philippines**	**11**	**19**
Brunei (1992)	**2**	**1**

Note
Rankings are by total merchandise trade. All figures exclude EU intra-trade. Figures for Hong Kong include re-exports of $107 billion and for Singapore re-exports of $27 billion (thus, excluding re-exports Singapore would rank tenth and Hong Kong twentieth). Figures for Russia are official national estimates which GATT reports to involve substantial undercounting. ASEAN members in bold print.
Source: GATT (1994), *International Trade, Trends and Statistics*, pp. 12, 98, 101.

Table 12.3 Trade matrix, 1993 ($ million)

X/M	*Brunei*	*Indonesia*	*Malaysia*	*Philippines*	*Singapore*	*Thailand*	*World*
Brunei		1	3	60	216	179	2 373
Indonesia	48		718	324	3 372	513	36 843
Malaysia	208	517		365	14 042	1 674	47 080
Philippines	3	57	219		504	181	11 279
Singapore	698	1 793	6 955	1 023		2 969	74 017
Thailand	40	235	1 134	175	3 518		37 111
World	2 601	28 333	45 552	17 965	85 393	46 065	3 686 700

Note
Rows indicate exports and columns imports. Thus, Indonesia's exports to Brunei were $48 million in 1993.
Source: Department of Foreign Affairs and Trade (Australia) (1994), *The APEC Region, Trade and Investment*, November.

Brunei

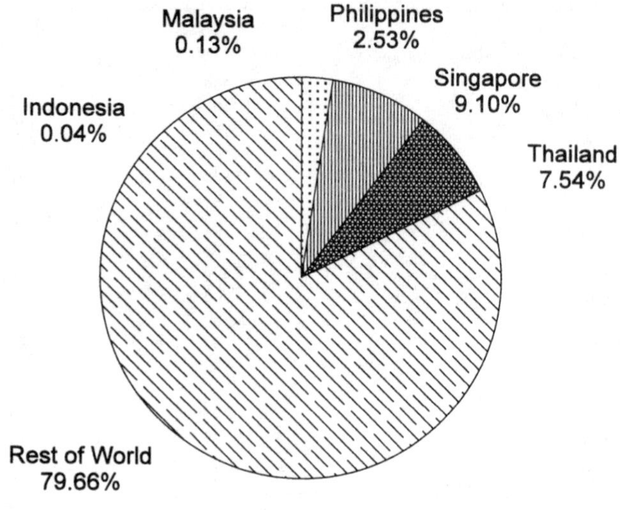

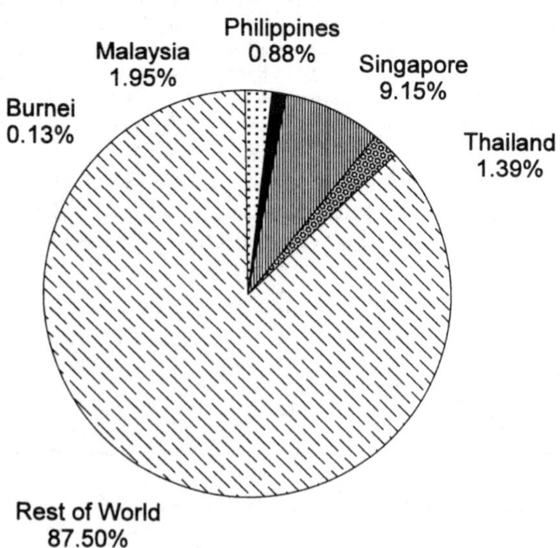

Figure 12.2 The destination of the exports of ASEAN nations

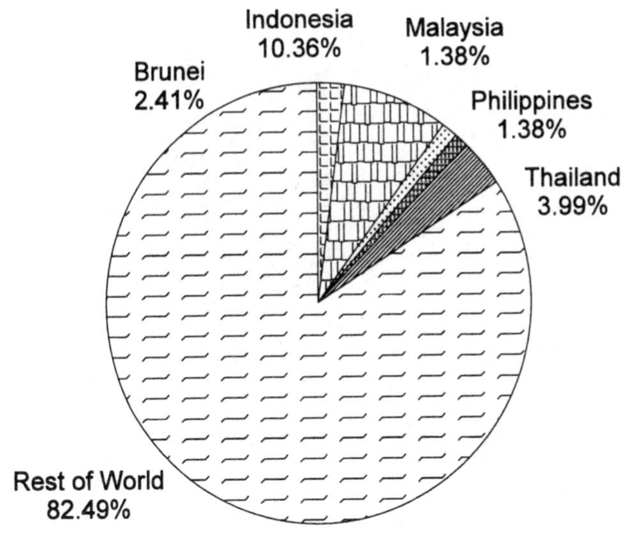
Singapore
Indonesia
10.36%
Malaysia
1.38%
Brunei
2.41%
Philippines
1.38%
Thailand
3.99%
Rest of World
82.49%

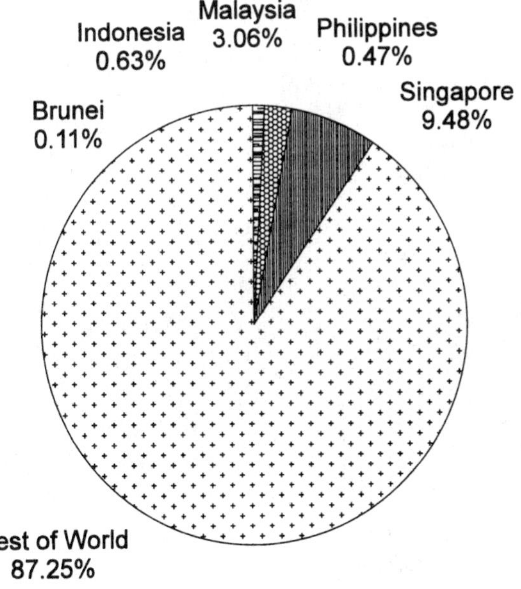
Thailand
Malaysia
3.06%
Indonesia
0.63%
Philippines
0.47%
Singapore
9.48%
Brunei
0.11%
Rest of World
87.25%

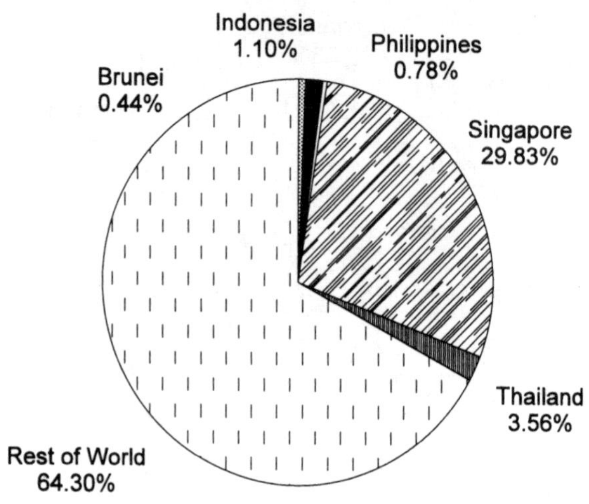
Malaysia
Indonesia
1.10%
Philippines
0.78%
Brunei
0.44%
Singapore
29.83%
Thailand
3.56%
Rest of World
64.30%

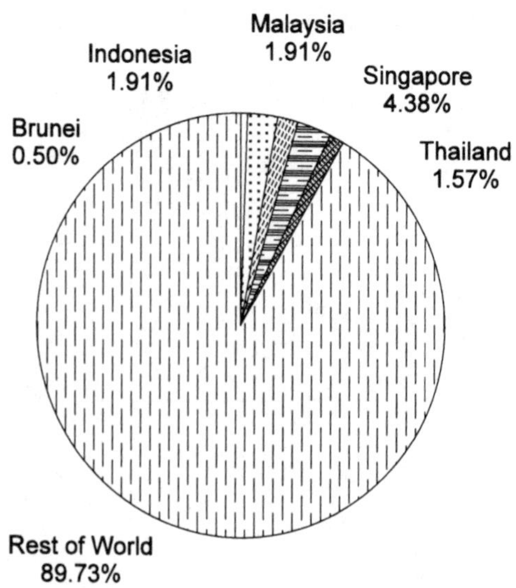
Philippines
Malaysia
1.91%
Indonesia
1.91%
Singapore
4.38%
Brunei
0.50%
Thailand
1.57%
Rest of World
89.73%

THE FIRST TWENTY-FIVE YEARS: ASEAN 1967–92

The creation of ASEAN in 1967 in the shadow of the escalating war in Indo-China had a strong political dimension, bringing together regimes opposed to communist expansion in South-East Asia. Until 1975 ASEAN's prime concern was geopolitical, and even after the end of the Indo-China War ASEAN continued to be a vehicle for common political action (e.g. in opposing the post-1978 Vietnamese military presence in Cambodia). Economic cooperation measures only came on the agenda after the first ASEAN summit in Bali, in February 1976.

In February 1977, the ASEAN Foreign Ministers signed an agreement on Preferential Trading Arrangements (PTA). The PTA envisaged a three-pronged process consisting of voluntary listing of products for preferential treatment, bilateral negotiation on a case-by-case basis, and across the board preferential tariff cuts on items with import trade value of less than $50 000. Progress was painfully slow as governments were reluctant to include reduction of tariffs which protected domestic producers – which, of course, meant almost all items where tariffs had significant economic impact. Members vied to announce large numbers of tariff cuts, but, by defining goods narrowly or by selecting irrelevant items,[4] they avoided increasing competitive pressures on their protected producers. By 1981 some 9000 preferential tariff reductions had been announced, but they covered only 2 per cent of intra-ASEAN trade, and even by the late 1980s only about 5 per cent of intra-ASEAN trade was covered by the PTA. Not surprisingly, all empirical studies of the PTA find that it had minimal impact on intra-ASEAN trade (Imada, 1993, pp. 4–8). Indeed, intra-ASEAN trade as a percentage of members' total trade was lower in 1989 than it had been in 1970 (Ariff and Tan, 1992, p. 254). Ariff (1994) points out that although intra-ASEAN trade did grow faster after the mid-1980s, this was due to unilateral liberalisation by the members and to the activities of transnational corporations following the investment boom.[5]

The ASEAN Industrial Projects (AIPs) programme was launched in 1977, aiming to promote industrial cooperation, especially in meeting regional requirements of essential commodities. Despite assignment of one AIP to each member state in March 1979 and Japanese financial aid for the programme, the first Project did not come on stream until 1984.[6] By that time Singapore had effectively dropped out of the programme and Thailand's position was anomalous.

Indonesia wanted modification of Singapore's original AIP, a diesel engine factory, because part of its output range would compete with an Indonesian plant. Limiting the output range would make the Singapore factory unprofitable, so Singapore replaced the engine project by a hepatitis B vaccine project, which was much smaller than the other AIPs and reduced its equity participation in other AIPs from 10 to 1 per cent.

After a long gestation period Thailand decided to drop its AIP, a soda ash plant, and built a urea fertiliser plant. The Philippines replaced its superphosphate AIP by a pulp and paper project which has yet to be built. Of the original AIPs, only the Indonesian and Malaysian urea fertiliser projects were eventually constructed and they faced unwanted competition from the new Thai national project.

The 1976 Bali Summit had called for complementarity agreements involving joint ventures among private firms in a regional context, and agreements were signed at ASEAN meetings in 1980 (Chee, 1987). A few such projects were approved and some were implemented, but their impact was small. Attempts to establish complementary production within sectors (known as Brand to Brand Complementarity, or BBC, agreements) began with automobile components, but the BBC scheme was undermined in the mid-1980s by Malaysia's decision to proceed with its own integrated automobile industry.

The Bali Summit also called for the creation of an ASEAN Finance Corporation. The corporation, established in 1981 by 140 commercial banks and individual shareholders, was to promote economic cooperation among ASEAN members, but it had little success and was restructured in 1987–8. The restructured corporation acts as a merchant bank, providing limited lending to bankable projects within ASEAN.

As a regional economic organisation, ASEAN made very little progress during the 1970s and 1980s and had limited economic impact. The major reason is that the five original members were pursuing different trade policy strategies. While Singapore had abandoned import-substitution following its independence in 1965, the other four countries retained import-substituting industrialisation strategies through the 1970s and only gradually (and at differing speeds) edged away from protectionism during the 1980s.

Table 12.4 illustrates the differences in trade policies. Singapore and Brunei have the lowest trade barriers, and Malaysia the next lowest. Indonesia, the Philippines and Thailand have the highest barriers, although it is difficult to rank them. Thailand has the highest tariffs, but the Philippines and especially Indonesia make more use of non-

Table 12.4 Levels of protection in ASEAN countries

	Indonesia	*Malaysia*	*Philippines*	*Singapore*	*Thailand*	*Brunei*
Early 1980s						
Ave tariff (%)	32.4	25.0	29.2	6.4	30.7	na
NTBs (number)	799	173	497	161	183	139
November 1992						
Ave tariff (%)	10.4	10.0	19.8	0.7	27.6	na

Notes
Tariff rates are weighted by imports; NTB measures are counts of the number of six-digit CCCN products affected by restrictive licensing, quotas, import prohibitions, restricted foreign exchange, and state import monopolies.
Sources: Early 1980s, Naya *et al.* (1989), pp. 38–40; November 1992, East Asia Analytical Unit (1994), p. 65 (the NTB data on pp. 63–4 have no date, but are identical to the Naya *et al.* figures for the early 1980s).

tariff barriers.[7] Pressures for regional trade liberalisation in the 1970s tended to come from Singapore with support from Malaysia and be blocked by Indonesia with the acquiescence of the Philippines and Thailand. The situation has, however, evolved as all of the ASEAN members unilaterally liberalised their trade regimes during the 1980s.

Regional trade liberalisation leading to trade creation was not possible as long as domestic producers had a sympathetic ear in the government whenever they voiced fears of competition from another ASEAN producer. In this setting the only acceptable regional projects were trade diverting ones, which would not directly compete with domestic producers elsewhere within ASEAN. Trade diverting projects are, however, by their nature costly because they involve purchasing goods from other than the least-cost supplier. Thus, while some countries wanted protected ASEAN-wide markets for their AIPs, the more outward-oriented economies were unwilling to bear the costs of such a programme.[8] In sum, while integration was lauded in general terms, both trade-creating integration via a PTA and trade-diverting integration via AIPs were rejected upon closer examination.[9]

The institution-building process did, however, bring some benefits. ASEAN's origins in 1967 were largely political, bringing together the South-East Asian countries resisting communist expansion beyond Indochina (Arndt and Garnaut, 1979), and ASEAN continued to act as a political force. United opposition to Vietnam's occupation of Cambodia contributed to negotiations being undertaken and to Vietnam's eventual withdrawal. On the economic front, the ASEAN countries increasingly negotiated with one voice, which added to their weight in trade negotiations, especially as individual countries experienced accelerated economic growth in the late 1980s. Thus, for example, ASEAN negotiated as a group with the European Union (EU) on the latter's trade restricting measures, and more importantly in the 1986–94 Uruguay Round of multilateral trade negotiations.[10]

THE SINGAPORE–JOHOR–RIAU GROWTH TRIANGLE[11]

From the beginning of ASEAN, private sector firms have operated across the national borders. Singapore and Malaysia had only separated two years before the founding of ASEAN and their economies remained closely tied. Conglomerates like Sime Darby operated throughout the region. The overseas Chinese communities spread throughout ASEAN also had cross-border activities. The Bangkok-based Charoen Pokphand group had 1983 sales of over $150 million from its animal feed and poultry operations in Indonesia, and operated poultry-farming and pig-raising joint ventures in Malaysia and Singapore (Chee, 1987, p. 109). Japanese corporations, whose presence in ASEAN expanded rapidly during the second half of the 1980s, increasingly coordinated operations across ASEAN borders (Ariff, 1994, p. 110). Such undirected regional integration was most starkly illustrated, however, by the spillover of Singaporean economic activity into neighbouring provinces of Indonesia and Malaysia in the late 1980s and early 1990s.

Between the mid-1960s and mid-1980s economic linkages between Singapore and its neighbours were not dynamic. After Singapore's separation from Malaysia, the Malaysian government actively sought to reduce the amount of trade flowing through Singapore. Links between Singapore and Indonesia were limited by the two countries' separate political histories, Indonesian restrictions on foreign investment, and the underdeveloped infrastructure in Riau province.

The emergence of a sub-regional economic zone (SRZ) involving Singapore, Johor and Batam first began to be noticed in the late 1980s. In Johor, approved foreign investment grew rapidly during the second half of the 1980s. Although Singaporeans played a significant role in this boom, Japanese investors were more important and investors from Taiwan, South Korea, Hong Kong, the USA and Western Europe also invested substantially in Johor. Proximity to Singapore seems critical, because Johor's share of foreign investment in Malaysia grew rapidly during this period. The role of governments in promoting links between Singapore and Johor was, however, negligible. The Malaysian central government has been lukewarm, although the Johor state government has advocated improved links with Singapore. The supporting physical infrastructure is overstrained, with heavy congestion on the causeway connecting Singapore with Johor. Discussions are under way for extending Singapore's rapid transit system to Johor and a second causeway linking Singapore to Johor is to be built, but infrastructure provision is obviously following demand rather than having contributed to the creation of the SRZ.

The Riau–Singapore link has been more influenced by government policy, but even in this case the formal agreements are minimal. In 1990 and 1991 bilateral agreements were signed on investment protection and on joint development of water resources in Riau, and on-going efforts to harmonise regulations and procedures are taking place. The crucial policy step, however, was unilateral. Creation of the Batam duty free zone in 1978 and subsequent liberalisation of foreign investment policy created a necessary condition for the upsurge of foreign investment. Actual growth in Batam accelerated in the second half of the 1980s, when exports increased from $21 million in 1986 to $210 million in 1991 and tourist arrivals (mainly from and through Singapore) grew from 60 000 in 1986 to over 600 000 in 1991.[12] Singapore accounts for over half of approved foreign investment in Batam both by number of projects and by value (US$532 million out of $1055 million cumulative total by the end of 1991), followed by the USA, Japan and Hong Kong, with Malaysia accounting for a mere 0.3 per cent of the total value.

The nature of the boom in both Johor and Batam is similar. It has been led by foreign investment, especially in labour-intensive and land-intensive activities. For both, Singapore, which is physically connected to Johor and a thirty to forty minute ferry journey from Batam, is the regional hub. The picture is of substantial shifting of labour-intensive activities from Singapore to neighbouring countries as wage rates have risen in the city, while keeping some functions in Singapore. Growth in incomes in Singapore has fuelled rising demand for land-intensive activities, especially tourism but also housing, which appears to be largely financed by Singaporean capital. Investors from Japan and the East Asian newly industrialising economies and from North America and Western Europe are relocating labour-intensive manufacturing activities to Johor and Batam. The attraction of these locations lies primarily in low-cost labour, and perhaps in low land costs in Batam,[13] but many other locations share these pluses and proximity to the urban services of Singapore is critical to tipping the balance in favour of Johor and Batam.

The balance between the importance of low wages and of proximity is one that varies between activities. The situation is a dynamic one; as wages and rents rise in Southern Johor and in Batam, some foreign investors are seeking locations further north in Malaysia and in other Riau islands, which are less convenient to Singapore but where land and labour are cheaper.[14] The development of Bintan Island involves the Indonesian government and Singapore's Public Utilities Board and the state-owned Jurong Town Corporation, but most of the estimated $7 billion development cost is expected to come from private sources.[15] Elsewhere the geographical expansion of the SRZ seems to be almost entirely driven by private entrepreneurs.

The concept of growth triangles caught the public imagination in Asia circa 1992.[16] As a picture of the Singapore–Johor–Riau SRZ the triangle image is, however, fundamentally misleading in so far as links between Riau and Johor are minimal. The popularity of the concept led to a growth industry in identifying other triangles, such as the 'Northern Growth Triangle' involving Southern Thailand, North-Western Malaysia and Northern Sumatra, or other geometric shapes, such as the 'Golden Quadrilateral' involving Northern Thailand, North-East Myanmar, North-West Laos and Yunnan. None of these has any substantive content, because they lack the key component of the Johor–Singapore–Riau SRZ, which is not its triangular shape but rather the central position of Singapore.[17]

Nevertheless, some ASEAN governments, notably Malaysia, have embraced the SRZ concept as a way of promoting regional integration without having to change national trade policies. The Malaysian government is actively promoting the Northern Growth Triangle and a SRZ incorporating Brunei, the Malaysian and Indonesian parts of Borneo (Kalimantan) and neighbouring islands of the Philippines. If this merely involves trade facilitation and other measures to reduce obstacles to trade then such initiatives may be helpful, but if governments try to supervise the geographical allocation of economic activity then their intervention could be harmful.[18]

THE ASEAN FREE TRADE AREA

In January 1992, the ASEAN members signed accords in Singapore which aimed at gradually establishing an ASEAN free trade area

(AFTA). AFTA involves reducing intra-ASEAN tariffs on manufactured goods to 0–5 per cent within fifteen years starting from 1 January 1993. It was also proposed to include elimination of non-tariff barriers to intra-ASEAN trade, although the mechanism for achieving this has not yet been specified.

AFTA was given greater credibility than the earlier PTA scheme by specifying mechanisms for moving towards the preferential tariff which required listing of exclusions, rather than detailed negotiation of what should be included.[19] Nevertheless, the original announcement had not been preceded by sufficient preparation at the national level, and during the next twenty months national governments responded to the concerns of protected domestic producers by drawing up long exclusion lists. A relaunch in October 1993 redressed the situation somewhat by bringing reductions on high tariffs (i.e. those over 20 per cent) forward to January 1994. Nevertheless, uncertainty remained over the extent to which members would follow through with preferential tariff reductions as deadlines (the ultimate one being in 2008) drew closer.

Studies of the impact of AFTA build on earlier work on the PTA. Imada (1993) finds that liberalising intra-ASEAN trade in manufactures will lead to greater specialisation, according to comparative advantage and increased intra-ASEAN trade due to both trade creation and trade diversion. The quantitative changes in trade flows are not large, and Imada does not estimate the welfare effects. Imada's estimates do, however, show significant trade balance effects, as the lower tariff countries (Singapore and Malaysia) will increase their intra-ASEAN exports by more than their imports, while Thailand will experience a large deterioration in its intra-ASEAN trade deficit. A key issue in practice will be how far internal trade really is freed, but even if AFTA goes much further than the PTA the potential gains are not large given the similarity of most of the members' economies.

A principal objective of AFTA is to increase ASEAN's attractiveness to foreign investors by creating an integrated regional market. To some extent this had already happened before AFTA as the multinational corporations, who increased their investment in ASEAN during the late 1980s, ensured that they would have the freedom to move components from factories in one ASEAN country to another without having to surmount trade barriers. Producing final consumer goods for the entire ASEAN market is more difficult, and will remain that way until governments are prepared to overrule calls for protection and open up their markets to foreign competition; if the experience of the 1980s is a guide, when this happens it is likely to be on a multilateral rather than a preferential basis in order to avoid trade diversion costs. Fears of investment diversion, voiced for example with respect to Australia (East Asia Analytical Unit, 1994, p. 112), seem misplaced, because AFTA itself is unlikely to have much impact on foreign investment.

EXPANDING ASEAN

The 1967 Bangkok Declaration states that ASEAN is open for participation by all states in the South-East Asian region subscribing to the association's aims, principles and purposes. After the 1973 Paris agreement between Vietnam and the USA, the ASEAN foreign ministers proposed expanding the association to include all countries in South-East Asia. Vietnam quickly rejected this proposal, alleging that ASEAN was a new version of the old anti-communist SEATO (Hoang, 1993, p. 284). After the fall of Saigon in 1975, all the ASEAN countries established diplomatic relations with Vietnam and sought to neutralise its potential dominance of the region. Over the next two years, however, regional tension increased (between Vietnam and Cambodia and between Vietnam and China) and the ASEAN countries grew concerned about the close relationship between Vietnam and the USSR. After Vietnamese troops invaded Cambodia in 1979, ASEAN–Vietnam relations deteriorated further.

Bilateral relations were maintained during Vietnam's occupation of Cambodia. In particular, Indonesia sought to accommodate Vietnam's leading role within Indochina by regular but unofficial contacts through the 1980s. The process culminated in President Soeharto's visit to Hanoi in November 1990, during which the Vietnamese Premier Do Muoi affirmed that Vietnam wished to join ASEAN.[20]

Malaysia also maintained a policy of constructive involvement, despite strains over Vietnam's responsibility for boat people arriving on Malaysian shores. In 1991 Malaysia removed restrictions on business travel to Vietnam. During the October visit of Prime Minister Vo Van Kiet to Malaysia, Prime Minister Mahathir supported the accession of the Indochinese countries and Myanmar to ASEAN. Early in 1992 the two countries' prime ministers made official visits to the other's country (Antolik, 1993, pp. 201–2). A joint venture branch of a Malaysian bank opened in Vietnam in April 1992 and the two countries announced a joint oil exploration agreement in June.

Thailand, with its long common border with Cambodia, felt most threatened by the Vietnamese occupation. Thailand's transition from opposing to embracing Vietnam occurred during the 1988–91 Chatichai government, after Vietnam's September 1989 withdrawal from Cambodia re-established a buffer zone between the two regional powers. The Anand government adopted the 'bridge' metaphor to characterise its more cautious approach towards Vietnam, centred on 'economic engagement'.[21] In October 1991 Premier Kiet visited Thailand, Indonesia and Singapore – the first such visit since 1978. Prime Minister Anand's January 1992 return visit was the first ever by a Thai head of government to unified Vietnam. In February 1993 Thailand, Vietnam, Laos and Cambodia signed an agreement on Cooperation and Development of the Mekong River.

Thailand has taken the lead as Laos's economic gateway to ASEAN. In 1991 they established a Lao–Thai Border Security Committee, and subsequently moved towards resolution of their dispute over the village of Baan Romklao, where fighting occurred in 1987. Foreign investment in Laos grew rapidly in 1992–3 from a low base; Thai manufacturing and trading companies and Thai banks became highly visible in Vientiane by 1994. Thai–Lao economic links were strengthened by the opening of the first bridge across the Mekong River in April 1994.

Singapore switched from suspicion of Vietnam to support after Premier Kiet's October 1991 visit. After the ban on investment in Vietnam was lifted in the next month, the Port of Singapore announced an agreement to help develop Vietnam's ports. Singapore quickly emerged as the largest ASEAN trading partner with Vietnam.

In Vietnam the Seventh Congress of the Communist Party in 1991 adopted a new outlook on foreign policy. The ideological approach to foreign policy was abandoned in favour of one based on national interest.

The foreign ministers of Laos and Vietnam attended the 1992 ASEAN Annual Ministerial Meeting in Manila, where their countries' accession to the Treaty of Amity and Cooperation marked the end of the Cold War in South-East Asia.[22] The meeting was also attended by China, which reflected the uncomfortable situation in the South China Sea and the difficulty of application of the treaty to this specific dispute.[23]

At the July 1995 ASEAN Summit Vietnam became the Association's seventh member, with an extension until 2006 for completing its AFTA tariff reductions. Laos and Cambodia are expected to become members in the near future. In Cambodia the principal obstacle to membership is the unsettled domestic political situation. The optimism following the 1991 Paris Agreement has disappeared. Despite the successful holding of elections in May 1993, the Khmer Rouge remain a potent force.

Beyond the three Indo-China countries, the next potential member of ASEAN is Myanmar (Burma). Indeed, by 1993–4 there were frequent references to the South-East Asian Ten (SEA-10) as the natural regional bloc. The ASEAN countries have led the cause for constructive engagement with the Myanmar regime, which many of the major trading nations prefer to treat as a leper.[24] Given some political easing and, more importantly, economic reforms in Myanmar, membership in ASEAN would face no major obstacles. The six pre-1995 ASEAN members have 330 million people; SEA-10 contains over 450 million, so expansion would make ASEAN larger in population than either the EU or NAFTA.

Once ASEAN includes the SEA-10 it will have reached its limits within mainland Asia, as there is no likelihood of India or China becoming members. Neither economic nor political connections between ASEAN and SAARC (South Asian Association for Regional Cooperation) members are substantial. Economic links with China are important, and Thailand and the four potential newcomers among the SEA-10 have cooperation agreements with Yunnan Province of China.[25] Nevertheless, ASEAN could not absorb a country the size of China, and, if ASEAN has a single uniting geopolitical theme in the 1990s, it is common concern about Chinese territorial claims in the South China Sea.

In 1993–4, there were some hints that ASEAN might consider Australia and New Zealand as future members.[26] These originated from Thailand within ASEAN and were taken up in the Australian government's East Asia Analytical Unit 1994 Report on AFTA (pp. 52, 130–4). On the economic front, an Australasian expansion would have to resolve the problems of marrying two regional organisations, ASEAN and the Closer Economic Relations (CER) agreement, which have so far moved at different speeds.[27] On the political front, a putative amalgamation of ASEAN and the CER raises the issue of where the ASEAN members see themselves within broader regional groupings.

ASEAN AND BROADER REGIONAL GROUPINGS

The revived activity within ASEAN in 1992 reflected not only internal frustration at the PTA and other integration schemes' lack of impact, but also the growing belief that the world economy was breaking up into regional blocs. Concerns about regionalism were fed by the European Community's 1992 programme for completing its internal market (EC92) and by the Canada–US Free Trade Area and subsequent negotiations to bring Mexico into a North American Free Trade Area (NAFTA). Meanwhile, in the early 1990s the Uruguay Round of multilateral trade negotiations appeared to be floundering. Thus, the GATT- based international trading system was being placed in doubt as the major trading nations of the Americas and Europe focused on regional arrangements, and Asia faced the prospect of being left defenceless in a world of trading blocs.

At the same time as ASEAN's leaders were rushing into AFTA, blueprints were being drawn up for wider Asian groupings. In 1989 Australia, fearful of being left out, had proposed APEC (Asia-Pacific Economic Cooperation), which would include not only the East Asian countries but also the Australasian and eastern Pacific countries. In December 1990 Malaysia proposed an East Asian Economic Group, bringing together the ASEAN countries and the North-East Asian economies. The name was subsequently modified to the East Asian Economic Caucus (EAEC) to emphasise its role as a forum rather than an exclusive trading group. Crucially, Japan threw its weight behind APEC, rather than the geographically narrower EAEC which might be viewed as confrontational by the USA, which took an active role in hosting the initial APEC summit. Participation at the highest political level in the first APEC summits at Seattle (1993) and Bogor (1994) indicated widespread support for APEC as a forum (Dobson and Lee, 1994). Nevertheless, APEC's economic content remains opaque. The best articulated economic philosophy behind APEC is open regionalism (see the contributions to Garnaut and Drysdale, 1994).

AFTA and APEC may turn out to have little impact. Both are symptoms of Asian reactions to NAFTA and the EC92, which might prove to be overeactions. Although policy-makers and the media feared the worst, academic economists pointed out that there was little reason to expect that Asian countries would suffer from these moves (Pomfret, 1992; Anderson and Snape, 1994). Empirical estimates of the negative effects of NAFTA and EC92 on ASEAN are small (Kim and Weston, 1993; Kreinin and Plummer, 1992; Pomfret, 1993).

To the extent that open regionalism can be subsumed under multilateral trade liberalisation, the immediate future for ASEAN may be a continuation of its recent economic past. The economic success of

Indonesia, Malaysia and Thailand since the mid-1980s has been based on unilateral trade liberalisation, plus stricter adherence to the GATT spirit on non-tariff issues (such as transparency, reducing bureaucratic obstacles to trade and respecting intellectual property rights). Continuation of this strategy will reduce the discriminatory impact of any preferential trade liberalisation within AFTA (and ultimately make AFTA irrelevant) and improve economic relations with APEC partners. In practice the most important economic organisation for the ASEAN members is likely to be the World Trade Organisation, while ASEAN remains an important forum for discussing regional issues and coordinating policies on geopolitical issues.

CONCLUSIONS

ASEAN seems to be perpetually at the crossroads, but never reaching a goal. In its first decade, ASEAN's main concerns were geopolitical and it was on the defensive in the face of military successes of communist movements in Indo-China. After the 1976 Bali summit ASEAN embraced regional economic integration, but in the late 1980s political leaders and commentators in the region were questioning why so little progress had been made towards establishing an Asian counterpart of the European Union. In the 1990s ASEAN is again contemplating basic issues, as would-be members knock on the door and balances have to be struck between South-East Asian regionalism and wider regional organisations.

One irony of all of this soul searching is that, with the exception of the Philippines, the ASEAN countries have been among the great economic success stories of recent years. This success, however, has had more to do with national policies and characteristics than with membership in ASEAN.[28] Regional integration has accelerated in the 1990s, but mainly as a result of unilateral (non-discriminatory) trade liberalisation and of economic growth. If the experience of other newly industrialised economies is a guide, this will become a virtuous circle as growth encourages liberalisation which leads to further growth. That will in turn generate more cross-border links among more specialised ASEAN firms, but will render AFTA nugatory in so far as multilateral liberalisation undermines the possibility of meaningful preferential trade liberalisation.

ASEAN leaders should cease worrying about failure to mimic the European Union. The situation is quite different in that the ASEAN countries have no dream of forming a federal state. A better model would be the European Free Trade Association (EFTA) of 1973–94, which brought together a handful of small to mid-sized countries whose main trading partners were non-members. The internal trade preferences of EFTA were of little significance, but the ability to speak when appropriate with one voice in international trade negotiations was very important (especially *vis-à-vis* the EC/EU). For the ASEAN countries successfully pursuing outward-oriented development strategies, almost all the gains from trade liberalisation can be achieved by unilateral action rather than creating a PTA/FTA (which will have negative side-effects), but securing and maintaining access to their most important external markets can better be achieved by joint action. At its current crossroads, ASEAN should keep on the path that most of its members have been following since the mid-1980s – a path which so far has been paved with gold.

Notes

* I am grateful to Gerald Tan, Hal Hill and Rolf Langhammer for helpful comments on an earlier draft. Financial support for the research upon which this chapter is based was provided by the Australian Research Council.

1. The crossroads image has been evoked during the last decade as the theme for a series of high-level meetings and conferences in 1987 (see the book containing the papers by Chee and by Tan), by semi-official US economic commentators (Naya and Plummer, 1991, p. 266), and by an Australian government think tank (East Asia Analytical Unit, 1994, p. 34).
2. The background and early history of ASEAN is analysed in Arndt and Garnaut (1979). Excellent recent surveys of the ASEAN economies are contained in Hill (1994) and Tan (1995).
3. Due to Singapore's importance as an entrepôt, much of the bilateral trade with other ASEAN members is for transhipment, so that the trade data in Figure 12.3 may even overstate the importance of intra-ASEAN trade, reflecting that these are competing rather than complementary economies. The major complementarity in merchandise trade appears to involve oil refining in Singapore. The discussion in the next section suggests that the complementarity of Singapore and its neighbours may have increased recently, but is represented in service and other 'invisible' exports from Singapore.

4. Tan (1987, p. 65) reports that 'for some product categories, up to two-thirds of the items granted preferential tariffs by some countries were not actually traded by them' and other 'preferential' reductions were offered on MFN tariffs of zero. Tan concludes: 'What started out as a serious attempt to stimulate trade between the Asean countries soon began to look more and more like a public relations exercise.' For more details on the shallowness of preferential tariff cuts see Tan (1982, p. 325–30) and on exclusions see Pangestu *et al.* (1992, p. 335–6).
5. According to International Monetary Fund data (*Balance of Payments Statistical Yearbook, 1992*) foreign direct investment in the five original ASEAN members was $2227 million in 1985, $2847m in 1986, $4303m in 1987, $6991m in 1988, $7459m in 1989, $10 442m in 1990 and $11 078m in 1991.
6. Each of the first set of AIPs was expected to require an investment of $250–300 million, and each ASEAN member was expected to be a share-holder in all AIPs (the host country would take up 60 per cent of total equity and the other four members would take up the remaining 40 per cent).
7. Since the average tariff rates are calculated using import weights, quantitative restrictions may bias the tariff measures downwards. For example, if Indonesia has a high tariff and a quantitative limit on an item, then imports of that good will be reduced by the quantitative limit, and hence the high tariff will be underweighted in calculating the tariff average.
8. The extended infant industry argument implicit in the AIP programme has underlaid many regional integration schemes in Latin America and in Africa, none of which had much success because members wanted the infant industries to be on their territory but did not want to be forced to buy the output of infant industries located on other members' territory (Pomfret, 1988, p. 158).
9. Apart from the issues raised in this paragraph, widely differing external trade policies pose a technical problem for free trade areas because they encourage trade deflection. An importer in a high tariff ASEAN member will be encouraged to source imports from outside ASEAN through Singapore in order to pay the low Singaporean customs duty. Internal customs barriers will be necessary in order to check that rules of origin are met, i.e. that goods coming from Singapore are indeed of ASEAN origin and not subject to the national tariff. The bigger the differences in tariff rates, the greater is the incentive to try to avoid the internal customs checks or to falsify origin statements, and the greater are the enforcement costs. It should be noted that within ASEAN geography is highly conductive to smuggling and enforcement of restrictions on intra-ASEAN trade is not easy.

10. Some ASEAN members were in overlapping pressure groups as Indonesia, Malaysia, the Philippines and Thailand were members of the Cairns Group which successfully brought agricultural trade back into the GATT/WTO regime.
11. This section relies heavily on Chia and Lee (1993). Pomfret (forthcoming 1996) provides a broader discussion of subregional economic zones.
12. Chia and Lee (1993, p. 248). By the early 1990s Batam had surpassed Bali as Indonesia's second tourist entry point, after Jakarta.
13. In 1989 land costs (in $US per square meter) were $4.3 in Singapore, $4.1 in Johor and $2.3 in Batam, while unskilled labour cost $350 per month in Singapore, $150 in Johor and $90 in Batam (Chia and Lee, 1993, p. 243).
14. Batam does not have abundant labour. Wages have been kept down only by substantial immigration from other parts of Indonesia, which increased the population from 7000 in the early 1970s to over 100 000 by the early 1990s.
15. The Public Utilities Board is involved in a $1 billion water development project. Water supply is a critical attraction for Singapore, which is currently dependent on Johor, but that should not obscure the enormous activity by private small-scale businesses.
16. The papers from a conference at the National University of Singapore, in April 1992, on Regional Cooperation and Growth Triangles in ASEAN were widely reported on in the press. They were published in the following year (Toh and Low, 1993).
17. Singapore's evolving economic role may have implications for the region beyond its immediate hinterland. Amelung (1992) found statistical evidence of regional integration in the 1980s among Indonesia, Malaysia, Singapore and Thailand, but ascribed the result to Singapore's role as a regional hub rather than to ASEAN.
18. Thailand's experience with regional devolution in the 1970s was disappointing. After the policy reforms of the early 1980s the Thai government largely left the spatial pattern of investment to the market. The result was huge rural–urban migration to greater Bangkok, accompanied by accelerated economic growth – a result which is consistent with some strands of endogenous growth theory (Pomfret, 1995).
19. East Asia Analytical Unit (1994) contains an accessible statement of the contents of AFTA and early progress in implementing AFTA, as well as the text of the agreements. Lee (1994) also analyses the AFTA implementation mechanisms. The 'padding' of exclusions was addressed by agreeing that inclusions would be defined at the 6-digit level while exclusions would be defined at the more disaggregated 8-digit level (Tan, 1995, chs 8). The enforcement of rules of origin, a special problem for ASEAN given that two member states (Singapore and

Brunei) operate close to free trade policies (see note 9 above), does not appear to have been adequately addressed.

20. *Far Eastern Economic Review*, 22 November 1990, p. 17.
21. Political suspicions, however, remained. When Vietnam requested permission to open a consulate in Udon Thani, Thailand resisted out of fear of contacts being made with Vietnamese living in the region.
22. The USSR and the USA had withdrawn their fleets from the bases at Cam Ranh Bay and Subic Bay.
23. Although Vietnam agreed to abide by the ASEAN Treaty of Amity and Cooperation, China's Foreign Minister Qian would only say that he 'appreciated some of the basic principles' (*Far Eastern Economic Review*, 6 August 1992, p. 9).
24. Thailand, the ASEAN member with a Burmese border, has taken the lead in advocating constructive engagement, but other members appear to share this view, especially when China appeared to be building up ties, including military links, with the Burmese regime in 1994. In July 1995 Than Shwe, the Burmese Prime Minister and chairman of the State Law and Order Restoration Council (SLORC), headed a high level delegation to Singapore and Jakarta where he signed bilateral agreements, which were viewed in the region as boosting ties with ASEAN.
25. Technical cooperation among the Mekong riparian states dates back to the establishment in 1957 of the ECAFE-fostered Lower Mekong Basin Committee, out of which the UNDP-supported Mekong Secretariat emerged in 1963. In the early 1990s, the narrow technical focus was broadened into conscious attempts to promote a growth sub-region consisting of Cambodia, Laos, Myanmar, Thailand, Vietnam and Yunnan Province of the People's Republic of China. The countries of the Greater Mekong Sub-region (GMS) have held a series of meetings since 1992 supported by the Asian Development Bank (ADB). The first two Conferences on Sub-regional Economic Cooperation were held at the ADB's headquarters in Manila in October 1992 and August 1993. At the third Conference held in April 1994 in Hanoi the main emphasis was on physical infrastructure, especially transport projects, and it was determined that donor agencies should be invited to the next meeting. The fourth GMS Conference in Chiang Mai, in September 1994, was attended by representatives of the ADB, the United Nations Economic and Social Commission for Asia and the Pacific (ESCAP), and Canadian and Japanese aid agencies. Although there was discussion of soft as well as hard infrastucture (i.e. trade facilitation as well as roads and bridges) and of energy issues, the top priority remained transport projects such as the link from eastern Thailand through Cambodia to southern Vietnam.

26. Papua New Guinea is another potential member, having already signed the ASEAN Treaty of Amity and Cooperation (Blomqvist, 1993).
27. McLean (1995) analyses the evolution of the CER.
28. ASEAN may have been an important institution for preserving political stability in a region where neighbours have many quarrels, and peace was an important prerequisite for the rapid growth of the last three decades (Tan, 1995, chs 2).

13 Integration Amongst Members of the Arab League

Ali M. El-Agraa

INTRODUCTION

Just two days after the formation of the Arab Cooperation Council (ACC), on 16 February 1989, the Arab world's latest scheme of integration was created under the title of the Arab Maghreb Union (AMU). The treaty founding the ACC was signed by Egypt, Iraq, Jordan and the Yemen Arab Republic (Yemen, hereafter) with the aim of boosting 'Arab solidarity' and, according to King Hussein of Jordan, acting as 'yet another link in the chain' of Arab efforts towards integration. President Saddam Hussein of Iraq described it as a more ambitious grouping than the European Community (EC, now the European Union – EU, see Chapter 5), but no details were provided to confirm this. However, the officials of all four nations later pointed out that the ACC aimed solely at bolstering economic ties, and was not intended as a military or political bloc that would compete with the League of Arab States (generally referred to as the Arab League; hereafter, simply the League), but no concrete measures were stated about the nature and extent of the economic ties, so one was, and still is, left in the dark about whether or not the comparison with the EU was an appropriate one.

Saddam Hussain of Iraq was elected to hold the ACC's rotating presidency for the first year, and was thus to chair its next meeting, for which no date was set and the Iraqi invasion of Kuwait ensured its not taking place to date. Also, it was later indicated that the ACC was open to other member nations of the League; indeed, on 21 February 1989 President Mubarak of Egypt visited the United Arab Emirates (UAE) to discuss cooperation between the ACC and the Gulf Cooperation Council (GCC – see p. 322).

The membership of the AMU comprises Algeria, Libya, Mauritania, Morocco and Tunisia. These countries feared that the creation by the EU of the single European market (SEM – see Chapter 5) by the end of 1992 would have adverse effects on their economies and felt that through unity they would be able to bargain effectively with the EU. They decided that unity should be interpreted to mean the creation of an organisation similar to the EU of 1992, by eliminating all barriers to the free movement of capital, people, goods and services across the borders of member nations. However, that put it in the textbook category of common markets and made it unlike the EU which is, as we have seen (Chapters 1 and 5 and El-Agraa, 1994) a much more complex scheme. King Hassan of Morocco, the first chairman of the group, stated a day after the formation of the AMU that the next six months could see rapid progress towards dismantling customs and immigration controls and that 'we are very optimistic about the speed with which we plan to move', but no precise details were provided.

The AMU was to have a Council of Heads of State with the chairmanship rotating every six months, a Council of Ministers, a Consultative Chamber of parliamentarians, a High Court consisting of ten members to settle disputes between the member nations, and a low-level Secretariat to run the affairs of the organisation. The founding members stated that the AMU was a stepping stone to union with other Arab countries, but were quick to add that all Arab and African countries, presumably with predominantly Arabic characteristics, were free to join. Therefore, one could safely state that the AMU seemed to have much clearer objectives than the ACC and had a firm institutional structure.

Those who were keen to promote economic and political integration as a matter of principle would no doubt have applauded the efforts of these countries. Before doing so, however, they needed to ask whether or not these schemes differed from previous attempts by these countries, and whether such regional groupings were the rational way forward for the Arab countries and the African countries closely connected with them. The purpose of this chapter is to seek some answers to these questions. Thus the chapter commences with a brief and selective history of previous attempts at the integration of the Arab nations to see if they are fundamentally different from these latest efforts, goes on to evaluate the prospects for the ACC and AMU and finishes by suggesting an appropriate framework.

PREVIOUS ATTEMPTS

The history of involuntary (imposed by foreign powers) cooperation between Arab countries (together with some other countries) goes back to the establishment of the Middle East Supply Centre (MESC) by Great Britain in 1940. The aim of the MESC was to guarantee and regulate the import of essential commodities into the region, to provide the necessary shipping in difficult wartime conditions and to promote local production and exchange within the area so as to curb the demand for imports. Voluntary cooperation between these nations began with the inauguration of the League in 1945, primarily on an Egyptian initiative. The aim of the League was to 'strengthen the close ties linking (sovereign Arab nations) and to coordinate their policies and activities and direct them to the common good of all the Arab countries', and to mediate in disputes between the member nations. In 1950, a convention on Joint Defence and Economic Cooperation committed the member nations to take, in the case of attack, 'individually and collectively, all steps available, including the use of armed forces, to repel the aggression and restore security and peace'.

These terms of reference are very demanding indeed and some would argue that their grand yet vague nature is the reason why the League has survived for so long. However, some less general but arguably equally vague schemes have also been introduced. The Arab Economic Council, whose membership consists of all Arab Ministers of Foreign Affairs, was entrusted with 'suggesting ways for economic development, cooperation, and organisation and coordination' (Sayigh, 1982, p. 123). The Council for Arab Economic Unity (CAEU), which was formed in 1957, had the aim of establishing an integrated economy of all member states of the League. Moreover, in 1964 the Arab Common Market (which became an Arab Free Trade Area in 1971) was formed by Egypt, Iraq, Jordan and Syria, and the GCC was established in 1981 between Bahrain, Kuwait, Oman, Qatar, Saudi Arabia and the UAE to bring together the Gulf states and to prepare the ground for them to join forces in the economic, political and military spheres. However, in spite of its elaborate institutional structure (GCC has a Supreme Council consisting of the rulers of the six member nations, a Ministerial Council of their foreign ministers or their delegates, a General Secretariat and specialised Ministerial Committees), the GCC has for a long time been preoccupied with administrative cooperation and has only recently (since the Iraqi invasion of Kuwait) embarked on economic cooperation. However, its member nations no longer require visas for their nationals, their citizens can use their driving licences in the whole area and their television planners coordinate programmes. Other than these schemes, a treaty was signed by Libya and Morocco in August 1984 to establish the Arab African Union, whose main aim was to tackle their political conflicts in the Sahara Desert.

Apart from these somewhat major initiatives, various institutions were created which fell under the general category of economic cooperation, rather than economic integration. Some of these are official specialised agencies created mainly under the League, such as the Arab League Educational, Cultural and Scientific Organisation and the Arab Organisation for Industrial Development. Others are autonomous bodies, for example the Organisation of Arab Petroleum Exporting Countries (OAPEC, established in January 1968 by Kuwait, Libya and Saudi Arabia, but were joined in May 1970 by Algeria, Bahrain, Qatar and the UAE, and in March 1972, by Egypt, Iraq and Syria), the Arab Fund for Economic and Social Development (AFESD), the Arab Monetary Fund (AMF) and the Arab Authority for Agricultural Investment and Development (AAAID). Yet others are professional organisations such as the federations of Arab bankers, economists, trade unions.

Most of these developments were confined to the eastern part of the League, the countries of the Mashreq (east), but this does not mean that the countries of the Maghreb (west) started cooperation only in 1984 with the Arab African Union. Before that there was the Maghreb Consultative Committee, founded in Tunis in 1964, with a Permanent Committee and Secretariat. At the beginning, Algeria, Libya, Morocco and Tunisia were members of the Permanent Committee, but Libya withdrew in 1970 and Mauritania joined in 1975.

The response by the member nations of the League to being accused of attempting grand gestures completely devoid of any practical significance would be to state that they have actually undertaken a number of joint projects and have expended fair sums of money on them. For example, by 1980, 427 projects had been undertaken in the fields of agriculture, extractive industry, finance, manufacturing industry, transport and communications, and tourism and related services. Of these projects, 164 were bilateral Arab with an aggregate capital of $8.85 billion, 73 were multilateral Arab with a total capital of $9.91 billion, 91 were bilateral Arab-cum-foreign involving $7.5

billion and 99 were multilateral Arab-cum-foreign using $5.28 billion. Thus the exclusively Arab projects had a total capital of $18.76 billion, but if the three regional financial institutions (AFESD, AMF and AAAID) were to be added, the total would have risen to $22 billion (Sayigh, 1983, p. 150). Thus it can be seen that there have been many attempts in the past to create schemes of economic integration and organisations in the field of economic cooperation, together with joint projects, between the member nations of the League.

Of course, the impression of separate developments in the east and west can be slightly misleading since one should not forget that both the Mashreq and Maghreb countries are participants in the League. However, one may rightly wonder why these new separate schemes are being undertaken when the League seems to be the only one to endure the test of time, while all other attempts, except for the GCC (now 14 years old), seem to get nowhere, that is, if they did manage to get off the ground in the first place.

The answer could be that the experience of the GCC has suggested that only limited schemes may provide a solid basis for a way forward, but, as we have seen, the GCC has not made substantial progress. It could also be that, as indeed is suggested by the earlier statements made about the ACC and AMU, a closer cooperation between a smaller number of the member nations of the League will eventually pave the way for a proper integration of the totality of its membership, but this is unconvincing particularly since the main reason put forward for the creation of the GCC is the common ancestry of its inhabitants, thus suggesting that only people of the same family or race can unite. Moreover, one can state that all efforts for integration or cooperation within the League have been for 'Arab unity'. Therefore, as long as Arab unity remains a clear objective, failure in the past does not exclude determined efforts in the future.

These considerations require careful examination, but before doing so, one needs to look closely at the general characteristics of the total membership of the League since it is the umbrella that shelters the totality of these various schemes, and whatever its failings, it seems to have weathered the storm of time. Of course, in examining the whole of the League, one is naturally taking a closer look at the basic features of the separate schemes which it encompasses. Needless to add, without knowledge of the basic characteristics of these countries, it would be pointless to try to present what is a coherent integration scheme for them.

GENERAL CHARACTERISTICS OF THE LEAGUE

The League comprises twenty-one independent nations plus Palestine. It has always been adamant on being referred to as the 'group of 22' on the understanding that the Palestinians will one day have their own country, a dream which has almost become a reality with the agreement between Israel and the Palestine Liberation Organisation (PLO) for self-rule and settlement in the West Bank, thus ensuring that Israel is a potential participant, justifying inclusion of its data in the tables below. The '22' extend from the Gulf in the East to Mauritania and Morocco in the West, or, in more popular terms, from the Strait of Gibraltar to the Strait of Hormuz. Hence, the geographical area covered by the group includes the whole of North Africa, a large part of the Middle East, plus Somalia and Djibouti.

The total population of the members of the League was about 53 million in 1930–1 (Sayigh, 1982). According to the World Bank's *World Development Report* for various years, it grew to about 160 million by 1979, reached about 170 million by mid-1981, exceeded 197 million by 1986 and, as can be calculated from Table 13.1, was about 240 million in mid-1993. Therefore, the average rate of population growth has been over 2.5 per cent per annum, and the World Bank does not expect it to change drastically by the end of this century. This is a very high percentage indeed when compared with that for advanced nations (about 1 per cent in Canada and the USA, 0.7 per cent in Japan, 0.5 per cent in France and the Netherlands and 1 per cent in the UK – see Tables 2.1 and 2.4) whose rates are expected to continue to decline. Moreover, the population of the League has a life expectancy at birth which varies from 79 years for Mauritania to between 75 and 70 years for members of the GCC to below 50 years for Djibouti and Somalia.

With the exception of Bahrain, Kuwait, Libya, Qatar, Saudi Arabia and the UAE, per capita income is very low indeed (see Table 13.2). At least five countries have per capita incomes of $780 or below, and another seven of between $781 and $2785. Thus the majority of the member countries of the League have per capita incomes of less than 12 per cent than that of the USA. The exceptions that fare well are the oil producers, with economies which are unbalanced and lacking in skilled labour and general infrastructure. When I last wrote on this subject (El-Agraa, 1990), in 1986, agriculture played an important role in the economies of Egypt (20 per cent), Maurtania (34 per cent), Sudan (35 per cent) and Yemen (34 per cent). Although the data in

Table 13.1 Arab League area and demographic data

Country	Area (thousands of sq. km)	Population (millions) mid-1993	Life expectancy at birth (years)	Average annual rate of population growth (%) 1970–80	1980–93	1993–2000
GCC						
Bahrain	0.7	0.5	72	na	na	na
Kuwait	18.0	1.8	75	6.1	1.9	0.4
Oman	212.0	2.0	70	4.2	4.5	4.0
Qatar	11.0	0.5	72	na	na	na
Saudi Arabia	2,150.0	17.4	70	5.1	4.4	3.1
UAE	84.0	1.8	74	15.2	4.4	2.2
ACC						
Egypt	1,001	56.4	64	2.2	2.0	na
Iraq	438.3	19.5	66	na	na	na
Jordan	89.0	4.1	70	3.7	4.9	3.3
Yemen, Rep.	528.0	13.2	51	2.6	3.6	na
AMU						
Algeria	2,382.0	26.7	67	3.1	2.7	2.2
Libya	1,759.5	5.0	64	na	na	na
Mauritania	1,026	2.2	52	2.4	2.6	2.5
Morocco	447	25.9	64	2.4	2.2	1.9
Tunisia	164.0	8.7	68	2.2	2.3	1.6
Rest of AL						
Djibouti	23.2	0.6	49	na	na	na
Lebanon	10.4	3.9	69	na	na	na
Somalia	637.7	9.0	47	na	na	na
Sudan	2,505.8	26.6	53	na	na	na
Syria	185.2	13.7	68	na	na	na
Israel	21.0	5.2	77	2.7	2.3	2.1

Note
na means not available.
Source: World Bank *World Development Report 1995.*

Table 13.3 record declines in these percentages, they remain high, with probably no change in the case of Sudan. In 1981, manufacturing accounted for zero per cent in Egypt and 26 per cent in Syria, while in 1986 it accounted for 14 per cent in Jordan, 17 per cent in Morocco, 15 per cent in Tunisia and 14 per cent in the Yemen PDR. The latest data in Table 13.3 show that Egypt has done very well while the others have experienced minor variations. Hence the major contribution to GNP comes from the 'services' sector and 'mining and construction'. Note that the term industry is misleading since it comprises mainly mining and construction. It is therefore not surprising when

Table 13.2 Arab League per capita GNP and inflation rates

Country	per capita GNP US$ 1993	per capita GNP Average annual rate of growth (%), 1980–93	Average annual rate of inflation (%) 1970–80	Average annual rate of inflation (%) 1980–93
GCC				
Bahrain	8,030	–2.9	na	–0.3
Kuwait	19,360	–4.3	21.9	na
Oman	4,850	3.4	28.0	–2.3
Qatar	15,030	–7.2	na	na
Saudi Arabia*	7,510	–3.6	24.5	–2.1
UAE	21,430	–4.4	na	na
ACC				
Egypt	660	2.8	9.6	13.6
Iraq	b	na	17.9	na
Jordan	1,190	na	na	na
Yemen, Rep.	na	na	na	na
AMU				
Algeria	1,780	–0.8	14.5	13.2
Libya	c	na	18.4	0.2
Mauritania	500	–0.8	9.9	8.2
Morocco	1,040	1.2	8.3	6.6
Tunisia	1,720	1.2	8.7	7.1
Rest of AL				
Djibouti	780	na	na	3.6
Lebanon	b	na	na	na
Somalia	a	na	15.2	49.7
Sudan	a	na	14.5	42.8
Syria	b	na	11.8	15.5
Israel	13,920	2.0	39.6	70.4

Notes
* Saudi Arabia's per capita GDP is for 1992.
a = Estimated to be low income ($695 or less).
b = Estimated to be lower middle income ($696 to $2785).
c = Estimated to be upper middle income ($2785 to $8625).
Source: As for Table 13.1.

Sayigh (1982, p. 58) states that 'after fifty years of change and a strong post-war drive for industrialisation, the contribution [of manufacturing] is still only 7.6 per cent of GDP for the Arab region as a whole, but 16.3 per cent if oil revenues are excluded from GDP', a picture which has not changed much since then. This is in sharp contrast with countries like China and India which have about the same level of

Table 13.3 Arab League structure of production, 1993

Country	*GDP US$m*	*Distribution of GDP (%)* Agriculture	Industry	Manufacturing[1]	Services, etc.[2]
GCC					
Bahrain	na	na	na	na	na
Kuwait	22,402	0	55	9	45
Oman	11,686	3	53	4	44
Qatar	na	na	na	na	na
Saudi Arabia[3]	121,530	4	50	9	46
UAE	34,935	2	57	8	40
ACC					
Egypt	35,784	18	22	16	60
Iraq	na	na	na	na	na
Jordan	4,444	8	26	15	66
Yemen, Rep.	11,985	21	24	11	55
AMU					
Algeria	39,836	13	43	11	43
Libya	na	na	na	na	na
Mauritania	859	28	30	12	42
Morocco[4]	26,635	14	32	18	53
Tunisia	12,784	18	31	19	51
Rest of AL					
Djibouti	na	na	na	na	na
Lebanon	na	na	na	na	na
Somalia	na	na	na	na	na
Sudan	na	na	na	na	na
Syria	na	na	na	na	na
Yemen PDR	11,958	21	24	11	55
Israel	69,739	na	na	na	na

Notes

1 Manufacturing is, of course, part of industry. It is shown separately because it is the most dynamic part.
2 Includes unallocated items.
3 Data is for 1986.
4 GDP and its components are at purchaser values.

Source: As for Table 13.1.

development as the majority of the member nations of the League. The contrast is even more striking if it is made with countries such as Japan, the UK and the USA (a valid comparison only because the rich member nations of the League live under the illusion that they are highly developed) where industry 'proper' accounts for about one-third (a declining figure, due to deindustrialisation; hence appropriate comparison should relate to the higher figures of the past when these advanced nations were at the same level of development that the member nations of the League are now at), and the large services sector is highly sophisticated.

Of particular significance is the rate of growth of per capita GNP. The average rate for the period 1965–86 was negative for Mauritania, Somalia and the Sudan. This was due to some fundamental difficulties concerning the management of their economies; indeed, Sudan became one of the major debtors of the International Monetary Fund (IMF) within the developing world during this period. Of course, there was and continues to be the refugee problem and there was the sudden drought in Africa, but according to the IMF these have aggravated an already worsening situation, which is why it refused to continue to assist the Sudan to the extent to which it did in the past. Kuwait also registered a negative rate, but that is simply a reflection of the decline in the world price of crude petroleum, which gives a clear indication of the hazardous nature of complete dependence on one product, especially one that has limited duration. All the other countries for which we have information have had rates in excess of 3 per cent, except for Morocco which registered only 1.9 per cent. However, the latest information, given in Table 13.2, shows a worsening of the situation since, except for Oman, all members of the GCC have been experiencing negative rates and the rest have had much lower rates.

Finally, one should add that most of these countries seem to have very high rates of inflation – see Table 13.2. It should be mentioned that Algeria, Saudi Arabia and the Sudan are very large countries while Bahrain, Djibouti, Kuwait, Lebanon and Qatar are very small in size (see Table 13.1). However, these absolute sizes do not mean very much particularly when deserts loom large in the larger member countries. When one is concerned with whether or not a region can become self-sufficient in agricultural production, especially food production, what is of significance is the proportion of total land that is arable and irrigated land as a percentage of arable land. A glance at the statistics (see Table 13.4) shows eight member nations to have a proportion of arable land of 3 per cent or less, and the number excludes three members of the GCC. Lebanon, Syria and Tunisia have a proportion of nearly one-third each, but these are small countries, hence their agricultural potential is limited: the 5 per cent for the Sudan is equivalent to about 12.5 million hectares which is roughly equal to half the size of the whole of Morocco. Of particular interest is the information given in column 3 of Table 13.4 relating to irrigated

Table 13.4 Arab League land use

Country	Arable land (% of total)	Irrigated land (% of arable)	Forest land (% of total)
GCC			
Bahrain	3.0	50.0	0.0
Kuwait	0.0	100.0	0.0
Oman	**	**	**
Qatar	**	**	**
Saudi Arabia	1.0	36.0	1.0
UAE	**	42.0	**
ACC			
Egypt	3.0	100.0	0.0
Iraq	13.0	32.0	3.0
Jordan	14.0	6.0	1.1
Yemen, Rep.	14.0	9.0	7.8
AMU			
Algeria	3.0	4.0	1.7
Libya	1.0	5.0	0.0
Mauritania	0.2	4.0	0.6
Morocco	17.0	6.0	20.1
Tunisia	32.0	3.0	4.3
Rest of AL			
Djibouti	**	**	**
Lebanon	34.0	24.0	7.0
Somalia	2.0	15.0	1.3
Sudan	5.0	14.0	17.2
Syria	31.0	9.0	1.1
Israel			4.8
Comparators			
China	11.0	50.0	13.0
India	57.0	23.0	15.7
Japan	13.0	66.0	63.0
UK	29.0	2.0	9.8
USA	21.0	9.0	30.2

Notes
1. The data is for various years between 1980 and 1990.
2. ** = insignificant figure.

Sources: various issues of FAO's *Yearbook for Food and Agricultural Statistics* and World Bank's *World Development Report*.

land as a percentage of arable land. Only 14 per cent of Sudan's arable land is irrigated while Egypt's is totally irrigated. Eight countries have a proportion of less than 10 per cent. A final point is that a population of nearly 240 million has to be supported by agricultural production from about half a million square kilometers; therefore, it should not come as a surprise to learn that the whole area is far less than self-sufficient in food production.

The period 1960–70 led to exceptional growth rates in the exports of Libya (67.5 per cent) and Mauritania (50.6 per cent). However, apart from Jordan, Lebanon and Saudi Arabia (all with double figures) the rest of the member nations of the League experienced only modest single figure growth rates. As for the period since then (see Table 13.5), roughly from 1980 to 1990, Syria was the star with a rate of 19.2 per cent, but Oman, UAE, Jordan, Mauritania and Tunisia all recorded rates of over 5 per cent. What is of particular significance, however, are the negative rates for Kuwait and Saudi Arabia. With regard to imports, with the exception of Oman, UAE, Mauritania, Morocco, Tunisia and Syria, all recorded negative rates. Again, of particular importance are those of Kuwait, Libya, Saudi Arabia and Sudan. The performance of Kuwait, Saudi Arabia and Libya during this period could be explained by the world oil situation which necessitated curtailment of oil production in order to sustain higher oil prices. The performance of Sudan could be explained by the detrimental effects of high energy costs since the country is heavily dependent on oil imports as its essential energy source, but the political turmoil there may also have been an important factor. As for the terms of trade, their movement during 1960–70 was particularly favourable to the countries one would expect: the oil producing countries; all the others, except for Egypt, Sudan and Syria, experienced some deterioration in their terms of trade. Similar factors would explain the reversal in the movement of the terms of trade since 1970 (see Table 13.5) for the oil exporters.

The structure of merchandise exports also reveals what one would expect. In 1986, the bulk of the exports of certain countries was concentrated in the category of 'fuels, minerals and metals': Algeria (97 per cent), Kuwait (87 per cent), Libya (99 per cent), Oman (92 per cent), Saudi Arabia (90 per cent) and UAE (78 per cent). Comparable data was not available for Iraq, but the 1965 figure was 95 per cent. Egypt also had a high percentage (74 per cent). 'Other primary commodities' also loomed large in the exports of a number of countries: Egypt (14 per cent), Jordan (20 per cent), Morocco (27 per cent),

Table 13.5 Arab League exports, imports and terms of trade

Country	Annual average growth rate (%) Exports	Imports	Structure of trade: Fuels, minerals and metals % of Exports	Other primary commodities % of Exports	Machinery and transport equipment % of Imports	Other manufactures % of Imports	1970 = 100 Terms of trade
GCC							
Bahrain	na	na	na	na	na	na	na
Kuwait	–6.0	–4.4	5[a]	7[a]	42	41	86
Oman	8.4	1.2	90	2	44	32	84
Qatar	na	na	na	na	na	na	na
Saudi Arabia	–4.2	–5.5	90	1	33	45[b]	98
UAE	6.0	1.9	95[b]	1[b]	31[b]	43[b]	98
ACC							
Egypt	0.8	–1.5	55	12	31	34	99
Iraq	na	na	35[a]	41[a]	48[a]	33[a]	na
Jordan	5.8	–2.4	27	22	27	37	123
Yemen, Rep.	1.2	–5.3	22[e]	6[e]	88[e]	1[e]	88
AMU							
Algeria	3.0	–5.1	96	1	31	34	95
Libya	1.8[c]	–10.4[c]	100[a]	0	37[a]	43[a]	97

Mauritania	5.1	5.1	52	47	42[b]	28[a]	115
Morocco	3.9	4.0	14	29	29	31	114
Tunisia	7.2	3.0	13	12	32	46	100
Rest of AL							
Djibouti	na	na	na	na	na	na	na
Lebanon	na	na	na	na	na	na	na
Somalia	−8.4	−7.0	0[b]	99[b]	50[b]	21[b]	87[b]
Sudan	0.2[d]	−4.8[d]	3[b]	96[b]	22[b]	37[b]	91[b]
Syria	19.4	4.6	45[b]	17[b]	26[b]	32[b]	89
Israel	7.9	6.4	2	7	33	49	99

Notes
na means not available.
[a] data is for 1990.
[b] data is for 1992.
[c] the rate is for 1980–90.
[d] the rate is for 1980–92.
[e] data is for 1988.
Source: various issues of the World Bank's *World Development Report*.

Somalia (98 per cent), Sudan (98 per cent) and Yemen (91 per cent in 1965). Allowing for the impact of the Iraqi invasion of Kuwait on the latter's oil exports, the latest information given in Table 13.5 shows that, on the whole, the picture has not changed much since 1986. In short, the structure of merchandise exports is such that member nations of the League are heavily dependent on fuels, minerals, metals and other primary commodities.

The structure of imports is more or less the reverse. 'Machinery and transport equipment' and 'other manufactures' figure prominently, with the latter category even more so. This is important and should be borne in mind since the category of 'other manufactures' tends to be primarily consumer goods. Of course, fuels are either prominent or not insignificant for countries like Jordan, Morocco, Sudan, Syria, Tunisia (7 per cent) and Yemen. Moreover, food imports are significant for all members of the League.

With regard to the destination of exports, Algeria, Egypt, Kuwait, Libya, Mauritania, Morocco, Saudi Arabia, Sudan, Syria, Tunisia and Yemen conduct more than half their export trade with industrial market economies (i.e. members of the OECD) and the Eastern European countries that used to be members of the CMEA. If one were to go back to 1960, only Jordan, Lebanon and Yemen PDR conducted less than 50 per cent of their export trade with these groups of countries. Moreover, in 1981, only Lebanon, Somalia, the UAE and Yemen PDR conducted a substantial or significant proportion of their export trade with the five League nations which were referred to as 'high income oil exporters' by the World Bank. In terms of export trade with the developing world in general, only Iraq, Jordan and Yemen conducted over 50 per cent of their trade with them. Although equivalent recent data is not available, one should not expect much change from this pattern. In short, the general picture is that member nations of the League, on the whole, rely heavily for their export markets on advanced nations and the former Eastern European nations of the CMEA. This is in sharp contrast with advanced and ex-CMEA nations who conduct a high proportion of their export trade amongst themselves.

Given that the richer member nations of the League rely almost entirely on oil revenues, it is instructive to take a closer look at the League's oil sector – see Table 13.6. The table clearly shows that in 1979 the major oil producers were Algeria, Iraq, Kuwait, Libya, Saudi Arabia and the UAE. There was modest production in Egypt, Oman and Qatar. The remaining countries either produced insignificant

Table 13.6 Arab League oil sector

Country	Crude oil production (thousand barrels per day) 1979	Proven reserves (million barrels) 1979	Oil consumption (thousand barrels per day) 1978	Refining capacity (thousand barrels per day) 1985
GCC				
Bahrain	50	240	5.6	250
Kuwait	2,600	65,400	36.8	644
Oman	295	2,400	23.0	—
Qatar	500	3,760	8.4	10
Saudi Arabia	10,200	163,350	225.5	1,625
UAE	1,776	29,400	10.9	135
ACC				
Egypt	550	3,100	187.7	410
Iraq	3,500	31,000	175.8	320
Jordan	—	—	28.6	75
Yemen	—	—	5.3	—
AMU				
Algeria	1,210	8,440	102.1	502
Libya	2,020	23,500	80.2	138
Mauritania	—	—	3.7	20
Morocco	—	—	61.4	148
Tunisia	108	2,250	38.1	85
Rest of AL				
Djibouti	—	—	1.2	—
Lebanon	—	—	42.8	30
Somalia	—	—	4.6	10
Sudan	—	—	38.7	51
Syria	170	2,000	86.0	237
Yemen PDR	—	—	12.9	—
Total Arab	22,979	334,840	1,179.4	4,859
Total World	64,324	641,600	na	na

Notes
1. The 1985 data are estimates.
2. na = not available.

Sources: compiled from various sources.

quantities or nothing at all. The second column of the table also indicates that this ranking according to absolute production levels was consistent with that for proven reserves, that is, the largest producers had the largest capacity for production. A comparison of the first and third columns reveals that practically all the oil producers are net exporters of oil. However, a degree of caution has to be exercised here since the production figures are for 1979 while the consumption data is for 1978, but it would have taken a drastic turn of events to change the consumption growth rate in such a way as to reverse this position. However, if one were to consider a longer period such as 1960–80, there would be some obvious variations. One should note that Jordan, Morocco, Sudan, Syria, Tunisia and Yemen depend heavily on oil imports.

The table also refers to refining capacity (final column). It shows Saudi Arabia and Kuwait continuing to head the ranking in this respect. However, other countries will also become of some significance. Hence this column reflects the changing oil fortunes of the individual member nations of the League.

From this very brief survey, one can see that the member nations of the League are either very poor developing countries, some with great potential for agriculture and industry, or financially rich nations with economies which will continue to be viable for as long as the oil revenues (or, depending on the stock of accumulated financial wealth, an adequate stream of revenues generated by their appropriate investment) last. It could also be seen that the economies of the League are heavily dependent on foreign trade, particularly on trade with advanced nations and the ex-CMEA Eastern European countries, that is, they conduct a very small proportion of their trade amongst themselves.

Therefore, despite the apparent financial prosperity of some of the member nations of the League, its totality can be described as poor, hence in need of economic development. This is because the financially rich countries have no secure future economic base (more on this in the next section) and are therefore subject to the same predicament. Thus, as has long been recognised in the literature on international economic integration (see Chapter 3; Robson, 1980; El-Agraa, 1981, 1982, 1989, 1994), the level of intra-area trade is irrelevant when one considers the economic integration of the League. What is needed is to increase the size of market so as to encourage optimum plant installations, hence the need for economic integration (see Robson, 1983 and El-Agraa, 1989 for a full discussion of this issue). To put it differently:

> the neoclassical analysis of [economic] integration among developing countries starts from an entirely different developmental stand-

> point. It is assumed that there is a valid case for protecting certain activities – particularly industry – either for the purpose of increasing income or the rate of growth, or in order to attain certain non-economic objectives that are sought for their own sake. To attain the latter may entail economic sacrifice, but that would not negate the argument. The implications of economic integration in these terms can best be considered within a broader framework than that often employed, in which account is formally taken of... economies of scale... and... divergencies between private and social costs of production. The gains from integration can then be analysed in the particularly relevant context of opportunities to exploit economies of scale that cannot be secured in single markets, and the implications of market imperfections can also be brought about. Imperfections typically arise when certain goods and services do not fully pass through the market, thus giving rise to external economies and diseconomies, or when government policies distort prices of factors and goods. (Robson, 1983, pp. 6–7)

The relevance of these issues to the League will become apparent after we have examined the oil revenues more closely.

OIL REVENUES

The world economy was subjected to severe shocks as a result of the oil price increases of 1973–4 and 1979–80. Beblawi (1984) correctly argued that these shocks led to increased savings by members of OPEC, including the Arab group within the organisation, which is roughly equivalent to OAPEC. Beblawi claimed that these increased savings could be disposed of in any of three ways: (i) an increase in the global rate of real investment; (ii) dissavings by the non-OPEC countries of the world to exactly offset OPEC's increased savings; and (iii) an increase in financial assets. He labelled (i) the 'investment' case, (ii) the 'distribution of wealth' case and (iii) the 'placement' case.

The first two cases are too obvious to warrant further consideration. Beblawi argued that the placement case meant that the increase in OPEC's financial assets had to be matched by a corresponding increase in the financial liabilities of deficit countries. Assuming that real capital stocks remained unchanged, the issuance of new financial assets meant that capital would now have a wider ownership. The new owners would expect to receive the *nominal* going rate of return on their assets (but the marginal *real* return must surely decline). Beblawi concluded that with nominal rewards being fixed, the increase in financial assets must result in a corresponding absolute increase in nominal earnings in property titles, that is, they must increase the share of profits. He asserted that the increase in OPEC's savings, unmatched by increased real investment, must necessarily be inflationary. Therefore, OPEC's gains from oil price increases would be eroded by this extra inflation. Beblawi recommended that OPEC countries should invest their newly acquired financial resources in the developing nations, since they are capital hungry but unable to secure adequate finance. Such a channelling of resources would ensure an increase in real investment with benefits all round.

I have taken issue with this analysis elsewhere (El-Agraa, 1984d), since a decline in the real marginal return may or may not increase the share of profits, indeed the share may even decline. Also, the three cases do not offer mutually exclusive alternatives. However, such an analysis will not negate Beblawi's recommendation for OPEC to invest in the developing countries (see p. 340). For our purposes, it is important to note that Beblawi's recommendation also applies to OAPEC: members of OAPEC should be encouraged to invest in developing countries. At present, OAPEC nations continue to deposit the bulk of their newly acquired financial assets in the financial markets of the advanced western nations. Admittedly, some of these resources are routed as investment in developing nations, but only a small proportion is invested in this way and with no coherent strategy in mind.

A relevant piece of information that should be mentioned in this context is that the total amount of assistance given by Arab donors to Arab nations is modest when compared with the financial resources accumulated in the advanced nations. For example, over the period 1970–82, it amounted to about $36 billion at a time when the financial resources accumulated by the Arabs in the advanced nations were estimated at $350 billion in 1982 (Kubursi, 1980 and van den Boogaerde, 1991). Moreover, the percentage of that aid which went to Arab countries declined from 100 per cent in the early 1970s to under 50 per cent during the 1980s. Equivalent recent information has proved impossible to obtain, but Tables 13.7a and 13.7b give the absolute and percentage figures for Official Development Assistance (ODA) provided by member nations of OAPEC between 1975 and 1993. The figures clearly show a sharp decline since 1982 which is no doubt attributable to the fall in the price of crude oil during this

Table 13.7a Arab League ODA (US$ millions)

Year	Algeria	Iraq	Kuwait	Libya	Qatar	Saudi Arabia	UAE	Total	% to Arabs
1975	41	215	946	259	338	2,756	1,046	5,601	76.9
1976	11	123	706	98	180	2,791	1,028	4,937	72.4
1977	35	103	1,032	130	127	2,900	1,091	5,418	81.3
1978	39	123	1,001	132	95	5,250	889	7,529	49.3
1979	281	658	971	145	282	3,941	968	7,246	60.0
1980	81	864	1,140	376	277	5,682	1,118	9,538	54.3
1981	55	207	1,163	257	246	5,514	805	8,247	53.0
1982	129	52	1,161	44	139	3,854	406	5,785	56.8
1983	37	−10	997	144	20	3,259	351	4,798	62.4
1984	52	−22	1,020	24	10	3,194	88	4,366	52.8
1985	54	−32	771	57	8	2,630	122	3,610	84.8
1986	114	−21	715	68	18	3,517	87	4,498	48.5
1987	39	−35	316	66	0	2,888	15	3,289	53.4
1988	13	−21	108	129	4	2,048	−17	2,264	40.9
1989	42	36	170	174	−3	1,171	65	1,655	49.4
1990	7	78	1,295	37	−2	3,692	888	5,995	na
1991	3	−3	389	15	1	1,704	558	2,667	na
1992	7	−28	202	40	1	962	169	1,395	na
1993	7	—	381	27	1	811	236	1,463	na

Source: various issues of World Bank's *World Development Report*, but the last column comes from Boogaerde (1991), p. 73, with some data variation due to the inclusion of other Arab countries.

period, but some would argue that the decline is due to the support given to Iraq during (and after?) its war with Iran, support which is not registered in the official statistics.

Before proceeding further, it is vital to examine the demand for investment in the poor nations of the League in order to compare it with the supply of financial assistance made available through the rich oil-producing Arab nations. A good and appropriate (in the sense of being realistic, but not necessarily economically rational) approximation to this is the demand for investment as determined by these countries' own development plans. Table 13.8 provides this information for the member nations of the League with such plans for varying periods during the 1970s.

The total investment required by the poorest nations of the League (Egypt, Jordan, Lebanon, Mauritania, Somalia, Sudan and the Yemen) was about $34 billion for an average of four years at 1974–8 world conditions, that is, about $8.5 billion per annum – see

Table 13.7b Arab League ODA (as percentage of donor GDP)

Year	Algeria	Iraq	Kuwait	Libya	Qatar	Saudi Arabia	UAE	Total
1975	0.28	1.62	7.18	2.29	15.58	7.76	11.68	5.73
1976	0.07	0.76	4.82	0.66	7.35	5.95	8.95	4.23
1977	0.18	0.55	8.19	0.73	5.09	4.93	7.50	3.95
1978	0.15	0.55	5.53	0.75	3.29	8.06	6.38	4.51
1979	0.90	1.97	3.52	0.60	6.07	5.16	5.08	1.75
1980	0.20	2.36	3.52	1.16	4.16	4.15	4.06	3.26
1981	0.13	0.94	3.65	0.81	3.50	3.45	2.57	2.52
1982	0.31	0.13	4.34	0.15	2.13	2.50	2.22	1.81
1983	0.08	−0.02	3.38	0.51	0.40	2.69	1.26	1.70
1984	0.10	−0.05	3.95	0.10	0.18	3.20	0.32	1.60
1985	0.10	−0.06	2.96	0.24	0.12	2.92	0.45	1.39
1986	0.19	−0.05	2.84	0.30	0.36	3.99	0.41	1.80
1987	0.07	−0.08	1.15	0.30	0.00	3.70	0.07	1.10
1988	0.02	−0.04	0.39	0.62	0.06	2.73	−0.07	0.85
1989	0.07	0.05	0.53	0.80	−0.04	1.64	0.23	0.56
1990	0.01	0.11	5.13	0.14	0.03	3.42	2.64	1.80
1991	0.01	0.00	2.45	0.05	0.01	1.60	1.64	—
1992	0.01	−0.04	0.87	0.15	0.01	0.80	0.48	—
1993	0.01	--	1.30	0.12	0.02	0.70	0.66	—

Source: various issues of World Bank's *World Development Report.*

Table 13.8a. The figure increases to about $40 billion if one were to add Morocco. During this period the total aid provided by OAPEC to other Arab countries was just over $15 billion, that is, less than half the amount required by the poorest nations or over a third if Algeria and Morocco were to be added. Hence, if all the investments that were required to finance the development plans of the poorest nations of the League were to be met by the richer members of OAPEC, all that would have been needed was a doubling of OAPEC's assistance to them. If Morocco were to be counted in, a trebling would have been necessary. The accumulated financial resources of OAPEC at the end of 1982 would have guaranteed such aid for about three decades. Of course, these figures are on the excessive side since they are based on the assumption that the poor member nations of the League do not have to provide any domestic resources towards these investments.

Again, it has proved difficult to obtain comparable recent information, especially on the investment required by national plans, but Table 13.8b shows that in the peak years, 1974–5, official Arab assistance to Arab aid recipient countries amounted to about one

Table 13.8a Arab League investment allocation by national plan

Country	*Plan period*	*Investment*	
		Total (US$ million)	*Average annual (US$ million)*
GCC			
Bahrain	—	—	—
Kuwait	1976–80	16,609	3,322
Oman	1976–80	3,922	748
Qatar	—	—	—
Saudi Arabia	1975–80	140,346	23,391
UAE	1977–79	4,385	1,462
ACC			
Egypt	1976–80	20,407	4,081
Iraq	1976–80	45,561	9,112
Jordan	1976–80	2,308	464
Yemen	1976–80	3,500	700
AMU			
Algeria	1974–77	27,575	6,894
Libya	1976–80	24,219	4,844
Mauritania	1976–80	206	41
Morocco	1973–77	6,197	1,236
Tunisia	1977–81	9,790	1,958
Rest of AL			
Djibouti	—	—	—
Lebanon	1972–77	539	90
Somalia	1974–78	615	123
Sudan	1977–83	6,030	1,005
Syria	1976–80	13,712	2,742
Yemen PDR	1974–79	216	43

Note
— = there was no development plan.
Sources: Kubursi (1980) and official national plans, with corrections.

quarter of the latter group's investment. This percentage has steadily declined over the years, for the reasons mentioned above, but a return to the peak percentage over the entire period from 1973 to 1989 would have provided official assistance of US$192 billion, that is, if all the investment by the Arab recipients were to be provided by the rich Arab nations US$668 billion would have been needed (calculated from van den Boogaerde 1991, table 39, p. 79). Given the data in the previous paragraph, this would not have been inconceivable.

Table 13.8b Total official Arab assistance as percentage of investment by Arab recipient countries

Year	*Total*	*Arab Middle East*[a]	*Arab Africa*[b]
1973	15.6	18.2	13.1
1974	24.0	29.2	20.6
1975	22.8	19.5	22.5
1976	16.8	16.3	14.1
1977	14.5	14.3	14.1
1978	10.5	12.7	8.7
1979	12.0	21.7	5.3
1980	11.3	17.9	5.7
1981	9.1	12.7	5.2
1982	5.5	8.2	2.4
1983	4.4	7.7	0.8
1984	3.7	7.4	0.6
1985	4.1	6.2	2.0
1986	3.2	7.0	0.4
1987	2.4	5.4	0.3
1988	1.5	1.9	0.8
1989	2.7	7.9	1.7

Notes
[a] These are Bahrain, Iraq, Jordan, Lebanon, Oman, Syria and the Republic of Yemen.
[b] These are Algeria, Egypt, Mauritania, Morocco, Somalia, Sudan and Tunisia.
Sources: Selected from Boogaerde (1991), p. 83.

If the richer nations of OAPEC are to provide the resources which are needed to finance the investment plans of the poorer member nations within the League, they will most certainly want some guarantees with regard to both the carrying out of the agreed investments and the securing of a reasonable rate of return on them, both equally important considerations. After all, they can always continue to earn the going nominal rate offered by the financial markets in the advanced world without too much risk of default. The problems with this will become clear after some consideration is given to the type of cooperation that is required by the League.

To propose that the richer nations within OAPEC should provide the investment funds needed by their poor member nations within the League is to suggest that the mere execution of the economic plans, which are conceived by each individual nation for its own economy, is economically rational for the whole of the League. Such a proposal also suffers from the practical problem that if each poor member nation is automatically guaranteed the financial resources to carry out whatever plan it desires, there would be every incentive for these nations to inflate their plans, hence their investment requirements. There is therefore a need not only to ensure against such temptation but also to secure the appropriate utilisation of the resources of the League for the totality of its membership; it should be apparent that what is good for one member nation need not be so for the whole of the League. Indeed, one can visualise situations where the overall strategy might seem like a complete calamity from the single member nation's original own point of view. This consideration is vital since it relates to the earlier point about an acceptable rate of return for the countries providing the fund.

APPROPRIATE ECONOMIC INTEGRATION

We have seen that the richer countries within the League depend heavily on oil revenues. These revenues cannot be guaranteed indefinitely: they will last as long as the oil lasts. Once oil is depleted, these countries will have to depend on the flow of income from their assets and accumulated financial resources, which will be no more than a fraction of the present flows. Moreover, the rate of increase in accumulated resources has been declining due to the sharp oil price reductions in the 1980s. Of course, these countries have made attempts to construct plants, at prohibitive running costs, to produce the food and products which they need and for which they are not naturally suited. However, such attempts are doomed to failure since their running costs are sustainable only for as long as the oil revenues last. What is needed, therefore, is an *overall* development plan which ensures that each nation within the League will be assigned the task of exploiting its potential to the full *provided* this is beneficial for the League as a whole. This does not mean that countries will be asked to produce only what is needed for consumption within the League; it also means that those countries which are capable of producing commodities for export to the rest of the world should be encouraged to do so.

As things stand at present, countries like Iraq, Mauritania and the Sudan have a tremendous potential for food and agricultural production; some claim that the Sudan can feed the whole of the Arab world and still have something left over to export. Countries like Egypt, Lebanon and Syria have some skilled labour and have started the process of industrialisation, so they may be most suitable for concentrating on industrial development. However, these are simply examples of resource allocation decisions, but what I really want to stress is that resources should be allocated in such a way that whenever there is a potential for the League as a whole, it should be exploited. Such an allocation procedure is necessarily dynamic, hence the decision-making authorities must be sufficiently flexible to exploit the potential as and when it arises. There will therefore be a need not only for resource appraisal but also for both short- and long-term planning.

This recommendation is tantamount to specifying that there should be a single and coherent economic development plan for the whole of the League, that is, national plans as presently understood should become regional sub-plans within the context of the overall strategy. Hence, what one member nation may envisage as the appropriate plan for itself may be deemed inappropriate for the good of the whole; indeed, the present trend of each member nation wanting to set up its own industry will be seen as utterly meaningless. It should then become apparent that such an overall plan cannot possibly be drawn up by a group of completely *independent* nations. In short, the acceptance of this recommendation is tantamount to the acceptance of some sort of political integration of the member countries of the League. This is because the recommendation does not mean that the rich OAPEC nations should dictate what the poor member nations within the League are to produce; it simply means that there should be a joint body to draw up an overall and dynamic economic strategy. This implies not only that some of the poor member countries will have to produce certain goods, but also that some OAPEC countries will be asked to discontinue production of certain commodities. Hence, the burden is equally shared: those countries which are poor will have to accept *common* decisions about what to produce, while the rich oil producers will have to accede to *common* decisions about their abstaining from simply depositing their financial resources with the financial centres of the advanced countries and about not utilising these resources within their own territories.

Finally, it should be stressed that this recommendation calls for a joint authority to determine the overall strategy as well as its regional implications. Such an authority will not be effective without the political (and military) backing necessary for any present-day government to enable it to carry out its mandate. Hence the type of integration that is needed involves a great deal of political unification; after all some sort of authority will be needed to guarantee the delivery of the agreed returns to the countries providing the necessary finance. This is a very serious issue indeed since member nations of the League follow widely differing political persuasions. On the other hand, as we have seen, although the member nations founded the League as an economic scheme, they have extended it to include joint military defence against attack on any member nation; thus one could argue that this effectively makes it a political organisation. Therefore, it is the most appropriate institution within which one should promote this recommendation, if only to test the member nations about the seriousness with which they take their organisation.

IMPLICATIONS AND CONCLUSION

The conclusion reached is that if members of the League are seriously concerned with their economic development and are prepared to use their military forces to defend each other, the best means of doing so, given their disparate fortunes, is to utilise their *own* resources for their *own* good. This recipe requires overall planning which can be effective only if the League becomes an economically as well as a politically integrated area since experience has shown that insistence on national sovereignty within the context of economic and political integration would simply not work, and the guarantee for the delivery of the goods and the required returns depends entirely on a common pooling of sovereignty. The implication of this is that although one is inclined to applaud the formation of the ACC and AMU, and the GCC before that, all three schemes fall far short of the ideal, particularly since none of them can be classified as a self-sufficient group in the sense adopted here, that is, as a viable long-term economic unit. This is because member nations of the GCC have neither an agricultural nor an industrial potential, member nations of the ACC have no major supplier of finance (unless Iraq returns to the fold and the world price of crude petroleum recovers its pre-1979 height which is plainly impossible), and the countries of the AMU have no adequate agricultural potential, which is why they wanted Sudan to join them soon.

One implication of this recommendation is that the position of the Sudan needs to be re-examined along the lines I suggested in the past (El-Agraa, 1969). All member nations of the League have something in common: the majority of their populations speak Arabic and are Muslim. Those who are Muslim but whose native tongue is not Arabic (Mauritania) are able to understand the language due to their daily recital of the *Koran*. The large Christian population of Lebanon does speak Arabic and the Orthodox Catholics (Coptics) of Egypt do likewise. However, the Sudan is unique in that its northern population speaks Arabic and is largely Muslim, but its southern population is neither Muslim nor speaks Arabic as a native tongue, and when Arabic is spoken, it is because it is obligatory at school. The fighting between the north and south of Sudan, which has been going on virtually since Sudan gained its independence, is a clear manifestation of the disharmony that prevails within that nation. One cannot go into this issue here, but what should be emphasised is that the peoples of southern Sudan resent being part of a country which has adopted Arabic as its official language and Islam as its constitutional religion. In short, the southern Sudanese do not see themselves as a part of this 'Arabness'. Hence, if the Sudan decides to follow the League along the lines recommended here, the logical implication would be that the south must be granted the independence it has been fighting for ever since 1957. It is ironic that member nations of the League have been complaining about irrational borders created by the colonial powers yet continue to preserve them at the risk of their own survival.

The second implication of this recommendation relates to its impact on the rest of the world economy. The non-participating countries can be split into two: the developing countries and advanced nations. The newly industrialising economies (NIEs) do not matter in this respect since they will have to fit into one or other of the two groups, for reasons that will become apparent in due course.

As far as the developing countries are concerned, it is difficult to detect any detrimental effect. This is because the recommendation envisages the League plan being financed by OAPEC resources, with the implication that aid from the advanced nations to the poor members of the League will be dispensed with. Therefore, these released resources can be allocated by the advanced nations to *other* developing countries. This is in the immediate short run. In the long-term, the enhancement of the League economy should enable it to trade more with these nations and in the process enhance the economies of the non-League developing world.

What will be the impact on the advanced world, especially on those countries like Switzerland, the UK and the USA where most of the financial resources and assets of the rich OAPEC countries are kept? The short-term effect may seem negative, but is actually far from being so. This is because the bulk of these resources will not be withdrawn at all, since they will be used to purchase the capital equipment made necessary by the overall plan. This should transfer some of the accumulated financial resources into the production of real goods, thus generating output and employment in the advanced nations. Of course, not all the countries of the advanced world can gain in this way since there would definitely be some redistribution, but the overall impact should be clear for the short term. However, the distribution may favour the ex-CMEA economies if these resources are used to buy capital goods from them, but experience suggests that, on the whole, this would be highly unlikely. In the long-term, the enhancement of the economies of the member nations of the League, as well as of the countries receiving the orders for the needed capital goods, should generate enough demand to benefit most. Of course, distributional effects cannot be ruled out but one can be certain that any adverse impact would be minor.

Finally, it should be apparent that the introduction of a third group to represent the NIEs would not alter this picture. If the NIEs were presently in receipt of OAPEC assistance, the implication for them would be the same as for the developing countries. If the NIEs were themselves donating assistance to some member nations of the League, they would fall into the category of advanced nations. Of course, enhanced economic growth in the League might favour trade with the NIEs at the expense of the advanced countries, but it should be obvious that this would have nothing to do with the recommendation put forward here; it would simply be a reflection of the natural development of the world economy.

14 Integration in Sub-Saharan Africa

Peter Robson

AN OVERALL VIEW

Reculer pour mieux sauter is not a dictum that seems to carry much weight among African governments involved in regional integration. On the contrary, if a certain level of integration cannot be made to work, the reaction of policy-makers has typically been to embark on something more elaborate, more advanced and more demanding in terms of administrative requirements and political commitment. Thus, although the Preferential Trading Area for East and Southern Africa (PTA) has conspicuously failed to deliver significant benefits, it has been replaced by the much more ambitious Common Market for Eastern and Southern Africa (COMESA) which additionally aims to create a monetary union. Likewise, although the West African Economic Community (CEAO – see Robson, 1988) was not fully implemented, it has been replaced by an Act constituting an economic and monetary union. In certain policy areas of which monetary union is the most notable, a big leap might well, as European experience and economic analysis both suggest, be an appropriate strategy. The alternative of a long gestation period during which exchange rates are fixed within a bloc and monetary policies are coordinated has been shown to pose immense operational difficulties. By contrast, with regard to trade and investment, it is difficult to find any grounds that would support a big leap strategy.

The context of African regional integration has changed greatly in the past decade and in some ways for the better. An emphasis on trade liberalisation and tariff reform in structural adjustment programmes, coupled with the results and commitments of the last round of tariff negotiations under the General Agreement on Tariffs and Trade (GATT now WTO) all point to a reduction of the costs of preferential arrangements and of customs unions for many countries. Fiscal reforms, too, involving a relative increase in the role of non-discriminatory indirect taxation, such as value-added tax (VAT) at the expense of customs duties levied on imports only, have also contributed to a significant alteration of the constraints and opportunities of regional integration. In the current context, many of the benefits of integration in Africa stem from what may be termed unorthodox sources, that is, they are of the kinds that the European Union (EU) has emphasised in its single European market (SEM) initiative–see Chapter 5. Among these, the traditional advantages that motivated early customs unions, namely savings in administrative and transactions costs, bulk large. To obtain these benefits, however, administrative and institutional reforms are a prerequisite. Unless these reforms can be introduced, so permitting an elimination of fiscal frontiers, and a consequent substantial reduction in rent-seeking activities, any wider benefits of regional trade integration will continue to elude African blocs.

Monetary integration is, however, one policy area where African experience has been relatively successful in terms of the promotion of trade and the delivery of macroeconomic stability. Indeed, African experience provides some of the longest standing and instructive examples of the problems of operating a single currency in groups of independent states (Cobham and Robson, 1994). Currently, three monetary unions exist in Africa. These embody some fifteen separate states, namely, the two francophone franc zone unions, in West and Central Africa, and the Common Monetary Area of Southern Africa. In this domain, the most notable event of recent years has been the devaluation of the CFA franc, in January 1994, by 50 per cent in foreign currency terms. For many years the francophone unions and their supposedly immutable fixed rate *vis-à-vis* the French franc assured their member states a better economic performance than their neighbours (Guillaumont *et al.*, 1988; Devarejan and de Melo, 1987, 1991). In recent years, however, the substantially overvalued CFA franc has constituted a major obstacle to structural reform and the export promotion efforts of francophone African countries. Apart from that, serious operational weaknesses of the previous system have been widely recognised. In an attempt to overcome those weaknesses, important initiatives in the fields of banking reform and macroeconomic surveillance have been elaborated in the regional reform programme of the World Bank for UDEAC which has become the Central African Economic and Monetary Community, and in initiatives with somewhat similar objectives that are in train for the

West African Economic and Monetary Union. These initiatives should have significantly favourable effects for the macroeconomic policies and financial institutions of the countries concerned if they are fully implemented (Guillaumont and Guillaumont-Jeanneney, 1993).

This chapter is only incidentally concerned with regional monetary integration in Sub-Saharan Africa. Its primary focus is on regional economic integration, in the sense of customs union and common market initiatives and related non-monetary measures aimed at integrating markets for goods and services. Initiatives for such purposes have been numerous, but with a few exceptions their outcomes have been disappointing. Not surprisingly, donors and international institutions remain for the most part conspicuously unenthusiastic about such policies. Nevertheless, they continue to support certain initiatives of a more or less traditional kind, apparently in the hope of making the best of a bad job. They also support certain more novel initiatives that seek to promote market integration by removing obstacles to cross-border investment. Cooperation in fields other than trade, such as transport, telecommunications, education, and so on, is also assisted. Indeed, the new conventional wisdom appears to be that it is through cooperation rather than integration that the path ahead lies. During the past decade, however, little or no substantive progress has been made in either dimension of integration (Langhammer and Hiemenz, 1990; Foroutan, 1993), despite support from the African Development Bank, the World Bank, and to some extent from the EU.

ECOWAS, the largest bloc, which includes the Nigerian giant and countries which generate much of the GDP of middle Africa, has made little substantive progress since its establishment in 1975 (Berg, 1993). In 1993 its 16 member states signed a revised Treaty. Among other things, this envisages the restructuring of the ECOWAS Fund for Cooperation, Compensation and Development. The transformation of the latter into a Development Bank has been mooted. As to COMESA, which in December 1994 succeeded the geographically far-reaching PTA, there are few grounds for expecting it to fare better than ECOWAS. The Southern African Development Community (SADC) which includes eleven Southern African countries together with Mauritius also aims to eliminate internal trade barriers and obstacles to free movement. At the time of writing, most SADC members with the significant exception of South Africa are also members of COMESA, although a SADC decision of August 1994 requires its members to withdraw from the PTA. Overlapping membership of often incompatible regional integration arrangements is not uncommon throughout Africa. Inevitably, where it is found, it invites doubt on the seriousness of the engagements in question. There are, nevertheless, at least two African schemes where, with some reshaping, commitment founded on established interests may allow a continued and enhanced integration role to be played. Each of the two schemes links countries having strong linguistic, historical, cultural and economic ties. The first is the Southern African Customs Union (SACU), which has an unbroken and, in its limited sphere, a quite successful history which goes back some eighty years. Indeed, SACU represents the only African instance of a customs union that is fully operational. This agreement is currently being renegotiated. Some see the renegotiation as an opportunity for creating a more flexible system around which a wider group of Southern African countries might coalesce (Maasdorp, 1994). All members of SACU except Botswana also participate in the Common Monetary Area which constitutes a form of monetary union. The second scheme which appears to be grounded in more than rhetoric is the West African Economic and Monetary Union (Union Economique et Monétaire Ouest-Africaine or UEMOA). This grouping was formally initiated in 1994. It aims to transform the existing quite successful monetary union of West Africa into a full economic union. This sequence does not really reverse the conventionally expected progression in regional integration from customs union towards a common market and beyond to economic and monetary union, because in effect the newly established UEMOA replaces the CEAO which had been faltering for more than a decade, and which was finally abolished with the creation of UEMOA. The Union's membership is initially limited to the countries of the monetary union and is thus not identical with that of CEAO. The treaty which creates UEMOA is largely concerned with the customs union and common market aspects of union, while the operation of the monetary union itself basically remains subject to the existing UMOA Treaty.

THE SOUTHERN AFRICAN CUSTOMS UNION

Introduction

Southern African integration arrangements encompass the Republic of South Africa, together with Botswana, Lesotho, Namibia and

Swaziland (BLNS). Except for Botswana, which has had its own currency for a number of years, all of these countries participate in both SACU and the Rand-based Common Monetary Area. The customs union arrangements themselves have an unbroken history going back some eighty years. The existing SACU Agreement was signed in 1969 and was amended in 1976. Moves to renegotiate it subsequently commenced in 1981. South Africa was on the verge of withdrawing from it in 1993, viewing the arrangement as too costly. Since then the attitude of South Africa has changed and the present government has accepted the importance of the customs union for itself, for BLNS and, potentially, for economic integration in the wider Southern African region. Renegotiation is currently in train under the auspices of a task team appointed in November 1994.

The main features of the present agreement are: (i) a revenue-sharing formula that was designed to compensate BLNS for trade diversion, polarisation of industrial development and the loss of fiscal sovereignty; (ii) a number of provisions designed to enable BLNS to develop industries and diversify their economies. The revenue formula was later amended to stabilise the revenues of BLNS. The amendment guarantees BLNS a minimum rate of revenue on imports of 17 per cent. Renegotiation will centre on the revenue allocation provisions, but the developmental provisions also seem likely to figure importantly. A further aspect will concern the administration of SACU, which, in terms of policies, has hitherto been a matter solely for its hegemonic member state. The recent GATT negotiations, for instance, were handled exclusively by South Africa with no apparent consideration being given to the special interests of its partners. The resulting tariff offer on its part was subsequently simply adopted *in toto* by each of the other partners. Explicit recognition of the interests of the other countries in any future tariff initiatives, to be reflected in institutional innovation in a revised agreement, is one of the objectives sought by BLNS in the current renegotiations. A brief review of the 1969 agreement serves to underline both its merits in customs union terms and its limitations as a development instrument from the standpoint of the smaller parties.

The 1969 Agreement

Until 1969, BLNS merely received the customs and excise revenues attributable to them in respect of their estimated imports from outside the customs union. Over time, the basis of estimation of imports itself had become empirically unsatisfactory. In addition, BLNS were suffering in revenue and real income terms from the effects of South Africa's highly protective industrial policy that had been adopted in 1925. On their independence, BLS sought a new agreement. The unilateral introduction of a sales tax by South Africa in March 1969 was a major contributory factor in inducing all parties to bring the protracted negotiations on a new agreement to an early conclusion. The new agreement was signed in December of the same year and came into force in March 1970.

The agreement sets out its general aim as being to ensure the continued economic development of the area as a whole and in particular the development of its less advanced members, and the diversification of their economies. The disadvantages to BLNS of a customs union with a much more advanced country were perceived to be the costs of trade diversion, of polarisation of development, and the loss of fiscal sovereignty. To compensate for these three disadvantages, a much improved revenue-sharing formula was introduced, which was then subject to enhancement. The resulting formula is unique in the experience of customs unions. All customs, excises and sales duties (but not general sales taxes) collected in the member countries are pooled at the South African Reserve Bank. Essentially, the formula seeks in the first place to divide that common revenue pool among BLNS in proportion to their annual imports from all sources, including South Africa, and in proportion to their consumption of excisable goods. This basis of division would in itself roughly compensate BLNS for the costs of trade diversion by providing those countries with the average rate of revenue for the area, even in respect of their imports from South Africa. However, the proceeds on that basis were then enhanced by 42 per cent. This enhancement can be taken to represent, at that time, compensation for the costs of polarisation and the loss of fiscal discretion, since there is evidence that, initially, basic revenue shares corresponded roughly to the amounts that BLNS could themselves have raised by the imposition of a tariff that would have left the prices of all goods unchanged by comparison with the position in the customs union (the so-called iso-price tariff).

Four important points may be noted in relation to this formula: (i) BLS exports to South Africa do not reduce their share of the pool; (ii) the inclusion of excise duties constitutes a step beyond customs union in the direction of fiscal union; (iii) the share of revenue of the so-called TVBC states, that is, of the homelands, was determined in the same way; and (iv) the share of South Africa itself is a residual after formula payments have been made to BLS, Namibia (and, until their demise, to the homelands).

From the standpoint of BLNS, the revenue-sharing formula turned out to have one important technical weakness, namely, it produced substantial fluctuations in their revenue receipts. To overcome this disadvantage, the formula was amended in the mid-1970s to incorporate a stabilisation factor. This operates so as to provide BLNS with receipts from the agreement amounting to a minimum rate of 17 per cent and a maximum of 23 per cent of the value of their imports and their production and consumption of excisable products.

The second important aspect of the 1969 agreement is the provision that was made – unusual in a customs union agreement – for encouraging the development of the less advanced countries of the customs union. This took a number of forms. In the first place, Article 6 permitted BLNS countries to protect new industries by imposing additional duties. They would collect the duties themselves and remit the proceeds to the common revenue pool. Secondly, Article 7 provided that a BLNS country could, by agreement, specify an industry as being of major economic importance, whereupon South Africa could not reduce import duty on its products without the consent of the government concerned.

During the late 1970s, SACU was subjected to considerable academic scrutiny. A highly critical appraisal based on its claimed detrimental developmental effects on BLS was presented by Mosley (1978) and Cobbe (1980). Mosley's appraisal was itself criticised by Robson (1978) and Landell-Mills (1979).

By the end of the decade it had become clear that neither South Africa nor the BLNS countries were satisfied with the agreement. For both sides much of this dissatisfaction centred on its revenue aspects. On the one hand, the BLNS countries sought an increase in the stabilised rate, arguing that the deal had for various reasons become less satisfactory from their standpoints. For its part, the South African government was concerned with its declining share, which had fallen from 96 per cent in 1969 to 75 per cent in 1980. It continued to fall to less than 40 per cent by 1992–3. South Africa's share of the pool has declined, however, mainly because of the slower rate of growth of its economy and hence of its imports in comparison with developments in BLNS. Under the influence of sanctions, the South African economy stagnated for two decades prior to 1993. If its exports had been 50 per cent higher – a not inconceivable outcome under the conditions of pre-1975 growth – its share of the larger pool (including

Transkei, Bophuthatswana, Venda and Ciskei, the so-called TBVC states which, since the new Constitution, no longer exist) would for 1992–3 have been nearly 80 per cent.

By the early 1980s, the South African government's concern with declining revenue shares led it to decide to renegotiate the whole agreement. With that in mind it commissioned a study by Professor McCarthy to investigate the issues. Among its important recommendations (McCarthy, 1986) were that an industrial strategy to counter polarisation should be formulated for SACU as a whole; that the enhancement element of BLNS receipts should be converted into conditional development finance; and that a so-called 'clean' formula should be introduced for revenue sharing without enhancement. (The present official position seems currently to favour such an approach.) McCarthy also recommended that BLNS should be represented on South Africa's Board of Tariffs and Trade.

For most of the following period leading up to the formation of the Government of National Unity, in May 1994, the possibility of reconciling the diverse economic and policy objectives of the then South African government and of BLNS appeared to be remote, and dissolution of SACU appeared to be not out of the question. Indeed, it was reported in May 1993 that the South African government was on the point of publishing a document recommending dissolution. Within a few months, however, the South African government had adopted a positive stance towards the value of SACU. That position, despite their own reservations on particular aspects, was echoed by the governments of BLNS. The African National Congress also, in the run-up to the 1994 elections, displayed a positive attitude to both SACU and the problems and aspirations of BLNS and recognised the responsibility of South Africa towards its neighbours. The upshot is that the political climate for renegotiation as far as BLNS are concerned is more favourable than it has been for some time. Moreover, there is growing awareness within South Africa of the considerable importance of the markets of BLNS for South African products. In 1992, for instance, BLNS took one quarter of South Africa's exports of manufactures. Without SACU, South African exporters could face severe competition in the markets of BLNS. There is a further danger that products dumped in BLNS could easily find their way through the permeable frontiers into South Africa. At the same time, both the changing global context and the redirection of South Africa's own economic strategy, coupled with its urgent need to promote development in its own less advanced regions, combine to suggest that difficult choices will have to be faced by all sides in the passage to a new agreement. In the following sections, the revenue and economic development contexts of the negotiations will be more specifically addressed.

The Revenue Formula

Despite the objections that have been made to it by BLNS and its apologists, by any reasonable criteria, the revenue deal, at least in the years immediately following the introduction of the 1969 agreement, produced an extremely generous outcome. This is because, at that period, the basic rate of duty for the customs area as a whole appears to have been approximately equivalent to the product of an iso-price tariff. Consequently, the enhancement factor of 42 per cent could be regarded as compensation for the costs of industrial polarisation and for the loss of fiscal discretion on the part of BLNS. The true compensation element would have been larger because the benefit of duty-free exportation to South Africa by BLNS was not taken into account in the formula. There is no parallel to payments on this scale in customs unions anywhere else in the world. In most of the rest of Africa indeed, compensation has never been more than the putative amount needed to offset the costs of trade diversion alone.

The South African view is that the deal is currently still too generous. It has been pointed out for instance, that in 1991–2, whereas the revenue rate for SACU as a whole was 8.8 per cent, as a result of applying the stabilisation factor it was 17 per cent for BLNS and only 7.2 per cent for South Africa itself. A recent unpublished study by the Central Economic Advisory Services of the South African government even goes so far as to claim that after stabilisation, the enhancement rate is nearer to 95 per cent than the original 42 per cent.

The South African government nevertheless recognises that the abolition of the stabilisation and enhancement factors would destabilise the economies of BLNS, and that any abolition (in the course of adopting a clean formula) could only occur over a long period. Some downward revision seems likely to be sought. With a less costly formula in mind, the Central Economic Advisory Services have calculated the financial implications of a range of alternative possibilities. These include the exclusion of excises from the formula, a reduction of the stabilisation minimum and the adoption of alternative levels of enhancement.

Although the South African position may appear persuasive, calculations undertaken on behalf of BLNS suggest that there may be good grounds on which BLNS could argue against any reduction in their receipts from the agreement. For instance, calculations of the proceeds of an iso-price tariff for Botswana for 1987, 1993 and 1994 (Clark Leith, 1992, 1993) and for Namibia for 1993 suggest that the real enhancement derived by those countries for those years from the present revenue arrangements is negligible or possibly negative. This result could be interpreted to mean that those two countries derive no net benefit from the customs union, that is, they would be as well off if they withdrew. An indicative calculation for Swaziland based on the new 1993 trade statistics points in the same direction. Of course, the revenue aspects of the customs union are by no means the only factor to consider in relation to the question of a possible withdrawal from SACU for the smaller members. For one thing, given the permeability of their frontiers, BLNS might not be able to collect all of the calculated revenues, and certainly would be unable to do so without making their customs services more effective, which could be costly. Nevertheless, if the calculations cited are at all near the mark, they provide a relevant input to the revenue aspects of the renegotiation.

In that connection one limitation of the calculations cited for Botswana and Namibia as a guide to future policy is that they provide evaluations of the outcomes derived from the present formula prior to the GATT negotiations. The renegotiations must, however, be viewed in the context of the SACU offers to the GATT, since those offers imply a substantial reduction in tariff rates which must affect the future costs and benefits of SACU. There are several relevant considerations. In the first place, the planned tariff cuts will reduce the input costs of most industries. Potentially, this impact, together with the increased pressures from external competition on final prices and on industrial efficiency, should have important positive effects on competitiveness and on domestic prices, so reducing the costs of trade diversion of SACU. To the extent that these costs were a major element that determined the 1969 settlement, it must be expected that South Africa would use their prospective reduction as supporting a lower stabilisation range, if the present basis is continued or a comparable reduction in the enhancement factor if the original basis is reverted to. However, the effects of the tariff cuts in prospect should make it possible for BLNS to raise sales duty to some extent, without increasing the cost of living. In that way they could partly offset any reduction in revenue that may ensue from a formula change. The change in tariff rates can also be expected to affect the size of the common revenue pool itself. At present, with the stabilisation agreement in force, the size of the revenue pool is not material to the revenue proceeds of BLNS. However, the South African negotiators might seek to restore the size of the revenue pool as a significant variable.

In principle, in the post GATT context, the revenues derived from an iso-price tariff at the new rates should provide an important input to the negotiations by providing BLNS countries with a major ingredient for evaluating their trade policy options. From that point of view, it is relevant that calculations for one country at least appear to suggest that the proceeds in 1993–4 of an iso-price tariff utilising the new GATT rates would yield as much as the stabilised proceeds actually payable for that period. This result, if generally applicable, would provide strong grounds for arguing that revenue proceeds for BLNS should not at present be reduced whatever formula change is adopted. However, the calculation in question ignores the significant benefits that BLNS enjoy from their ability to export to South Africa free of duty since the existing formula disregards those exports.

One proposal which may be put forward by South Africa in the negotiations is the possibility of adopting a differentiated formula, which would treat different countries differently. South Africa argued for differentiation in 1969 but this was resisted by BLNS. Customs revenue is the major budgetary resource for all countries, but it is not uniformly important. Also, the four countries differ substantially in their per capita GDPs and growth potential. If payments to BLNS are to be made over and above what is implicit in a clean formula, South Africa may wish to reflect the relative prosperity and fiscal dependence of the recipients in the level of its transfers. There would be a strong case, certainly in terms of need, for providing Lesotho, the poorest and least developed member, with more generous treatment.

Economic Development Aspects

Regional balance is an important issue in most forms of regional economic integration. In the EU it is reflected in its Regional Policy and its policies for convergence. In blocs of developing countries it has also been a central issue, and often the one over which several promising arrangements for integration have come to grief.

A number of provisions of the 1969 agreement were intended to assist BLNS to promote their industrial development. In particular, additional import duties could be imposed by Botswana, Lesotho or Swaziland under certain conditions to protect local infant industries.

However, the proceeds of such protective duties had to be paid into the common revenue pool, and the additional duties provided no protection against products from South Africa.

Little or no use was made of these provisions. Such industrial development as has taken place in BLNS since 1969 owes little to the provisions of the customs agreement. It has been stimulated by various factors: the relatively low wage rates in those countries; the effects of sanctions on South Africa; the access to EU markets provided by Lomé (see Chapter 6); and by the activities of national Industrial Development Corporations. It has in any case been limited in scale. Moreover, when such developments have involved significant sales in the South African market, rather than merely serving the domestic markets of BLNS, the reaction of South African manufacturers and of the Board of Tariffs and Trade has often been to discourage any such industries by overt and covert hindrances to their exports to South Africa. The hostile reaction of the South African vehicle industry and of the South African government to the small vehicle assembly plants set up in Botswana is only one case of several, which suggests that few if any new industries set up in BLNS could rely on unimpeded access to what is nominally a single market in the absence of the introduction of new safeguards in a revised agreement.

Other problems have also hindered attempts on the part of BLNS to develop industrially. For instance, under South Africa's Regional Industrial Development Programme (RIDP), industries were offered very generous incentives for decentralising from the main industrial centres. BLNS could not match these incentives. The pressure to decentralise under the new Provincial structure of the new South African Constitution will be different, but is unlikely to be less strong.

In the context of improving arrangements for the promotion of a more balanced development in Southern Africa, the question of fiscal incentives, rather than of tariff protection, would be a more appropriate focus for negotiation for several reasons. For one thing, GATT bindings and other commitments would virtually exclude any possibility of imposing additional protective duties by BLNS. In any case, the current climate is hostile to the use of tariffs to protect uncompetitive industries. In the context of international commitments and the hopes placed on the efficient economic development of the Southern African region as a whole, the best that BLNS could hope for would be to ensure that their ability to compete within a Southern African single market would not be nullified by the provision of regional incentives within South Africa.

EU experience is instructive in this connection. In the EU the harmonised system of regional incentives permits agreed differentiation which operates in favour of more backward countries and regions. In that framework, Ireland, Portugal and other countries have been able to offer more favourable incentives countrywide than all but the least favoured regions of the most advanced countries receive. These more generous incentives have improved the ability of those less advanced countries to attract foreign direct investment to serve EU markets. It is important for the efficient operation of SACU that the ability of member states to distort competition by the provision of fiscal and other investment incentives should be limited. Above all, however, it is important that such incentives as are provided should contribute to the objective of balanced development. From that point of view it will be important that BLNS should seek a deal that would ensure that regional aid provided by any country in SACU is transparent, measurable and related to agreed objectives, and properly monitored.

One other issue has been raised from time to time in connection with the development objectives of SACU. South Africa has in the past suggested that the BLNS countries should use a greater proportion of their customs union receipts to stimulate their development. The McCarthy Report itself, in the context of the introduction of a so-called clean revenue formula, suggested the possibility of providing conditional development finance through SACU in partial substitution for enhancement. In that connection a possible role has been seen for the Development Bank of Southern Africa (DBSA), as a vehicle for the payment and administration of such funds paid out of the common revenue pool, but 'earmarked' for 'development'. At present, BLNS are not members of the Development Bank which is a purely South African institution hitherto geared to the development of the TBVC states. An extension of the role of DBSA in this and other ways may conceivably be proposed in the renegotiations. There are precedents in regional integration for channelling some part of compensation receipts into a development fund (as in the case of the former West African Community's FOSIDEC). However, it seems clear from the stance adopted by the BLNS countries in relation to the McCarthy Report's proposals, that they would resist strongly any suggestion that the payment of funds to BLNS from the common revenue pool should be channelled through the bank. A reshaped DBSA could only be of interest to those countries if it could be expected to expand their access to technical assistance and aid.

THE WEST AFRICAN ECONOMIC AND MONETARY UNION

The Background

Most of the francophone West African states have since independence been linked in a monetary union (Union Monétaire Ouest-Africaine), as well as in a separate economic community (CEAO) with a largely similar membership. It is widely accepted that the monetary union has operated remarkably successfully from many points of view, although the machinery for macroeconomic coordination and the supervision of financial institutions left much to be desired. Also, over the years, the currency (the CFA franc) became progressively overvalued. It was eventually devalued by 50 per cent early in 1994. The CEAO was fully discussed in Robson (1988). It achieved a limited amount of regional integration, but there was no common external tariff (CET), its trade liberalisation programme was *ad hoc*, and effectively each member country could determine the degree of protection accorded to the industries of its partners. Trade liberalisation was coupled with a system of fiscal compensation that was linked to the degree of preference that countries offered and received, and to net intra-CEAO trade balances. Ivory Coast and Senegal, the principal net exporters in intra-CEAO trade, were the contributors to the compensation funds. In no sense, however, did the region constitute a single market, and it is clear that transnational enterprises did not treat the area as such (Robson, 1993). There was a failure to exploit the economies of scale that showed itself in a replication of plants. In other fields of shared interest, such as transport and agriculture, cooperation was limited. The community did however succeed in maintaining what was, by African standards, a relatively high level of intra-community trade. By the end of the last decade, financial and other pressures had combined to produce the abandonment of the trade preferences and compensation arrangements and thus the virtual demise of the CEAO.

In 1990, the seven Heads of State of UMOA decided to transform the monetary union into an economic and monetary union (UEMOA). This was in part a response to the deficiencies of CEAO, and in part a response to manifested operational weaknesses of the monetary union itself that have already been referred to. To deal with these weaknesses, the project calls for the introduction of arrangements for the multilateral surveillance of macroeconomic policies, but apart from that, the existing monetary union and its central bank remain intact and subject to the existing arrangements and treaty. Most of the treaty of January 1994 is therefore concerned with the requirements for economic union. Here, the treaty provides for the institution of a customs union and the establishment of a single market together with a variety of measures to give effect to these objectives. As a preliminary to the establishment of the union, the CEAO was formally abolished shortly after the signature of the treaty, although, as noted above, it had already ceased to function. This section focuses on the approach of the treaty to the economic union aspects of integration and the issues that have to be resolved before a sustainable single market can be operated. Essentially, the approach of the treaty to the attainment of this objective builds on the objectives and practices of previous Communities in Africa, in particular so far as concerns its provision for fiscal compensation. Unlike CEAO and ECOWAS, however, compensation is to be purely transitional. In the longer term, the treaty provides for the establishment of structural and development funds, but the object of these would not be to compensate for experienced disparities in costs and benefits but rather to finance mechanisms to encourage the balanced development of UEMOA in order to make it sustainable.

The UEMOA confronts three major tasks in relation to the implementation of the customs union and the institution of a sustainable single market. The first is to put in place a CET and fiscal harmonisation measures that would enable a single market to operate without fiscal frontiers within the UEMOA. The second task is to put into effect a system for compensating for certain revenue losses associated with the introduction of a CET. The third is to elaborate longer-term instruments and mechanisms that would enable the union to be sustainable and effective in the face of existing economic disparities and the structural forces that have already produced a polarisation of development upon Ivory Coast and Senegal, and that may be strengthened by an effective single market. The treaty provides general guidelines, but specific approaches remain to be worked out, adopted and applied before practical effect can be given to the treaty.

The Common External Tariff and Fiscal Harmonisation

A basic task will be to elaborate fiscal harmonisation measures, including a CET and internal indirect tax structures that will reduce to a minimum the need for border tax adjustments and inspections.

The establishment of a CET would involve a shift from the CEAO system of a free trade area for agricultural products combined with preferential trading arrangements for approved manufactures, and would involve revenue changes for some member states and changes in the relative competitivenes of industries in certain countries. A simplified tariff, of a kind that the prospective member countries have been urged to adopt in the course of structural adjustment, and with rates of 5, 20 and 30 per cent on necessities, intermediate inputs and other final products for example, would permit a modest reduction in tariff levels while maintaining or even increasing revenues for the principal countries (Gagey *et al.*, 1994). For the low tariff countries of Benin and Togo which 're-export' taxed products outside the zone, there could be serious revenue problems, since those re-exports would be put in question.

If a CET and harmonised rates of VAT and excise are adopted, one major advantage is that rent-seeking trade and arbitrage can be expected to decline, so reducing a principal motive for frontier controls inside the UEMOA. The importance of this should not be underrated since experience in Africa strongly points to the conclusion that if any border tax adjustments whatsoever are maintained, the operation of regional markets is apt to be significantly impeded. This would suggest the desirability of adopting mechanisms in the UEMOA that would make it possible to shift any adjustments that would still be required in connection with the activities of registered traders away from the borders themselves. One approach for VAT would be to adopt a direct transfer mechanism in conjunction with a clearing house, involving a switch to the origin system for imposing the tax. An alternative would be to retain the destination system for trade between registered traders but to institute an improved documentation system and exchange of information among the national tax authorities. It remains to be seen whether either of these approaches, which correspond to the transitional and definitive systems of the EU, would be practicable in West Africa, having regard to their preconditions in terms of trust and of administrative requirements. In their absence, and without a unified fiscal administration, the chances of removing frontier controls in the UEMOA would not appear to be high.

Compensation

A second urgent task for UEMOA is to elaborate a system of compensation for revenue losses arising from the institution of the customs union, as is required by the treaty. In the absence of intra-UEMOA tariff free trade, the adoption of a CET itself at contemplated levels would not involve revenue losses, except perhaps for Benin and Togo. In the light of the very different levels of participation in intra-CEAO trade in the past, however, it must be expected that the adoption of a CET coupled with free trade would entail very different fiscal costs for the different members, with Benin, Togo, Burkina Faso, Niger and Mali standing to lose considerably in their capacity as likely net importers from Senegal and Ivory Coast, in the absence of the payment of compensation.

The treaty provides few guidelines in relation to this issue, but its implication is that payments would be made through a special fund. The most appropriate basis for compensation would be to base it on the static real income losses that would be associated with the institution of tariff free trade. These losses would equate to the additional revenue that could be raised by an iso-price tariff. It may be argued that this would not be very different from the basis adopted in the former CEAO (Robson, 1987), and which proved, ultimately, to be unacceptable to the net contributory countries. However, unlike the CEAO arrangement, the UEMOA arrangement is to be transitional. Moreover, a fully effective single market can be expected to be much more attractive to the prospective net contributors than the previous *ad hoc* arrangements.

There are in any case few instances of blocs of developing countries successfully operating simple customs unions without compensation. It is true that a CET has been negotiated in MERCOSUR (see Chapters 9 and 10) without compensation, but a principal trade-off is that exceptions have had to be accepted in liberalising intra-MERCOSUR trade. If such exceptions are numerous, the outcome begins to look like a free trade area. Resort to any such an arrangement in UEMOA would inevitably hinder the operation of a single market. Nevertheless, analysis and experience suggest that the payment of compensation is fraught with difficulties. It is unlikely that UEMOA will be able to escape these, whatever basis is employed. It would therefore be desirable if any such payments could be avoided in the longer term. That indeed is envisaged in the treaty.

Structural Policies and Funds

After a transitional period, compensation for revenue losses is to disappear. In their place, the treaty envisages the institution of structural and development funds. These, in conjunction with the eventual system to be adopted for financing the UEMOA's budget (a share of

VAT proceeds) and the operations of any separate funds, could contribute to convergence and balanced development, as well as to ameliorating any real income losses that might result from disequalising effects from implementing a customs union and common market. The existence of significant provision for structural funds could be a decisive factor for the internal and external credibility of UEMOA. The importance of credibility for securing the favourable effects of a union, particularly in relation to the restructuring of investment, has frequently been emphasised in the EU. A recent survey of the intentions of transnationals in UEMOA as between the alternatives of concentrating production or continuing to operate several enterprises, each serving mainly the individual national markets, makes it clear, unsurprisingly, that this factor is paramount in the UEMOA context.

Up to the present time, the UEMOA does not appear to have determined at all precisely the policy objectives that are to be pursued through its structural funds. The structural operations are apparently to be led by distributional considerations, and thus the size, use and distribution of the funds must be expected to be defined in the course of a process of political negotiation that will reflect the degree of political and social solidarity within UEMOA. At the same time, if convergence is to be encouraged, a crucial role must be assigned to efficiency considerations. There appears to be a good deal of scope for doing so. For instance, the provision of infrastructure from a purely national perspective typically results in insufficient investment in cross-border transport links. The correction of such a shortfall through the intercession of structural funds could be expected to contribute to improved balance within the bloc. Structural funds might also be used to help to provide the UEMOA's less developed members with levels of infrastructure and of investment in human capital more comparable with those enjoyed in the more advanced countries. The utility of following such an approach in the context of regional policy is underlined by the increasing weight of evidence that links public investment in infrastructure with observed rates of economic growth.

Conclusion

At the present time, UEMOA is in a formative stage, so far as concerns its customs union and common market. In favour of an optimistic prognosis, there may be cited the evident political commitment to the maintenance of established links which have an unbroken history since independence, coupled with the new awareness of the many benefits of reducing transactions costs through the institution of a single market. At the same time, a number of the sources of conflicts of interest that have bedevilled earlier less ambitious initiatives among the countries are unlikely to disappear. In particular there is no painless way of financing either compensation or regional policies that depend on expenditure. There is, nevertheless, a better understanding of the issues on all sides and a sensible emphasis on finding solutions through structural approaches. But the fundamental problem of financing the burden of any required expenditures is unaffected, except to the extent that an effective single market may yield substantial net benefits that were not forthcoming in previous arrangements, or to the extent that additional donor support might be made available for financing regional policies that would not be available for financing direct intra-UEMOA compensatory transfers.

THE PROSPECT

Many arrangements have been established for regional economic integration in Africa since the initial enthusiasm for bloc formation in the early 1960s. Hardly any of the trade blocs have succeeded in generating significant tangible benefits. Orthodox theorists would find this unsurprising, since the structural characteristics of African countries – including high external trade dependence on agricultural and mineral products, small domestic markets and large income disparities – would suggest to them that countries with such characteristics do not constitute optimal trading areas. The progress of structural adjustment, and the character of that process, including its emphasis on outward-looking policies seems to place further question marks over the merits of regional integration in Africa. For instance, de Melo and Panagariya (1993), who employ essentially orthodox appraisal criteria, argue that with outward-looking policies and trade liberalisation any gains from trade creation through market integration among developing countries must be negligible.

Such arguments may be valid but they wholly neglect important dimensions that underlie the renewed thrust for regional integration that has recently been evident, particularly in Europe. Underlying this thrust has been an emphasis on sources of benefits from regional integration that are neglected by orthodox analysis. In the first place, apart from the static allocational effects on which orthodox theory exclusively focuses, there are administrative, efficiency (via increased competition) and transactions costs savings to consider. For the EU, these gains were put, in the lead-up to the SEM, at several times larger than orthodox trade creation gains (Commission of the European Communities, 1988 and Chapter 4). In Africa, the transactions costs involved in a failure to integrate policies and to take measures to eliminate fiscal frontiers have demonstrably contributed to market fragmentation and avoidable costs and inefficiencies. In West Africa, for instance, the transactions costs per ton–kilometre associated with unilateral policies towards transport has been estimated to be considerably more than the cost of transport itself (Badiane, 1992). It can take a month for a vehicle to make the round trip from Mombasa to Bujumbura. Settling payments through African banks outside monetary unions can take months. Secondly, economies of scale in the provision of infrastructure provide many well-documented instances of the substantial gains that can be procured from cooperation. Thirdly, the provision of certain public goods and the use of many policy instruments typically gives rise to significant external repercussions. In such cases, too, regional integration or harmonisation or coordination can offer the prospect of substantial benefits. At the level of policy instruments, tax structures and revenue adjustments, and a variety of supervisory activities in financial market regulation and transport are cases in point. A degree of regional market protection may also have merit as a means of supporting SAPs. The argument is that the costs of adjustment would be reduced if firms were first exposed to competition from other firms in the region before exposing them to the full force of world competition. Some of the evidence for that argument is assembled by Langhammer and Hiemenz (1990).

The integration policies required to secure gains from these sources do not depend on cost-raising regional market protection and are not inconsistent with outward-looking policies and structural adjustment. At the same time, for a variety of practical reasons, most could not be implemented other than on a regional basis. Evidently a crucial question is whether the size of the potential benefits from these unorthodox sources would justify the costs of negotiation, adjustment and administration, over and above the benefits from the pursuit of purely unilateral policies. In the end, only convincing empirical evidence of the wider benefits of regional economic integration can decide the issue, and that is lacking for some of the blocs in Africa that are at a formative stage.

15 'Fortresses' and Three Trading Blocs?

Ali M. El-Agraa

INTRODUCTION

The deepening and widening of integration in the EU and the formation of NAFTA and its possible extension to include Latin American countries have prompted two questions: will the two groups become inward looking and increase their protection *vis-à-vis* the outside world (*à la* 'Fortress Europe')? and will East Asia have to create a third force in response? The first question is of great interest to countries like Japan, but has actually been voiced by the smaller non-participating countries, especially those in East Asia and Australasia. Japan's concern does not warrant explanation since obviously it simply cannot afford to be left out of these two lucrative markets, especially when its exports–GDP ratio is the highest amongst the advanced nations and the two blocs absorb most of them. East Asia and Australasia are worried because they fear that the EU and NAFTA will become closed markets for their exports, and that foreign investment will not only be diverted away from them towards the two regional blocs but also their own efforts to investment there may be deterred. Although the major focus of this book is on actual schemes of economic integration, I think one may be justified in briefly considering these two issues, if only because they may shed light on the external effects of the two most important economic integration schemes in the world.

FORTRESSES?

The North Americans seem genuinely surprised by the concern of East Asia and Australasia. They admit that some non-participating nations may be adversely affected by trade and investment diversion due to the expansion of CUFTA to include Mexico. However, because Canada and the US have for a long time been highly integrated economies and because the Mexican economy is relatively small, they expect these effects to be insignificant. The same point is often made by the EU over the admission of EFTA countries, especially since, as we have seen, practically all of them belong to the EEA and the EC–EFTA Agreements before that.

However, these direct effects are only part of the outsiders' concern. The much more important aspects have to do with fear of:

(a) external trade barriers being raised by these blocs;
(b) preferential access to the EU market being extended to more products from the former Eastern European members of the CMEA;
(c) NAFTA admitting other members from Latin America and elsewhere;
(d) more confident US and EU leaders being more agressive unilaterally in their relations with other, especially East Asian countries; and
(e) the cumulative effects of these developments, in addition to those associated with other recent and prospective economic integration agreements, in eroding the WTO (GATT before it) rules-based multilateral trading system on which the prosperity of open economies depends.

Anderson and Snape (1994) address several questions raised by these general concerns. The first relates to whether there is evidence from the past that suggests that the direct and indirect effects of regional blocs on trade and investment have been income-reducing for excluded countries. They argue that many would answer positively and some would cite the increasing regionalisation of world trade to support that view. However, their analysis suggests that this answer is probably unwarranted since although it is true that the share of world trade that is intra-regional has been increasing, it is also true that the proportion of GDP traded has been increasing sufficiently rapidly for there to be growth also not just in trade with other regions but also in the share of GDP traded extra-regionally – see Table 15.1. Nevertheless, they are quick to state that whether the extra-regional trade volume would have been larger in the absence of regional blocs would depend on how restrictive the counterfactual trade policy would have been, adding that about this consideration 'we are able to say little

Table 15.1 Trade shares and the regionalisation of world merchandise trade, 1963–90

	1963	*1973*	*1983*	*1990*
Intra-regional trade share				
Western Europe	61	68	65	72
North America	35	39	36	40
Asia	47	42	43	48
– Japan	31	32	31	35
– Australasia	30	41	53	51
– Developing Asia	63	50	51	56
World total	44	49	45	52
Share of GDP traded (%)				
Western Europe	31	43	43	46
North America	8	13	16	20
Asia	22	23	27	29
– Japan	16	20	22	18
– Australasia	29	29	24	30
– Developing Asia	24	25	33	47
World total	21	28	31	34
Share (%) of GDP traded extra-regionally				
Western Europe	12	14	15	13
North America	6	8	11	12
Asia	14	16	15	15
– Japan	11	14	15	12
– Australasia	27	27	22	28
– Developing Asia	13	19	24	31
World total	12	14	17	16

Notes

1. Throughout the table, 'trade' refers to the average of the merchandise export and import shares, except that the share of GDP traded refers to exports plus imports of merchandise. All values are measured in current US dollars. North America refers to Canada, the US and Mexico. Australasia refers to Australia and New Zealand.
2. The rows for Australasia, Developing Asia and Japan differ from the other rows in that they are treated not as regions themselves but as part of their sum which is the Asian region including South Asia.
3. The world total is the weighted average across the world's seven regions (Africa, Eastern Europe, Latin America and the Middle East are not shown), using the regions' shares of world trade as weights.

Source: Norheim, Finger and Anderson (1993).

with our present understanding of the political economy of trade policy' (ibid.) – see El-Agraa (1989) and Chapter 4 for elaboration.

They then turn to a consideration of whether the widening of the EU and NAFTA is likely to contribute to or slow this past trend for increasing economic integration across regions as well as within regions. Their answer is that not all the signs are positive and the net effect may indeed be negative, but they are convinced that on balance the concerns of the excluded countries relating to trade and investment probably are exaggerated.

They then consider the broader systemic question that is worrying excluded small open economies regarding whether the proliferation of regional blocs will erode the WTO rules-based multilateral trading system, a system which has served them moderately well in the past. They argue that there is indeed cause for this systemic concern, not least because the texts of recent trading blocs tend to be many hundreds of, rather than a few dozen, pages. In other words, some of them contain many qualifications and exceptions, hence falling a long way short of creating literally free trade (see WTO Article XXIV, appended to Chapter 2). They also add that discussions to expand the EU and NAFTA membership 'have a distinct hub-and-spoke element, suggesting that future enlargements... could cause rules of origin and dispute settlement problems to dominate world trade' (Anderson and Snape, 1994).

Naturally then they turn to the question of how might East Asian and other excluded countries respond to these regional blocs. They argue that some obvious ways include continuing to search imaginatively for ways to circumvent the barriers of these blocs against imports and foreign investment, and to invest more both in lobbying for better market access and in actual manufacturing within them. However, they also suggest the more radical possibility of trying to take up the offer made by former US President Bush to seek NAFTA membership. They believe that the outsiders are also likely to consider forming closer links and perhaps even new regional blocs with other countries. As examples they suggest Malaysian Prime Minister Mahathir's East Asian Economic Caucus (EAEC) and the various attempts to give more life to the Asia Pacific Economic Cooperation (APEC) forum. They are of the opinion that the

> likelihood is that these initiatives will lead to a strengthening of the MFN-based open regionalism that has characterized the Western

> Pacific region in recent decades and set it apart from the more discriminatory regionalism elsewhere. Since the interests of Western Pacific (and other) economies will continue to be served best by a strong open multilateral trading system, they should continue not only to seek a strengthening of the WTO but also to liberalize their markets unilaterally. Fortuitously, even if this is done on a non-discriminatory, most-favoured-nation basis, most of the benefits of APEC liberalization would be reaped within the APEC region. (Ibid., p. 473)

However, one should not finish here since it is important to ask: why do countries have to belong to a group in order to force free multilateral trade? that is, is not open regionalism a contradiction in terms. One possible answer is that with a membership of about 150 nations, the WTO will become a hopeless forum for positive action: the shere size will make it difficult to reach consensus except at the lowest common denominator. The response to this is that if a group of nations is willing to offer unilateral trade reductions to the outsiders, why should the latter group feel the need to respond likewise? After all, as long as countries continue to believe that offers to lower their protection are concessions, it would be irrational for them to reciprocate. In short, if open regionalism is expected to succeed, why should not a drastic change in WTO's Article XXIV be equally possible? The following section has more to offer on these issues, so it is appropriate to turn to it now.

THREE BLOCS?

Now consider the second question: should East Asia form a region-wide trading bloc of its own? Panagariya (1994) believes that, on the whole, both economics and politics are against such an idea. His rationale is that, historically, East Asia has benefited greatly from an open world trading system. Indeed, despite a redirection of trade towards itself, East Asia still sends two-thirds of its exports to the rest of the world, including, in 1990, about 32 and 21 per cent going, respectively, to North America and Europe (see Table 15.2). Adding the fact that, almost without exception, studies of the NIEs draw a direct connection between growth in exports and growth in GDP and that China, Indonesia, Malaysia and Thailand have been repeating the experience of the NIEs must reinforce this reality.

Table 15.2 Destination of East Asian exports (percentages)

Exporter	*Year*	*North America*	*Western Europe*	*Europe*	*Partner* *East Asia*[1]	*Latin America*	*Africa*	*Middle East*	*South Asia*
North America	1980	33.5	25.2	27.4	15.8	8.9	3.3	4.2	1.0
	1985	44.4	19.3	21.0	15.5	5.9	2.5	3.2	1.0
	1990	41.9	22.3	23.4	20.4	5.0	1.7	2.6	0.8
Western Europe	1980	6.7	67.1	71.9	2.9	2.4	7.2	5.5	0.7
	1985	11.3	64.9	68.9	3.6	1.6	5.2	5.0	0.9
	1990	8.3	71.0	74.4	5.3	1.1	3.3	3.3	0.7
Europe	1980	6.3	63.7	72.7	2.7	2.3	6.9	5.5	0.7
	1985	11.0	63.5	69.2	3.4	1.6	5.1	5.0	0.9
	1990	8.2	70.6	74.5	5.2	1.1	3.3	3.3	0.7
East Asia[1]	1980	26.0	16.8	18.9	29.9	4.1	4.4	7.4	1.8
	1985	37.8	13.6	15.5	25.3	2.8	2.2	5.1	2.0
	1990	31.9	19.8	20.7	32.3	1.9	1.6	3.0	1.5
Latin America	1980	27.2	26.5	35.1	5.4	16.6	2.7	1.9	0.5
	1985	35.8	25.9	30.4	7.1	12.1	3.7	3.0	0.7
	1990	22.9	25.3	27.6	10.3	14.0	2.1	2.4	0.4
Africa	1980	27.4	43.6	46.1	4.3	3.2	1.8	1.7	0.3
	1985	14.8	64.9	69.3	1.8	4.2	5.1	2.2	0.7
	1990	3.0	66.0	68.0	4.6	0.6	12.8	4.4	3.6
Middle East	1980	11.5	40.3	41.5	28.7	5.0	1.5	4.1	2.5
	1985	6.2	15.0	17.7	1.5	0.3	1.4	8.7	0.4
	1990	17.8	48.6	53.0	9.1	1.2	3.6	8.5	0.9
South Asia	1980	10.9	24.6	39.4	14.5	0.5	6.8	14.5	1.0
	1985	18.4	20.8	37.0	16.4	0.4	4.6	11.0	1.0
	1990	17.1	30.1	46.6	18.3	0.3	2.7	6.5	0.8

Note
[1] Excludes China due to lack of data for 1980 and 1985.
Source: Panagariya, A (1994).

Given the importance of open markets to East Asia's economic growth, Panagariya (1994) argues that the case for an East Asian trading bloc should be evaluated primarily in terms of the impact such a bloc would have on the world trading system: the region's future interests will be best served by a strategy that promotes an open world trading system; a discriminatory one would not help.

Panagariya then asks if there is a role for an alternative form of regionalism in East Asia. He believes that an approach that encourages regionwide trade liberalisation on a non-discriminatory basis may still hold some promise since, in the long run, it could serve as a stepping stone for Japan and China to assume a leadership role in promoting global free trade similar to that played by England in the nineteenth century and the US in the post-war era. However, such liberalisation is unfortunately not likely due to the short-term adverse effects on East Asia's terms of trade.

These points merit further consideration.

The countries in the region are at very different levels of development. Japan, with a per capita income of $31 490 in 1993, is the richest. Per capita incomes for the other countries in the region range from a low of $490 in China to $19 850 in Singapore, with Hong Kong not far behind at $18 060 (see Table 2.4). Broadly speaking, Japan is followed by Singapore, Hong Kong and Taiwan, in that order and all three with per capita incomes in excess of $10 000, then by Brunei and South Korea, both with per capita incomes in excess of $5000 and the rest far behind, especially China, Indonesia and the Philippines with per capita incomes of less than $1000.

As well as being the richest, the Japanese economy is by far the largest. In 1990, its share of GDP was 13.2 per cent and within Asia its share was about 70 per cent. Without Japan, the share of Asia in world GDP drops from one-fifth to one-twentieth. China lags behind Japan but is rapidly becoming another major player in the region. Indeed, using GDP figures based on purchasing power parity (PPP, i.e. exchange rates adjusted for variations in buying power across countries) for 1990, the IMF puts China's share of world GDP at 6 per cent, just below Japan (7.6 per cent) but above Germany (4.3 per cent).

On the whole, trade regimes in the region can be described as open, although the level of protection varies widely across countries. In terms of trade–GDP ratios, the smaller economies of East Asia are very open, with exports and imports as percentages of GDP being high for all countries except for Japan and China. Singapore has by far the highest levels, rising in 1990 to more than 100 per cent. For the NIEs, they are both close to 40 per cent.

Hong Kong and Singapore are textbook examples of economies which practice free trade since they have low tariffs and no quantitative restrictions. South Korea, Malaysia, the Philippines and Thailand almost completely eliminated their quantitative restrictions on manufactures in the 1980s. However, their tariff rate reductions were not as dramatic, and in some of these countries, especially Indonesia and Thailand, they remain high. Although China has liberalised its import regime considerably since the early 1980s, its remaining formal restrictions place it amongst the most protected countries in the region. Indeed, even when China succeeds in fulfilling its promise to APEC to lower its tariffs unilaterally by a third in the future, it would still have an average tariff level of 25 per cent.

The openness of Japan's trade regime has been a matter of some controversy (see El-Agraa, 1986, 1995). In terms of formal barriers, Japan's trade regime is as open as those of other advanced nations since its tariff rates are very low, if not the lowest in the world and, apart from rice imports, it has virtually no quantitative restrictions. However, because Japan's import–GDP ratio is far below those of other countries of comparable size and with similar income levels, some analysts have argued that Japan's markets are protected by informal trade barriers and are thus relatively closed to outsiders. One should hasten to add that there are also those who disagree with this interpretation (see the contributions to the mini-symposium on Japan's trade policy, edited by El-Agraa, for *The World Economy*, vol. 18, no. 2, 1995).

While proponents of an East Asian trading bloc argue that economics favours their position, detractors claim that both economics and politics are against such a discriminatory scheme. The economic desirability of such a scheme depends on two considerations: (i) the effects on real incomes in member countries, assuming that the world trading system is unaltered; and (ii) the effects on incomes resulting from the scheme's impact on the openness of the trading system. Panagariya (1994) argues that because the second factor is the most significant for large regions like East Asia, such a scheme must be evaluated primarily in terms of its impact on the global trading system.

Advocates of such a trading bloc can offer two arguments in their support. First, such a scheme may serve as a deterrent to the formation of closed trading blocs worldwide. The rationale for this runs in the following manner. The world is already divided into trading blocs. To ensure that they do not become overly protective of and limit access to their markets, East Asia should be united and in a position to retaliate. For example, unilateral actions such as those taken by the US under its 'Super 301' provisions would be harder to implement. Second, the formation of economic integration schemes could facilitate rounds of WTO similar to those conducted under GATT, its predecessor. The Uruguay Round was protracted partly because of the large number of participants and the 'free rider' problem such a number generates. One reason for the success of previous rounds was that the US could deal with the EC as a single unit. Thus a small number of trading blocs could make future rounds more manageable. Moreover, a limited number of schemes would enable them to assume responsibility for many intra-regional trade issues, thus allowing the WTO process to be used mainly for resolving problems between them, and to lower trade restrictions, swiftly and efficiently. In short, a world composed mainly of the EU, an extended NAFTA plus an East Asian trading bloc could speed up the opening of global markets.

However, there are those who claim that these arguments are contenious. They stress that such schemes enjoy more market power than individual nations, hence, in principle, nothing can prevent them from raising rather than lowering trade restrictions. As a deterrent, then, trading schemes function only as long as they do not carry out the threat to raise trade barriers. Once the threat becomes a reality and a trade war breaks out, retaliatory actions are likely to be more severe than they would be without them. They also argue that a smaller number of schemes does not necessarily mean faster progress in trade talks, citing as evidence the fact that although the EU was established in 1957 (as the EEC), it is still to achieve a single market, and that, in the meantime, its non-tariff trade barriers have proliferated with their coverage expanding fivefold between 1966 and 1986.

With regard to the political feasibility of an East Asian trading bloc, there are at least three interrelated factors working against it. First, the major players in the region have historically been political rivals. Although time, trade and intra-regional investment have gone a long way towards bringing these former enemies together, they do not appear to be ready for such a venture. Second, these countries have very different levels of protection and are at very different levels of development. This suggests that the distribution of the gains from economic integration would be uneven, with the poorer and often highly protected nations being more likely either to lose more or to gain less than their relatively richer and more open counterparts. The rationale for this is that participants in economic integration eliminate tariffs against each other but not against the outside world, hence members' gains accrue largely from preferential access to each other's markets rather than from domestic liberalisation: by definition, the high-tariff countries provide a greater margin of preference than they receive from their low-tariff counterparts and consequently gain less. This unevenness raises the issue of compensation, a barrier not easily overcome. Third, the region comprises a large number of countries, making the negotiation for such a scheme a daunting task. With only six members and after twenty-five years, ASEAN has been able to make very little progress with trade promotion. Although the formation of NAFTA has prompted ASEAN to go for an ASEAN Free Trade Area (AFTA), serious preferential liberalisation has hardly begun. Considering this background, it is not clear how disparate countries such as China, Japan, South Korea and members of ASEAN can be expected to form such a trading bloc.

Panagariya (1994) believes that the external factors working against the scheme are even more formidable. Because many countries believe that Japan has closed markets, for over two decades the US has made it the target of unilateral policy actions, including voluntary export restraints (VERs), the *Structural Impediments Initiative* (SII), *Super 301* and, presently, the *Framework Talks*. Countries in the region with relatively small economies, such as China and South Korea, not only face an environment hostile to an East Asian trading bloc, but are also vulnerable to retaliatory actions by the US. In 1990, China and South Korea both sold a quarter of their exports to the US, hence they face immense risks in participating in a trading bloc that could divert trade from the US.

Given these difficulties, Panagariya (1994) goes along with the 'open regionalism' approach centred around WTO-style of non-discriminatory liberalisation. What this means is that the East Asian nations should form an association which would negotiate reductions in trade restrictions on a MFN basis, that is, any concessions one country makes to another would automatically be extended to all members. There are four arguments in support of such an approach. First, under such a scheme there will be no trade diversion. Second, since this approach will improve its access to East Asian markets, the US will have no reason to challenge it. Third, because liberalisation would occur simultaneously in all the major countries in the region, short-term adjustment costs would be minimised; in true WTO-style, liberalisation would take place in areas of mutual interest, hence export prospects would improve for all countries at the same time that import-competing industries were exposed to more foreign competition. Fourth, the economies in the region, especially Japan and greater China (China, Hong Kong and Taiwan), could become the leaders in global economic affairs.

However, Panagariya is quick to add that these long-run gains are countered by short- to medium-term adverse economic effects, also for four reasons. First, because existing tariffs levels, at least in Japan, are relatively low, potential gains from lowering them are limited.

Japan also extends extensive trade preferences to its East Asian trading partners under the Generalised System of Preferences (GSP). For example, 88 per cent of the Japanese tariff lines for South Korean goods are either at zero or below the MFN level; for about two-thirds of the tariff lines, the GSP gives South Korea duty free access. A similar pattern applies to other East Asian nations. If Japan were to lower its tariffs in a non-discriminatory fashion, these developing countries would lose the tariff preferences they currently enjoy. Second, because tariff levels across the other countries are highly variable, the scope for negotiating reduced barriers is limited. Indonesia, Thailand and arguably China have the highest tariff levels; those of the Philippines and South Korea are moderate (generally below 20 per cent); and Hong Kong and Singapore are virtually tariff free. Given this varied structure, the scope for reciprocal reductions is limited. Third, in any East Asian negotiations, Japan must assume the leadership role the US played during the GATT negotiations. However, with so few barriers, Japan may have difficulty. It must either find a way to negotiate non-tariff barriers or use its aid and investment leverage in the region to induce other countries to liberalise their regimes. Fourth, and perhaps most important, even if substantial trade barriers in Japan and other countries could be identified and negotiated away on a non-discriminatory basis, the likely decline in the region's terms of trade with the rest of the world would be substantial. Because two-thirds of the region's goods are traded with outsider countries, a major liberalisation would involve unilateral concessions. The GATT negotiations side-stepped this problem, as the EC, US and Japan negotiated tariff reductions simultaneously. They were able to carry out substantial liberalisation without making major concessions to negotiators, most of which were developing countries.

16 Policy Directives, Pertinent Questions, Overall Conclusions and Prognostications

Ali M. El-Agraa

In this concluding chapter I wish to highlight the policy implications of the theory of economic integration, ask the LDCs which either already belong to or are contemplating the formation of economic integration schemes to ask themselves some pertinent questions, bring together the conclusions that emerge from the book as a whole, and finally to prognosticate about the future for economic integration. The reader may be disappointed to learn that this chapter does not include a section devoted to a cross-sectional and comprehensives summary of the experiences of the various schemes considered in this book. However, given that these experiences are so varied, it is impossible to draw a unified set of experiences from them, and, in any case, the reader who has come to this chapter after having tackled the rest of the book will most certainly not appreciate such a section.

THE POLICY DIRECTIVES

Given the qualifications specified in Chapter 2, it should be clear that the economic rationale for customs union formation depends almost entirely on economies of scale bringing net benefits to the partners. The policy implications of this are equally clear: either industries should be equitably distributed in terms of location (in the case of vertically integrated industries and an equal provision of infrastructure), via some sort of authority, or a mechanism should be created to ensure an equitable distribution of the gains (where the industries are horizontally integrated). In the latter case, the mechanism should be a built-in fiscal and financial one or an agent which operates as such, rather than an authority without any specified criteria and/or guidelines. If these policy implications are ignored, the very rationale for customs union formation is undermined, unless those countries which stand to lose from the customs union consciously accept the outcome, maybe for non-economic objectives.

Needless to add that a scattering amongst the various member nations of a horizontally integrated industry or the setting up of a built-in fiscal and financial mechanism when industries are vertically integrated would be measures which are in direct contradiction to these policy specifications. Simple as these may seem, some of the schemes discussed in this book do not indicate a grasp of this basic message, for example, the Andean Pact's earlier decision to make an equal allocation of car factories when the car industry is not vertically integrated, and the EU's lack of a built-in fiscal and financial mechanism for the distribution of either industrial location or the gains from economies of scale.

Note that these policy requirements apply irrespective of whether the countries concerned are advanced or developing nations. However, for the latter, the built-in fiscal and financial mechanism should be the most appropriate since the lack of infrastructure means that the possibilities for the locational distribution of industries would be very limited indeed.

If one were to proceed beyond the simple criteria of trade creation and trade diversion to include terms of trade effects, the policy requirements are also quite clear: the customs union partners must 'speak with one voice' if they are to ensure that the terms of trade at least do not turn against them, or, if the outside world is too large and is able to act in unison, it is necessary to do so if only to minimise the extent of the possible damage that may be inflicted upon them. Again, simple as this may seem, there is no single scheme of economic integration which has demonstrated a real grasp of this basic message, since each member country seems to continue to conduct its international transactions in isolation.

In the case of economic unions, one needs to incorporate the policy directives regarding factor mobility and monetary integration. Theoretical considerations clearly demonstrate that monetary integration should not be contemplated without the establishment of a powerful central bank, which pools together all the foreign exchange reserves of all the participating nations and coordinates their monetary policies in such a manner as to benefit the totality of the economic union's membership. When monetary integration is combined with free factor mobility, the powers delegated to the common central bank have to extend beyond the mere execution of coordinated monetary policies, since a very strong fiscal policy will also be needed to ensure that no single participating nation gets out of line and becomes a completely or permanently depressed area. Of course, this part of fiscal policy could be labelled a 'powerful regional policy' or a 'cohesion policy', but what really matters is not so much the actual choice of words as the exact nature of the policy impact. Note here that the MacDougall Report (1977) showed quite clearly that a 'proper' monetary union needs an appropriate fiscal policy in order to ensure that the normal redistributional effects which are commonly generated in federal and national economies take place. In short, both free factor mobility and monetary integration have policy directives for the participating nations which are closely interrelated. Hence, to assign monetary coordination to a common central bank and the factor mobility aspects to some sort of 'regional/cohesion' agency is to miss the whole point regarding this strong interdependence. These are very clear policy directives, yet even in such a powerful and deeply involved scheme as the EU this interdependence is not only not evident, but the EU, which has decided to have a full EMU with a single currency in place by the end of this century, is still to develop a common fiscal policy.

Highlighting the policy directives in this manner suggests that governments are either irrational or simply act in an irresponsible manner in this particular context. Of course, governments may have their own political rationale for taking actions which may appear as such, but it is difficult to understand why governments commit themselves to schemes of economic integration without abiding by even the very basic requirements for their success. This suggests that some schemes were established in response to some mysterious notion that the simple act of creating or joining such a schemes is a panacea for serious and deep-seated economic ills. Of course, it could be the case that although countries create or join such schemes for the common good, each nation still has to strive to ensure the best outcome for itself alone. However, this would be like the classic economics textbook case of duopoly where profit maximisation requires collusion (joint and coordinated action by the two monopolists) but where the pursuit by each duopolist to maximise his/her share would lead to both incurring losses instead.

PERTINENT QUESTIONS

We have seen not only the proliferation and multiplicity of integration schemes amongst the LDCs but, especially in the case of Africa, also persistent swapping of membership as well as miserable economic performances. One therefore wonders what advice they should be given. Without intending to offend in any way, one should not hesitate to ask the LDCs to ask themselves some searching questions before they contemplate the formation of or joining any such bloc (Hazlewood, 1982). These are:

1. Are the members prepared to agree on a common system of fiscal incentives to encourage an acceptable distribution of investment between them and to prevent the competitive offering of concessions to investors?
2. Is a substantial degree of regional planning over such matters as the location of new industries and the pattern of industrial specialisation essential to achieve an acceptable distribution of the benefits of integration? If so, are members prepared to accept the constraints imposed on them by such planning? How does such planning cope with the strong preferences by potential investors about the location of production?
3. Are members willing to take a long-term view and to see the benefits from cooperation grow with the growth of trade between them, or do their assessments inevitably have a short horizon within which transactions between them, and hence the benefits from integration, are likely to be small?
4. If there are gains from the scheme for the members as a whole and for every member individually, can it be ensured that they all perceive the benefit, and do not have incompatible perceptions of the distribution of the benefits?
5. Is it necessary only that all members should benefit, or must they benefit equally, or must the poorer or less developed members gain most, or must even the gap between the members in their wealth and level of development actually narrow over time? The last is a very strong requirement since it is perfectly possible for the gap to widen even though the integration arrangements themselves may have a strong equalising element.
6. Are the expected benefits from industrialisation to serve a protected regional market great enough to make it worthwhile surmounting the difficulties, given the possibilities for manufacturing

for extra-bloc exports to advanced countries through multinational (transnational) corporations? The expectation will differ from country to country according to the size of its domestic market and its competitive ability internationally. Is a firmly affirmative answer from every member necessary if a grouping is to have strong prospects of success?

7. Is continuing political harmony between the members essential and must it go beyond a minimum of goodwill without which cooperation would be impossible?

OVERALL CONCLUSIONS

One of the overall conclusions is that the so-called *types* of economic integration are appropriate only for textbook exposition purposes since they do not represent any single actual scheme. Even at the simple 'free trade area' level some administrative mechanism has to be incorporated to ensure the proper carrying out of 'rules of origin' in order to eliminate trade deflection. Hence cooperation in general and coordination of certain policies in particular are not matters strictly confined to 'economic unions', that is, to more involved levels of economic integration.

A second overall conclusion is that it is not entirely true that customs union theory suffers from a *general* lack of applicability to the real world; this is only partially so. As was pointed out in the previous section, the theory suggests that the most likely benefits of economic integration are essentially those due to economies of scale. Economies of scale can come about in several ways, some of which are due to managerial and organisational efficiency so that plants do not have to be physically located in a concentrated area. Once allowance is made for several plants to manufacture the same product, the location of such plants within an integrated area becomes of crucial importance. The experience of a number of schemes has clearly demonstrated that decisions regarding the location of industry have been the main source of frustration, hindering progress in some cases and leading to complete collapse in at least one case. Hence the theory does have some bearing on reality but this does not mean that it is entirely satisfactory because, despite some initial efforts (El-Agraa, 1979a, 1980; El-Agraa and Jones, 1981, ch. 6; Jones, 1983), it has not yet come to terms with unemployment and economic growth.

A third overall conclusion is that the term economic integration does not seem to mean the same thing for every type of scheme in existence. In advanced Western economies it is about resource reallocation as determined by the law of comparative advantage defined basically in a *static* sense. For developing countries it is about promoting or enhancing economic development and is advanced basically in terms of a *dynamic* infant-industry argument. In the former CMEA it was about production planning and plant location, also defined in a context of dynamic development.

It is probably somewhat unfair to suggest that advanced Western economies are preoccupied with the static resource reallocation effects of integration, since they do in fact recognise the dynamic effects and hope to achieve them. However, their predominant behaviour seems to be in contradiction to this recognition. For example, most of the publicised discussion is conducted in terms of possible trade creation which is basically about replacing a particular nation's own expensive production by cheaper imports from a partner. In spite of this, participants are outraged when they find they are losing production in certain items accompanied by increased imports from a partner of the same item! One of my previous colleagues used to stress to his students that joining the EC meant that British Leyland (then the leading UK car manufacturer) would 'go bust'. Of course, this was an over-exaggeration since what the theory suggests is that sections of that company would have to cut back production or shut down altogether while other sections may get a boost. The point to stress is that the theory, despite its limitations, does point to possible redundancies in certain industrial sectors and to expansion in other sectors, but if redundancies are not acceptable then, in a fully employed world, expansion is impossible. This argument is intuitively reinforced in a world of less than full employment: redundancies here will be vigorously resisted and expansion is impossible since unemployment is basically structural, that is, the pool of unemployed labour does not contain the 'right' skills required in the expanding industrial sector. Alternatively, using modern jargon, one could say that large parts of the unemployment rates are 'natural', hence one should not expect them to be cured through any fiscal policy mix. In short, participating nations seem to enter into arrangements for the possible gains which they then proceed actively to undermine.

Related to the last issue is a point which, hopefully, might become a thing of the past. It is that although economic integration should be pursued for wider economic aims, participants should not be preoccupied with their 'net contribution' to a central budget which pays for specified administrative tasks and, in particular instances, finances certain policies. For example, during the late 1970s and early 1980s, practically every participant in the EC other than West Germany seemed to want to be a 'net recipient' from the EC General Budget; this was a very peculiar demand given that the budget had to be balanced. Admittedly some countries like the UK were making unfair contributions but a situation where each participant had to make a nil net contribution did not make sense. More generally, contributions had to be assessed in the wider context of economic gains and losses and must be discussed with reference to the terms of entry negotiated prior to accession to a scheme; unduly unfair contributions seem to reflect the short-sightedness of those who negotiated the accession treaties in the first place. Of course, they could also be viewed as merely the price that had to be paid for joining an already successful club, especially when the rationale for joining is purely economic.

A very significant overall conclusion is that the global experience of economic integration has clearly demonstrated the ease with which *negative* integration can be achieved and the difficulties involved in making any progress, if at all, in terms of *positive* integration. This should not be surprising, however, since the dismantling of tariff barriers and import quota restrictions is easy, particularly in a world where these have been gradually reduced through multilateral trade negotiations (the Dillon, Kennedy, Tokyo and Uruguay Rounds conducted under the auspices of GATT, now WTO) and the GSP (Generalised System of Preferences) whereby certain industrial exports by developing nations are granted preferential treatment in certain advanced countries. Positive integration, on the other hand, is mainly about non-tariff trade barriers and here harmonisation is of paramount importance. However, harmonisation is a positive act which requires not only concerted action but also, in a number of areas, a certain degree of political commitment with implications for the sensitive issue of sovereignty as, for example, is the case in fiscal harmonisation, monetary integration and the coordination of employment policies.

PROGNOSTICATIONS

Finally, let me prognosticate about the future of economic integration. In 1988 I wrote:

> Haberler described the 1960s as the decade of integration. In this book we have discussed eleven schemes of integration and have omitted almost twice as many. Those left out are very insignificant and the schemes covered encompass practically the whole world except for such large countries as China, India, Japan and the USA. Given that the basic justification for economic integration, particularly for developing nations, is in terms of increased size of market, it would seem that the prospects for further schemes are very limited. Of course there are prospects for higher levels of integration and for different rearrangements of groupings but these will not add significantly to the actual *number* of countries involved. Moreover, as the experience of the European Community has clearly demonstrated, economic integration is very attractive when participants are experiencing very high rates of [economic] growth because under such conditions even the 'regional problem' loses some of its importance. But in a stagnating world, particularly one suffering from stagflation, national interests will predominate in any discussion and will, therefore, cloud the issues. Thus, given these two considerations, it would seem that Haberler's statement is here to stay.
>
> This, however, does not mean that the world has exhausted the possibilities for integration in the future. On the contrary, in terms of achieving *positive* integration the world is at an embryonic stage. Hence, the true challenges of integration are still to be faced and the day that one can look back and say that such a period was 'the decade of positive integration' should be awaited with extreme fascination. (El-Agraa, 1988, pp. 334–5)

As we have seen since then the US, together with Canada, formed CUFTA and then added Mexico to create NAFTA. Moreover, the US, its NAFTA partners, China, Japan and thirteen other Asia-Pacific nations established the APEC forum. Hence, it would seem that my predictions were completely off the mark. However, Mexico was a member of LAFTA, six of the eighteen APEC nations are members of ASEAN, Chile belonged to LAFTA and Australia and New Zealand are together in the CER. Furthermore, the US and Canada have always been considered as one market, Hong Kong is set to revert to China in 1997 and Papua New Guinea has always been regarded as a member of the CER. Of course, the addition of China, Japan, South Korea and Taiwan does nullify my prediction regarding the *actual* number of nations. Nevertheless, apart from this reality, I do believe that the *gist* of my previous statement has remained intact.

Bibliography

Agarwal, J. P., Dippl, M. and Langhammer, R. J. (1985), *EC Trade Policies Towards Associated Developing Countries: Barriers to Success*, (Tubingen: Mohr).

Amelung, T. (1992), 'Regionalization of Trade in the Asia- Pacific: A Statistical Approach', *ASEAN Economic Bulletin*, vol. 9.

Anderson, K. and Snape R. (1994), 'European and American Regionalism: Effects on and Options for Asia', *Journal of the Japanese and International Economies*, vol. 8.

Anglin, D. (1961), 'The Political Development of the West Indies', in D. Lowenthal (ed.), *The West Indies Federation* (New York: Columbia University Press).

Antolik, M. (1993), 'ASEAN's Bridges to Vietnam and Laos', *Contemporary Southeast Asia*, vol. 15.

Anyadike-Danes, M. K. and Anyadike-Danes, M. N. (1992), 'The Geographic Distribution of the European Development Fund under the Lomé Conventions', in *World Development*, vol. 20.

Ariff, M. *et al.* (eds) (1977), *ASEAN Cooperation in Industrial Projects* (Kuala Lumpur: Malaysian Economic Association).

Ariff, M. (1980), 'Malaysia's Trade and Industrialisation Strategy with Special Reference to ASEAN Industrial Cooperation', in R. Garnaut (ed.), *ASEAN in a Changing Pacific and World Economy* (Canberra: Australian National University Press).

Ariff, M. (1994), 'Open Regionalism a la ASEAN', *Journal of Asian Economics*, vol. 5.

Ariff, M. and Tan, G. (1992), 'ASEAN-Pacific Trade Relations', *ASEAN Economic Bulletin*, vol. 8.

Arndt, S. W. (1968), 'On Discriminatory Versus Non-preferential Tariff Policies', *Economic Journal*, vol. 78.

Arndt, H. W. and Garnaut, R. (1979), 'ASEAN and the Industrialisation of East Asia', *Journal of Common Market Studies*, vol. 17, no. 3.

ASEAN Secretariat (1978), *10 Years ASEAN* (Jakarta: ASEAN).

Axline, W. A. (1978), 'Integration and Development in the Commonwealth Caribbean: The Politics of Regional Negotiations', *International Organization*, vol. 32, no. 4.

Axline, W. (1979), *Caribbean Integration: The Politics of Regionalism* (New York: Nichols).

Bacha, E. and Taylor, L. (1971), 'Foreign Exchange Shadow Prices: A Critical Review of Current Theories', *Quarterly Journal of Economics*, vol. 85.

Badiane, O. (1992), 'Regional Integration in West Africa: The Importance of Country Macroeconomic and Sector Policies' (Washington: International Food Policy Research Institute), mimeo.

Baerresen, D. Carnoy, M. and Grunwald, J. (1965), *Latin American Trade Patterns* (Washington, DC: Brookings Institution).

Balassa, B. (1962), *The Theory of Economic Integration* (London: Allen & Unwin).

Balassa, B. (1967), 'Trade Creation and Trade Diversion in the European Common Market', *Economic Journal*, vol. 77.

Balassa, B. (1974), 'Trade Creation and Trade Diversion in the European Common Market: An Appraisal of the Evidence', *Manchester School*, vol. 42, no. 2.

Balassa, B. (ed.) (1975), *European Economic Integration* (Amsterdam: North-Holland).

Balassa, B. (1977), 'Avantages comparés et perspectives de l'intégration Économique Afrique de l'Quest', unpublished.

Balassa, B. (1989), 'Europe 1992 and its Possible Implications for Nonmember Countries', in J. H. Schott (ed.), *Free Trade Areas and US Trade Policy*, (Washington, DC: Institute for International Economics).

Baldinelli, E. (1977), 'A New Road to Latin American Integration', *Comercio Exterior de Mexico*, vol. 23, no. 1.

Baldwin, Richard. E. (1970), *Non-tariff distortions of Trade* (Washington, DC: Brookings Institution, London: Allen & Unwin).

Baldwin, Robert. E. (1989), 'The Growth Effects of 1992', *Economic Policy*, October.

Baldwin, Robert. E. and Murray, T. (1977), 'MFN Tariff Reductions and Developing Country Trade Benefits under the GSP', in *The Economic Journal*, vol. 87.

Banco de México (1995), *Informe Anual 1994* (Mexico, D.F.: Banco de México).

Banco Nacional de Comercio Exterior (1963), *La integración económica Latinoamericana* (Mexico).

Bandawe, H. and Glen, L. (1991), 'A Case for Regional Exchange Rate Management for CARICOM', *Social and Economic Studies*, vol. 40.

Barker, T. S. (1970), 'Aggregation Error and Estimates of the UK Import Demand Function', in K. Hilton and D. Heathfield (eds), *The Econometric Study of the United Kingdom* (London: Macmillan).

Barrell, R., Sefton, J. and In't Veld, J. (1996), 'Fiscal Policy and the Maastricht Solvency Criteria', *Manchester School*, vol. 66.

Barrett, F. A. (1981), 'The Rise and Demise of the Federation of the West Indies', in R. M. Delson (ed.), *Readings in Caribbean History and Economics: An Introduction to the Region* (New York: Gordon & Breach).

Barten, A. P., D'Alcantra, G. and Cairn, G. J. (1976), 'COMET, a Medium-term Macroeconomic Model for the European Economic Community', *European Economic Review*, vol. 7, no. 1.

Barsotti, F. (1991), 'CARICOM: Facing the Question of Survival in the 21st Century', *Caribbean Affairs*, vol. 4.

Bayliss, B. T. (1985), 'Competition and Industrial Policy', in A. M. El-Agraa (ed.), *The Economics of the European Community* (Oxford: Philip Allan).

Beblawi, H. (1984), *The Arab Gulf Economy in a Turbulent Age* (Bechenkam: Croom Helm).

Beckford, G. (1976), *Caribbean Economy* (Mona, Jamaica: Institute of Social and Economic Research).

Begg, I. G. and Mayes, D. G. (1993), 'Cohesion in the European Community: A Key Imperative for the 1990s?', *Regional Science and Urban Economics*, vol. 23.

Begg, I. G., Mayes, D. G., Levitt, M. and Shipman, A. (1991), 'A Strategy for Social and Economic Cohesion after 1992', *European Parliament Research Papers*, no. 44 (Brussels/Luxembourg: European Union).

Behrman, J. N. (1972), *The Role of International Companies in Latin American Integration* (Lexington, Mass.: Heath).

Bennett, K. (1982a), 'An Evaluation of the Contribution of CARICOM to Intra-regional Caribbean Trade', *Social and Economic Studies*, vol. 31.

Bennett, K. (1982b), *Trade and Payments in the Caribbean Community* (Mona: ISER, UWI).

Bennett, K. (1983), 'Exchange Rate Policy and External Imbalance: The Jamaican Experience 1973–1982', *Social and Economic Studies*, vol. 32.

Bennett, K. (1985), 'A Note on Exchange Rate Policy and Caribbean Integration', *Social and Economic Studies*, vol. 34.

Bennett, K. (1990), 'Monetary Integration in CARICOM', Sixth Adlith Brown Memorial Lecture, Regional Programme of Monetary Studies, Georgetown, Guyana.

Berg, E. (1993), 'L'Intégration economique en Afrique de l'Ouest: problèmes et stratégies', *Revue d'Economie du Développement*, vol. 1.

Berglas, E. (1983), 'The Case of Unilateral Tariff Preductions: Foreign Tariffs Reconsidered', *American Economic Review*, vol. 73.

Bergsten, C. F. and Krause, L. B. (eds) (1975), *World Politics and International Economics* (Washington, DC: Brookings Institution).

Bhagwati, J. N. (1969), *Trade, Tariffs and Growth* (London: Weidenfeld & Nicolson).

Bhagwati, J. N. (1971), 'Customs Unions and Welfare Improvement', *Economic Journal*, vol. 81.

Binswanger, H. C. and Mayrzedt, H. M. (1972), *Europa Politik der Rest-EFTA Staaten*, Schultheses Poligraphischer Verlag, Zurich (Vienna: Wilhelm Braumüller).

Blackman, C. (1989), 'The Exchange Rate in the Balance of Payments Adjustment Process of CARICOM States', *CEMLA Monetary Affairs*, vol. 11.

Blades, H. (1993), 'A Proposal for a CARICOM Customs Tariff – the CCT', *Caribbean Affairs*, vol. 6.

Blake, B. (1976), *Anti-polarisation and Distribution Mechanism in CARICOM* (Georgetown, Guyana: CARICOM Secretariat).

Blake, B. (1979), *The Caribbean Community: An Assessment* (Georgetown, Guyana: CARICOM Secretariat).

Blankart, F. A. (1979), 'Interdépendance et intégration', paper presented to a conference on 'la Suisse et la Communauté élargie: perspectives à long terme', held at the Battelle Institute, Geneva, November.

Blomqvist, H. (1993), 'ASEAN as a Model for Third World Regional Economic Co-operation?' *ASEAN Economic Bulletin*, vol. 10, July.

Bobb, L. E. (1966), 'The Federal Principle in the British West Indies: An Appraisal of its use', *Social and Economic Studies*, vol. 15.

Booz, A. and Booz, H. (1986), 'The Cost of Europe's Fragmented Markets', *Wall Street Journal*.

Borchardt, K.-D. (1995), *European Integration: the Origin and Growth of the European Union*, 4th edn (Luxembourg: Office for Official Publications of the EU).

Bourne, C. (1988), *Caribbean Development to the year 2000: Challenges, Prospects and Policies* (London: Commonwealth Secretariat).

Bourne, C. and Oumade Singh, R. (1988), 'External Debt and Adjustment in Caribbean Countries', *Social and Economic Studies*, vol. 37.

Bourne, C. and Nicholls, S. M. A. (1990), 'The Real Debt Service Capacity of Commonwealth Caribbean Countries: A Preliminary Econometric Study of Barbados and Trinidad and Tobago', *Social and Economic Studies*, vol. 39.

Bourne, C., St Cyr, E., Howard, M. and Clarke, C. (1987), 'Industrialization and Foreign Trade in the Caribbean Basin: The Case of CARICOM Countries', report prepared for the Inter-American Development Bank, mimeo.

Brainard, L. J. (1980), 'CMEA Financial System and Integration', in P. Marer and J. M. Montias (eds), *East European Integration and East–West Trade* (Bloomington: Indiana University Press).

Braithwaite, L. (1957a), 'Progress towards Federation, 1938–1956', *Social and Economic Studies*, vol. 6.

Braithwaite, L. (1957b), '"Federal" Association and Institutions in the West Indies', *Social and Economic Studies*, vol. 6.

Brewster, H. (1971), 'Caribbean Economic Integration: Problems and Perspectives', *Journal of Common Market Studies*, vol. 9.

Brewster, H. (1977), 'Focus on CARICOM: An Overview of the Political Power', *Caribbean Contact*, vol. 5, no. 4.

Brewster, H. (1992), 'The Caribbean Community in a Changing International Environment: Towards the Next Century', Eighth Adlith Brown Memorial Lecture, Regional Programme of Monetary Studies, ISER, UWI.

Brewster, H. and Thomas, C. Y. (1967), *Dynamics of West Indian Integration* (Mona, Jamaica: Institute of Social and Economic Research).

Brewster, H. and Thomas, C. Y. (1969a), 'El Liberalismo Economico y Concepto de Integracion', *Foro International*, no. 36.

Brewster, H. and Thomas, C. Y. (1969b), 'Aspects of the Theory of Economic Integration', *Journal of Common Market Studies*, vol. 8.

Brown, A. J. (1961), 'Economic Separatism Versus a Common Market in Developing Countries', *Bulletin of Economic Research*, vol. 13.

Brown, A. J. (1972), *The Framework of Regional Economics in the United Kingdom* (Cambridge: Cambridge University Press).

Brown, A. J. (1980), 'Fiscal Policy: II the Budget', in A. M. El-Agraa (ed.), *The Economics of the European Community* (Oxford: Philip Allan).

Brown, A. J. (1985), 'The General Budget', in A. M. El-Agraa (ed.), *The Economics of the European Community*, 2nd edn (Oxford: Philip Allan).

Brown, D. K. (1989), 'Trade and Welfare Effects of the European Schemes of the Generalized System of Preferences', in *Economic Development and Cultural Change*, vol. 37.

Brus, W. (1979), 'Economic Reform and COMECON Integration in the decade 1966–75', *Wirtschaft und Gesellschaft: Kritik und Alternativen* (Berlin: Dunker & Humbolt).

Buckley, P. J. and Casson, M. (1976), *The Future of the Multinational Enterprise* (London: Macmillan).

Buigues, P. and Sheehy, J. (1993), 'Recent Developments and Trends of European Integration', paper prepared for a seminar 'Latin America's Competitive Position in the Enlarged European Market', Hamburg, March.

Bulmer-Thomas, V. G. (1976), 'The Structure of Protection in Costa Rica – a New Approach to Calculating the Effective Rate of Protection', *Journal of Economic Studies*, vol. 3.

Bulmer-Thomas, V. G. (1979), 'Import Substitution v. Export Promotion in the Central American Common Market', *Journal of Economic Studies*, vol. 6.

Bulmer-Thomas, V. G. (1983), 'Economic Development over the Long Run – Central America since 1920', *Journal of Latin American Studies*, vol. 15.

Bulmer-Thomas, V. G. (1987a), 'The Balance of Payments Crisis and Adjustment Programmes in Central America', in R. Thorp and L. Whitehead (eds), *Latin American Debt and the Adjustment Crisis* (London: Macmillan).

Bulmer-Thomas, V. G. (1987b), *The Political Economy of Central America since 1920* (Cambridge University Press).

Bulmer-Thomas, V. (1988), 'The Central American Common Market', in El-Agraa, A. M. (ed.), *International Economic Integration*, 2nd edn (London: Macmillan).

Bulmer-Thomas, V. (1992), *Regional Integration in Central America: Impact of Free Trade in Basic Grains* (Miami: Iberian Studies Institute, University of Miami).

Bulmer-Thomas, V. (1994), *The Economic History of Latin America since Independence* (Cambridge: Cambridge University Press).

Bulmer-Thomas, V., Cerdas Cruz, R., Gallardo, E. and Seligson, M. (1992), *Central American Integration* (Miami: European Community Research Institute, University of Miami).

Bureau of Economic Analysis, US Department of Commerce (1993), *US Direct Investment Abroad: Operations of US Parent Companies and Their Foreign Affiliates* (Washington, DC: US Government Printing Office).

Burns, J. (1984), 'Latin American Moves Towards Common Market', *Financial Times*, London, 9 May.

Burridge, M. and Mayes, D. G. (1990), 'Industrial Change for 1992', in D. Driver and P. Dunne (eds), *Structural Change and the UK Economy* (Cambridge: Cambridge University Press).

Burridge, M. and Mayes, D. G. (1993), 'The Impact of the Internal Market Programme on European Economic Structure and Performance', *European Parliament Working Paper*, E-2, July.

Burridge, M. Dhar, S., Mayes, D. G., Meen, G., Neal, E., Tyrell, G. and Walker, J. (1991), 'Oxford Economic Forecasting's System of Models', *Economic Modelling*, vol. 8.

Byé, M. (1950), 'Unions douaniéres et données nationales', *Economie Appliquée*, vol. 3; reprinted in translation as 'Customs Unions and National Interests', *International Economic Papers*, no. 3, 1953.

Bywater, M. (1990), *Andean Integration: A New Lease of Life?* Special Report No. 2018 (London: Economist Intelligence Unit).

Cable, V. (1969), 'The Football War and the Central American Common Market', *International Affairs*, October.

Caceres, L. R. (1979), 'Economic Integration and Export Instability in Central America: A Portfolio Model', in S. Smith and J. Toye (eds), *Trade and Poor Economies* (London: Frank Cass).

Cairncross, A. *et al.* (1974), *Economic Policy for the European Economic Community: The Way Forward* (London: Macmillan).

Caribbean Commission (1954), 'The Nature and Direction of Caribbean Trade', *Caribbean Economic Review*, vol. 6.

CARICOM SECRETARIAT (1971), *CARIFTA and the New Caribbean* (Georgetown: CARICOM Secretariat).

CARICOM SECRETARIAT (1972), *From CARIFTA to the Caribbean Community* (Georgetown: CARICOM Secretariat).

CARICOM SECRETARIAT (1973), *The Caribbean Community: A Guide* (Georgetown: CARICOM Secretariat).

CARICOM SECRETARIAT (1973), *Treaty of Chaguaramas* (Georgetown: CARICOM Secretariat).

CARICOM SECRETARIAT (1977), *Review of the Special Regime for the LDCs* (Georgetown: CARICOM Secretariat).

CARICOM SECRETARIAT (1980), *Developments in CARICOM since 1973* (Georgetown: CARICOM Secretariat).

CARICOM Secretariat (1981), *Caribbean Common Market: A Guide to the Common Market Rules* (Georgetown: CARICOM Secretariat).

CARICOM Secretariat (1991a), *Common External Tariff of the CARICOM Market: An Explanation of its Scope and Operational Features* (Georgetown: CARICOM Secretariat).

CARICOM Secretariat (1991b), 'Purpose, Scope, Application of CET', *Caribbean Affairs*, vol. 4.

CARICOM Secretariat (1992), *CARICOM: Single Market and Economy* (Georgetown: CARICOM).

Casson, M. (1980), 'The Theory of Foreign Direct Investment', in *Conference Proceedings*, International Economics Study Group (Brighton: University of Sussex).

CEAO (1973), *Traité Instituant la Communauté Economique de l'Afrique de l'Quest* (Ougadougon).

CEAO, *Journal Officiel*, various years (Ougadougon).

CEAO (1979), *Statistiques des Produits Agréés à la T. C. R.* (Ougadougon).

CEAO (1979), *Tarif d'Usage T. C. R.* (Ougadougon).

CEAO (1983), 'Balance preliminar de la economia latinoamericana durante 1983', Information Document, December 16, Santiago de Chille.

Cecchini, P. (1988), *The European Challenge 1992: The Benefits of a Single Market* (Aldershot: Wildwood House).

CEPAL (1976), *América Latina: Relación de Precios del Intercambio*. Cuadernos Estadísticos de la CEPAL (Santiago, Chile: United Nations).

CEPAL (1979), *Reexamen de la integración económica en América Latina y busqueda de nuevas orientaciones*, E/CEPAL/R. 209, October, Santiago de Chille.

CEPAL (1995), *Centroamérica: Evolución de la Integración Económica durante 1994 y avances en los primeros meses de 1995* (Santiago, Chile: United Nations).

Chee, P. L. (1987), 'Asean Co-operation in Industry: Looking Back and Looking Forward', in N. Sopiee, L. S. Chew and S. J. Lim (eds), *ASEAN at the Crossroads: Obstacles, Options and Opportunities for Economic Co-operation* (Kuala Lumpur: Institute of Strategic and International Studies).

Chenery, H. B. (1960), 'Patterns of Industrial Growth', *American Economic Review*, vol. 50.

Chernick S. (1978), *The Commonwealth Caribbean: The Integration Experience* (A World Bank Country Report) (Baltimore: Johns Hopkins Press).

Chia, S. Y. and Lee, T. Y. (1993), 'Subregional Economic Zones: A New Motive Force in Asia-Pacific Development', in C. F. Bergsten and M. Noland (eds), *Pacific Dynamism and the International Economic System* (Washington, DC: Institute for International Economics).

Choi, J-Y. and Yu, E. S. H. (1985), 'Technical Progress, Terms of Trade and Welfare under Variable Returns to Scale', *Economica*, vol. 52, no. 257.

Clark Leith, J. (1992), 'The Static Welfare Effects of a Small Developing Country's Membership in a Customs Union: Botswana in the Southern African Customs Union', *World Development*, vol. 20.

Clark Leith, J. (1993), 'A Simple Measure for the Evaluation of Trade Policy Options with Application for Botswana', *Development Discussion Paper*, No 452 (Cambridge, Mass: Harvard Institute for International Development).

Cline, W. R. (1978), 'Benefits and Costs of Economic Integration in Central America', in W. R. Cline and E. Delgado (eds), *Economic Integration in Central America* (Washington, DC: Brookings Institution).

Cline, W. R. and Rapoport, A. (1978a), 'Industrial Comparative Advantage in the Central American Common Market', in W. R. Cline and E. Delgado (eds), *Economic Integration in Central America* (Washington, DC: Brookings Institution).

Cline, W. R. and Rapoport, A. (1978b), 'Industrial Comparative Advantage: Supplementary Tables', Appendix F of W. R. Cline and E. Delgado (eds), *Economic Integration in Latin America* (Washington, DC: Brookings Institution).

Cobbe, J. H. (1980), 'Integration among Unequals: The Southern African Customs Union and Development', *World Development*, vol. 8.

Cobham, D. and Robson, P. (1994), 'Monetary Integration in Africa: A Deliberately European Perspective', *World Development*, vol. 22.

Codrington, H. (1992), 'The Common Currency Decisions: Some Implication for Barbados' (Central Bank of Barbados), mimeo.

Cohen Orantes, I. (1972), *Regional Integration in Central America* (Lexington, Mass.: Lexington Books).

Collins, C. D. E. (1980), 'History and Institutions of the EC', in A. M. El-Agraa (ed.), *The Economics of the European Community*, 1st edn (Oxford: Philip Allan).

Collins, C. D. E. (1985), 'Social Policy', in A. M. El-Agraa (ed.), *The Economics of the European Community*, 2nd edn (Oxford: Philip Allan).

Collins, C. D. E. (1994), 'History and Institutions of the EC', in A. M. El-Agraa, *The Economics of the European Community*, 4th edn (Hemel Hempstead: Harvester Wheatsheaf; New York: Prentice Hall Int.).

Comercio Exterior de México, monthly report on Latin American Integration.

Comercio Exterior de México, (1983), 'Asociación Latinoamericana de integración – prevalence el bilaterisme', vol. 33, no. 6, July.

Commission of the European communities (1970), 'Report to the Council and the Commission on the Realisation by Stages of Economic and Monetary Union in the Community', *Bulletin of the European Communities*, Supplement 11 (The Werner Report).

Commission of the European Communities (1975), *Report of the Study Group Economic and Monetary Union 1980*, Brussels, March (The Marjolin Report).

Commission of the European Communities (1977), *Report of the Study Group on the Role of Public Finance in European Integration*, 2 vols, Brussels, April (The MacDougall Report).

Commission of the European Communities (1980), *La Suisse et la Communauté* (Brussels).

Commission of the European Communities (1985), 'Completing the Internal Market', *White Paper* from the Commission to the European Council, Brussels.

Commission of the European Communities (1988), 'The Economics of 1992', *European Economy*, no. 35.

Commission of the European Communities (1989), *Research on the Costs of Non-Europe*, 16 volumes. This is known as The Cecchini Report.

Commission of the European Communities (1990), 'One market, one money: an evaluation of the potential benefits and costs of forming an economic and monetary union', *European Economy*.

Commission of the European Communities (1992), 'Development Cooperation Policy in the Run-up to 2000', *Report SEC(92) 915 final*, Brussels.

Commission of the European Communities (1993a), 'The European Community as a World Trading Partner', *European Economy*, no. 53.

Commission of the European Communities (1993b), 'Memorandum on the Community's Development Aid in 1991', Brussels, unpublished.

Commission of the European Communities (1993c), 'The Run-up to 2000: Identifying Priority areas for the Coordination of Development Cooperation Policies Between the Community and the Member States', *Doc. COM(93)123 final*, Brussels.

Commission of the European Communities (1993d), 'Eleventh Annual Report of the Commission on the Community's Antidumping and Antisubsidy Activities', *Report COM(93)156*, Brussels.

Commission of the European Communities (1993e), 'Procedures for Coordination Between the Community and its Member States at Policy and Operational Levels', *Doc. COM(93)195 final*, Brussels.

Commission of the European Communities (1994a), 'Integration of the Developing Countries in the International Trading System: The Role of GSPs – 1995 to 2004', *Doc COM(94)212*, Brussels.

Commission of the European Communities (1994b), *The Uruguay Round: Global Agreement, Global Benefits* (Luxembourg: Office for Official Publications of the European Communities).

Commission of the European Union (1995a), 'Financial Cooperation Under Lomé: Review of Aid at the end of 1993', *Doc. DE 179*, Brussels.

Commission of the European Union (1995b), *General Report of the Activities of the European Union 1994*, Brussels.

Cooper, C. A. and Massell, B. F. (1965a), 'A New Look at Customs Union Theory', *Economic Journal*, vol. 75.

Cooper, C. A. and Massell, B. F. (1965b), 'Towards a General Theory of Customs Unions in Developing Countries', *Journal of Political Economy*, vol. 73.

Corden, W. M. (1972a), 'Economies of Scale and Customs Union Theory', *Journal of Political Economy*, vol. 80.

Corden, W. M. (1972b), 'Monetary Integration', *Essays in International Finance*, no. 93, April (Princeton University).

Corden, W. M. (1977), *Inflation, Exchange Rates and the World Economy* (Oxford: Oxford University Press).

Corner, D. C. and Stafford, D. C. (1977), *Open-ended Investment Funds in the EEC and Switzerland* (London: Macmillan).

Cosgrove-Twitchett, C. (1978), *Europe and Africa: From Association to Partnership* (Westmead: Saxon House).

Court of Auditors of the EC/EU (1982), *Annual Report Concerning the Financial Year 1981*, Part II, Official Journal of the European Communities, 31 December, Brussels.

Court of Auditors of the EC/EU (1994), *Annual Report Concerning the Financial Year 1993*, Official Journal of the European Communities, 24 November, Brussels.

Court of Auditors of the EC/EU (1995), 'The Stabex Fund in the Context of the First Financial Protocol of the Fourth Lomé Convention', *Special Report No. 2/95*, Luxembourg.

Cuthberston, K. C., Henry, S. G. B., Mayes, D. G. and Savage, D. (1980), 'Modelling and Forecasting the Rate of Exchange', *Conference Proceedings*, International Economics Study Group (University of Sussex).

Dam, K. W. (1970), *The GATT: Law and International Economic Organization* (Chicago: University of Chicago Press).

Danns, D. (1990), *History of the Bank of Guyana, 1965–1990* (Georgetown: Bank of Guyana).

Deardorff, A. V. and Stern, R. (1985), Methods of Measurement of NTBs, *UNCTAD Doc. STD/MD/28*, Geneva, United Nations Conference on Trade and Development.

de Clercq, W. (1988), 'European into the 1990's and Beyond: Opportunities and Constraints', in J. Jamar and H. Wallace (eds), *EEC–EFTA: More than Just Good Friends*? (Bruges Collège d'Europe.)

De Grauwe, P. (1975), 'Conditions for Monetary Integration: A Geometric Interpretation', *Weltwirtschaftliches Archiv*, vol. 111.

Delgado, E. (1978), 'Institutional Evolution of the Central American Common Market and the Principle of Balanced Development', in W. R. Cline and E. Delgado (eds), *Economic Integration in Central America* (Washington, DC: Brookings Institution).

Dell, S. (1966), *A Latin American Common Market?* (Oxford: Oxford University Press).

Demas, W. (1960), 'The Economies of West Indies Customs Union', *Social and Economic Studies*, vol. 9.

Demas, W. (1965), *The Economics of Development in Small Countries with Special Reference to the Caribbean* (Montreal: McGill University Press).

Demas, W. (1974a), *West Indian Nationhood and Caribbean Integration* (Barbados: CCC Publishing House).

Demas, W. (1974b), *Some Thoughts on the Caribbean Community* (Georgetown, Guyana: CARICOM Secretariat).

Demas, W. (1976), *Essays on Caribbean Integration and Development* (Mona, Jamaica: Institute of Social and Economic Research).

Demas, W. (1978), 'The Caribbean and the New International Economic Order', *Journal of Inter-American Studies and World Affairs*, vol. 10, no. 3.

de Melo, J. and Panagariya, A. (eds) (1993), *New Dimensions in Regional Integration* (Cambridge: Cambridge University Press).

Denison, E. F. (assisted by J-P Poullier) (1967), *Why Growth Rates Differ: Post-war Experience in Nine Western Countries* (Washington, DC: Brookings Institution).

de Paiva Abreu, M. (1995), 'Trade in Manufactures: The Outcome of the Uruguay Round and Developing Countries' Interests', paper presented at the World Bank Conference on the Uruguay Round, Washington, DC.

Department of Foreign Affairs and Trade (Australia) (1994), *The APEC Region, Trade and Investment*, November (Canberra: DFAT).

Deppler, M. C. and Ripley, D. M. (1978), 'The World Trade Model: Merchandise Trade', *IMF Staff Papers*, vol. 25, no. 1, March.

de Vries, B. A. (1977), 'Exports in the New World Environment: The Case of Latin America', *CEPAL Review*, vol. 3.

Devarejan, S. and de Melo, J. (1987), 'Evaluating Participation in African Monetary Zones: A Statistical Analysis of the CFA Zones', *World Development*, vol. 15.

Devarejan, S. and de Melo, J. (1991), 'Membership in the CFA Zone: Odyssean Journey or Trojan Horse?', in A. Chhibber and S. Fischer (eds), *Economic Reform in Sub-Saharan Africa* (Washington, DC: World Bank).

Diaz-Alejandro, C. and Helleiner, G. K. (1987), 'Developing Countries and the Reform of the World Trading System', in D. Salvatore (ed.), *The New Protectionist Threat to World Welfare* (Amsterdam: North Holland).

Dobson, W. and Yuan, L. T. (1994), 'APEC: Co-operation amidst Diversity', *ASEAN Economic Bulletin*, vol. 10.

Dosser, D. (1973), 'Tax Harmonisation in the European Community', *Three Banks Review*, no. 98.

Dunning, J. H. (1977), 'Trade Location of Economic Activity and the MNE: A Search for an Eclectic Approach', in B. Ohlin, P. Hesselborn and P. M. Wijkman (eds), *The International Allocation of Economic Activity* (London: Macmillan).

Dunning, J. H. (1980), 'Explaining the International Direct Investment Position of Countries: Towards a Dynamic or Developmental Approach', *Conference Proceedings*, International Economics Study Group (Brighton University of Sussex).

Durham, W. H. (1979), *Scarcity and Survival in Central America* (Stanford: Stanford University Press).

East Asia Analytical Unit (1994), *ASEAN Free Trade Area: Trading Bloc or Building Block?* (Canberra: Australian Government Publishing Service).

Echegaray, S. (1983), 'El proceso de revisión de los mecanismos financieros de la ALADI', *Integración Latinoamericana*, year VIII, no. 83, September.

ECLA, see UN Commission for Latin America.

Economic Commission for Europe (1995), 'Economic Integration in Europe and North America', *Economic Studies*, no. 5, edited by M. Panić and A. M. Vacic (New York and Geneva: United Nations).

EFTA Secretariat (1966), *Building EFTA: A Free Trade Area in Europe (Geneva).*
EFTA Secretariat (1968), *The Effects on Prices of Tariff Dismantling in EFTA (Geneva).*
EFTA Secretariat (1969), *The Effects of EFTA on the Economies of Member States* (Geneva).
EFTA Secretariat (1980a), *EFTA – Past and Future* (Geneva).
EFTA Secretariat (1980b), *The European Free Trade Association* (Geneva).
EFTA Secretariat (1984), *EFTA Trade 1984* (Geneva).
EFTA Secretariat (1985), *EFTA Trade 1985* (Geneva).
El-Agraa, A. M. (1969) 'The Sudan and the Arab Common Market: A Conflict', *Eastern Africa Economic Review*, vol. 3.
El-Agraa, A. M. (1979a) 'Common Markets in Developing Countries', in J. K. Bowers (ed.), *Inflation, Development and Integration: Essays in Honour of A. J. Brown* (Leeds: Leeds University Press).
El-Agraa, A. M. (1979b), 'On Tariff Bargaining', *Bulletin of Economic Research*, vol. 31.
El-Agraa, A. M. (ed.) (1980), *The Economics of the European Community* (Oxford: Philip Allan).
El-Agraa, A. M. (1981) 'Customs unions in developing countries', in A. M. El-Agraa and A. J. Jones, *Theory of Customs Unions* (Oxford: Philip Allon; New York: St Martin's Press).
El-Agraa, A. M. (ed.) (1982), *International Economic Integration* (London: Macmillan).
El-Agraa, A. M. (ed.) (1983a), *Britain Within the European Community: The Way Forward* (London: Macmillan).
El-Agraa, A. M. (1983b), *The Theory of International Trade* (Beckenham: Croom Helm).
El-Agraa, A. M. (1984a), *Trade Theory and Policy: Some Topical Issues* (London: Macmillan).
El-Agraa, A. M. (1984b), 'The Distributional Implications of Economic Integration in Developing Countries', *Kashmir Economic Review*, vol. 1, no. 1.
El-Agraa, A. M. (1984c), 'Has Membership of the European Communities Been a Disaster for Britain?', *Applied Economics*, vol. 16, no. 1.
El-Agraa, A. M. (1984d), Review of *The Arab Gulf Economy in a Turbulent Age* by H. Beblawi, in *Arabia*, September.
El-Agraa, A. M. (ed.) (1985a), *The Economics of the European Community*, 2nd edn (Oxford: Philip Allan).
El-Agraa, A. M. (1985b), 'Assessments of the Burdens of the CAP', *Kokusai Mondai* (International Affairs), no. 308, November.
El-Agraa, A. M. (1985c), 'On Measuring the Economic Consequences of British Membership of the EC by Pomfret', *Applied Economics*, vol. 17, no. 4.
El-Agraa, A. M. (1986), 'An Equitable Budget for the European Community?', in A. M. El-Agraa (ed.), *Protection, Cooperation, Development and Integration: Essays in Honour of Professor Hiroshi Kitamura* (London: Macmillan).
El-Agraa, A. M. (ed.) (1988a), *International Economic Integration* (London: Macmillan), 2nd edition.

El-Agraa, A. M. (1988b), *Japan's Trade Frictions: Realities or Misconceptions?* (London: Macmillan).

El-Agraa, A. M. (1989), *The Theory and Measurement of International Economic Integration* (London: Macmillan).

El-Agraa, A. M. (1990), 'The Need for Rationalisation of Arab League Integration Attempts', *The Middle East Business and Economic Review*, vol. 2.

El-Agraa, A. M. (1994a), 'The Economics of the Single Market', in A. M. El-Agraa, *The Economics of the European Community* (New York, Harvester Wheatsheaf).

El-Agraa, A. M. (1994b), 'Economic Integration', in E. Grilli and D. Salvatore (eds), *Economic Development*, Handbook of Comparative Economic Policies vol. 4 (Westport Conn. and London: Greenwood Press).

El-Agraa, A. M. (1994c), *The Economics of the European Community* (Hemel Hempstead: Harvester Wheatsheaf).

El-Agraa, A. M. (1995), 'Mini-symposium on Japan's Trade Policy', *The World Economy*, vol. 18.

El-Agraa, A. M. and Goodrich, P. S. (1980), 'Factor Mobility With Specific Reference to the Accounting Profession', in A. M. El-Agraa (ed.), *The Economics of the European Community* (Oxford: Philip Allan).

El-Agraa, A. M. and Jones, A. J. (1981), *Theory of Customs Unions* (Oxford: Philip Allan).

El-Agraa, A. M. and Majocchi, A. (1983), 'Devising a Proper Fiscal Stance for the European Community', *Revista Di Diritto Finanziario E Scienza Delle Finanze*, Anno XLII–N. 3, September.

El-Agraa, A. M. and Hu, Y.-S. (1984), 'National Versus Superanational Interests and the Problems of Establishing an Effective EC Energy Policy', *Journal of Common Market Studies*, vol. 22, no. 4.

El-Agraa, A. M. and Hu, Y.-S. (1985), 'Energy Policy', in A. M. El-Agraa (ed.), *The Economics of the European Community*, 2nd edn (Oxford: Philip Allan).

El-Agraa, A. M. and Hojman, D. (1988) 'The Andean Pact', in El-Agraa, A. M. (ed.), *International Economic Integration*, 2nd edn (London: Macmillan).

El Azhary, M. S. (ed.) (1984), *The Impact of Oil Revenues on Arab Gulf Development* (Beckenham: Croom Helm).

Emerson, M. (1979) 'The European Monetary System in the Broader Setting of the Community's Economic and Political Development', in P. H. Trezise (ed.), *The European Monetary System: Its Promise and Prospects* (Washington, DC: Brookings Institution).

Emerson, M., Aujean, M., Catinat, M., Goybet, P. and Jacquemin, A. (1988), 'The Economics of 1992', *European Economy*, no. 35 (reissued by Oxford University Press).

Eminent Persons Group (1994), *Achieving the APEC Vision: Free and Open Trade in the Asia-Pacific*, Second Report (Singapore: APEC).

European Research Associates (1983), *The European Community and EFTA in the 1980s: How can the West European Free Trade System be Preserved and Expanded?* A Report to the EC Commission (Brussels: EC Commission).

Faini, R. and Portes, R. (eds) (1995), *European Union Trade with Eastern Europe* (London: Centre for Economic Policy Research).

Farrell, T. (1977), 'Why CARICOM Will Fail: What Can Be Done About It?', *Caribbean Contact*, vol. 5, no. 2, July.

Farrell T. (1980), 'Arthur Lewis and the Case for Caribbean Industrialization', *Social and Economic Studies*, vol. 29.

Farrell, T. (1991), 'The Political Economy of Caribbean Monetary and Financial Integration', *Caribbean Affairs*, Vol. 4.

Felix, D. and Caskey, J. P. (1990), 'The Road to Default: An Assessment of Debt Crisis Management in Latin America', in Felix, D. (ed.), *Debt and Transfiguration? Prospects for Latin America's Economic Revival* (Armonk, NY: M. E. Sharpe).

Fennell, R. (1985), 'A Reconsideration of the Objectives of the Common Agricultural Policy', *Journal of Common Market Studies*, vol. 23, no. 3.

Ffrench-Davies, R. and Griffith-Jones, S. (eds.) (1995), *Coping with Capital Surges: The Return of Finance to Latin America* (Boulder: Lynne Rÿnner).

Field-Ridley, D. (1991), *Towards a Single CARICOM Market and Economy* (Georgetown: CARICOM Secretariat).

Finch, E. A. (1973), *The Politics of Regional Integration: A Study of Uruguay's Decision to Join LAFTA*, Monograph No. 4, Centre for Latin American Studies, University of Liverpool.

Finch, M. H. J. (1988), 'The Latin American Free Trade Association', in A. M. El-Agraa, (ed.), *International Economic Integration*, 2nd edn (London: Macmillan).

Fink, G. (1977), 'Measuring Integration: A Diagnostic Scale, Applied to EEC, CMEA, and East–West Trade', *Forschungsberichte*, no. 42, August (Vienna: Wiener Institute für Internationale Wirtschaftsvergleiche).

Fishlow, A. (1991), 'Some Reflections on Comparative Latin American Economic Performance and Policy', in T. Banuri, (ed.), *Economic Liberalization: No Panancea. The Experience of Latin America and Asia* (Oxford: Clarendon Press).

FitzGerald, E. V. K. (1996), 'The New Trade Regime, Macroeconomic Behaviour and Income Distribution in Latin America', in V. Bulmer-Thomas, (ed.), *The New Economic Model in Latin America and Its Impact on Income Distribution and Poverty* (London: Macmillan and Institute of Latin American Studies).

Fleming, M. (1971) 'On Exchange Rate Unification', *Economic Journal*, vol. 81.

Fonds de Solidarité et d'Intervention pour le Développément de la Communauté Economique de l'Afrique de l'Quest (1983), *Rapport final de la sé session du counseil d'administration* (Ouagadougou: FOSIDEC).

Foroutan, F. (1993), 'Regional Integration in Sub-Saharan Africa; Past Experience and Future Prospects', in J. de Melo and A. Panagariya (eds), *New Dimensions in Regional Integration* (Cambridge: Cambridge University Press).

Frank, C. (1978), 'The Demand for Labour in Manufacturing Industry in Central America', in W. R. Cline and E. Delgado (eds), *Economic Integration in Central America* (Washington, DC: Brookings Institution).

Franzmeyer, F., Hrubesch, P. Seidel, B., Weise, C. and Schweiger, I. (1991), 'The Regional Impact of Community Policies', *European Parliament*

Research Paper no. 19 (Luxembourg: European Communities Publications Office).

Friedman, M. (1975), *Unemployment Versus Inflation?: An Evaluation of the Phillips Curve* (London: Institute of Economic Affairs).

Gagey, F., Grapinet, G. and Duhamel, S. (1994), *Rapport sur l'harmonisation de fiscalités douanières dans l'Union Economique et Monétaire Ouest Africaine* (Paris: Ministère de la Coopération).

Ganga, R. (1991), 'Structural Adjustment in Guyana: The Human Impact', *Caribbean Labour Journal*, vol. 1.

Garland, J. and Marer, P. (1981), 'US Multinationals in Poland: Case Study of the International Harvester – BUMAR Cooperation in Construction Machinery', in *East European Economic Assessment*, a Compendium of Papers, submitted to the Joint Economics Committee, US Congress (Washington, DC: Government Printing Office).

Garnaut, R. and Drysdale, P. (eds) (1994), *Asia Pacific Regionalism* (Sydney: HarperCollins).

GATT (1991 and 1993), *Trade Policy Review Mechanism: European Community* (Geneva: GATT).

GATT (1994), 'Increases in Market Access Resulting from the Uruguay Round', *News of the Uruguay Round*, April.

Gehrels, F. (1956–7), 'Customs Unions from a Single Country Viewpoint', *Review of Economic Studies*, vol. 24.

Geiser, H., Alleyne, P. and Gajraj, C. (1976), *Legal Problems of Caribbean Integration: A Study on the Legal Problems of CARICOM* (Leyden: Sijthoff).

Geroski, P.A. (1989), 'The Choice Between Diversity and Scale', in E. Davis *et al.* (eds) *1992: Myths and Realities*, Centre for Business Strategy (London: London Business School).

Girvan, N. P. (1991), 'Labour and Caribbean Integration', *Caribbean Labour Journal*, vol. 1.

Girvan, N. P. and Jefferson, O. (eds) (1971), *Readings in the Political Economy of the Caribbean* (Mona, Jamaica: New World).

Girvan, N. and Jefferson, O. (1977), 'Three Areas of Our Regional Crisis', *Caribbean Contact*, vol. 5, no. 5, p. 5, August.

Glezakos, C. (1973), 'Export Instability and Economic Growth: A Statistical Verification', *Economic Development and Cultural Change*, vol. 21.

Godwin, G. and Lake, Y. (1977), *The LDCs in Integration Schemes: The CARICOM Experience* (Antigua: ECCM Secretariat).

Grey, H. P. (1980), 'Towards a Unified Theory of International Trade, International Production, and Direct Foreign Investment', International Economics Study Group, *Conference Proceedings* (Brighton: University of Sussex).

Grey, H. P. (1981), 'Conditional Protection for "Embattled" Industries: An Analysis', mimeo.

Griffith, W. (1990), 'Crisis in Caribbean Integration', *Caribbean Studies*, vol. 23.

Griffith-Jones, S. (1984), *International Finance and Latin America* (London: Croom Helm).

Grilli, E. (1990a), 'Protectionism and the Developing Countries', in E. Grilli and E. Sassoon (eds), *The New Protectionist Wave* (London: Macmillan).

Grilli, E. (1990b), 'Responses of Developing Countries to Trade Protectionism in Industrial Countries', in C. S. Pearson and J. Riedel (eds), *The Direction of Trade Policy* (Oxford: Basil Blackwell).

Grilli, E. (1991), 'EC Development Policies and Their Effects on Developing Countries: A Review', in A. B. Atkinson and R. Brunetta (eds), *Economics for the New Europe* (London: Macmillan).

Grilli, E. (1993), *The European Community and the Developing World* (Cambridge: Cambridge University Press).

Grilli, E. (1995) 'Creativity of Europe's Trade Policies Towards Developing and Eastern European Countries', *Development Studies Working Paper*, No. 81, (Centro Studi Luca d'Agliano - Queen Elizabeth House: Oxford).

Grilli, E. and Daveri, F. (1993), 'Modelli di Distribuzione Geografica degli Aiuti Pubblici allo Sviluppo', in C.M. Santoro (ed.), *I Problemi della Cooperazione Allo Sviluppo Negli Anni 90* (Bologna: Il Mulino).

Grilli, E. and Riess, M. (1992), 'EC Aid to Associated Countries: Distribution and Determinants', *Weltwirtschftliches Archiv*, vol. 128.

Group of Experts (1981), *The Caribbean Community in the 1980s* (Georgetown: CARICOM Secretariat).

Grubel, H. C., and Lloyd, P. J. (1975), *Intra-industry Trade* (London: Macmillan).

Gruben, W. G. and Welch, J. H. (1994), 'Is NAFTA Economic Integration?', *Economic Review* of the Federal Reserve Bank of Dallas, second quarter.

Grundwald, J., Wionczek, M. S. and Carnoy, M. (1972), *Latin American Economic Integration and U.S. Policy* (Washington, DC: Brookings Institution).

Guillaumont, P., Guillaumont, S. and Plane, P. (1988), 'Participating in African Monetary Unions: An Alternative Evaluation', *World Development*, vol. 16.

Guillaumont, P. and Guillaumont-Jeanneney, S. (1993), 'L'intégration économique: un nouvel enjeu pour le zone franc', *Revue d'Economie du Développment*, vol. 1.

Gwilliam, K. M. (1985), 'The Transport Policy', in A. M. El-Agraa (ed.), *The Economics of the European Community* (Oxford: Philip Allan).

Haberler, G. (1964), 'Integration and Growth in the World Economy in Historical Perspective', *American Economic Review*, vol. 54.

Haines-Ferrari, M. (1993), 'MERCOSUR: A New Model of Latin American Economic Integration?', *Journal of International Law*, vol. 25.

Hall, K. O. (1979), 'Collective Self-reliance: The Case of CARICOM', *IFDA Dossier*, no. 7.

Hall, K. O. and Blake, B. (1976), 'Major Development in CARICOM 1975', in L. Manigat (ed.), *The Caribbean Yearbook of International Relations* (Leyden: Sijthoff).

Hall, K. O. and Blake, B. (1978), 'The Caribbean Community: Administrative and Institutional Aspects', *Journal of Common Market Studies*, vol. 16, no. 3.

Hansen, R. (1967), *Central America: Regional Integration and Economic Development* (Washington, DC: National Planning Association).

Harberger, A. (1965), 'Survey of Literature on Cost Benefit Analysis for Industrial Project Evaluation', paper presented at the UN Inter-Regional Symposium in Industrial Project Evaluation, Prague.

Hart, M. (1994), *What's Next: Canada, the Global Economy and the New Trade Policy* (Ottawa: Centre for Trade Policy and Law of Carleton University and the Université d'Ottawa).

Hazlewood, A. (1964), *Rail and Road in East Africa: Transport Coordination in Underdeveloped Countries* (Oxford: Blackwell).

Hazlewood, A. (1967), *African Integration and Disintegration* (Oxford: Oxford University Press).

Hazlewood, A. (1975), *Economic Integration: The East African Experience* (London: Heinemann).

Hazlewood, A. (1982), 'The East African Community', in A. M. El-Agraa (ed.), *International Economic Integration* (London: Macmillan; New York: St. Martin's Press). Also in the second edition (1988).

Herin, J. (1986), 'Rules of Origin and Differences Between Tariff Levels in EFTA and the EC', *Occasional Paper No. 13*, Economic Affairs Department (Geneva: EFTA).

Hewett, E. (1974), *Foreign Trade Prices in the Council for Mutual Economic Assistance* (Cambridge: Cambridge University Press).

Hewitt, A. (1982), 'The European Development Fund and its Functions in the EEC's Development Aid Policy', *ODI Working Paper*, no. 11 (London: Overseas Development Institute).

Hiemenz, U. (1993), 'EC Protectionism Against Developing Countries', in I. Yamazawa and A. Hirata (eds), *Trade Policies Towards Developing Countries*, (London: Macmillan).

Hilaire, A. H., Codrington, H., Robinson, J. and Samuel, W. (1991) 'Options for Monetary Integration in the Caribbean – An Evaluation of Current Proposals', *Report for Central Bank Governors* (Georgetown: CARICOM Secretariat).

Hill, H. (1994), 'ASEAN Economic Development: An Analytical Survey', *Journal of Asian Studies* vol. 53.

Hindley, B. (1992), 'Exports from Eastern and Central Europe and Contingent Protection', in J. Fleming and J. Rollo (eds), *Trade Payments and Adjustment in Central and Eastern Europe* (London: Royal Institute for International Affairs).

Hine, R. C. (1985), *The Political Economy of European Trade* (Brighton: Wheatsheaf Books).

Hine, R. C. (1991), 'Protection in the European Community Before and After 1992', in D. Greenaway *et al.* (eds), *Global Protectionism* (London: Macmillan).

Hoang, A. T. (1993), 'Why Hasn't Vietnam Gained ASEAN Membership?', *Contemporary Southeast Asia,* vol. 15.

Holmes, P. and Shepherd, G. (1983), 'Protectionist Policies of the EEC', paper presented to the International Economics Study Group confernece at Sussex University.

Holzman, F. (1974), *Foreign Trade Under Central Planning* (Cambridge, Mass.: Harvard University Press).

Hope, K. R. (1986), 'A Macroeconomic Overview of the Trade Impact of CARICOM', in K. R. Hope, *Economic Development in the Caribbean* (New York: Praeger).

Horn, P. V. and Bice, H. E. (1949), *Latin American Trade and Economics* (New York: Prentice Hall).

Houthakker, H. S. and Magee, S. P. (1969), 'Income and Price Elasticities in World Trade', *Review of Economics and Statistics*, vol. 51.

Hu, Yao-Su (1979), 'German Agricultural Power: The Impact on France and Britain', *The World Today*, vol. 35.

Hufbauer, G. C. (1989), *The Free Trade Debate* (New York: Twentieth Century Fund Press).

Hufbauer, G. C. and Chilas, J. G. (1974), 'Specialization by Industrial Countries: Extent and Consequences', in H. Giersch (ed.), *The International Division of Labour: Problems and Perspectives* (Mohr: Tübingen).

Hufbauer, G. C. and Schott, J. J. (1992), *North American Free Trade: Issues and Recommendations* (Washington, DC: Institute for International Economics).

Hufbauer, G. C. and Schott, J. J. (1993), *NAFTA: An Assessment*, rev. edn (Washington, DC: Institute for International Economics).

Hufbauer, G. and Schott, J. J. (1995), *Western Hemisphere Economic Integration* (Washington, DC: Institute for International Economics).

Hughes, H. and Waelbroeck, J. (1981), 'Can Developing Country Exports Keep Growing in the 1980s?', *The World Economy*, vol. 4.

Hughes Hallett, A. J. (1992), 'The Impact of EC-92 on Developing Countries' Trade: A Dissenting View', *World Bank Policy Research Working Paper*, no. 885 (Washington, DC).

Imada, P. (1993) 'Production and Trade Effects of the ASEAN Free Trade Area', *The Developing Economies*, vol. 31.

Imada, P. and Naya, S. N. (eds) (1992), *AFTA: The Way Ahead* (Singapore: Institute of Southeast Asian Studies).

Ingram, J. C. (1973), 'The Case for European Monetary Integration', *Essays in International Finance*, no. 98 April, (Princeton University).

Instituto para la integración de America Latina (INTAL), *El proceso de integración en América Latina*, annual.

INTAL (1983a), *El proceso de integración en América Latina en 1982* (Buenos Aires).

INTAL (1983b), *Estadisticas de expotación de los paises de la ALADI 1980–83* (Buenos Aires).

INTAL, various issues of the magazine *Integración Latinoamericana* (Buenos Aires) and the official quarterly *Sintesis ALADI* (Montevideo).

Inter-American Development Bank (1981), *Economic and Social Progress in Latin America: 1980–1 Report* (Washington, DC: Inter-American Development Bank).

Inter-American Development Bank (1990), *Economic and Social Progress in Latin America: 1990 Report* (Washington, DC: Inter-American Development Bank).

Inter-American Development Bank (1992), *Economic and Social Progress in Latin America: 1992 Report* (Washington, DC: Inter-American Development Bank).

Inter-American Development Bank (1994), *Economic and Social Progress in Latin America: 1994 Report* (Washington, DC: Inter-American Development Bank).

Inter-American Development Bank (1995), *Economic and Social Progress in Latin America: 1995 Report* (Washington, DC: Inter-American Development Bank).

International Monetary Fund (1995), *Direction of Trade Statistics* (Washington, DC: IMF) August.

Joel, C. (1971), 'Tax Incentives in Central American Development', *Economic Development and Cultural Change*, vol. 19.

Johnson, H. G. (1965a), 'An Economic Theory of Protectionism, Tariff Bargaining and the Formation of Customs Unions', *Journal of Political Economy*, vol. 73.

Johnson, H. G. (1965b), 'Optimal intervention in the presence of domestic distortions', in R. E. Baldwin *et al.* (eds), *Trade, Growth and the Balance of Payments* (New York: Rand McNally).

Johnson, H. G. (1974), 'Trade Diverting Customs Unions: A Comment', *Economic Journal*, vol. 81.

Johnson, H. G. and Krauss, M. B. (1974) *General Equilibrium Analysis* (London: Allen & Unwin).

Jones, A. J. (1979), 'The Theory of Economic Integration', in J. K. Bowers (ed.), *Inflation, Development and Integration: Essays in Honour of A. J. Brown* (Leeds: Leeds University Press).

Jones, A. J. (1980), 'Domestic Distortions and Customs Union Theory', *Bulletin of Economic Research*, vol. 32.

Jones, A. J. (1983), 'Withdrawal from a Customs Union: A Macroeconomic Analysis', in A. M. El-Agraa (ed.), *Britain Within the European Community: The Way Forward* (London: Macmillan).

Kaldor, N. (1971), 'The Dynamics of European Integration', in D. Evans (ed.), *Destiny or Delusion* (London: Gollancz).

Kaminski, B. (1994), *The Significance of the 'Europe Agreements' for Central European Exports* (Washington, DC: World Bank) (processed).

Karnes, T. L. (1961), *The Failure of Union: Central America, 1824–1960* (Chapel Hill: University of North Carolina Press).

Karsenty, G. and Laird, S. (1987), 'The GSP, Policy Options and the New Round', *Weltwirtschaftliches Archiv*, vol. 123.

Kaser, M. (1967), *COMECON: Integration Problems of Planned Economies* (Oxford: Oxford University Press).

Keesing, D. B. (1980), 'Exports and Policy in Latin American Countries: Prospects for the World Economy and for Latin American Exports 1980–90' (Sao Paulo), March (mimeo).

Kern, D. (1978), 'An International Comparison of Major Economic Trends, 1953–76', *National Westminster Bank Quarterly Review*, May.

Kim, H. S. and Weston, A. (1993), 'A North American Free Trade Agreement and East Asian Developing Countries', *ASEAN Economic Bulletin*, vol. 9.

Kleppe, P. (1991), 'EFTA and EC's Internal Market', in F. Laursen (ed.), *Europe 1992: World Partner?* (Maastricht: European Institute of Public Administration).

Koskinen, M. (1983), 'Excess Documentation Costs as a Non-tariff Trade Measure: An Empirical Analysis of the Imports Effects of Documentation Costs', working paper, Swedish School of Economics and Business Administration (Stockholm).

Kramer, H. (1993), 'The European Community's Response to the New Eastern Europe', *Journal of Common Market Studies*, vol. 31.

Krause, L. B. (1968), *European Economic Integration and the United States* (Washington, DC: Brookings Institution).

Krauss, M. B. (1972), 'Recent Developments in Customs Union Theory: An Interpretative Survey', *Journal of Economic Literature*, vol. 10.

Kreinen, M. E. (1961), 'The Effects of Tariff Changes on the Prices and Volumes of imports', *American Economic Review*, vol. 51.

Kreinen, M. E. (1972), 'Effects of the EEC on Imports of Manufactures', *Economic Journal*, vol. 82.

Kreinen, M. E. (1973), 'The Static Effects of EEC Enlargement on Trade Flows', *Southern Economic Journal*, vol. 39, no. 4, April.

Kreinen, M. E. (1979), 'Effects of European Integration on Trade Flows in Manufactures', European-American Seminar, University of Tilburg, June.

Kreinin, M. and Plummer, M. (1992), 'Effects of Economic Integration in Industrial Countries on ASEAN and Asian NIEs', *World Development*, vol. 20.

Krugman, P. R. (1986), *Strategic Trade Policy and the New Industrial Economics* (Cambridge, Mass.: MIT Press).

Kubursi, A. A. (1980), 'Arab Economic Prospects in the 1980s', *Institute of Palestine Studies Papers*, no. 8(E) (Beirut: Institute of Palestine Studies).

Laird, S. and Yeats, S. (1990), 'Trends in Non-Tariff Barriers of Developed Countries', *Weltwirtschaftliches Archiv*, vol. 126.

Landell-Mills, P.M. (1979), 'The Southern African Customs Union: A Comment on Mosley's Reappraisal', *World Development*, vol. 7.

Langhammer, R.J. (1992), 'EC Integration Widening Towards Eastern Europe', *Kiel Working Paper*, no. 524, Kiel Institute of World Economics.

Langhammer, R. J. and Hiemenz, U. (1990), *Regional Integration among Developing Countries*, Kieler Studien (Tübingen: Mohr).

Langhammer, R.J. and Sapir, A. (1987), *Economic Impact of Generalized Tariff Preferences* (Aldershot: Gower) (for the Trade Policy Research Center).

Lavigne, M. (1975), 'The Problem of the Multinational Socialist Enterprise', *The ACES Bulletin*, vol. XVIII.

Lee, T. Y. (1994), 'The ASEAN Free Trade Area; The Search for a Common Prosperity', *Asian-Pacific Economic Literature* vol. 8.

Lewis, G. (1968), *The Growth of the Modern West Indies* (New York: Modern Reader Paperbacks).

Lewis, V. (1976), 'Problems and Possibilities of the Caribbean Community', *Social Studies Education*, vol. 7.

Lewis, W. A. (1949), 'Industrial Development in Puerto Rico', *Caribbean Economic Review*, vol. 1.

Lewis, W. A. (1950a), *Industrial Development in the British Caribbean* (Port of Spain: Kent House, Trinidad).

Lewis, W. A. (1950b), 'The Industrialisation of the British West Indies', *Caribbean Economic Review*, vol. 2.

Lipgens, W. (1982) *A History of European Integration, vol. 1* 1945–47: *The Formation of the European Unity Movement* (Oxford: OUP)

Lipsey, R. G. (1957), 'The Theory of Customs Unions, Trade Diversion and Welfare', *Economica*, vol. 24.

Lipsey, R. G. (1960), 'The Theory of Customs Unions: A General Survey', *Economic Journal*, vol. 70.

Lipsey, R. G. and Lancaster, K. (1956–57) 'The general theory of the second best', *Review of Economic Studies*, vol. 24.

Lister, M. (1988), *The European Community and the Developing Countries* (Aldershot: Avebury).

Lizano, E. and Willmore, L. N. (1975), 'Second Thoughts on Central America: The Rosenthal Report', *Journal of Common Market Studies*, vol. 13.

Llewellyn J., Potter, S. and Samuelson, L. (1985), *Economic Forecasting and Policy: The International Dimension* (Routledge & Kegan Paul).

Low, P. (1993), *Trading Free: The GATT and US Trade Policy* (New York: Twentieth Century Fund Press).

Lysy, F. and Taylor, L. (1979), 'Vanishing Income Redistributions: Keynesian Clues About Model Surprises in the Short Run', *Journal of Development Economics*, vol. 6.

Maasdorp, G. (1994), *A Vision for Economic Integration and Cooperation in Southern Africa*, report for Department of Trade and Industry, Pretoria.

McAleese, D. (1994), 'EC External Trade Policies', in A.M.El-Agraa, *The Economics of the European Community* (New York: Harvester Wheatsheaf).

MacBean, A. (1966), *Export Instability and Economic Development* (New York: Allen & Unwin).

McCarthy, C. L. (1986), *The Southern African Customs Union*, report prepared for the Central Economic Advisory Services, Pretoria.

McClelland, D. H. (1972), *The Central American Common Market: Economic Growth and Choices for the Future* (New York: Praeger).

MacDougall, G. D. A. (1960), 'The Benefits and Costs of Private Investment from Abroad: A Theoretical Approach', *Economic Record*, vol. 36.

MacDougall Report (1977) *see* Commission of the European Communities (1977).

Machlup, F. (1977), *A History of Thought on Economic Integration* (London: Macmillan).

Machowski, H. (1977), 'International Economic Organizations Within COMECON: Status, Problems, Prospects', in NATO Directorate of Economic Affairs, *COMECON: Progress and Prospects* (Brussels).

McIntyre, A. (1965), 'De-colonialization and Trade Policy in the West Indies', in F. M. Andić and T. C. Matthews (eds), *The Caribbean Transition* (Rio Piedras, Puerto Rico: Institute of Caribbean Studies).

McIntyre, A. (1971), '*The Effects of Alternative Trade Groupings on the United Kingdom*', Ph.D. thesis, University of Bristol.

McIntyre, A. (1976a), *Evolution of the Process of Integration in the Caribbean* (Georgetown: CARICOM Secretariat).

McIntyre, A. (1976b), *The Current Situation and Perspectives of CARICOM* (Georgetown: CARICOM Secretariat).

McIntyre, A. (1977), 'CARICOM – Setting the Records Straight', *Caribbean Contact*, vol. 5, no. 4, July.

McLean, I. (1995), 'Trans-Tasman Trade Relations: Decline and Rise', in R. Pomfret (ed.), *Australia's Trade Policies* (Melbourne: Oxford University Press).

McManus, J. G. (1972), 'The Theory of the International Firm', in G. Paquet (ed.), *The Multinational Firm and the Nation State* (Ontario: Collier Macmillan).

McMillan, C. H. (1978), 'Some Thoughts on the Relationship Between Regional Integration in Eastern Europe and East–West Economic Relations', in F. Levcik (ed.), *International Economics: Comparisons and Interdependencies* (Vienna: Springer Verlag).

MacPhee, C. R. and Rosenbaum, D. I. (1989), 'Has the European Community GSP Increased LDC Exports?', *Applied Economics*, vol. 21.

McQueen, M. (1992), 'European Community Trade Policies Towards the Developing Countries: A Survey', *Discussion Paper in Economics*, no. 248, Department of Economics, University of Reading.

McQueen, M. and Stevens, C. (1989), 'Trade Preferences Under Lome IV: Non-traditional ACP Exports to the EC', *Development Policy Review*, vol. 7.

Marer, P. (1972), *Postwar Pricing and Price Patterns in Socialist Foreign Trade*, International Development Research Centre, Report 1 (Bloomington, Indiana).

Marer, P. (1976), 'Prospects for Integration in Eastern Europe: Council for Mutual Economic Assistance', *International Organisation*, vol. 3, no. 4, reprinted in J. F. Triska and P. M. Cocks (eds), *Political Development in Eastern Europe* (New York: Praeger, 1977).

Marer, P. (1980), 'Western Multinational Corporations in Eastern Europe and CMEA Integration', in Z. Fallenbuchl and C. McMillan (eds), *Partners in East–West Economic Relations* (New York: Pergamon Press).

Marer, P. (1981), 'The Mechanism and Performance of Hungary's Foreign Trade, 1968–1979', in P. Hare, H. Radice and N. Swain (eds), *Hungary: A Decade of Reform* (London: Allen & Unwin).

Marer, P. and Montias, J. M. (1980), 'Theory and Measurement of East European Integration', in P. Marer and J. M. Montias (eds), *East European Integration and East–West Trade* (Bloomington: Indiana University Press).

Marer, P. and Montias, J. M. (1981), 'CMEA Integration: Theory and Practice', in *East European Economic Assessment* (Washington: Joint Economic Committee, Congress of the United States).

Marer, M. and Montias, J. M. (1988) 'The Council for Mutual Economic Assistance', chapter 6 of A. M. El-Agraa (ed.), *International Economic Integration* (London: Macmillan), 2nd edition.

Marjolin Report (1975) *see* Commission of the European Communities (1975).

Mateo, F. (1983), 'Alternativas instrumentales para la complementación industrial argentino-andina', *Integración Latinoamericana*, year VIII, no. 81, July.

Mayes, D. G. (1971) 'The effects of alternative trade groupings on the United Kingdom', *PhD Thesis*, University of Bristol, UK.

Mayes, D. G. (1978), 'The Effects of Economic Integration on Trade', *Journal of Common Market Studies*, vol. 17, no. 1.

Mayes, D. G. (1983), 'EC Trade Effects and Factor Mobility', in A. M. El-Agraa (ed.), *Britain Within the European Community: The Way Forward* (London: Macmillan).

Mayes, D. G. (1984), Memorandum of Evidence in House of Lords Select Committee on the European Communities, *Trade Patterns: The United Kingdom's Changing Trade Patterns Subsequent to Membership of the European Community*, HL(41) 7th Report Session 1983–4 (London: HMSO).

Mayes, D. G. (1985), 'Factor Mobility', in A. M. El-Agraa (ed.), *The Economics of the European Community*, 2nd edn (Oxford: Philip Allan).

Meade, J. E. (1955), *The Theory of Customs Unions* (Amsterdam: North-Holland).

Meirelles, J. G. P. (1995), *Economic Cooperation and Integration Between Argentina and Brazil, 1939–92*, unpublished Ph.D. thesis, University of London.

Messerlin, P. (1989), 'The EC Antidumping Regulations: A First Economic Appraisal, 1980–85', *Weltwirtschaftliches Archiv*, vol. 125.

Messerlin, P. (1992), 'The Association Agreements Between the EC and Eastern Europe: Trade Liberalization vs. Constitutional Failure', in J. Flemming and J. M. C. Rollo (eds), *Trade, Payments and Adjustment in Central and Eastern Europe* (London: Royal Institute of International Affairs).

Messerlin, P. (1993), 'The EC and Central Europe: The Missed Rendez-Vous of 1992?', *Economics of Transition*, vol. I.

Middle East Economic Survey (1968) vol. XI, no. 13.

Milenky, E. S. (1973), *The Politics of Regional Organisation in Latin America* (New York: Praeger).

Mills, G., Burton, C., Lewis, J. O. and Sorhaindor, C. (1990), *Report on a Review of Regional Programmes and Organisations of the Caribbean Community* (Georgetown: CARICOM Secretariat).

Mingst, K. A. (1977–8), 'Regional Sectoral Economic Integration: The Case of OAPEC', *Journal of Common Market Studies*, vol. XVI.

Mishalani, P., *et al.* (1981), 'The Pyramid of Privilege', in C. Stevens (ed.), *EEC and the Third World: A Survey* (New York: Holmes & Meier).

Mitchell, C. (1967), 'The Role of Technocrats in Latin American Integration', *Inter-American Economic Affairs*, vol. 21, no. 1.

Mitrofanova, N. M. (1979), 'The Economic Nature of Contract Prices in Mutual Collaboration of CMEA Countries', *Izvestiia Akademii nauk SSSR*, translated in *Soviet and East European Trade*, vol. XV, no. 1, Spring.

Monteforte Toledo, M. (1972), *Centro America: Subdesarrollo y Dependencia*, 2 vols. (Mexico City: Instituto de Investigaciones Sociales).

Montias, J. M. (1967), *Economic Development in Communist Rumania* (Cambridge, Mass.: MIT Press).

Montias, J. M. (1969), 'Obstacles to Economic Integration of Eastern Europe', *Studies in Comparative Communism*, July–October.

Moore, L. (1994), 'Developments in [EU] Trade and Trade Policy', in J. Artis and N. Lee (eds), *The Economics of the European Union* (Oxford: Oxford University Press).

Mordecai, J. (1968a), *Federation of the West Indies* (Evanston, Ill.: Northwestern University Press).

Mordecai, J. (1968b), *The West Indies: The Federal Negotiations* (London: Allen & Unwin).

Morgan, A. D. (1970), 'Income and Price Elasticities in World Trade: A Comment', *Manchester School*, vol. 38.

Morgan, R. (1983), 'Political Cooperation in Europe', in R. Jenkins (ed.), *Britain and the EEC* (London: Macmillan).

Morgenstern, K. (1978), 'The International Specialization of Production and Its Concentration in CMEA Countries', *Voprosy ekonomiki*, no. 2, translated in *Soviet and East European Trade*, vol. XV, no. 1, Spring 1979.

Morris, C. N. (1980), 'The Common Agricultural Policy', *Fiscal Studies*, vol. 1, no. 2, March.

Mosley, P. (1978) 'The Southern African Customs Union: A Reappraisal', *World Development*, vol. 6.

Moss, J. and Ravenhill, J. (1987), 'The Evolution of Trade Between the ACPs and the EEC', in C. Stevens and J. V. van Themaat (eds), *Europe and the International Division of Labor* (London: Hodder & Stoughton).

Mundell, R. A. (1967), 'Tariff Preferences and the Terms of Trade', *Manchester School*, vol. 32.

Musgrave, R. A. and Musgrave, P. B. (1976), *Public Finance in Theory and Practice* (Homewood, Ill.: McGraw-Hill).

Nam, C. and Reuter, J. (1991), 'The Impact of 1992 and Associated Legislation on the Less Favoured Regions of the European Community', *European Parliament Research Paper*, no. 18 (Luxembourg: European Communities Publications Office).

Naya, S. (1977), 'ASEAN Trade and Development Cooperation: Preferential Trading Arrangements and Trade Liberalisation', for UNCTAD and UNDP (Project RAS/77/015A/40).

Naya, S. and Plummer, M. (1991), 'ASEAN Economic Cooperation in the New International Economic Environment', *ASEAN Economic Bulletin* vol. 7.

Naya, S., Plummer, M., Sandhu, K. S. and Akrasanee, N. (1989), *ASEAN–US Initiative: Assessment and Recommendations for Improved Economic Relations* (Singapore: Institute of Southeast Asian Studies; Honolulu: East-West Center).

Nevin, E. T. (1985), 'Regional Policy', in A. M. El-Agraa (ed.), *The Economics of the European Community* (Oxford: Philip Allann).

Nicholls, S. M. A. (1995) *Economic Integration in the Caribbean Community: From Federation to the Single Market*, PhD Thesis (Queen Mary and Westfield College, University of London).

Niesr (1995), *The National Institute World Model Users Manual*, May.

Noël, E. (1991) *Working Together – The Institutions of the European Community* (Luxembourg: Office of official publications of the EU).

Norheim, H., Finger, K.-M. and Anderson, K. (1993), 'Trends in the Regionalization of World Trade, 1928 to 1990', Appendix in K. Anderson and R. Blackhurst (eds), *Regional Integration and the Global Trading System* (Hemel Hempstead: Harvester Wheatsheaf; New York: St Martin's Press).

Nugent, J. B. (1974) *Economic Integration in Central America* (Baltimore: Johns Hopkins University Press).

OECD (1979), 'The OECD International Linkage Model', *OECD Economic Outlook*, January.

OECD (1992, 1993, 1994 and 1995), *Development Cooperation: DAC Annual Reports 1991, 1992, 1993, 1994* (Paris: OECD).

Orcutt, G. H. (1950) 'Measurement of Price Elasticities in International Trade', *Review of Economics and Statistics*, vol. 32.

Orrego Vicuna, F. (1981), 'Hacia nuevas formas de integración económica en América Latina: lecciones de una experiencia', *Estudios Internacionales* (Santiago de Chille), year XIV, no. 56, October–December.

Owen, N. (1983), *Economies of Scale, Competitiveness and Trade Patterns Within the European Community* (Oxford: Oxford University Press).

Panagariya, A. (1994), 'Should East Asia Go Regional? No, No, and Maybe', *Working Paper Series*, no. 1209, Policy Research Department (Washington, DC: World Bank).

Pan-American Union (1952), *The Foreign Trade of Latin America since 1913* (Washington, DC: Pan-American Union).

Pangestu, M., Soesastro, H. and Ahmad, M. (1992), 'A New Look at Intra-ASEAN Economic Cooperation', *ASEAN Economic Bulletin*, vol. 8.

Panić, M. (1980), 'Some Longer Term Effects of Short-run Adjustment Policies: Behaviour of UK Direct Investment Since the 1960s', International Economics Study Group, *Conference Proceedings* (Brighton: University of Sussex).

Pantin, D. (1991), *Into the Valley of Debt: An Alternative Road to the IMF/World Bank Path* (Trinidad: Gloria Ferguson).

Paterno, V. T. (1982), 'ASEAN Industrial Complementation', for UNIDO (UNIDO/IS 282 of 25.1.82).

Payne, A. (1981), 'The Rise and Fall of Caribbean Regionalisation', *Journal of Common Market Studies*, vol. 19.

Payne, A. and Sutton, P. (1984), *Dependency under Challenge: The Political Economy of the Commonwealth Caribbean* (Manchester: Manchester University Press).

Peacock, A. T. and Wiseman, J. (1967) *The Growth of Public Expenditure in the UK* (London: Allen & Unwin).

Pearce, D. W. and Westoby, R. (1983), 'Energy and the EC', in A. M. El-Agraa (ed.), *Britain Within the European Community: The Way Forward* (London: Macmillan).

Pécsi, K. (1977), *A KGST Termelési Integráció Közgazdásagi Kérdései* (Economic Issues of CMEA's Production Integration), Közgazdaságí es Jogi Könyvkiadó, Budapest. An English translation of a revised and updated edition was published by M. E. Sharpe (New York: White Plains, 1981).

Pelkmans, J. (1984), *Market Integration in the EC* (Hague: Martinus Nijhoff).

Pelkmans, J. (1987), 'The European Community's Trade Policy Towards Developing Countries', in C. Stevens and J. V. van Themaat (eds), *Europe and the International Division of Labor* (London: Hodder & Stoughton).

Pena, F. (1984), 'Y después de Quito? La Conferencia Económica Latinoamericana y sus resultados pràcticos', *Integración Latinoamericana*, no. 88.

Petersmann, E. (1994), 'Why Do Governments Need the Uruguay Round Agreements, NAFTA and the EEA?', *Aussenwirtschaft*, vol. 49.

Petith, H. C. (1977), 'European Integration and the Terms of Trade', *Economic Journal*, vol. 87.

Phelps, E. S. (1968), 'Money-wage Dynamics and Labor Market Equilibrium', *Journal of Political Economy*, vol. 76.

Phillips, A. W. (1958), 'The Relation Between Unemployment and the Rate of Change of Money Wages in the United Kingdom 1862–1957', *Economica*, vol. 25.

Pinder, J. (1968), 'Positive and Negative Integration: Some Problems of Economic Union in the EEC', *The World Today*, vol. 24.

Pinder, J. (ed.) (1971), *The Economics of Europe* (London: Knight).

Pinder, J. (1991), *The European Community and Eastern Europe* (New York: The Council on Foreign Relations Press).

Pollard, D. (1976), 'Institutional and Legal Aspects of the Caribbean Community', *Caribbean Studies*, vol. 14, no. 1.

Pomfret, R. (1988), *Unequal Trade: The Economics of Discriminatory International Trade Policies* (Oxford: Basil Blackwell).

Pomfret, R. (1992), 'Are Regional Trading Arrangements Hurting Australia?', in R. Leach (ed.), *National Strategies for Australasian Countries: The Impact of the Asian/Pacific Economy* (Brisbane: Queensland University of Technology).

Pomfret, R. (1993), 'Measuring the Effects of Economic Integration on Third Countries: A Comment on Kreinin and Plummer', *World Development* vol. 21.

Pomfret, R. (1995), 'Strategic Trade and Industrial Policy as an Approach to Locational Competitiveness: What Lessons from Asia?', in H. Siebert (ed.), *Locational Competition in the World Economy* (Tubingen: J. C. B. Mohr).

Pomfret, R. (1996), 'Subregional Economic Zones', in B. Bora and C. Findlay (eds), *Regionalism in the Asia-Pacific Region* (Melbourne: Oxford University Press).

Premdas, R. and St Cyr E. B. A. (eds) (1991), *Sir Arthur Lewis: An Economic and Political Portrait* (Mona: ISER).

Prest, A. R. (1972) 'Government revenue, the national income and all that', in R. M. Bird and J. G. Read (eds), *Modern Fiscal Issues* (Toronto: Toronto University Press).

Prest, A. R. (1979), 'Fiscal Policy', in P. Coffey (ed.), *Economic Policies of the Common Market* (London: Macmillan).

Prest, A. R. (1983), 'Fiscal Policy', in P. Coffey (ed.), *Main Economic Policy Areas of the EEC* (The Hague: Martinus Nijhoff).

Price, V. Curzon (1974), *The Essentials of Economic Integration* (London: Macmillan).

Price, V. Curzon (1995), 'The European Economic Area: Implications for Nonmembers in General and Mediterranean Countries in Particular', in E. Ahiram and A. Tovias (eds), *Wither EU–Israeli Relations? Common and Divergent Interests* (Frankfurt: Peter Lang).

Proctor, J. (1956), 'Britain's Pro-federation Policy in the Caribbean: An Inquiry into Motivation', *Canadian Journal of Economics and Political Science*, vol. 4.

Puyana, A. (1982), 'De la ALALC y el Grupo Andino a la ALADI: de la cooperación integral al bilaterismo comercial', *Economia de América Latina*, CIDE (Mexico), no. 8, first semester.

Raddavero, B. C. (1978), 'La Promoción y el Desarrollo de Proyectos Multinacionales en América Latina', *Integración Latinoamericana*, January–February.

Raisman Report, Colonial Office (1961), *East Africa: Report of the Economic and Fiscal Commission*, Cmnd 1279 (London: HMSO).

Ramsaran, R. (1978), 'CARICOM: The Integration Process in Crisis', *Journal of World Trade Law*, vol. 12, no. 3.

Ramsaran, R. (1989), *The Commonwealth Caribbean in the World Economy* (London: Macmillan).

Ramsett, D. (1969), *Regional Industrial Development in Central America: A Case Study of the Integration Industries Scheme* (New York: Praeger).

Rapoport, A. (1978), 'Effective Protection Rates in Central America', Appendix K of W. R. Cline and E. Delgado (eds), *Economic Integration in Central America* (Washington, DC: Brookings Institution).

Reid, G. (1984), 'The Evolving Structure of the CARICOM Trade Regime', in IADB, *Ten Years of CARICOM* (Washington, DC: IADB).

Republic of Trinidad and Tobago (1979), *White Paper on CARICOM, 1973–78* (Port of Spain: Government Printery).

Reynolds, C. and Leiva, G. (1978) 'Employment Problems of Export Economies in a Common Market: The Case of Central America', in W. R. Cline and E. Delgado (eds), *Economic Integration in Central America* (Washington, DC: Brookings Institution).

Riding, A. (1985), *Distant Neighbors: A Portrait of the Mexicans* (New York: Knopf).

Rielly, J. E. (ed.) (1955), *American Public Opinion and US Foreign Policy, 1955* (Waukegan, Ill.: Lake County Press for the Chicago Council on Foreign Relations).

Robson, P. (1968), *Economic Integration in Africa* (London: Allen & Unwin).

Robson, P. (ed.) (1972), *International Economic Integration* (Harmondsworth: Penguin).

Robson, P. (1978), 'Reappraising the Southern African Customs Union: A Comment', *World Development*, vol. 6.

Robson, P. (1980), *The Economics of International Integration*, 2nd edn, 1984; 3rd edn, 1985 (London: Allen & Unwin).

Robson, P. (1983), *Integration, Development and Equity: Economic Integration in West Africa* (London: Allen & Unwin).

Robson, P. (1984), *The Economics of International Integration*, 2nd edn (London: Allen & Unwin).

Robson, P. (1985), 'Performance and Priorities for Regional Integration With Special Reference to West Africa', in T. Rose (ed.), *Crisis and Recovery in Sub-Saharan Africa* (Paris: OECD).

Robson, P. (1987), *Intégration, développement et equité* (Paris: Economica).

Robson, P. (1988), 'The West African Economic Community', in A. M. El-Agraa (ed.), *International Economic Integration*, 2nd edn (London: Macmillan).

Robson, P. (1993), *Transnational Corporations and Regional Economic Integration* (London: Routledge).

Rosenblatt, J. *et al.* (1988), 'The Common Agricultural Policy of the European Community', *Occasional Paper*, no. 62 (Washington, DC: International Monetary Fund).

Rosenthal, G. (1973), 'The Role of Private Foreign Investment in the Development of the Central American Common Market', mimeo (SIECA: Guatemala City). Guatemala.

Sackey, J. (1978), 'The Structure and Performance of CARICOM: Lessons for the Development of ECOWAS', *Canadian Journal of African Studies*, vol. 12, no. 2.

Salgado Penaherra, G. (1983), 'Progreso y problemas de la integración económica: una visión de conjunto', paper presented at the Fourth Congress of the International Economic Association, Madrid, September.

Sapir, A. (1981), 'Trade Benefits Under the EEC Generalized System of Preferences', *European Economic Review*, vol. 15.

Sarna, A. J. (1985), 'The Impact of a Canada–US Free Trade Area', *Journal of Common Market Studies*, vol. 23, no. 4.

Sayigh, Y. A. (1982), *The Arab Economy* (Oxford: Oxford University Press).

Sayigh, Y. A. (1983) 'A New Framework for Complementarity Among the Arab Economies', in I. Ibrahim (ed.), *Arab Resources: The Transformation of a Society* (Beckenham: Croom Helm).

Scaperlanda, A. (1967), 'The EEC and US Foreign Investment: Some Empirical Evidence', *Economic Journal*, vol. 77, March.

Schmitter, P. C. and Haas, E. B. (1964), *Mexico and Latin American Economic Integration*, Research Series no. 5, Institute of International Studies (Berkeley: University of California).

Schwamm, H. (1990) 'EEE–Union dounaière à terme?', *Tribüne der Wissenschaft, Basler Zeitung*, vol. 4.

Schwanen, D. (1993), *A Growing Success: Canada's Performance under Free Trade* (Toronto: C.D. Howe Institute).

Schweitzer, I. (1977), 'Some Particularities of Hungarian Machine Imports from the Soviet Union', *Acta Oeconomica*, vol. 18.

Schwok, R. (1989), 'Horizon 1992: La Suisse et le grand marché européen', *Journal de Genève and Georg*, Institut universitaire d'études européennes, Geneva.

Scitovsky, T. (1958), *Economic Theory and Western European Integration* (London: Allen & Unwin).

Scott, C. (1996), 'The Distributive Impact of the New Economic Model in Chile', in V. Bulmer-Thomas (ed.), *The New Economic Model in Latin America and Its Impact on Income Distribution and Poverty* (London: Macmillan and Institute of Latin American Studies).

Scott, N. (1993), 'Protectionism in Western Europe', in D. Salvatore (ed.), *Protectionism and World Welfare* (Cambridge: Cambridge University Press).

Secchi, C. (1995), 'The Political Economy of the Uruguay Round: Groups, Strategies, Interests and Results', in R. Faini and E. Grilli (eds), *Multilateralism and Regionalism After the Uruguay Round* (London: Macmillan).

Seers, D. (1957), 'Federation of the British West Indies: The Economic and Financial Aspects', *Social and Economic Studies*, vol. 6.

Shanks, M. (1977), *European Social Policy, Today and Tomorrow* (Oxford: Pergamon Press).

Shibata, H. (1971), 'The Theory of Economic Unions: Comparative Analysis of Customs Unions, Free Trade Areas and Tax Unions', in C. S. Shoup (ed.), *Fiscal Harmonisation in Common Markets* (New York: Columbia University Press 1967), reproduced, amended, in P. Robson (ed.), *International Economic Integration* (Harmondsworth: Penguin).

SIECA (1973), *El desarrollo integrado de centroamérica en la presente Década: bases y propuestas para el perfeccionamienro, y la reestructuración del mercado comun centroamericano*, 13 vols, Institute for Latin American Integration (Buenos Aires: Inter-American Development Bank).

SIECA (1995), *Centroamérica: Balanza de Comercio, 1990–4* (Guatemala: Dirección de Sistemas y Estadística, SIECA).

Siri, G. (1978), 'Calculation of the Shadow Price of Foreign Exchange Based on the Central American Econometric Model', in W. R. Cline and E. Delgado (eds), *Economic Integration in Central America* (Washington, DC: Brookings Institution).

Smith, Adam (1776), *An Enquiry into the Nature and Causes of the Wealth of Nations* (Glasgow: Chapman).

Smith, A. J. (1977), 'The Council of Mutual Economic Assistance in 1977: New Economic Power, New Political Perspectives and Some Old and New Problems', in US Congress Joint Economic Committee, *East European Economies Post-Helsinki* (Washington, DC: Government Printing Office).

Smith, A. and Venables, A. (1988), 'The Costs of Non-Europe: An Assessment Based on a Formal Model of Imperfect Competition and Economies of Scale', in vol. 2 of The Commission of the European Community's *Research the Costs of Non-Europe*, The Cecchini Report (Luxembourg: European Communities).

Smith, G. E., Maggs, P. E. and Ginsburgs, G. (eds) (1981), *Soviet and East European Law and the Scientific and Technical Revolution* (New York: Pergamon Press).

Soutar, G. (1977), 'Export Instability and Economic Growth', *Journal of Development Economics*, vol. 4.

Sowell, T. (1980), *Knowledge and Decisions* (New York: Basic Books).

St Cyr, E. B. A. (1980), 'On Lewis's Theory of Growth and Development', *Social and Economic Studies*, vol. 29.

Stoeckel, A., Pearce, D. and Banks, G. (1990), *Western Trade Blocs: Game Set or Match for Asia-Pacific and the World Economy?* (Canberra: Centre for International Economics).

Sumner, M. T. and Zis, G. (eds) (1982), *European Monetary Union* (London: Macmillan).

Sundelius, B. and Wiklund, C. (1979), 'The Nordic Community: the Ugly Duckling of Regional Cooperation', *Journal of Common Market Studies*, September, vol. 18, no. 1.

Swann, D. (1978), *The Economics of the Common Market*, 2nd edn (Harmondsworth: Penguin).

Swann, D. (1988), *The Economics of the Common Market*, 3rd edn (Harmondsworth: Penguin).

Tan, G. (1982), 'Trade Liberalisation in ASEAN', *AER Research Notes and Discussion Paper*, no. 32 (Singapore: Institute of Southeast Asian Studies).

Tan, G. (1982), 'Intra-ASEAN Trade Liberalisation, *Journal of Common Market Studies*, vol. 20.

Tan, G. (1987), 'Asean Preferential Trading Arrangements: An Overview', in N. Sopiee, C. L. See, and L. S. Jin (eds), *ASEAN at the Crossroads: Obstacles, Options and Opportunities for Economic Co-operation* (Kuala Lumpur: Institute of Strategic and International Studies).

Tan, G. (1995), *ASEAN: Economic Development and Cooperation* (Singapore, Times Academic Press).

Ten Kate, A. (1994), 'Is Mexico a Backdoor to the US Market or a Niche in the World's Largest Free Trade Area?', in V. Bulmer-Thomas, N. Craske and M. Serrano (eds), *Mexico and the North American Free Trade Agreement: Who will Benefit?* (Basingstoke: Macmillan and Institute of Latin American Studies).

Thomas, C. Y. (1977), 'The Community is a Big Paper Tiger', *Caribbean Contact*, vol. 5, no. 4, July.

Thomas, C. Y. (1979), 'Neo-colonialism and Caribbean Integration', in B. Ince (ed.), *Contemporary International Relations of the Caribbean* (St Augustine: *Institute of International Relations*, UWI).

Thomas, C. Y. and Rampersaud, R. (1991), 'The Cambio-system of an Independent Exchange Rate Float: The Case of Guyana', *Social and Economic Studies*, vol. 40.

Thoumi, F. E. (1989), *Las exportaciones intraregionales y la integración Latinoamericana y del Caribe en perspectiva* (Washington, DC: Banco Interamericano del Desarrollo).

Tin, O. G. (1981), *ASEAN Preferential Trading Arrangements (PTA): An Analysis of Potential Effects on Intra-ASEAN Trade* (Singapore: Institute of Southeast Asian Studies).

Tinbergen, J. (1952), *On the Theory of Economic Policy* (Amsterdam: North-Holland).

Tinbergen, J. (1954), *International Economic Integration* (Amsterdam: Elsevier).

Toh, M. H. and Low, L. (eds) (1993), *Regional Cooperation and Growth Triangles in ASEAN* (Singapore: Times Academic Press).

Trend, H. (1977), 'Economic Integration and Plan Coordination under COMECON', in K. Robert and J. F. Brown (eds), *Eastern Europe's Uncertain Future* (New York: Praeger).

UN (1974), 'Economic Cooperation Among Member Countries of ASEAN', *Journal of Development Planning*, no. 7.

UN (1995), 'Strengthening Capacities in Trade, Investment and the Environment for the Comprehensive Development of Indo-China', *ESCAP Studies in Trade and Investment*, vol. 1. (New York: United Nations).

UN Economic Commission for Africa (1983), *Rapport annuel* (Ouagadougou: CEAO).

UN Economic Commission for Africa (1984), *Proposals for Strengthening Economic Integration in West Africa* (Addis Ababa: ECA).

UN Economic Commission for Europe (1971), 'Note on the Projection of the Matrices of International Trade', *Economic Bulletin for Europe*, vol. 22, no. 1.

UN Economic Commission for Latin America (1957), *Los problemas actuales del comercio interlatinoamericano*, E/CN 12/423.

UN Economic Commission for Latin America (1959), *The Latin American Common Market* (New York: United Nations).

UN Economic Commission for Latin America (1962), *Multilateral Economic Cooperation in Latin America*, vol. 1, E/CN 12/621.

UN Economic Commission for Latin America (1989), *Preliminary Overview of the Economy of Latin America and the Caribbean 1989* (Santiago, Chile: United Nations).

UN Economic Commission for Latin America (1992), *Statistical Yearbook for Latin America and the Caribbean* (Santiago, Chile: United Nations).

UN Economic Commission for Latin America (1994a), *Statistical Yearbook for Latin America and the Caribbean* (Santiago, Chile: United Nations).

UN Economic Commission for Latin America (1994b), *Open Regionalism in Latin America and the Caribbean* (Santiago, Chile: United Nations).

UNCTAD (1983), *Trade and Development Report, 1983*, Part 1, *The Current Economic Crisis*, TOR/3, Geneva, September.

UNCTAD (1987 and 1992), *Handbook of International Trade and Development Statistics* (New York: United Nations).

UNCTAD (1990), 'Selected Issues on Trade Restrictions', *UNCTAD ITO/24*, Geneva.

US Department of Commerce (various issues), *Survey of Current Business*, a monthly publication.

Vaitsos, C. V. (1978), 'Crisis in Regional Economic Cooperation (Integration) Among Developing Countries: A Survey', *World Development*, vol. 6.

Van Brabant, J. M. (1980), *Socialist Economic Integration* (Cambridge: Cambridge University Press).

Van Den Boogaerde, P. (1991), *Financial Assistance from Arab Countries and Arab Regional Institutions* (Washington, DC: IMF).

Vanek, J. (1965), *General Equilibrium of International Discrimination: the Case of Customs Unions* (Cambridge, Mass.: Harvard University Press).

Vargas-Hidalgo, R. (1979), 'The Crisis of the Andean Pact: Lessons for Integration Among Developing Countries', *Journal of Common Market Studies*, vol. 17, no. 3, March.

Verdoorn, P. J. and Schwartz, A. N. R. (1972), 'Two Alternative Estimates of the Effects of EEC and EFTA on the Pattern of Trade', *European Economic Review*, vol. 3.

Viner, J. (1950), *The Customs Union Issue* (New York: Carnegie Endowment for International Peace).

Wallace, E. (1977), *The British Caribbean: From the Decline of Colonialism to the End of the Federation* (Toronto: University of Toronto Press).

Wallace, W. (1980), (ed.), *Britain in Europe* (London: Heinemann).

Weintraub, S. (ed.) (1993), *The ANNALS of the American Academy of Political and Social Science*, issue on 'Free Trade in the Western Hemisphere', vol. 526, March.

Weintraub, S. (1994), *NAFTA: What Comes Next?* (Westport, Conn.: Praeger for the Center for Strategic and International Studies).

Weintraub, S. (1995a), 'Mexico's Foreign Economic Policy: From Admiration to Disappointment', *Challenge*, vol. 38.

Weintraub, S. (1995b), 'The Depth of Economic Integration Between Mexico and the United States', *Washington Quarterly*, vol. 18.

Werner Report (1970) *see* Commission of the European Communities (1970).

West Indian Commission (1992a), *Time for Action. The Report of the West Indian Commission: A Synopsis* (Black Rock: West Indian Commission Secretariat).

West Indian Commission (1992b), *Overview of the Report of the West Indian Commission: Time for Action* (Black Rock: West Indian Commission Secretariat).

West Indian Commission (1992c), *Time for Action: The Report of the West Indian Commission*, (Black Rock: West Indian Commission Secretariat).

Wijkman, P. M. (1995), 'The Winding Voyage to and Beyond the EEA', in E. Ems (ed.), *35 Years of Free Trade in Europe: Messages for the Future*, Proceedings of EFTA's 35th Anniversary Workshop, Geneva, 9–10 March 1995 (Geneva: EFTA Secretariat).

Wilford, W. T. (1970), 'Trade Creation in the Central American Common Market', *Western Economic Journal*, vol. 8.

Wilford, W. T. (1978), 'On Revenue Performance and Revenue-income Stability in the Third World', *Economic Development and Cultural Change*, April.

Wilkie, J. W. and Reich, R. (1978, 1980), *Statistical Abstract of Latin America*, vols 19, 20 (Los Angeles: UCLA).

Williams, M. (1985), 'An Analysis of Regional Trade and Payments Arrangements in CARICOM 1971–1983', *Social and Economic Studies*, vol. 34.

Williams, R. (1978), 'Economies of the Scale Parameters for Central American Manufacturing Industry', in W. R. Cline and E. Delgado (eds), *Economic Integration in Central America* (Washington, DC: Brookings Institution).

Willmore, L. N. (1975/76), 'Trade Creation, Trade Diversion and Effective Protection in the Central American Common Market', *Journal of Development Studies*, vol. 12, no. 4.

Willmore, L. N. (1976), 'Direct Foreign Investment in Central American Manufacturing', *World Development*, vol. 4.

Winters, L. A. (1989), 'The So-called Non-Economic Objectives of Agricultural Policy', *OECD Economic Studies*, no. 13.

Winters, L. A. (1992), 'Goals and Own Goals in European Trade Policy', *The World Economy*, vol. 15.

Wionczek, M. S. (ed.) (1966), *Latin American Economic Integration* (New York: Praeger).

Wionczek, M. S. (ed.) (1969), *Economic Cooperation in Latin America, Africa and Asia: A Handbook of Documents* (Cambridge Mass.: MIT Press).

Wionczek, M. S. (1970), 'The Rise and the Decline of Latin American Economic Integration', *Journal of Common Market Studies*, vol. 9.

Wionczek, M. S. (1972), 'The Central American Common Market', in P. Robson (ed.), *International Economic Integration* (Harmondsworth: Penguin).

Wionczek, M. S. (1980), 'La evaluación del tratado de Montevideo 1980 y las perspectivas de las acciones de alcance parcial de la ALADI', *Integracion Latinoamericana*, year V, no. 50.

Witter, M. (1983), 'Exchange Rate Policy in Jamaica: A Critical Assessment', *Social and Economic Studies*, vol. 32.

Wolf, M. (1983), 'The European Community's Trade Policy', in R. Jenkins (ed.), *Britain and the EEC* (London: Macmillan).

Wong, J. (1979), *ASEAN Economies in Perspective: A Comparative Study of Indonesia, Malaysia, the Philippines, Singapore and Thailand* (London: Macmillan).

Wong, J. (1985), 'ASEAN's Experience in Regional Economic Cooperation', *Asian Development Review*, vol. 3, no. 1.

Wonnacott, R. J. (1991), *The Economics of Overlapping Free Trade Areas and the Mexican Challenge* (Toronto: C.D. Howe Institute).

Wonnacott, G. P. and Wonnacott, R. J. (1981), 'Is Unilateral Tariff Reduction Preferable to a Customs Union? The Curious Case of the Missing Foreign Tariffs', *American Economic Review*, vol. 71.

World Bank (various years), *World Development Report* (New York: Oxford University Press).

World Bank (1990), *The Caribbean Common Market: Trade Policies and Regional Integration in the 1990s* (Washington, DC: World Bank).

World Bank (1993), *Reassessing Namibia's Membership of the Southern African Customs Union* (Washington, DC: World Bank).

Worrell, D. (1991), 'A Common Currency for the Caribbean', paper presented to the West Indian Commission (George town: CARICOM Secretariat).

Xafa, M., Kronenberg, R. P. and Landell-Mills, J. (1992), 'The European Community's Trade and Trade-related Industrial Policies', *IMF Working Paper*, no. WP/92/94 (Washington, DC: The International Monetary Fund).

Yah, L. C. (1978), 'ASEAN Economic Cooperation and Economic Reality', *UMBC Economic Review*, no. 1.

Yotopoulos, P. and Nugent, J. (1976), *The Economics of Development: Empirical Investigations* (New York: Harper & Row).

Name Index

Subject Index

POINT LOMA NAZARENE COLLEGE
RYAN LIBRARY